# Dame Philology's Charrette:
## Approaching Medieval Textuality through Chrétien's *Lancelot*

## Essays in Memory of Karl D. Uitti

# Medieval and Renaissance
# Texts and Studies
## Volume 408

# Dame Philology's Charrette:

## Approaching Medieval Textuality through Chrétien's *Lancelot*

## Essays in Memory of Karl D. Uitti

*Edited by*

Gina L. Greco
Ellen M. Thorington

ACMRS
(Arizona Center for Medieval and Renaissance Studies)
Tempe, Arizona
2012

*Funding and material support for the volume were provided by:*
*The Florence Gould Foundation*
*Ball State University*
*Portland State University*

---

Published by ACMRS (Arizona Center for Medieval and Renaissance Studies)
Tempe, Arizona
© 2012 Arizona Board of Regents for Arizona State University.
All Rights Reserved.

**Library of Congress Cataloging-in-Publication Data**

Dame philology's charrette : approaching medieval textuality through Chrétien's Lancelot : essays in memory of Karl D. Uitti / edited by Gina L. Greco, Ellen M. Thorington.
    p. cm. -- (Medieval and renaissance texts and studies ; v. 408)
    Includes bibliographical references.
    ISBN 978-0-86698-456-0 (acid-free paper)
    1. Chrétien, de Troyes, 12th cent. Chevalier de la charrette. 2. Lancelot (Legendary character)--Romances--History and criticism. 3. Arthurian romances--Criticism, Textual. I. Greco, Gina L. II. Thorington, Ellen Moffat, 1969- III. Uitti, Karl D.
    PQ1445.L5D36 2011
    841'.1--dc23

                                                                2011047950

**Front Cover:**
Portrait of Marie de Champagne. MS BNF fr. 794 fol. 27r.
*Credit: The Bibliothèque Nationale de France, Paris.*

∞
This book is made to last. It is set in Adobe Caslon Pro,
smyth-sewn and printed on acid-free paper to library specifications.
*Printed in the United States of America*

*In memoriam*
*Karl D. Uitti*

# Table of Contents

# ACKNOWLEDGMENTS

We would like to express our sincere gratitude to Michelle Freeman for her assistance and encouragement at the outset of this project. Special thanks for their intellectual and moral support are also due to Gaetano DeLeonibus, Donald Gilman, Jennifer Margulis, Christine Rose, Dorothy Stegman, Nicolas Renet, and Caroline, Katherine, and Richard Thorington. We are particularly grateful to those who read articles for us: Rafael Alvarado, Peter Shoemaker, and Maud Simon. Most importantly, we wish to thank each of our contributors, who wrote with both head and heart for the volume. Our combined efforts are dedicated to the memory of Karl D. Uitti.

# Introduction

Chrétien de Troyes's *Le Chevalier de la Charrette* is both a masterpiece of Old French poetry and the earliest extant tale to recount the great love between Lancelot and Queen Guinevere. As such, it has served as a text of reference since shortly after its composition. Within a generation, the redactors of the thirteenth-century prose Lancelot cycle placed Chrétien's romance at the center of an extensive project which recast the hero as unworthy of accomplishing the ultimate adventure due to his adulterous past. The prose authors thus initiated a quest to understand, explicate, and at times even control the meaning of the *Charrette*. While a variety of medieval writers, such as the authors of the Vulgate romances and certain medieval sermons, condemned Lancelot for his amorous relations with Guinevere, other writers and artists celebrated the hero and his love for his lady. Chrétien's romance has continued to play a central role in the scholarly debate and study of medieval narrative and Old French language.

Thanks to its unique position within Arthurian and Old French studies, this romance has exerted influence on the literary traditions of Western Europe as a whole. This, in addition to its relatively compact manuscript tradition, has allowed the *Charrette* to become a kind of ideal "test case" for philologists and literary historians. Gaston Paris, for example, opened the critical conversation with his analysis of *Le Chevalier de la Charrette* in his landmark articles on courtly love, in which he coined the term *amour courtois* and launched generations of scholarly discussions.[1] The romance has also received the attention of a distinguished line of textual scholars who have maintained a lively conversation of sorts through their editions. With the advent of electronic editions, moreover, *Le Chevalier de la Charrette* has become one of the most represented Old French texts among scholarly electronic projects. The *Princeton Charrette Project*,[2] for example, is a multi-media digital archive that encompasses the entire manuscript tradition of the romance as well as grammatical and poetico-rhetorical databases.

---

[1] Gaston Paris, "Études sur les romans de la Table Ronde: *Lancelot*," *Romania* 12 (1883): 459–534.

[2] *The Princeton Charrette Project*, ed. Karl D. Uitti, 1994, Trustees of Princeton University, 2006, Dept. of French and Italian, Princeton University, 3 April 2007. http://www.princeton.edu/~lancelot. Hereafter referred to as the *Charrette Project*.

In keeping with the spirit of experimentation that has surrounded the *Charrette* since its inception ca. 1170, we present *Dame Philology's Charrette: Approaching Medieval Textuality through Chrétien's* Lancelot. The essays in this volume continue the discussion of the *Charrette* from a variety of philological and literary perspectives, and apply techniques learned from the *Charrette* to other works of medieval literature. We emphasize the interaction between established philological methods and emergent digital techniques as a way to provide avenues for further exploration of both Chrétien's *Charrette* and medieval textuality.

In many respects, this volume originated in the research of the late Karl D. Uitti of Princeton University. His scholarship on the *Charrette* poem and other works was inspired by the complementary application of all the tools available to the philologist. As the architect of the *Charrette Project*, his work came from a conviction that the scholar-reader was the best interpreter of medieval romance, but that the eye of the reader could be further informed through the use of evolving technological tools. Rather than seeing these methods as a mere means to an end, he recognized their ability to provide alternative ways to approach the text. The present volume builds upon his vision and his scholarly example. It presents a variety of innovative approaches to medieval narrative that focus on but also reach beyond Chrétien's *Charrette*. These approaches, which encompass both established and evolving techniques, share an appreciation of the material culture of medieval textual production. The collection therefore situates these articles within the perspective of the larger philological tradition out of which the *Charrette Project* evolved. *Dame Philology's Charrette* memorializes and continues Professor Uitti's important work by providing models for the solution of philological problems and by opening up avenues for research.

Using both Chrétien's *Charrette* and the *Charrette Project* as examples, the following essays demonstrate the coming together of both established methodologies and electronic techniques to further the philological study of medieval narrative. With the rise of digital tools, scholarly electronic editions, and technologically-inspired research since the early 1980s, we have noted the development of two separate types of scholarship, digital and non-digital, frequently published in distinct venues. Yet this separation, based on the tools of research rather than the results, is more illusory than real. The present volume seeks to bridge this gap to reflect the current reality in philological practice. Each contribution in the volume affirms the value of sound philological study, asking and answering questions of interest to all medievalists.

By bringing together scholars of various methodological orientations (both digital and non-digital), the collection creates a conversation across disciplines and provides fruitful avenues for scholarship in both medieval studies and humanities computing. Yet, as the volume's organization reflects, no one approach can provide all the answers. Moreover, in choosing to present the articles thematically, between those that are concerned with context and language and those that deal explicitly with digital philology, one can still see the type of divide that we endeavor to bridge. Yet in placing these articles together, we begin a dialogue that integrates approaches. It is through such dialogue, and through the developing marriage of electronic analysis and enduring theoretical concerns, that philology proves its continuing relevance to all readers.

*Dame Philology's Charrette* opens with Part I, Le Chevalier de la Charrette: *An Introduction to the Romance*. Intended for those less familiar with the poem, Peter Dembowski's "The *Sens* of the *Charrette*: A General Introduction to the *Charrette* Poem and its Significance" offers both a review of the poem and an overview of selected critical issues useful to the student and scholar alike. In presenting the text, Dembowski argues that the significance of the *Charrette* lies in Lancelot's heroism and selfless virtue. He highlights episodes of Chrétien's romance that will serve as the focus of analysis in subsequent essays. In particular, Dembowski discusses Lancelot's hesitation before entering the cart, his crossing of the Sword Bridge, the night of love, and the tournament of Noauz. The essays in the volume demonstrate that although such passages have been much discussed in past scholarship, they still deserve and invite further attention.

The essays in Part II, Translatio: *Contextualizing the Romance*, return to questions raised by Dembowski to reassess our understanding of the *Charrette's* place within the chain of medieval textual production. The authors of the essays in this section employ methodologies that reveal affinities between their approaches and the *Charrette Project's* presentation of medieval textuality. John Fleming's article sets Chrétien's Old French poem within the larger context of medieval literature, while examining anew three conventions found in the opening lines of the *Charrette*—the contrasts between infancy and maturity, jest and earnest, and Reason and Love. He views these conventions both through parallel imagery from such fourteenth-century works as *Sir Gawain and the Green Knight*, Chaucer's "Knight's Tale," and his *Troilus and Criseyde*, and through a philological lens, then illustrates the way in which such binary oppositions signal the moral complexity of the poem and invite the reader to explore the ambiguities. Using Augustine's distinction, made in the *Confessions*, between *pectus* and *lingua* to revisit Lancelot's conflict at the moment of hesitation before the infamous cart, Fleming looks backward as well as forward to situate the *Charrette* within the evolving literary context of the Middle Ages.

Continuing these thoughts, Lori Walters suggests that Augustine's transformation of his mother Monnica into an image of the Church can help us understand both Lancelot and Guinevere's coupling as a "holy adultery" and Guinevere herself as a symbol of the City of Cities, Jerusalem. Walters's innovative rereading of the Sword Bridge and night of love scenes as an exhortation to the reader to support the Crusades draws on evidence from manuscript BNF fr. 794. She draws attention to the Pauline echoes within the *Charrette* to show how carnal love can be transformed into the spiritual, thereby supporting the idea of earthly queen as crusading symbol. In particular, she explores the connections between the manuscript's compiler, Guiot, and Marie de Champagne and her illustrious family of royal crusaders and literary patrons.

The role of the scribe in manuscript compilation serves also as the inspiration to Douglas Kelly's reassessment of the tradition of medieval textual transmission. In examining the question of *Rigomer*'s radical rewriting of the *Charrette*, he points to manuscript Chantilly 472, which juxtaposes these diametrically opposed versions of Lancelot. Kelly suggests that the frequency of incomplete romances in the codex, together with the juxtapositions of seemingly contradictory representations of Arthurian characters, demonstrates the medieval audience's willingness to explore "parallel universes." Grace Armstrong further analyzes the relationship between a source text and its epigonal romance through a study of the recasting of the *Charrette*'s Sword Bridge scene in the Vulgate Cycle's *La Queste del Saint Graal.* Her essay uses this key episode to elucidate the workings of romance, especially the re-evaluation of source texts which results from the interpretive process of textual transmission. Like Walters, she also explores Pauline language, but emphasizes its presence in the *Queste*, where, in contrast to Chrétien's romance, it serves to emphasize the imperfections of the worldly.

The Sword Bridge episode also receives attention in Ellen Thorington's essay, which opens Part III, *Weighing Words: The Language of the* Charrette. The contributions in this section focus on Chrétien's language, his poetic technique, and linguistic evolution, using electronic texts as a support to literary and linguistic interpretation. Thorington presents a detailed analysis of the poetics of rich rhyme in the scene, leading her to conclude that Chrétien employs the figure of rich rhyme in word play that highlights significant sections of the narrative. Her argument is supported with textual evidence generated through the *Charrette Project.* Similarly, Christiane Marchello-Nizia and Alexei Lavrentiev draw on the resources of the *Charrette Project* in their study of the development of the demonstrative "ce." Use of data from the searchable manuscript transcriptions provides a clearer idea of the evolution of the system of determiners in Old French. Further, these data allow them to formulate and support their hypothesis that the demonstrative pronoun *ce* is a form introduced into the textual tradition by the scribes and did not figure in Chrétien's own language.

These two articles offer a segue into the next set of essays, Part IV, *Historical Perspectives on Digital Philology*, which investigate the history and theoretical underpinnings of the *Charrette Project* and discuss the implications of digital approaches within medieval studies. This section, which illustrates how digital philology was informed from the start by the philological and interpretative principles of literary study, begins with a brief reflection by Robert Hollander that considers the influence of the *Dartmouth Dante Project* on Karl Uitti's initial work on the *Charrette Project*, thus situating the latter project within a line of digital *translatio.* Hollander concludes by raising issues of broad concern in humanities computing regarding funding, citation, and intellectual property in the electronic domain. Gina Greco then provides a history of the *Charrette Project*, presenting the variety of theoretical and philological questions that inspired early team members, and highlights the project collaborators' original guiding principles. Greco's essay demonstrates the way in which collaborators' differing concerns (discussions of *mouvance* and *variance* as well as an intimate knowledge of the poem's manuscript tradition) coalesced to form a shared vision. The result, she maintains, is a project that acknowledges the roles of both author and scribe in textual production, and recognizes the value both of a good edition and of access to a complete manuscript tradition.

Cinzia Pignatelli revisits the Project's original approach to manuscript transcription and argues that some of the early decisions should be reconsidered. Those choices, grounded in a desire to reflect manuscript variation fully, have sometimes resulted in such a complex set of data that the non-specialist finds it difficult to manipulate. In light of her own use of the archive and of more recent paleographical work, she provides a number of guidelines that serve both for a rereading of the *Charrette*'s archive of transcriptions and for the development of similar archives elsewhere. The typology of transcription errors she presents will serve all medievalists as the basis for a theory and methodology of transcription.

Part V, *Digital Poetics: The* Charrette Project *and Beyond*, explores the ways in which digital scholarship has influenced scholars' ways of seeing and questioning a text, and in so doing illustrates that digital scholarship is as much — or more — a question of a theory, or of a poetics, as a question of tools. Rafael Alvarado's essay presents a rationale for *Figura*, an application he wrote to resolve the technical difficulties that arise from complex philological problems. After describing his data model, Alvarado proposes a study of the relationship between Lancelot and Méléagant and their associations with particular rhetorical-poetic figures as an example of the kind of questions that can be asked of the database, and the textual evidence that is produced by such queries. This example leads to his final observations on how criticism changes, or perhaps ought to change, when the text becomes a database.

The final two essays, by Katherine Brown and Juliet O'Brien, explore new texts, the fabliau *La Damoiselle qui ne pooit oïr parler de foutre* and *Flamenca* respectively, using methodology inspired directly from their past work on the *Charrette Project*. Working with the digital version of *La Damoiselle qui ne pooit oïr parler de foutre* available through the Base de Français Médiéval, Brown analyzes the *fabliau*'s inversion of courtly paradigms and diction. This approach leads her to re-examine the fabliau tradition and its relationship to *courtoisie*; in particular, she demonstrates that parody within these texts serves to reinforce rather than undermine courtly ideals. O'Brien uses digital analysis of the *Flamenca* to study how the text juxtaposes *amor cortes*, "courtly love," with *amor coral*, "love of the heart." Employing an experimental electronic edition she produced of the romance, she identifies the various layers and voices of this polyphonic narrative. This reading supports her thesis that the romance is both critical of courtly love and composed in a debating and critical mode in which the debate and discussion of an idea—in this case, love—lies at the actual heart of the narrative. O'Brien concludes with a reexamination of the longstanding debate over courtly love, providing support to Karl Uitti's stance on the issue, a stance he elaborated most clearly through his study of the *Charrette*.

In the Afterword, K. Sarah-Jane Murray and Matthieu Boyd return to questions of interest to students as well as scholars, approaching Chrétien's romance through a pedagogical lens that echoes that with which Dembowski opens the volume. Their essay offers a review of past translations of the poem, and suggests a new methodology of translation that exploits the availability of electronic texts and tools. Next, they examine contemporary Old French scholarship's emphasis on the materiality of the medieval text in both its codicological and literary context. In so doing they illustrate the increasing interrelationship between digital and non-digital methodologies. In particular, they argue that the *Charrette Project*, and projects like it, should grow in ways that reflect current interest in the codex and offer a concrete example for such development. The creation of the types of tools they propose will allow for a more complete dissolution of the digital/non-digital divide when scholars interested in questions related to *translatio* and codicology have electronic archives designed for their needs. Their Afterword concludes with an overview of future avenues of research for students and scholars of Chrétien.

Taken as a whole, these essays illustrate that key debates surrounding Chrétien's text continue to invite critical attention, and show that the *bele conjointure* of complementary methodologies, including digital philology, can expand our appreciation of medieval textuality and tradition. From "reading" the text in new ways to comprehending the influences on and technique of medieval poets and scribes, these essays together forge their way over the Sword Bridge and its illusory obstacles towards a reaffirmation of the value of philological study.

# Part I.

## *Le Chevalier de la Charrette*:
## An Introduction to the Romance

# THE SENS OF THE CHARRETTE:
# A GENERAL INTRODUCTION TO THE
# CHARRETTE POEM AND ITS SIGNIFICANCE

PETER F. DEMBOWSKI
UNIVERSITY OF CHICAGO

The significance of *Lancelot* or the *Chevalier de la Charrette* by Chrétien de Troyes[1] has been discussed both by medieval audiences and by modern critics. In the Middle Ages, the discussions frequently took the form of alternatives to Chrétien's texts: elaborations, revisions, and continuation—discussions by juxtaposition with new versions of the romance. In modern times Chrétien's text became the object of extensive analytic and critical literature. I understand fully that the *Charrette* permits—if not invites—various kinds of figurative or symbolic interpretation of its significance. But here, I shall stress not so much the "deep" sense (or senses) of the romance, but, its "surface" significance.[2] The subject matter of the romance is presented in a series of episodes which could easily be divided into two parts. The first part presents Lancelot's search for the queen and his love encounter with her (31–5063); the second part presents Lancelot's captivity, his suffering, and his final triumph (5064–7119). The romance is preceded by an important Prologue (1–30) and concludes with a brief Epilogue (7120–7134) in which Godefroi de Leigni announces that, following Chrétien's wishes, he composed the last section of the romance.

In the Prologue, Chrétien himself draws our attention to significance as something to be sought in the subject matter of his romance. In the first lines, he tells us that "ma dame de Chanpaigne," that is, Countess Marie (1145–1198),[3]

---

[1] I follow the Alfred Foulet and Karl D. Uitti edition: Chrétien de Troyes, *Le Chevalier de la Charrette (Lancelot)*, ed. Alfred Foulet and Karl D. Uitti (Paris: Bordas, 1989). English translations are mine. They strive to be literal.

[2] For a typical example of the *Charrette* seen in its rich "deep" and fundamentally Christian significance, see Jacques Ribard, *Chrétien de Troyes, Le* Chevalier de la Charrette*: essai d'interprétation symbolique* (Paris: Nizet, 1972).

[3] Wife of Henry the Liberal, Count of Champagne (1152–1181), and daughter of Louis VII King of France and Aliénor d'Aquitaine (1122–1204), the famous patron of

Gina L. Greco and Ellen M. Thorington, eds., *Dame Philology's Charrette: Approaching Medieval Textuality through Crétien's 'Lancelot': Essays in Memory of Karl D. Uitti*. MRTS 408. Tempe: ACMRS, 2012. [ISBN 978-0-86698-456-0]

wishes him to begin a romance. Chrétien's words resemble here Lancelot's attitude towards Guenièvre: "Je l'anprendrai mout volentiers, / Come cil qui est suens antiers" (3–4) [I will undertake it most willingly / As one who is entirely hers]. While denying any intention of flattery, Chrétien proceeds (8–19) with a series of hyperbolic compliments of Marie. He then goes back to her wishes: "Mes tant dirai je que mialz oevre / Ses comandemanz an cest oevre / Que *sans* ne paine que g'i mete" (21–23, my emphasis) [But I will say that her commandment / works more effectively in this work / Than my own *sans* and the effort that I put into it].

Switching to the third person singular, Chrétien concludes his Prologue:

Del CHEVALIER DE LA CHARRETE
Comance Chrestïens son livre;
*Matiere* et *san* li done et livre
La Contesse, et il s'antremet
De *panser*, si que rien n'i met
Fors sa painne et *s'antancion*. (24–29, my emphasis)

[Chrétien begins his book / About the KNIGHT OF THE CART / Subject matter and significance is furnished / By the Countess, and he undertakes / To take care, and he does not bring into it anything / Except his effort and attention.]

Our (recent) habit of offering English translation tends to hide a real problem within these lines. The words in italics are polyvalent and, for us at least, imprecise in meaning. But even if we are not quite sure whether Chrétien's *sans* (23) and Marie's *san* (26)[4] are synonymous, and what they signify (sense, intelligence, meaning, significance, main idea, direction, orientation, etc.), the passage indicates, first, that Marie wished him to write a romance; then, that her choice of subject and its significance are given to Chrétien by her; and finally, that her contributions are deemed by Chrétien to be more important than his own care, effort, and *antancion* = intention (?). The last point could have been influenced by Chrétien's use of the topos of humility, consonant with his flattering of the countess, for indeed Chrétien's treatment of the countess in the Prologue resembles Lancelot's treatment of the queen in the romance.

---

the troubadours, of Wace, and of Benoît de Sainte-Maure, and granddaughter of the first troubadour, Guillaume (Guilhem) IX d'Aquitaine, Count of Poitiers (1071–1226).

[4] The term is derived from a polyvalent Latin *sensus* and the Germanic *sin* 'direction' (see this acceptation in v. 1393). But even without the Germanic semantic input, the descendent of the Latin *sensus* was sufficiently rich in meaning to make the interpretation of Chrétien's Prologue difficult. See Albert Gier, "Das Verwandschaftsverhältnis von afr. *sens* und *sen*," *Romanistisches Jahrbuch* 28 (1977): 54–72.

We know that, generally speaking, romance writers did not invent *ex nihilo* the subject matter of their stories, but recomposed, or pretended to recompose, previous stories. We also know that the *Charrette* takes as its model certain Celtic stories of abductions of queens and the subsequent efforts of their husbands to rescue them. The late twelfth-century German poet Ulrich von Zatzikoven claims that his *Lancelet* followed a *welsches buoch*, that is, a French book—certainly not the *Charrette*, but a lost Old French (OF) romance. What is important for us is that in Ulrich's story—and presumably in his French source—Lancelot is not the queen's lover. All seems to indicate that it was the countess who suggested to her poet to interpret the Celtic story (or stories) in a way that would make the queen and her rescuer lovers.

Before continuing on to an analysis of the particular significance of the *Charrette* and its lyric themes, it would be useful to review the main points of the tale. My summary follows the natural division of the romance into two parts.

## Part One

The romance opens at King Arthur's court, Camaalot, in his kingdom of Logres (the Celtic name for England). The festivities are suddenly interrupted by the arrival of a fully armed knight whose name, Méléagant, we do not learn until v. 641. He holds many captives from Logres in his father's domain of Gorre and offers a condition for freeing them: a knight must accompany the queen to the forest and there fight a duel with him. If the knight wins, the queen and the captives will be freed; if not, the queen will join the other captives in Gorre.

Keu becomes the queen's first champion. Before leaving with him, she whispers: ". . . se vos ce seüssiez, / Ja, ce croi, ne me leissessiez / Sanz chalonge mener un pas!" (211–213) [. . . if you only knew (what is happening), / I do not believe that you would permit / (Anybody) to take me one step away without challenge].[5] Gauvain leaves the court in search of Guenièvre. He finds Keu's charger without the rider (273) and suddenly runs into a knight whose horse is dying of exhaustion. It is thus that we meet Lancelot, and although we do not learn his name here, it will be revealed by the queen herself very near to the mid-point of the romance (3676–3677). Gauvain offers him one of his chargers and, having accepted it, Lancelot rides off ahead. Gauvain soon comes upon the scene of a combat and finds that

---

[5] This important phrase is different in the Guiot manuscript, where the queen addresses herself to Arthur: "King, if you knew it, you would not permit Keu to lead me one step." Her words in that form are incoherent, because certainly Arthur knew about his wife's predicament. I have profited from Douglas Kelly's pioneering work, Sens *and* Conjointure, which strives to underscore the coherence of the romance. The early criticism stressed its contradictions and incoherence. See Sens *and* Conjointure *in the Chevalier de la Charrette* (The Hague: Mouton, 1966).

same charger lying dead. The action of the opening scenes moves with an eerie rapidity: in the space of nine verses (298–307) two of Lancelot's chargers die.

Next, Gauvain meets Lancelot fully armed, but on foot, standing before a cart driven by a dwarf; at this point Chrétien (323–346) informs the reader that such carts were used as pillories for criminals. When Lancelot asks the dwarf whether he has seen the queen, the dwarf promises to find her the next day if Lancelot will get into his cart. Lancelot hesitates for the time required to take two steps (363–364),[6] but then enters it, thereby becoming *le Chevalier de la Charrette*.

Gauvain follows the cart on his horse, and at nightfall they arrive at a castle whose inhabitants deride Lancelot for having ridden in the shameful cart. Nevertheless, Gauvain and Lancelot are well received by the lady of the castle. She is the first of five nameless young ladies that Lancelot will meet during his quest. After dinner, the knights go to bed; at midnight, a mysterious flaming lance flies down from the ceiling, wounding Lancelot's side and setting the bed on fire. Lancelot extinguishes the fire and goes back to sleep. The next day, he looks out the window and sees a knight being carried on a bier; the knight is accompanied by weeping damsels and another knight leading a lady whom Lancelot recognizes as Guenièvre. When she can no longer be seen, Gauvain saves Lancelot from falling out the window in his despair over losing sight of her.

Gauvain and Lancelot follow the road taken by the queen and her abductor. They encounter the second damsel, who knows where the queen is to be found. But before she will agree to impart the information, she extracts two promises from them: Gauvain will become her loyal servant, and Lancelot will fulfill all her wishes. The damsel tells them that Méléagant, the son of King Bademagu, is the abductor of the queen and that he has taken her to Gorre, "Don nus estranges ne retorne" (645) [From where no stranger returns]. Reaching Bademagu's capital of Bath (*Bade*) will be dangerous: one must cross the same dangerous current either by the Underwater Bridge, or by the Sword Bridge. Gauvain chooses the former, Lancelot the latter. The second damsel disappears from the romance, and the two companions part ways.

Lancelot rides until afternoon, when he comes to a river. His thirsty horse takes him straight to the ford defended by a nameless knight. Lost in amorous thought, Lancelot comes back to his senses only after being unhorsed and thrown into the stream (779). He defeats the knight, but the third damsel, who accompanies the guardian of the ford, saves his life.

Lancelot continues his quest until nightfall. Soon (943), he meets the fourth of the five nameless damsels. This maiden has been named the Immodest Damsel by critics, for she offers Lancelot a night's lodging provided that he sleep with her

---

[6] Again, these dramatically important verses are missing from the Guiot manuscript. See Alfred Foulet and Karl D. Uitti, "On Editing Chrétien de Troyes: *Lancelot*. Two Steps and their Concern," *Speculum* 63 (1988): 271–92.

(954). After dinner, Lancelot hears screams coming from the bedroom (1069) and sees the maiden thrown on the bed by an attacking knight. Six men-at-arms guard the door. Lancelot defends the damsel in distress, but suddenly she dismisses the attacker and his men (1196–1197). Later, Lancelot finds her in his bed, where he fulfills his agreement: they lie together, but nothing else happens.

The next day, the Immodest Damsel proposes to accompany Lancelot according to the custom of Logres. At this moment, Chrétien makes another authorial comment, explaining this *costume* (1313–1328): no knight should assault a woman traveling alone upon pain of banishment. If she traveled in the company of a knight, this knight had to respect her, but any other knight could fight for her, and defeating her companion could "Sa volenté an . . . faire / Sanz honte et sanz blasme retraire" (1327–1328) [Do as he wishes with her / Without incurring dishonor or blame]. *Costume*, or custom, is thus an unwritten set of courtly rules of behavior.[7]

Soon, Lancelot discovers a fine comb with a strand of blond hair in it, which the damsel recognizes as belonging to Guenièvre. Lancelot ". . . comance a aorer" (1474) [he begins his adoration of the hair]. Suddenly, an unwanted suitor of the damsel arrives. He wishes to win her in a duel (according to the custom of Logres), but the father of the suitor prevents the duel from taking place.

The next episode offers a clear prediction of the larger dimensions of Lancelot's heroic role. He and the Immodest Damsel arrive at a monastery where, in the adjoining cemetery, lie the graves of Arthurian heroes. Some of them bear the names of living knights: Gauvain, Louis, and Yvain, but others are unnamed. The most sumptuous tombstone bears the following inscription: "*Cil qui levera / cele lamme seus par son cors / gitera ces et celes fors / qui sont an la terre an prison, / Don n'ist ne sers ne gentix hon*" (1912–1916) [He who will lift this tombstone all by himself / Will free those men and women / Who are captives in the land / From where neither serf nor nobleman escapes]. Lancelot lifts the stone easily.

After leaving the cemetery, Lancelot rides alone until evening, when he meets the first vavasseur, who offers him hospitality for the night. Lancelot is already in the territory of Gorre and his reputation has grown among the captives. The next morning, accompanied by two of the sons of the first vavasseur, he arrives at the Stone Passage, which is protected by an armed knight and two sergeants. Lancelot defeats the knight (2240), and goes through the Stone Passage. We learn that because of the news of Lancelot's great deeds of arms, the captives have taken arms against their oppressors.

Here Chrétien introduces another aspect of the supernatural. Arriving at a fortress, Lancelot consults a magic ring to ascertain whether or not the place is enchanted. Evoking the name of the fairy who raised him and gave him the ring (2357–2359), he learns that the fortress is free from enchantment. He and

---

[7] For the important concept of *costume* see Donald Maddox, "*Lancelot* et le sens de la coutume," *Cahiers de Civilisation Médiévale* 29 (1986): 330–53.

his companion join a battle between the captives, now in armed revolt, and the knights of Gorre. The arrival of Lancelot inspires the rebels, and before long they are victorious.

Lancelot is received that night by the second vavasseur as a hero and liberator. However, a fully-armed, uncourtly knight interrupts supper: the knight taunts Lancelot for planning to pass the Sword Bridge and an arduous duel ensues. As the winner, Lancelot would ordinarily spare the life of the knight on condition that he ride in a cart (2773). Yet suddenly, the fifth nameless damsel arrives and asks Lancelot for the head of the defeated knight as a gift. Lancelot grants the knight another duel, which he again wins, but this time Lancelot cuts off the knight's head. The damsel promises to reward Lancelot for his deed, and indeed she will.

The next morning, Lancelot arrives at the Sword Bridge. Passing it (3108–3131) is a frightful adventure in which he cuts his hands, feet, and knees to ribbons. Once across, his magic ring allows him to realize that the lions he had seen from the other bank were merely the result of an enchantment. The Bridge is close to King Bademagu's castle where the queen lies captive. Bademagu and Méléagant witness Lancelot's crossing and Bademagu now considers Lancelot "[li] mieudres chevaliers del monde" (3233) [the best knight in the world]. He tries in vain to convince his son to give up Guenièvre and to convince Lancelot to postpone the duel with Méléagant, both without success. News of the duel has spread: the young women captives have been praying and fasting three days for Lancelot's victory. Everyone watches the battle, even the queen. At the beginning, Lancelot appears weakened by the wounds he sustained while crossing the Bridge, and the duel goes badly for him. At this moment, the queen—for the first time—reveals the identity of her knight, saying to a maiden: "Lanceloz del Lac a a non / Li chevaliers . . ." (3676–3677) [Lancelot du Lac / Is the knight's name]. The maiden cries out: ". . . Lancelot! / Trestorne toi et si esgarde / Qui est qui de toi prent garde!" (3682–3684) [. . . Lancelot! / Turn around and look / Who is watching you!]. Seeing his lady-love gives him new strength. He positions himself so that Méléagant is between him and Guenièvre and fights, gazing constantly at the object of his love. As Méléagant begins to weaken, Bademagu begs the queen's permission to put an end to the fight. When she agrees, he stops the duel, even though Méléagant does not consider himself vanquished. A compromise is reached: Méléagant frees the queen with the rest of the captives on the condition that another duel will be fought in Arthur's court in one year's time; this duel will decide their final fate. Guenièvre and Lancelot consent to the accord (3902–3903) and everyone hails Lancelot the Liberator.

Lancelot wishes to see the queen, but to his astonishment she refuses, saying to King Bademagu: "De son veoir n'ai ge que faire" (3964) [I do not care to see him]. But Lancelot, like a perfect lover, accepts her decision. He goes to see Keu, who is still recovering from his wounds, and then leaves in search of Gauvain, accompanied by some of the former captives. The inhabitants of Gorre follow, however, and in keeping with their "custom" of unfaithfulness and treason, they seize Lancelot and hand him over to Bademagu (4150). The false rumor (*"novele,"* 4158–4160) of Lancelot's death begins to circulate and reaches Guenièvre's ears. So desperate that "A po qu'ele ne s'est occise" (4178) [She almost killed herself], she realizes, and we with her, that she has always loved Lancelot. In a long monologue (4185–4262), she blames herself for her cruel treatment of him and subsequently ceases to eat and drink. She appears so ill that another false rumor, this time of her death, reaches Lancelot (4268) when he is brought back to Bath. He tries to kill himself, but fails, and eventually the news reaches him that she is not dead. Similarly, the information that Lancelot is alive also reaches first Bademagu and later Guenièvre; the queen's reconciliation with her knight is now inevitable.

Bademagu himself arranges their meeting. Inspired by Love, the two speak joyously. Lancelot wishes to know the mysterious reasons for Guenièvre's previous angry reception. She answers clearly "Molt a gerant enviz i montastes" (4504) [You hesitated to enter (the cart)]. Guenièvre invites him to talk to her that night at her window; while they speak, she points the window out to him with her eyes (4525).

Nighttime arrives; Lancelot comes stealthily to the iron-barred window where Guenièvre awaits. They greet each other eagerly, "Que molt estoient desirrant / Il de li et ele de lui" (4606–4607) [Because they desired each other greatly / He desired her, and she him]. Lancelot asks permission to enter the room, and she replies, "Certes, fet ele, je voel bien" (4634) [Certainly, she says, I wish it]. Lancelot twists apart the solid bars covering the window and in the process cuts his finger, which bleeds profusely. He comes to Guenièvre's bed, "Si l'aore et se li ancline, / Car an nus cors saint ne croit tant" (4670–4671) [He bends down to her in adoration, / Because he does not believe in any holy relic as much as he believes in her]. But Guenièvre takes the initiative: she extends her arms and draws him to her: "Que d'Amors et del cuer li muet. / D'Amors vient qu'ele le conjot" (4678–4679) [Because Love and her heart dictate her action. / Love makes her receive him thus]. They pass the night in each other's arms, but the poet insists that their delights and joys should be kept hidden from the reader (4702). Lancelot leaves his lover unwillingly, straightens up the bars of the window, and arrives in his lodgings without being seen by anyone. He has, however, left a sign of his presence: the sheets of the bed are stained with his blood.

The next day, Méléagant visits Guenièvre and discovers the stains. Because Keu's wound has opened during the night and there are stains on his bed as well as the queen's, Méléagant promptly accuses Keu of sleeping with the queen. She denies vehemently—and truthfully—her involvement with Keu. Méléagant, who has always desired the queen, accuses her formally before his father, but Lancelot offers to defend Keu in a judiciary duel. Méléagant swears Keu's guilt and Lancelot his innocence. The duel is fought fiercely, but Bademagu again asks Guenièvre to interrupt. Her secret and her honor are saved by this request.

## Part Two

The second part of the romance opens with Lancelot again in search of Gauvain. He meets (another) dwarf who promises to take him to a "molt boen leu" (5095) [very good place], provided that nobody follows him. Lancelot does not suspect the treacherous dwarf, who delivers him into the hands of his enemies (5104–5105). Distressed by Lancelot's disappearance, his companions continue on without him and find Gauvain in the water, close to the Underwater Bridge. Gauvain immediately inquires about the queen and is told about Lancelot and his exploits; the company of knights then returns to Bath. The queen and the former captives rejoice in Gauvain's safe return, but their joy is marred by anxiety about Lancelot's fate.

Bademagu organizes a search party for Lancelot, but at this very moment a messenger arrives with a letter (5272). The letter, supposedly written by Lancelot, claims that he has returned to King Arthur's court safe and sound. The next day, the queen and the other former captives leave Bath. Arthur and the people of Logres greet the queen joyfully.

During Guenièvre's absence from the court, some young noble ladies had planned a great tournament. The participants are to be divided between two camps: the lady of Noauz is in charge of the first camp, and the lady of Pomelegoi of the second. As Chrétien explains, the aim of the ladies is not only competitive and chivalric, but also matrimonial: the winners of the tournament will be chosen as husbands.

The news of the tournament spreads beyond the kingdom of Logres until it reaches Lancelot, who has been imprisoned by Méléagant in the latter's seneschal's house. Lancelot begs the seneschal's wife—whose husband is temporarily absent—to let him go to the tournament, and swears that he will return to his prison afterwards. Acting on a clear understanding of the rules of courtesy, she extracts the promise of Lancelot's love upon his return, and he in turn assures her of ". . . tote celi que j'ai" (5502) [all (the love) that is at my disposal]. Although she understands perfectly that another has his heart, she lends him red armor and a charger.

Lancelot arrives at the court incognito. The herald immediately cries out the appellation under which Lancelot will participate in the tournament: "Or est venuz qui l'aunera!" (5583) [Now comes the one who will measure!]. Chrétien explains that the expression *qui l'aunera* is used for the first time on this occasion.[8] The splendid tournament is attended by many spectators including the queen. She suspects that "he who will measure" might be Lancelot, and, to verify her suspicion, sends him a message requesting that he fight "au noauz" (5664–5665).

---

[8] There have been many discussions as to the possible figurative meanings of *aunera*. However, the literal meaning of *auner* (two syllables) is transparent: 'to measure,' from *aune* 'yardstick.'

The adverb (and adjective) *noauz* (*noals)* means "bad," "worse," therefore *au noauz* means "in a worse manner." Where any other knight would have interpreted *au noauz* simply to mean being part of the "team" of the lady of Noauz, Lancelot understands and is ready to compromise his knightly status once again for the sake of love. Love wins over honor, for now he fights badly. The onlookers mock him, but Guenièvre is delighted, for she knows that the knight must be Lancelot. His performance "au noauz" continues for the rest of the day and part of the second.

The queen, absolutely certain that he is "cil cui ele est tote" (5894) [the one to whom she belongs entirely], immediately sends him message to do "au mialz" (5899) [his best]. Lancelot obeys again, and now jousts like a champion. He is proclaimed the true winner of the tournament (6047) but must, however, obey the promise given to the seneschal's wife. He leaves the field stealthily to return to his prison (6078).

After the tournament, Méléagant and his treacheries take center stage in the *Charrette*. To prevent the final duel between Lancelot and himself, he orders the construction of a stone tower on a remote sea island in the wilds of Gorre and has Lancelot walled up inside. There is only a small window through which Lancelot receives his meager rations of food and drink, which are hauled up on a rope. We shall learn in the Epilogue that Chrétien ends his section of the *Charrette* here; from this moment on, the romance was composed by Godefroi de Leigni.

When the space of one year draws to a close and the appointed time arrives, Méléagant goes to Arthur's court and demands that the promised duel with Lancelot be arranged. No one except the traitor knows where Lancelot is, and so Gauvain offers to fight in Lancelot's place if the latter cannot be found. Méléagant returns to Bath during the celebration of Bademagu's birthday, and, in the hearing of all the barons, brags that he is feared by everybody in Arthur's court. The king tries in vain to teach him humility.

One of Bademagu's daughters, who is none other than the fifth unnamed damsel, overhears the conversation. Alone, she leaves in search of Lancelot. After a month of traveling, she arrives close to the tower, and, seeing it, is astonished by the lack of doors and windows. Suddenly (6480), she hears a weak and sad voice coming from the small window. It is poor Lancelot complaining (6488–6549) against cruel Fortune and the inability of his friend Gauvain to find him. The helpful maiden finds a strong pickax, sends it up with the rope, and in the space of four verses (6642–6645), Lancelot makes a breach in the wall large enough to escape. The rescuing maiden takes him to a dwelling that she knows to be nearby, and nurses him back to health. Soon they separate and Lancelot rides alone to avenge the traitorous Méléagant.

The poet now returns us to Arthur's court, where Méléagant demands a duel. Gauvain, fully armed, is prepared to fight, when suddenly Lancelot appears (6809). A general joy greets his arrival and Guenièvre conceals her intense emotion with difficulty. The duel is hard-fought, but finally Méléagant falls to the ground and Lancelot cuts off his head (7109). To general rejoicing, they disarm

Lancelot and lead him from the field of battle: "Ci faut li romans . . ." (7123) [Here ends the romance . . .].

I hold with an important segment of critical opinion that the principal significance of the *Charrette* lies in the fact that the queen's rescuer is her lover. Lancelot appears in v. 273, so to speak, out of nowhere. We do not know who he is, but we learn that he is known to the perfect knight, Gauvain. Most importantly, he is the *ami* of Guenièvre, who hopes to be rescued by him. At the end of the romance he disappears again.

Love in the *Charrette* is presented in the lyric tradition of the troubadours and *trouvères*: the love between Lancelot and Guenièvre not only stresses the joy of a passionate desire, but includes what the troubadours called *lo plus*, that is, the sexual union of the lovers. In all probability this shocking idea of an adulterous and treasonable union was furnished to Chrétien by his patron's *san*. It was perhaps shocking to Chrétien himself, because in his other romances he defends the doctrine of love in marriage.

Prior to the *Charrette*, another story known in OF literature of an adulterous union between a queen and her husband's subject is found in the *Roman de Brut*. In this tale, the usurper of Arthur's kingdom, Mordred, seduces Guenièvre. This seduction is presented in the romance and in its Latin model as a "natural" outcome of Mordred's far more serious crime: political treason and usurpation.[9] Even more important to an understanding of the *Charrette* is the representation of love in *Tristan et Iseut*, for there is an indication that Chrétien disapproved of this tale.[10] In all the known versions of that famous legend, the love between Tristan and Iseut has a magical source: the fatal potion. The lovers are somewhat excused by the fatal power of the *philtre* and made pathetic by their painful exile from the court and their attempts to return. Nevertheless, their magic love must end in death.

In the *Charrette*, however, love subsists without any magico-chemical prompt. It is a pure and obsessive love, but a *courtly* love. Unlike the involuntary love in *Tristan*,[11] the union of Lancelot and Guenièvre is consciously accepted by both lovers. Lancelot loves Guenièvre before the action of the *Charrette* begins:

---

[9] See Wace, *Le Roman de Brut*, ed. Ivor Arnold, 2 vols. (Paris: SATF, 1938–1940), 2: 11175–11187, 13025–13030. Mordred is anything but a *fin amant*: he is a traitor in politics and in love.

[10] In *Cligès*, Chrétien presents a magical potion twice to spare his heroine Iseut's humiliating role of belonging to two men. In the Prologue to that romance (1–7), Chrétien states that he is the author of *Erec et Enide* and of some Ovidian tales, and an elaboration of the Tristan story bearing the intriguing title *Del roi Marc et Iseut la blonde*. Could it have been a Tristan story defending the principle of marriage?

[11] Shades of the Tristan legend—the association of love and death—are perhaps to be found in the *Charrette* in Lancelot's attempt at suicide, and in the queen's final realization of her love brought about by the false "noveles" of Lancelot's death.

he rushes to her rescue as soon as he hears that Méléagant has taken her from
the court. We have seen that in the moment of being handed over to Méléagant,
she whispers, addressing herself to an absent "vos" (var. "amis") (211), and her
words obviously refer to the absent Lancelot. From subsequent events, we can assume her words indicate that she has loved Lancelot before the opening of the
*Charrette*.[12] This, incidentally, should excuse Godefroi de Leigni's abrupt ending
of the *Charrette*. Having obtained the ultimate victory over his mortal enemy,
Lancelot cannot encounter Guenièvre in her normal hierarchical situation. Their
love and their memories of the ineffable happiness of their night together will
go on, but they cannot seek a prolongation or repetition of their experiences any
more than a lyric poem can continue after the prescribed number of stanzas.

The love in the *Charrette* is also a mutual one. While it is easy to see that
Lancelot loves Guenièvre, one must also realize that she loves him from the very
beginning of the romance. Her whispered words (cited above), uttered just before
she leaves Camaalot with Méléagant, furnish proof of this mutuality. (Incidentally, her words point to the importance of variants, and hence to one of the central tenets of endeavors such as the *Charrette Project*.) Their love, unlike the love
in *Tristan*, does not lead to a conflict between love and society. There are no *los-
engiers* in the *Charrette*:[13] Lancelot and Guenièvre's love is not suspected by anyone. Their love is protected by the courtly principles of control and discretion. I
believe that, for the medieval audience, their absolute prudence and discretion in
fulfilling their love could constitute a certain excuse for their behavior. The conflict between love and society is avoided by Lancelot's obedience to his *domna*,
who insists upon and herself practices the principle of discretion and secrecy.

Guenièvre's love for Lancelot and her conviction that he loves her completely
makes her decide to choose, in troubadour terminology, *lo plus*, that is, sexual
consummation of her love. Her haughty behavior rightfully belongs to her rank,
both as wife of Lancelot's sovereign and as courtly beloved who is the natural
object of her lover's affection, devotion, and obedience. In the troubadour language she is Lancelot's *midons*, that is, his feudal lord. Yet her haughty behavior
also signifies something more important. Before choosing *lo plus*—because it is,
in fact, she who decides and arranges their encounter—she must be absolutely
sure that Lancelot loves her completely and without reservation. Love of the
queen can be bestowed only on an extraordinary man. This explains her chiding
of Lancelot for hesitating slightly to enter the infamous and dishonoring cart.
During the tournament, her order to him to fight *au noauz* was based on her

---

[12] See Alfred Foulet, "Guenevere's Enigmatic Words: *Lancelot*, vv. 211–13," in *Jean
Misrahi Memorial Volume: Studies in Medieval Literature* (Columbia, SC: French Literature Publications, 1977), 175–79.

[13] If Méléagant is a *losengier* or *jalos*, his suspicion falls on the perfectly innocent
Keu, permitting Lancelot to be technically a legitimate defender of the queen's honor.

desire to penetrate his incognito, for she knows now that no other knight except Lancelot would sacrifice his chivalric honor to his love.

Courtly love, presented in its absolute form, constitutes thus the main explanation and perhaps justification for Lancelot and Guenièvre's adulterous union—*amor vincit omnia*. Nonetheless, it is possible that Chrétien presents mitigating circumstances when he explains the *costume* of Logres pertaining to traveling ladies. Lancelot wins the queen from Méléagant, her abductor. Furthermore, her matrimonial (and political) status is somewhat compromised by the fact that she—a captive—and her lover are outside of Logres, and that Arthur allowed her to be taken from there.

Lancelot's chivalry, like his love, is extraordinary. As we have seen, it is sometimes presented in religious terms. In the Judeo-Christian tradition, the love of God has all the attributes of human love, pushed to its extreme. An absolute human love participates in aspects of the love of the divine. Some modern readers of the *Charrette* discern humor in seeing Lancelot "exaggerating" his state: i.e., being lost in his amorous meditations, forgetting the reality around him, adoring Guenièvre's strand of hair, or treating her—while she awaits him in her bed—more reverently than any holy relic. We have been taught by our post-courtly tradition to smile gently, if not laugh derisively, at the conflicts between love's desires and daily reality. I believe, however, that Chrétien's public—those numerous ladies with their mastery of the courteous French language—did not smile indulgently or laugh derisively at these situations. Lancelot's adventures in general and his great love adventure in particular were taken seriously by Chrétien's medieval audience. When the Lancelot of the *Charrette* or of its later continuations is mentioned in other medieval works, it is always with a respect due to a chivalric and courtly paragon. A rather obvious observation is perhaps in order: neither Chrétien nor his audience had heard about *Don Quixote*, but without the *Charrette* and its tradition Cervantes could never have written his masterpiece in the same way.

The first part of the *Charrette* is dominated by five damsels who both help Lancelot and test his character. Again, modern readers have a tendency to consider the actions of these ladies as somewhat "remote-controlled" by the queen, who is anxious to test Lancelot. But Chrétien never says or suggests this. Instead, things happen to our hero *par aventure*. If there is a certain amount of "logic" to events in the *Charrette,* it can be explained in part by the spreading of knowledge of what happens. It is based on the principle that the actions of the main protagonists become known through the circulation of *noveles*, in which the false reports can be as important as the true ones. It is thus through the *noveles*, rather than the communication with the ugly dwarf, that the queen learns about Lancelot's momentary hesitation to get into the cart. The damsels, even the most extravagant and extraordinary damsel of them all, are fundamentally supporters of the *costume* of Logres with its insistence on chivalric and courtly virtues and values.

Older critics interested in explaining the sense of the *Charrette* from the vantage point of Celtic or, for that matter, classical origins[14] saw in the passage into Gorre the passage to the Other World. Chrétien depicts this Other World as one dominated by culture and values opposite to the *costume* of Logres. Accordingly, the significance of the second part is dominated by Lancelot's incessant (but often suspended) struggle against the uncourtly *costume* of Gorre and its chief representative, the truly diabolical Méléagant. He portrays all Lancelot's virtues in their opposite vices. Where Lancelot is faithful, truthful, and selfless, Méléagant is faithless, mendacious, and self-seeking.

Perhaps as an echo of the Celtic lore behind the *Charrette*, there are supernatural elements injected into the story. The flaming lance, the mysterious cemetery, and the magic ring inherited by Lancelot from his adoptive mother, the *Dame del Lac*, are indeed magical. Foulet and Uitti suppose, perhaps with reason, that the Immodest Damsel is a fairy.[15] Although such elements of the *merveilleux* add to a certain coloring of "surrealism" proper to many romances, they contribute little to the significance of the *Charrette*. Lancelot's ring furnishes a particularly good illustration of this point: Lancelot uses it not to create magic, but rather to test whether the magic he encounters is real.

In this Other World of Gorre, there are people who instinctively support Lancelot and, by extension, the *costume* of Logres. Bademagu, his daughter who becomes Lancelot's rescuer, and the wife of Méléagant's seneschal represent potential "candidates" for membership in a realm of courtesy and chivalry that is the realm of the *costume* of Logres.

This brings us to the most important aspect of the significance of the *Charrette*. By striving to free the object of his love, Lancelot becomes the Liberator of the people. His role as the archetypal hero who frees the people from bondage follows naturally from his role as an ideal lover. Lancelot would not have become the Liberator without his unconditional love for the queen. Unlike Tristan, whose adulterous love separates him from society, Lancelot's selfless, courtly love leads him to be integrated fully among the people of Logres and to become the chief defender and champion of their *costume*. Thus the significance of the *Charrette* is an extension of the courtly idea: the noble heart guiding his noble deeds will ultimately lead to common good. Such a role was hinted at in *Erec et Enide* and in *Yvain*, but it is fully developed in the *Charrette*. And this is indeed the main significance of this magnificent romance: that deeds based on selfless virtue will follow the hero. Blessed be such a hero.

---

[14] For example, Tom P. Cross and William A. Nitze, *Lancelot and Guenevere: A Study on the Origins of Courtly Love* (Chicago: University of Chicago Press, 1930) and Roger Sherman Loomis, *Celtic Myth and Arthurian Romance* (New York: Columbia University Press, 1927).

[15] See their note to v. 2023, 115.

# PART II.

## *TRANSLATIO*:
## CONTEXTUALIZING THE ROMANCE

# Intimations of Ambiguity in some Initial Images of the *Chevalier de la Charrette*[1]

John V. Fleming
Princeton University

Most great writers make conscious artistic use of ambiguities, contrasts, shifting perceptions, competing levels of perception. This was perhaps especially true of medieval Christian writers, whose broader literary culture found its center in scriptural exposition, the search for a "spirit" to be found within the "letter," and featured among its most influential vernacular compositions formal allegories such as the *Roman de la Rose*, the *Divine Comedy*, or *Piers Plowman*. While Chrétien de Troyes's romances belong to another genre, they characteristically include narrative elements, often accompanied by symbolic actions, of ambiguous import. It is in such a contested symbolic action that Chrétien grounds the very title of his poem, when in its early lines a knight—we do not as yet know that it is Lancelot—after but a brief hesitation mounts a cart customarily used to expose criminals to public opprobrium. He does so, of course, because the sinister dwarf who is driving the cart proposes that by mounting it he will be able to find out what has become of the queen, whom he loves passionately.

To climb into the cart is to incur a strong social stigma, but he does so, virtually without a qualm, at the behest of the god of Love. We have here an orchestrated clash of values in which Love triumphs over social propriety. Lancelot appropriates what is widely regarded as a symbol of shame into a symbol of his obeisance to Love. Yet the conventional view thus contested is by no means silenced. Gawain, given the same invitation, regards what Lancelot has done as

---

[1] It would not have been possible to be a colleague of Karl Uitti's for so many years as I was without developing a keen admiration, sometimes threatening to descend into vulgar envy, for the long succession of his talented graduate students, many of whom are today among the world's foremost scholars of medieval French literature. It is a particular pleasure, therefore, to have been invited to join forces with a number of them in an enterprise dedicated to Karl's memory and centered on a great poem with which his name will long be associated, the *Chevalier de la Charrette* of Chrétien de Troyes.

Gina L. Greco and Ellen M. Thorington, eds., *Dame Philology's Charrette: Approaching Medieval Textuality through Crétien's 'Lancelot': Essays in Memory of Karl D. Uitti.* MRTS 408. Tempe: ACMRS, 2012. [ISBN 978-0-86698-456-0]

great folly (*molt grant folie*, 393).[2] Hence the moral problem is raised on the poem's formal agenda. It is not simply that one man's meat is another man's poison. The reader is forced to take a stand as to whether Lancelot has chosen wisely or, indeed, whether he has any choice at all.

For, after all, what is shameful and foolish from one perspective may be most glorious and wise from another. The doctrine of Christ crucified, "foolishness to the Greeks" was for the elect "the power of God and the wisdom of God" (1 Cor. 1: 23–24). The central symbol of the Christian faith, the cross, was a badge of shame transformed to a sign of triumph. Many medieval poems explore that paradox, but none more brilliantly than the Old English "Dream of the Rood." In that poem the speaker is the cross, thought of as a member of the warrior band of Christ's Germanic *comitatus*. His primary recognized social duty, therefore, is to defend the life of his lord. Instead a revolutionary obedience demands that he become the slayer of his lord.

An analogue more appropriate to Chrétien is to be found in the brilliant fourteenth-century English romance *Sir Gawain and the Green Knight*. In that poem the questing hero accepts as a gift from his temptress an intimate garment, a girdle, which he believes (or at any rate hopes) to have magical life-saving properties. Since he is facing imminent decapitation, we may forgive him; but he is not able to forgive himself. The girdle becomes for him a shameful symbol of his cowardice and his "covetise" for his life—a symbol of his failure. But the members of Arthur's court do not let that judgment stand. Instead, they adopt the girdle as a talisman of the highest chivalry. There is good reason to believe that the ambiguities of romance were continuous with the ambiguities of lived experience. The cryptic colophon of the unique manuscript of the *Gawain* is "HONI SOIT QUI MAL PENCE." This is a version of the motto of the Order of the Garter, among the most chivalric societies in Europe. A garter is very like a girdle, as the etymons suggest. The legendary founding of the Order of the Garter dates from an episode in the life of Edward III, who chivalrously retrieved a garter that had slipped from a lady's leg on the dance floor. It might be possible to interpret in more ways than one the gesture of royal address to an intimate item of female clothing, with some interpretations more carnal than others. The king uttered a famous "courtly saying" to remove all doubt. *Honi soit qui mal y pense*: Shame on him who evil thinks.

In this essay I propose to take note of three images of ambiguity or contrast that decorate the rather complex opening of Chrétien's poem. The contrasts are between infancy and maturity, jest and earnest, and mouth and heart. The last is the strangest and most fecund of them, but all three invite the reader to question and to adjudicate the moral behavior of the poem's hero and the moral ethos

---

[2] All quotations from Chrétien's *Lancelot* are taken from Chétien de Troyes, *Le Chevalier de la Charrette (Lancelot)*, ed. Alfred Foulet and Karl D. Uitti (Paris: Bordas, 1989).

of the court to which he is attached. The method will be to adduce parallel images or ideas in the three greatest English romances of the fourteenth century: *Sir Gawain and the Green Knight*, Chaucer's "Knight's Tale," and his *Troilus and Criseyde*. The authors are the two in the medieval English canon who are most closely related to Chrétien in their humanistic spirit, their ethical dexterity, and, especially, in their interrogation of courtly and chivalric ideals.

Yet there will be of course no claim of direct genetic influence. Though the young Chaucer was deeply immersed in the French literary culture in which he was raised and seems to have read most of the important French authors who preceded him, there is no irrefutable evidence that he read Chrétien. As for the *Gawain*-poet, it is probable that he was as familiar as Malory would be in the fifteenth century with the old "French books" that were the classics of romance and gave the genre its name, but the only French romance he alludes to by name is the *Roman de la Rose*. Nor do I suppose any two instances of a literary phenomenon separated by two centuries and a wide expanse of intellectual history define a "topos" any more than two swallows proclaim a summer. But all three poets are deeply invested in definable literary traditions. Indeed the originality of each is defined precisely in terms of a relationship with definable literary tradition. What Horace has said of the poetry of tradition in the first Augustan Age was paraphrased by Pope in the second: "True wit is Nature to advantage dress'd, / What oft was thought but ne'er so well expressed." Let us turn to a few instances of what "oft was thought" by writers of medieval romance.

## I. Infancy and Maturity

Chrétien's *Lancelot* begins with a sequence of beginnings. There are in fact three of them, characterized by what might be called incremental confusion. In what is usually regarded as the "Introduction" the author identifies the occasion of his project. Madame de Champagne has asked him to write. The worthiness of the patron must trump the inadequacy of the poet, so he will here begin a book called "The Knight in the Cart." The "Introduction" is, comparatively speaking, lucid and uncomplicated.

Then we have what might be called the beginning proper, an account of the troubled festivities at Arthur's Ascension Day Court, in which the narrative's subject seems at first undecided. The poem initially suggests, perhaps, that it will be about someone unexpectedly *entering* the court: an unidentified knight who brusquely issues threats, insults, and finally a challenge. The mystery knight holds several of Arthur's people in thrall; and the king answers, feebly, that if he cannot repair the situation, he will simply have to endure it. The knight's brutal challenge is this: if the king has a single knight in whom he has sufficient confidence to send out against him, *accompanied by the queen*, he may regain the captives. Of course if he loses, the queen too will fall into his power.

Then the narrative becomes one concerning someone unexpectedly *exiting* the court. Kay tells the king that, after long years of service, he wants out. The king seems to forget all about the intrusive knight. He implores him to stay, but Kay is adamant. Then the queen begs Kay to stay. Now Kay relents, provided that the queen will promise, in the king's name, to grant a request, as yet unspecified, that Kay will make. This she promises to do.

When it comes to the point of course, the queen and others fault the king for honoring a rash promise made to satisfy Kay's "orguel, outrage et desreison" (188); but for the king a promise is a promise. Gawain's rebuke of the king likewise points to his unreasonable behavior: "'Sire', fet il, 'mout grant anfance / Avez feite, et mout m'an mervoil . . .'" (228–229). The meaning of *anfance*, which is a noun and is something that Arthur has "done" or "made," has to be "childishness," "childish behavior," "a childish act," or the like. Uitti and Foulet say "ce que vous avez fait est bien puéril."[3] Deborah Rogers has "you've done something extremely childish."[4] The Pléiade translation turns it into an adverb (Arthur has behaved *bien naïvement*).[5] While this by no means misses the sense, I prefer those translations that keep the child in the text, because it helps us see in the topos a possible biblical echo of a famous Pauline passage (1 Cor. 13:11). But first we must realize that Arthur's childishness is indeed a topos, if by that we mean it is a theme that occurs in more than one romance. In the greatest of the English Arthurian poems, *Sir Gawain and the Green Knight*, we find, in strikingly similar context, the following passage. This poem, too, begins with the king's court gathered for a festival meal.

> But Arthure wolde not ete til al were serued,
> He wats so joly of his joyfness, and sumquat childgered:
> His life liked hym lyȝt, he louied the lasse
> Auther to longe lye or to longe sitte,
> So busied him his ȝonge blod and his brayn wylde. (85–89)[6]

The poet goes on to explain that it is not merely courtesy that keeps Arthur from beginning his meal before all have been served. He has made it a point of honor not to eat a high holiday meal until he has heard, "Of sum auenturus thing an vncouthe tale, / Of sum mayn meruayle, that he myȝt trawe . . ." (93–94). Of

---

³ *Le Chevalier de la Charrette*, ed. Foulet and Uitti, ad loc.

⁴ Chrétien de Troyes, *Lancelot, The Knight of the Cart*, ed. Deborah Webster Rogers, intro. W. T. H. Jackson, Records of Civilization: Sources and Studies 97 (New York: Columbia University Press, 1984).

⁵ Chrétien de Troyes, *Lancelot, ou Le Chevalier de la Charrette*, ed. Daniel Poirion, in *Œuvres complètes*, Bibliothèque de la Pléiade (Paris: Gallimard, 1994), 505–682.

⁶ All quotations from *Sir Gawain* are taken from *Sir Gawain and the Green Knight*, ed. J. R. R. Tolkien and E. V. Gordon, 2ⁿᵈ ed., rev. Norman Davis (Oxford: Clarendon Press, 1967).

course he gets a dilly of a pre-prandial adventure in the form of a visit from the Green Knight, "uncouth" in both its medieval and its modern senses. Indeed the opening actions of the *Lancelot* and the *Green Knight* are so similar that it is impossible not to suppose the direct or mediated influence of the former upon the latter. In each a hostile knight appears to disturb Arthur's revels, and in each Gawain sets out as the king's champion. It is at least possible that Gawain's astonishment at the king's "childish behavior" in Chrétien (*mout* m'an *mervoil*) is linguistically echoed by the Gawain-poet (sum *mayn meruayle*). This possibility of course points to another: that Arthurian "childishness" may be thematically linked in the two poems.

Is regal childishness a thing good, bad, or indifferent? When Chrétien's Gawain says "mout grant anfance avez feite," it is clearly a reprimand. The *anfance*—agreeing to honor Guinevere's rash vow—appears to have placed his wife in jeopardy. That the English romance's Arthur is "sumquat childgered" seems at first perhaps less censorious. The condition manifests a kind of coltishness, youthful exuberance, the product of "his 30nge blod and his brayn wylde." Yet again in the narrative context it is an invitation to danger and disorder.

It might be useful here to adopt one of Karl Uitti's characteristic procedures and follow a frankly philological excursus. Though the meaning of "childgered" is fairly clear, the word itself remains mysterious. Tolkien's learned note convincingly argues that it is a compound, the second element of which comes from the noun *gere(s)*, of obscure etymology, meaning customary mode(s) of behavior, usually with the implication that the behavior is immature, extreme, or irrational. Tolkien draws attention to a well-known passage in Chaucer's most famous romance, the "Knight's Tale," dealing with the mad behavior of Arcite, a sufferer from the "lover's malady of Hereos."[7]

> What that Arcite hadde romed al his fille,
> And songen al the roundel lustily,
> Into a studie he fil sodeynly,
> As doon this lovers in hir queynte *geres*,
> Now in the crope, now doun in the breres,
> Now up, now doun, as boket in a welle. (KT 1528–1533)[8]

In this text *geres* denotes the curious, mercurial, indeed bipolar modes of behavior characteristic of pathological love. The lover's malady of Hereos, as D.W. Robertson and others have shown, is the specific medical and scientific version of the "love" defined by Andreas Capellanus as a *passio mentis* and by Lady Reason

---

[7] *Sir Gawain*, ed. Tolkien and Gordon, 75.

[8] All quotations from *The Canterbury Tales* are taken from *The Works of Geoffrey Chaucer*, ed. F. N. Robinson, The New Cambridge Edition, 2nd ed. (Boston: Houghton Mifflin, 1957).

in the *Roman de la Rose* as a *maladie de pensee.*[9] In the romance context, Arthurian "childishness" is a topic wholly congruent to the major themes of all three authors—Chrétien, the *Gawain*-poet, and Chaucer—which is an exploration of eroticism as a complication of chivalric behavior.

This is the sense also of *gere(s)* in the early English text Tolkien cites to explicate the word. That text is the *Ormulum*, written at Bourne Abbey in Lincolnshire about 1175—roughly contemporaneous with Chrétien's *Charrette*, indeed. I offer that somewhat gratuitous observation only because it seems unlikely that any other comparison between the two works is likely to come forward. The *Ormulum*, a collection of versified homilies, is "drasty rhyming" of a rather oppressive kind. Its importance is unrelated to its conceptual or aesthetic achievement. It is a rare extended example of early Middle English that, because of the customized orthography adopted by Orm, its Anglo-Scandinavian author, is invaluable for the study of the history of English pronunciation. But Orm incidentally makes clear a biblical allusion that is probably latent in Chrétien as well.

> For Latin boc uss seȝȝth full wel
> That tatt man iss forrwarrȝedd
> That iss an hunndredd winnterr ald,
> & follȝhethth childes gæress. (8047–8050)[10]

This means: "For the Latin book tells us clearly that that man is cursed who, though a hundred years old, behaves in a childlike manner (follows *childes gæress*)." Now the Latin book is either the Vulgate itself or, more likely, a Vulgate text with an actual or implied gloss surrounding it. It is indeed clear that Orm has in mind a specific scriptural citation—Isaiah 65:20—but the *clarity* of that text itself may be in the eye of the beholder. "Non erit ibi amplius infans dierum, et senex qui non impleat dies suos, quoniam puer centum annorum morietur, et peccator centum annorum maledictus erit"—in the Douay translation: "There shall no more be an infant of days there, nor an old man that shall not fill up his days: for the child shall die a hundred years old, and the sinner being a hundred years old shall be accursed."

In its context as the prologue to one of the most famous of Messianic prophecies ("The wolf and the lamb shall feed together: the lion and the ox shall eat straw. . .," Isaiah 65:25), the meaning appears to be that in a blessed future time there will be no infant mortality, all men will live to a ripe old age, and justice

---

[9] D.W. Robertson, *A Preface to Chaucer* (Princeton: Princeton University Press, 1962), 108–10; M.A. Wells, *The Secret Wound: Love-Melancholy and Early Modern Romance* (Stanford: Stanford University Press, 2007).

[10] All citations from *The Ormulum* are taken from Orm, *The Ormulum, with the Notes and Glossary of Dr. R. M. White*, ed. Robert Holt, vol. 1 (Oxford: Clarendon Press, 1879).

will escape no one.[11] But the passage is obscure. The medieval exegetical consensus is recorded, as it so often is, by the Renaissance scholar Cornelius à Lapide. He cites his fellow Jesuit Sanchez to gloss the phrase *infans dierum*: "scilicet multorum est is qui ætatis multos dies et annos habet, sed quoad sapientiam et mores est infans."[12] The matter is somewhat tricky from the biblical point of view, for of course there is a "good" childishness. In a well-known passage Jesus said that only the childlike can enter the kingdom of heaven (Matthew 18:3). But nowhere in the exegetical tradition is the *infans dierum* an *infans in bono*. On the contrary, he is the one who, though ostensibly of mature years, continues to behave as a child. That is certainly Gawain's charge against Arthur. And for a grown man to behave as a child "in terms of mores and wisdom" inevitably invites another and more famous biblical text: the Apostle Paul's contrast between childishness and maturity. Hence Orm continues thus:

> & of thiss illke se33de thuss
> the posstell Sannte Pawell;
> A33 whil that I wass litell child
> Icc held of childess thæwess,
> and son summ icc wass waxenn mann,
> that flæh I childess cosstess. (8051–8056)

That is, "When I was a child, I spoke as a child, I understood as a child, I thought as a child. But when I became a man, I put away the things of a child" (1 Cor. 13: 11). This verse is immediately followed by two of the most famous in Saint Paul: "We see now through a glass in a dark manner; but then face to face. Now I know in part: but then I shall know even as I am known. And now there remain faith, hope, and charity, these three: but the greatest of these is charity" (1 Cor. 13:12–13). The verses clarify the meaning of Paul's similes of infancy and adulthood. The latter is a condition that corrects, displaces, supersedes, the former. The phrase "through a glass darkly" (*per speculum in aenigmate*) is among the most privileged phrases in the vocabulary of medieval allegory.[13] Nor is the explanation of the privilege difficult to adduce. What we see now is cloudy, partial, vague, imprecise. It may indeed be wholly deceptive. The anagogic vision will be very different: plenary, true. In literary terms the vision of the spiritual sense is appropriate to maturity. That of the literal or carnal sense is characteristic of childishness. But since these are images of spiritual qualities, it is of course

---

[11] Thus the *Jerusalem Bible*: ". . . no more will be found the infant living a few days only, or the old man not living to the end of his days. To die at the age of a hundred will be dying young; not to live to be a hundred will be the sign of a curse."

[12] Cornelius à Lapide, *Commentaria in quatuor prophetas maiores* (Antwerp, 1703), 537.

[13] See Robert Javelet, *Image et ressemblance au douzième siècle: de Saint Anselme à Alain de Lille* (Paris: Letouzey et Ané, 1967), 1: 211–56.

possible for a literal adult man to speak, to understand, to think as a child, in short to follow *childes gæress*, to commit *anfances*, to be *sumquat childgered*.

## II. Earnest and Game

A second convention is what I shall call, following Chaucer, "earnest and game." When Kay tells Arthur he intends to leave his court, the king is dumbfounded. He can scarcely believe his ears. Surely his seneschal must be kidding! ('Est ce a certes ou a gas?' [98]). But Kay answers immediately that he is deadly earnest: "Je n'ai or cure de gabois, / Einz praing congié trestot a certes . . ." (100–101). There is an extended tragic-comic treatment of this theme at the beginning of Chaucer's "Knight's Tale," an inventive "translation" of Boccaccio's *Teseida*. The poem begins as Duke Theseus is riding home in triumph with his conquered bride-to-be, the Amazon Hippolyta, and her sister Emily. He is briefly distracted *en route* by the necessity of fighting and defeating the Theban tyrant Creon. He finds two Theban knights, Palamon and Arcite, still alive on the field of slaughter. He takes them back to Athens, where he incarcerates them—under life sentences excluding any possibility of parole—in a shared cell in a tower. The tower overlooks a garden in which Emily is wont to disport herself. One day Palamon looks out of the window, sees Emily, and falls in love with a speed and violence rarely paralleled even in the most "courtly" of erotic documents. Alerted by Palamon's extravagant groans, Arcite in turn goes to the window, looks down, and if possible falls even more deeply in love than did Palamon. When Arcite expresses his passion Palamon, who clearly believes in the principle "First come, first served," is indignant.

> This Palamoun, whan he tho wordes herde,
> Dispitously he looked and answerde,
> "Wheither seistow this in ernest or in pley?"
> "Nay," quod Arcite, "in ernest by my fey!
> God helpe me so, me lest ful yvele pley." (1123–1127)

We shall return to this passage presently. It may prove useful in preparation to take cognizance of two levels of Chaucerian context, the global and the local. In terms of the global, the poles of "earnest" and "game" provide the defining parameters of the *Canterbury Tales* as a whole. The tale-telling contest is perceived as a recreational activity that might mitigate the difficult business of peregrination. The recreational nature of poetry or song is a classical theme widely diffused in medieval literature. According to a frequently remarked passage in Virgil's ninth eclogue, song makes every highway more bearable: *minus via laedit*. Chaucer's Host may actually echo this very line with his phrase "to shorte with oure weye" (791). The rigors of the medieval road are adequately suggested by the etymological relationships between English *travel* and French *travail*. There is also a sacramental structure to the institution of pilgrimage itself. The physical journey is an external event that is in theory answered by a more important, inward motion of the soul. But Chaucer took particular pains to link the ideas of earnest and game (play) with notions of literary merit. The prize in the storytelling contest will go to "tales of best sentence and moost solaas" (GP 798). We have here a medieval reflex of the famous Horatian dictum that the successful poet must both please and instruct: *omne tulit punctum, qui miscuit utile dulci* (*Ars poetica* 343).[14] The best tale will be the one that has the most impressive moral significance *and* the most pleasing narrative. It is important to grasp that, in this way of thinking, moral meaning and literary construction are not the same thing, nor is one dependent upon the other. It is implicitly possible to have a pleasing poem that is not edifying and to have edification that is not poetically pleasing. Chaucer the pilgrim, the only narrator within the pilgrimage who tells two tales, seems to play a joke upon "himself" by telling one tale that has no *sentence* ("Sir Thopas") and one that is all *sentence* ("Melibee").

Though the Chaucerian terminology of *sentence* and *solaas* has no direct parallel in Chrétien, the commonplace ideas that underlie it may well bind the two poets together. Certain terms in Chretién's technical literary vocabulary—particularly *sens* and *conjointure*—have been much debated. Having accepted the obligation of reviewing the "literature" for the preparation of this essay, I conclude that the debate, insofar as it centers on the attempt to explicate Chrétien's vernacular terms in relation to an anterior Latin technical literary vocabulary, is not resolvable. In fact no significant new primary materials have been adduced since the publication in 1951 of a classic article by D. W. Robertson, which was itself responding to a classic article of 1915 by William Nitze.[15] Both scholars connected *sens (san)* with medieval Latin *sensus*. But that did not take us too far given the fact that in different contexts in the twelfth century *sensus* could mean either "the doctrinal content of a text" or "the superficial meaning of a text."[16] As to *conjointure*, Nitze preferred to connect it with the idea of *junctura* in Horace's *Ars poetica*. Robertson, on the other hand, found the more precise *conjunctura* in a highly relevant context in the *De planctu Naturae* of Alain de Lille, one of the

---

[14] Horace, *Satires, Epistles and Ars poetica, with an English Translation*, ed. and trans. H. Rushton Fairclough, Loeb Classical Library 194 (Cambridge, MA: Harvard University Press, 1929).

[15] See William A. Nitze, "*Sans* et *matière* dans les œuvres de Chrétien de Troyes," *Romania* 44 (1915): 14–36 and D. W. Robertson, "Some Medieval Literary Terminology, with Special Reference to Chrétien de Troyes," *Studies in Philology* 48 (1951): 669–92.

[16] Robertson, "Terminology," 692.

great school poems of the twelfth century.[17] Horatian *iunctura* appears to refer
to the effect of the combination of *words* within a poem. Alainian *conjunctura* in
its context referred to the wedding of words with the ideas or themes they ani-
mate. It should be obvious that *junctura* and *conjunctura* are lexical relatives, just
as junction and conjunction are. Still it may be possible to honor nuances. One
does not change trains at a conjunction nor link independent clauses with a junction. Robertson was pursuing an exegetical theme, Nitze a rhetorical one. The
striking artistic arrangement of words by which Horace ends his line ". . . utile
dulci" is perhaps *iunctura*. The way in which a poet expresses what is morally useful through what is verbally pleasing is perhaps *conjunctura*.

The more local significance of the themes of earnest and game in the
"Knight's Tale" also claims our attention. The idea of the *Canterbury Tales* is
founded in play, and play of a problematical nature.

> Greet chiere made oure Hoost us everichon,
> And to the soper sette he us anon.
> He served us with vitaille att the beste;
> Strong was the wyn, and wel to drynke us leste. . . .
> And after soper pleyen he bigan . . . (747–750, 758)

This is one of several places in the "Prologue" that create a tension between the
supposedly ascetic nature of the pilgrimage and its actual carnival tendencies. It
is also one of many textual reminiscences of the pilgrimage *par excellence*—the
Exodus. The line "And after soper pleyen he bigan" alludes to a famous text in
Exodus (32:6), "The people sat down to eat and drink, and they rose up to play."
I call it "famous" because it features prominently in Paul's "typological" interpretation of the events of the Exodus (1 Cor. 10). We recall that the "play" to which
the people arose was the shaping of a golden calf. "Neither become ye idolators,
as some of them, as it is written, *The people sat down to eat and drink, and rose up to
play*" (1 Cor. 10:7; emphasis mine). At the stunning conclusion of the "Pardoner's
Tale," when the Pardoner is trying to mulct his fellow pilgrims with his phony
relics and worthless pardons, Chaucer actually has him remember the golden
calf with another kind of play, word-play: "Boweth youre heed under this hooly
bulle!" (909). The Knight is chosen to be the initial narrator through the game
of "drawing straws"—a form of gaming that in the "Pardoner's Tale" reveals a
sinister potential.

The themes of earnest and game in the relationship between Palamon and
Arcite is developed within a context hardly less extravagant in its eroticism than
is the episode of Lancelot's mounting the tumbrel. Palamon and Arcite are fellow

---

[17] See William A. Nitze, *"Conjointure* in *Erec,* vs. 14," *Modern Language Notes* 69
(1954): 180–81 and D. W. Robertson's riposte, "A Further Note on *Conjointure,*" *Modern
Language Notes* 70 (1955): 415–16.

Theban knights and actual kinsmen—the originals, indeed, of the "two noble kinsmen." They are sworn blood-brothers and fellow prisoners condemned to share a common cell in their Athenian prison in perpetuity. One day, several years into their life sentence, a beautiful woman appears in a garden, a view of which is commanded by a barred window of the dungeon tower. Through this window Palamon chances to see her—with immediate and disastrous erotic results: "He cast his eye upon Emelya, / And therwithal he bleynte and cride, 'A!'" Amazingly, it has proved possible for some readers to come upon this couplet without laughing out loud. Palamon is for a moment uncertain whether the female vision is woman or goddess, though he soon enough plumps for divinity and, falling on his knees, worships her as Venus. Eventually Arcite too strolls over to the window, views the lady, and falls immediately and violently in love with her as well. It is his report of his own sudden erotic wound that causes Palamon to ask "Whether seistow this in ernest or in pley?"

Thus arises the strenuous erotic competition that is at the center of this story in many versions. Chaucer alone exposes the risible aspects of its tragicomedy through Virgilian and Boethian intertextual decorations. The two sworn blood-brothers, under life sentences of strait confinement, are now at each other's throats over which of them is to "get" the girl—whom they have never met, but only seen for a matter of a few seconds at a distance unspecified but implicitly considerable. Palamon's argument is that he saw her first. Arcite's finds that claim without force seeing as how Palamon cannot tell the difference between a woman and a goddess whereas he, Arcite, knows a succulent female mortal when he sees one.

## III. Mouth and Heart

The conflict of the heart and the head is one of the great matters of our literature, and the central matter of the vast body of European erotic lyric poetry in the Petrarchan tradition. The conflict of heart and mouth, on the other hand, seems quite rare. Yet Chretien tells us that Lancelot followed Love and not Reason, as the former was in his *cuer*, the latter only in his *bouche*. Context shows that *bouche* is here used in its relationship to words and human speech. The counsel of the god of Love was in the core of Lancelot's sensibility, that of Reason only on his lips. To Love Lancelot pays the service of a vassal. To Reason he pays only what we still call lip-service—a superficial and external acquiescence that denies the internal and the essential.

I know of only one parallel in medieval literature, but it is so famous and authoritative as necessarily to command our attention. It is to be found in the *Confessions* of Augustine. The third book of the *Confessions* begins with the young Augustine's arrival in Carthage, "a frying pan of evil loves." These are typified by the immoralities of the stage. But not all of his studies lacked moral edification. In the regular course of his rhetorical studies he came upon the *Hortensius* of Cicero, one of his set texts. "Inter hos ego imbecilla tunc ætate discebam libros eloquentiæ . . . peruemeram in librum cuiusdam Ciceronis, cuius linguam fere omnes mirantur, pectus non ita. Sed liber ille ipsius exhortationem continet ad philosophiam et uocatur Hortensius" [In the midst of all this at that tender age I was studying manuals of eloquence . . . I came upon a book of a certain Cicero, the *lingua* of which was admired by practically everybody, the *pectus* not so. But that very book contains an exhortation to philosophy, and it is called *Hortensius* . . .].[18]

This famous passage of the *Confessions* is full of complexities. The remarkable phrase *cuiusdam Ciceronis*—roughly the equivalent of "a certain Shakespeare"—seems designed to distance the intellectual posture of the bishop who writes from that of the young sinner of whom he writes. The terms *lingua* and *pectus*, however, seem quite clear, despite the fact that *pectus* is an odd word. The *lingua* is the book's style, the *pectus* is moral doctrine. Almost everyone praised the style, but very few understood its "message." The young Augustine, who did understand it, found that the book turned his prayers to the true God. That *pectus* means heart—the heart of the matter of the *Hortensius*—is obvious; but it is still an odd word. We should expect *cor*. The *pectus*, anatomically, is the chest cavity or rib-cage in which the heart is protected and enclosed. I am persuaded by a brilliant suggestion of Christine Mohrmann. The word *cor* appears very frequently in the Latin Bible, the word *pectus* infrequently. Augustine wishes to signal that while Cicero's work has a sound philosophical heart of truth, that heart is not identical with the truth of the Gospel. Its use is patronizing, a kind of lexical condescension.[19]

The archness that the mature Augustine displays with regard to his youthful enthusiasm for Cicero is matched by a certain archness with regard to Virgil. Though his own book competes with the *Æneid*, it never names that book. Instead we get the extraordinary periphrasis "Æneæ nescio cuius errores"—"the *errores* of I know not what Æneas" (1. 13. 20). The phrasing of "I know not what Æneas" is similar in its condescending tone to "a certain Cicero," but Augustine obviously wants the benefit of the pun on *errores*—the wanderings of Aeneas, the mistakes of Aeneas. He parallels them with his own topographic and moral errancy.[20] For even as in Carthage Aeneas was temporarily diverted from his sa-

---

[18] *Confessions*, 3.4.7. All quotations from the *Confessions* are taken from Augustine, *Confessiones, Books I-IV*, ed. Gillian Clark, Cambridge Greek and Latin Classics (Cambridge: Cambridge University Press, 1996). All English translations are taken from *Saint Augustine: Confessions*, trans. Henry Chadwick (Oxford: Oxford University Press, 1998 [1st ed. 1991]).

[19] See Maurice Testard, *Saint Augustin et Cicéron*, 2 vols. (Paris: Etudes Augustiniennes, 1958), 1:28, and Christine Mohrmann's review, *Vigiliæ Christianæ* 13 (1959): 239.

[20] Ronald Knox titled his autobiographical work, not 'A Spiritual Odyssey,' but *A Spiritual Aeneid* (London: Burns and Oates, 1950)—bringing him at last to Rome.

cred mission by the lusts of the flesh, so also was the young Augustine. The third book of the *Confessions* in particular seems to be structured around the idea of *error*, a spiritual zigging and zagging from the lubricity of the theater to the search for wisdom through Cicero to its misdirection with the Manichaeans, and at last to the Bible — on and on, back and forth. Thus the dim discovery of wisdom in the *Hortensius* is lost among the Manichaeans in rhetorical terms that make us see the relationship between the two episodes.[21]

> Itaque incidi in homines superbe delirantes, carnales nimis et loquaces, in quorum ore laquei diaboli et uiscum confectum conmixtione syllabarum nominis tui et domini Iesu Christi et paracleti consolatoris nostri spiritus sancti. Hæc nomina non recedebant de ore eorum, sed tenus sono et strepitu linguæ; ceterum cor inane ueri. (3.6.10)

> [Thus it was that I fell into the midst of men mad in their pride, carnal, and most garrulous. In their mouth were the devil's snares and a lime made up of a mixture of syllables: Thy name, and that of the Lord Jesus Christ and of the Paraclete, our consoler the Holy Spirit. These were never absent from their mouth, though merely as a noise and the clacking of the tongue; as for the rest, a heart empty of the truth.]

It was perhaps this passage the bishops had in mind when in the seventeenth century they wrote the beautiful "General Thanksgiving" in the *Book of Common Prayer* with its petition that the gospel be "not only on our lips, but in our lives." In any event in both of the Augustinian passages the *os* or *lingua* stands for what is said, a thing external and literal, indeed a "concoction of syllables," while the *pectus* or *cor* stands for something internal and spiritual.

The contrast of the mouth and the heart, where the mouth is a metonymy for an allegiance literal and external and the heart for something spiritual and internal, is sufficiently striking and unusual to lead us at least to entertain the possibility of a specific Augustinian influence on Chrétien. But however we resolve that suggestion, or more likely recognize its imponderability and leave it unresolved, the conflict between Reason, to whom Lancelot owes lip-service, and Love, to whom he owes a service far more profound, brings us very early to the moral problem at the center of the poem.

Twenty-five years ago in *Reason and the Lover*[22] I addressed the conflict between Love and Reason in the *Roman de la Rose*, a poem in which that debate is one of the two episodes that most clearly link the design of Guillaume de Lorris, possibly around 1240, with that of its more robust and Gothic continuator, Jean

---

[21] See Patrice Cambronne, "Augustin et l'Eglise Manichéenne: jalons d'un itinéraire," *Vita Latina* 115 (1989): 22–36.

[22] John V. Fleming, *Reason and the Lover* (Princeton: Princeton University Press, 1984).

de Meun, probably around 1280. (The other is the transformation of Ovid's story of Narcissus.) In Guillaume, as in Chrétien, the contest is merely suggested.

One of Chaucer's principal original interventions in his "translation" of Boccacio's story of Troilus is his injection of Boethian ideas, situations, and textual allusions. These begin in the first book, in the scene in which Pandarus, like Lady Philosophy, visits the bedside of his sick friend, and continue throughout the work.[23] It is probably that Chaucer's entirely new five-book structure invokes not merely the genre of the classical tragedy announced in the poem's opening lines but also the structure of the *Consolation of Philosophy*.

From the structural and intellectual points of view, one of the most obvious textual seams will be found in the relationships between books four and five of the two works. At the end of the fourth book of the *Consolation*, Lady Philosophy proposes the compatibility of God's foreknowledge and the liberty of the individual human will as a problem too difficult even for the greatest of the pagan sages. In the fifth book she and Boethius in dialogue do resolve the problem. This is precisely the question over which Troilus despairs in Chaucer's fourth book. Pandarus finds the hero alone in a temple (pagan, obviously) where he is praying to "the pitous goddes evrichone" that they would "doon hym sone out of the world to pace." His stated desire for a speedy death is perhaps compromised, perhaps exemplified by what next follows: a lengthy, point-by-point rehearsal of the preliminary parts of the Boethian argument.[24]

But of course Troilus, like all the other pagan philosophers, fails to crack this hard nut. In fact his approach to the problem is, from the philosophical point of view, feeble in the extreme. His enlightenment, such as it is, will be posthumous; and his fifth book is given over not to consolation but to misery, despair, and a hopeless death. It is accordingly in the mental drama of the fourth book that the contested moral ground of the poem is most clearly discerned. As Siegfried Wenzel has pointed out, that drama is defined by a contest between Love and Reason.[25] There are in fact three explicit invocations of the topos, the first of which alone has a textual basis in Boccaccio. It comes in the description of Troilus's agonized response to the proposal raised in the Trojan Parliament to exchange Criseyde for the Trojan warrior Antenor, held captive in the Greek camp.

---

[23] Alan Gaylord, "Uncle Pandarus as Lady Philosophy," *Papers of the Michigan Academy of Science, Arts, and Letters* 46 (1961): 571–95.

[24] See Geoffrey Chaucer, *Troilus and Criseyde*, ed. Robert K. Root (Princeton: Princeton University Press, 1926), 517. All quotations from *Troilus and Criseyde* are taken from Root's edition.

[25] Siegfried Wenzel, "Chaucer's Troilus of Book IV," *PMLA* 79 (1964): 542–47. Though in what follows I depend on Wenzel's scrupulous presentation of the textual data, including its relationship to the Italian of the *Filostrato*, I diverge from him somewhat in its interpretation.

Love hym made al prest to don hir bide,
Or rather dyen than she sholde go;
But resoun seyde hym on that other syde:
"Withoute assent of hir ne do nat so,
And seyd, that thorugh thy medlynge is iblowe
Youre other love, ther it was erst unknowe." (4. 162–168)

Chaucer's stanza begins in responsible translation of the *Filostrato*. Boccacio's verse paragraph begins:

Amore il facea pronto ad ogni cosa
doversi oppore, ma d'altra parte era
ragion che 'l contrastava. . .[26]

It is not possible to say whether Boccaccio's conflict between *Amore* and *Ragion* is a meaningful allusion to the *Roman de la Rose*. It is quite possibly a mere commonplace. But Chaucer's text is another matter, for in it there are numerous silent allusions to or quotations from that poem. In the second book, when Pandarus is analyzing the conflicting forces probably working within Criseyde, he uses the poetic personifications Kynde (Nature in its aspect of natural sexual desire) and Daunger (the social and psychological resistance to sexual advance). It is of course impossible to think about the strange personification Danger without thinking of the *Roman de la Rose*.[27]

Yet there is a significant change in content. What is at stake here is the Parliament's proposal of an unchivalrous act of oppression against Criseyde. The manly thing to do is to oppose the exchange, and this is precisely what Hector does. He observes that "she nys no prisoner"—a point hardly subtle, but one nonetheless overlooked by the parliamentarians—and that, furthermore "We usen here no wommen for to selle." That latter noble thought, uttered in ironic innocence, runs counter to the history of the Trojan War, as we know it, and counter also to the intrigue Pandarus has undertaken, unbeknownst to Hector, to bring his niece to Troilus's bed. The Parliament acts not out of legal constraint or chivalric purpose but swayed by mere vulgar opinion. Chaucer's phrase, to which we must return in a moment, is "the noyse of people."

The second appearance of the "love and reason" theme in the fourth book is much more closely dependent upon the *Roman de la Rose*. It comes in a passage in which Pandarus returns to his Boethian role of a limping Lady Philosophy. He offers three specific arguments by way of philosophical consolation. All three hover in an uncertain middleground between low comedy and outright burlesque. (1) Troilus has already gotten the sexual pleasure he sought in the ar-

---

[26] Giovanni Boccaccio, *Il Filostrato e il Ninfale fiesolano*, ed. Vincenzo Pernicone (Bari: Laterza, 1937).

[27] See *Troilus and Criseyde*, 2. 1373–1376.

rangement and that is more than he, Pandarus, has ever been able to achieve. (2) Since women are a dime a dozen, all Troilus need do is find another one. (3) If he insists on Criseyde, why not just rape her? After all, this *is* Troy.

All three of these arguments are Ovidian in spirit, and the second is Ovidian in content. The aphorism "The newe love out chaceth ofte the olde," attributed to "Zanxis," will actually be found in the *Remedia Amoris* (452, 462). Troilus's response is that he is doomed to inaction, jostled between reason and desire.

> Thus am I lost, for aught that I kan see.
> For certain is, syn that I am hire knight,
> I most hire honour lever han than me
> In every case, as lovere ought of right.
> Thus am I with desir and reson twight:
> Desir for to destourben hire me redeth
> And reson nyl nat; so my herte dredeth. (4.568–574)

Here the inspiration is not Ovid, but his thirteenth-century French imitators, Guillaume de Lorris and Jean de Meun. When at the very beginning of Jean's continuation of the poem Lady Reason reappears on the scene, the Lover describes himself as the subject of what is nearly a literal tug-of-war between Reason and the God of Love. Reason stands on one side preaching good advice in one ear while Amors stands at the other, armed with the shovel he needs to pitch it out at the other. "Ainsinc Reson me preescheit, / Mes Amors tout enpeescheit . . ." (4599–4600) [Thus Reason preached to me. But Love prevented anything from being put into practice].[28]

Chaucer's word *twight*, the past participle of what has become in modern English "to twitch," means something like "jerked this way and that," capturing the tug-of-war theme.

The most striking appearance of the topos is found at the very end of the book, in the lovers' last recorded conversation on their last night together. In a speech constructed of noble rhetoric Criseyde tells Troilus why she did, and why she did not, fall in love with him. She dismisses such possible reasons as might relate to his exalted social status along with healthy physical carnality.

> But moral virtue grounded upon trouthe,
> That was the cause I first hadde on yow routhe
> Eke gentil herte and manhood that ye hadde,
> And hat ye hadde, as me thoughte, in despit
> Everythyng that souned into bade,

---

[28] *Le Roman de la Rose*, ed. Félix Lecoy, 3 vols. (Paris: Champion, 1965). English translation from Guillaume de Lorris and Jean de Meun, *The Romance of the Rose*, trans. Charles Dahlberg (Princeton: Princeton University Press, 1971; repr. Amherst: University Press of New England, 1983).

As rudeness and poeplissh appetit,
And that youre resoun bridled youre delit
This made, aboven every creature,
That I was youre, and shal be while I may dure. (4.1671–1680)

But if the appearance of the topos here is striking, it is also heavily freighted with irony. Neither the claim of Troilus's "moral virtue grounded upon trouthe" nor the extravagant fidelity it supposedly inspires can withstand close scrutiny for even a sidelong glance, for that matter. Troilus is a very emblem of *un*reason, and Criseyde's sworn eternal devotion fails to make it through the first thousand lines of the fifth book, let alone a lifetime. But we also see that the passage is linked to that of the Parliament scene precisely through the idea of "vulgar appetite." It is the "noyse of people" against which Troilus shows himself so spineless.

In all the three instances here examined the effect of the contrastive theme is to complicate and make more ambiguous the moral adjudications to which a reader of romance is otherwise so urgently invited. The final subject of *Sir Gawain and the Green Knight*, as its ending suggests, is social. The story of a lone, individual quest is given its final relevance in the meaning that the community (Arthur's court) finds in it. That is a meaning very different from the one reached by the protagonist himself. That the quest has its origins in the "childishness" of Arthur himself complicates the reader's adjudication of the competing perspectives. In the "Knight's Tale" the initial comic conflict of earnest and game is at once an index of the disordered passion which has captivated Palamon and Arcite and, at the same time, the thematic key to our understanding of the poem's exploration of chivalry as a stately and grandiose monument of human artifice. Finally, the debate between reason and desire that wracks Troilus in the crucial fourth book renders truly tragic, from the philosophical point of view, what the narrator so often seems naively to want to treat as a "love story."

In these instances taken from fourteenth-century English romance the ambiguity of perception latent in three binaries — maturity and infancy, earnest and game, Reason and Love — are developed, confirmed, or expanded in clarifying fashion in the larger narrative. It is of interest that all three are clustered together in the initial lines of the *Charrette*. To trace their workings through the larger poem might help guide our adjudication of the wisdom or unwisdom of climbing up into the tumbrel.

# Holy Adultery: The *Charrette*, Crusader Queens, and the Guiot Manuscript (Paris, BNF fr. 794)

Lori Walters
Florida State University

The paradoxical nature of Lancelot and Guinevere's love in Chrétien de Troyes's *Chevalier de la Charrette* has long frustrated readers' attempts at interpretation.[1] In the past I have characterized their love as an adulterous relationship that strangely enough both ennobles the lovers and is beneficial to others.[2] Matilda Bruckner has more recently observed that

> Lancelot and Guenevere's love is and is not adultery—that is to say, viewed from a certain angle, of course, it is an act of treason against Arthur as husband and king. Viewed from another angle, the question of adultery—a word never used in the romance—disappears and then reappears along another route, which turns it into a conundrum that requires reflection and resists resolution. How to make sense of an apparent impossibility, the paradox in which Lancelot is Arthur's best knight and Guenevere's lover, not one or the other but both, not Arthur's best knight in spite of, but because of his love for the queen?[3]

I have come to make sense of this "apparent impossibility" by viewing Lancelot and Guinevere's coupling as a "holy adultery," an illicit love that paradoxically signifies

---

[1] See Matilda T. Bruckner, "Why Are There So Many Interpretations of *Le Chevalier de la Charrette*?," in *Lancelot and Guinevere: A Casebook*, ed. Lori J. Walters (New York: Garland, 1996; repr. London: Routledge, 2002), 55–78; orig. in *Romance Philology* 40 (1986): 159–80.

[2] Walters, *Lancelot and Guinevere*, xiii, xx.

[3] Matilda T. Bruckner, "*Le Chevalier de la Charrette*: That Obscure Object of Desire, Lancelot," in *A Companion to Chrétien de Troyes*, ed. Joan Grimbert and Norris J. Lacy (Cambridge: Boydell and Brewer, 2005), 137–55, here 154.

Gina L. Greco and Ellen M. Thorington, eds., *Dame Philology's Charrette: Approaching Medieval Textuality through Crétien's 'Lancelot': Essays in Memory of Karl D. Uitti.* MRTS 408. Tempe: ACMRS, 2012. [ISBN 978-0-86698-456-0]

a spiritual marriage.[4] This interpretation runs counter to the widespread opinion that Chrétien's patroness, the Countess Marie de Champagne (1145–1198), wanted him to compose a narrative endorsing adultery in real life.[5] Yet a story about a knight who accomplishes impossible or improbable exploits would seem to call out for a reading other than a literal one. My paper thus proposes interpreting the *Charrette* in quite a different way, as a tale designed to inspire fervor for the Crusades by provoking reflection upon the "theoerotic" relationship between Christ and his Church.[6] According to such an interpretation, Chrétien would be placing Lancelot and Guinevere in the tradition that cast as *figurae* of Christ and the Church the adulterous couple David and Bathsheba,[7] whose wise son Solomon would compose the quintessential mystical epithalamium, the *Song of Songs* (hereafter *Song*).[8] This allegorical interpretation of the romance has particular relevance for Chrétien's patroness. Besides hailing from a long line of crusaders,[9] Marie de Champagne commissioned the *Eructavit*, a vernacular paraphrase of Psalm 44, a mystical epithalamium[10] that David supposedly pronounced when repenting of his crimes of adultery and murder. As we will see, this twelfth-century text recommends crusading activities as means of expiating sin.

---

[4] This situation at once mirrors Mary's legal marriage to Joseph versus her bond with Christ, the "heavenly bridegroom," and, on a more general level, humans' yoking to the flesh versus their true destiny to be united with the spirit.

[5] I do not consider here whether Marie's attitude reflected a change of heart relative to the opinions expressed by the character bearing her name in the *De arte honeste amandi* of Andreas Capellanus. Such a change might have been influenced by her husband's decision to undertake a Crusade.

[6] See Richard Kieckhefer, "Mystical Experience and the Definition of Christian Mysticism," in *The Comity and Grace of Method: Essays in Honor of Edmund F. Perry*, ed. Thomas Ryba, George D. Bond, and Herman Tull (Evanston, IL: Northwestern University Press, 2004), 198–234. I prefer the term "theoeroticism" to "bridal mysticism" because of its broader connotations. Kieckhefer's view of mysticism is compatible with the ideological use of it that I am proposing here.

[7] A. J. Minnis, *Medieval Theory of Authorship: Scholastic Literary Attitudes in the Later Middle Ages* (London: Scolar Press, 1984), 104–5. Pseudo-Bede, St. Ambrose, and Honorius Augustodunensis all stressed the exemplary and allegorical implications of their relationship. Bathsheba's example is especially pertinent to Marie in that she exercised a regency for Solomon and his success is partially credited to his mother's instruction and counsel; see Minnis, *Theory of Authorship*, 150. Despite his sins, David was to be regarded, "not as a sinner, but as a true penitent and, indeed, a just man": Minnis, *Theory*, 109.

[8] All biblical references will be made to the Douai-Rheims translation of the Vulgate.

[9] I glean the general facts of Marie's life from the notice written by William Provost in *Women in the Middle Ages: An Encyclopedia*, ed. Nadia Margolis and Katharina M. Wilson, 2 vols. (Westport, CT: Greenwood Press, 2004), 2: 596–99.

[10] Minnis, *Theory of Authorship*, 88, adduces St. Jerome's understanding of the psalms, which "at once designate events which were actual to the psalmist (*res gestae*) and prefigure or foreshadow various things concerning Christ or the Church."

I argue that if we have been unable to understand the *Charrette*'s many paradoxes, it is because we have not properly assessed all the information at our disposal. My interpretation establishes connections between textual analysis and factual knowledge about Chrétien's patrons and manuscripts of his texts. The only reliable historical information we have about Chrétien is that he was associated with Marie's Champagne court. I accordingly base my analysis upon a recent study of that court, focusing in particular on Patricia Stirnemann's painstaking survey of the library of the Champagne counts that housed BNF fr. 794, the most complete copy of the five romances ascribed to Chrétien. Her belief that our author spent his entire career at the Champagne court places even greater emphasis on understanding his relationship with the countess.[11] Two other scholars have influenced my approach. One is Gilbert Ouy, who explains that dealing with the actual libraries to which writers had access eliminates the contingency of identifying possible textual sources.[12] The other is Karl D. Uitti, who in conceiving of the original *Charrette Project* was convinced that the manuscript context of medieval literature has a great deal to tell us about medieval texts, despite the difficulty of evaluating the evidence.

This study is thus as much about method as about content. If I bring out the Augustinian and Bernardian bent of Chrétien and two other authors writing for Marie, it is because these Latin-educated writers would have had ready access to copies of works of these Church authorities.[13] If I assume, as I will do here, that in portraying the lovers Chrétien adopted Bernard de Clairvaux's allegorical method of scriptural analysis grounded in exposition of *Song*, it is because the latter had preached the First Crusade to Marie's parents and maintained close relations with the countess and her husband.[14] If I treat the *Eructavit* and *Genesis*, it is because they were in Marie's book collection. If I consider BNF fr. 794, it is because I believe that it contains clues to the way that Chrétien wanted adultery to be viewed in the *Charrette*.

Taking off, then, from the insights of Stirnemann, Ouy, and Uitti, I structure my demonstration on our historical knowledge of Marie, her relatives, and books associated with them. The opening section traces the crusader mentality of Marie's extended family and its relevance for the developing ideology of the

---

[11] Patricia Stirnemann, Thierry Delcourt, Xavier de la Salle, and Danielle Quéruel, eds., *Splendeurs de la cour de Champagne au temps de Chrétien de Troyes: Catalogue de l'exposition de la Bibliothèque municipale de Troyes (18 juin–11 septembre 1999)* (Troyes: Association Champagne historique, 1999), 65.

[12] Gilbert Ouy, *La librairie des frères captifs: Les manuscrits de Charles d'Orléans et Jean d'Angoulême* (Turnhout: Brepols, 2007), "Introduction," 7–25.

[13] P. Stirnemann, "Une bibliothèque princière au XIIᵉ siècle," in *Splendeurs,* 36–42, here 42.

[14] Two of Bernard's works were also present in the library, as well as the *Grande Bible de Clairvaux*. See Stirnemann et al., *Splendeurs,* 56, entries #13 and #14.

French royal house.[15] The second section is devoted to the presence of a crusading mentality in the *Charrette*, composed by Chrétien in the late 1170s,[16] and to the extension of this mentality in *Le Conte du Graal* and its Continuations (ca. 1185–1191). Section three establishes similarities between the *Charrette* and two free French adaptations of Scripture made for or dedicated to the widowed countess: the *Eructavit*, composed for her around 1184–1185 by her Cistercian confessor Adam de Perseigne,[17] and a vernacular paraphrase of Genesis begun for her in 1192 by Evrat, one of seventy-two secular canons of the collegial church of St. Etienne de Troyes adjoining Marie's palace.[18] It will become clear that meditational and devotional practices underlying the scriptural adaptations made for Marie[19] are also present in the *Charrette*. The countess's interest in Psalm 44 is, moreover, of special note, since both the psalm and Augustine's glosses on it associate noblewomen like her with the Church's task of moral edification and promote the need to defend Christianity with pen and sword, two concepts that underlie the *Charrette*. The fourth section treats the presence of a crusading mentality in Paris, BNF fr. 794,[20] a manuscript connected to Marie through its scribe Guiot.[21] This section includes a comparison of the image of Marie found in BNF fr. 794 with the picture of her niece, the French queen

---

[15] For an ideological interpretation of the Round Table, see Lori J. Walters, "Re-Examining Wace's Round Table," in *Courtly Arts and the Art of Courtliness: Selected Papers from the Eleventh Triennial Congress of the International Courtly Literature Society, University of Wisconsin-Madison, 29 July–4 August 2004*, ed. Keith Busby and Christopher Kleinhenz (Cambridge: Boydell and Brewer, 2006), 721–44.

[16] Karl D. Uitti, "Background Information on Chrétien de Troyes's *Le Chevalier de la Charrette*," 1997, *The Princeton Charrette Project*, Trustees of Princeton University, 1 October 2006, http://www.princeton.edu/~lancelot.

[17] June Hall McCash, "Chrétien's Patrons," in *A Companion to Chrétien de Troyes*, ed. Grimbert and Lacy, 15–29; eadem, "*Eructavit cor meum*: Sacred Love in a Secular Context at the Court of Marie de Champagne," in *Earthly Love, Spiritual Love, Love of the Saints*, ed. Susan J. Ridyard (Sewanee, TN: University Press of the South, 1999), 159–78, here 163. Whereas McCash, "Chrétien's Patrons," considers the attribution to Adam provisional, Stirnemann et al. accept it. Below I give other reasons for accepting it.

[18] Willy Boers, "La Genèse d'Evrat," *Scriptorium* 61 (2007): 74–149, here 75. On 91 Boers speculates that Evrat may have also served as a notary at her court. McCash, "*Eructavit cor meum*," 177, refers to him as priest of the court's Lady Chapel.

[19] These are characteristic of *lectio divina*. Meaning "divine" or "holy reading," this is a traditional form of spiritual reading and prayer.

[20] Keith Busby, Terry Nixon, Alison Stones, and Lori Walters, eds., *Les Manuscrits de Chrétien de Troyes–The Manuscripts of Chrétien de Troyes*, 2 vols. (Amsterdam: Rodopi, 1993), 1: 28–31.

[21] Ad Putter, "Knights and Clerics at the Court of Champagne: Chrétien de Troyes's Romances in Context," in *Medieval Knighthood: Papers from the Fifth Strawberry Hill Conference*, ed. S. Church and R. Harvey (Woodbridge: Boydell and Brewer, 1994), 243–66, here 251.

Blanche de Castille (1188–1252), included in a moralized Bible of the same time period. The analysis concludes with some final words about crusader queens and Chrétien's depiction of "holy adultery" in the *Charrette*.

## I. The crusader mentality of Marie de Champagne's extended family and its relevance for the ideology of the French royal house

By basing my study on knowledge of the Champagne court, I distance myself from the idea, expressed by Sarah Kay, that Chrétien de Troyes's name functions as an "anonym," a mark of Christian anonymity.[22] I argue instead that the name refers to an actual person, and one who moreover says he took his identity from his patroness. That we cannot tell if our Chrétien was one of the two clerics noted in historical records named "Christianus" is no reason to assume, as does Kay, that he was not the author of the five romances traditionally ascribed to him.[23] Somebody did compose these romances, and that person could well have been actually called "Christianus." We are reminded of the early fifteenth-century writer Christine de Pizan, whose trials led her to reinterpret her name as a female version of Christ's. Nevertheless, her identity as a representative Christian woman in no way negates her historical identity. In other words, that the names "Christine" and "Chrétien" are descriptive of their bearers' identities as Christian men and women does not exclude the possibility that these were their own given names. Chrétien in fact implied the double significance of his name when in the final verses of the prologue to his first extant romance, *Erec et Enide* (ca. 1270), he connected his name to the perpetuity of Christianity. With these words he expressed his realization that his destiny as a Christian writer was to foster the ideology of the royal house, which was dedicated to a strong Church-State alliance. That ideology was emanating from Troyes[24] under the leadership of Countess Marie and her husband Henri le Libéral, who were to be the great-aunt and great-uncle of France's most famous crusader, the *"rex christianissimus"* St. Louis (1214–1270).

---

[22] Sarah Kay, "Who was Chrétien de Troyes?" *Arthurian Literature* 15 (1997): 1–35, here 34.

[23] Kay, "Chrétien de Troyes?", 2, n. 5. The two were a regular canon, Christianus of Saint-Loup-de-Troyes mentioned in a charter of 1173, and a chaplain, Christianus of Saint-Maclou in Bar-sur-Aube. The notion that Godefroi de Laigni was a pseudonym assumed by Chrétien (or vice versa), which Kay also entertains (34), is placed in question by the presence in the Champagne library of texts by a certain "Magister Godefroi."

[24] The city's name evokes memory of the supposed Trojan origins of the French monarchy touted by the authors of the *Grandes Chroniques de France*.

Marie's extended family was heavily invested in the Crusades. The countess was the great-granddaughter of Guilhem IX (1071–1126) and the grandmother of Thibaut IV de Champagne (1201–1253), both distinguished crusaders. In the approximately two centuries that spanned 1097 to 1270, most of the French kings who led a total of eight Crusades were Marie's blood relatives.[25] Marie was the eldest daughter of crusader parents, France's King Louis VII (1120–1180) and his queen, Aliénor d'Aquitaine (1122–1204). But most pertinent to this study, she was also the wife and mother of crusaders. Marie was regent when her husband, Count Henri I le Libéral (1127–1181), undertook a personal Crusade to Constantinople from 1179 to 1181, during which he was captured and ransomed by the emperor of Constantinople and returned ill and dying.[26] Left a widow in 1181, Marie acted as regent twice again, the first time during the minority (1181–1187) of her son Henri II (1166–1197), the second time (1190–1197) when he left to go on the Third Crusade with Philippe de Flandre and her half-brothers Philippe II Auguste and Richard Coeur de Lion. After Henri was killed by accident at Acre on 10 September 1197, Marie entered the nunnery of Fontaines-les-Nones near Meaux, where six months later she died of inconsolable grief.[27]

June Hall McCash has posited a direct connection between the *Charrette* and the crusading mentality of Marie's family. She proposes the date of 1179–1181 for the romance, reasoning that Henri's absence gave the countess the opportunity to assume an active political role for the first time.[28] Considered in this historical context, it seems reasonable to believe that Marie asked Chrétien to undertake a Bernardian-inspired narrative to encourage the crusading efforts of her immediate family and their descendants. Bernard (1090–1153) preached the First Crusade at Vezelay on 31 March 1146 to a crowd that included Marie's parents. Her father Louis VII received the cross from the preacher's own hands, and her mother Aliénor wrapped herself in the banner of the cross.[29] Bernard was a key figure in Marie's life. He was even thought to have been responsible for her birth! Aliénor had made a bargain with the preacher, whereby in return for his prayers to the Virgin for the birth of an heir, she agreed to encourage Louis to work out his differences with the Church. When her daughter was born,

---

[25] French kings were leaders of the 3rd Crusade, 1188–1192; the 4th Crusade, 1202–1204; the 5th Crusade, 1215–1221; the 6th Crusade, 1227–1229; and the 7th Crusade, 1248–1254.

[26] I thank June Hall McCash for having supplied me with this piece of information.

[27] McCash, "*Eructavit cor meum*," 165.

[28] McCash, "Chrétien's Patrons," 19–20. Marie's interest in the Crusades is also indicated by her relationship with Geoffroi de Villehardouin, one of her chief advisors and marshal of Champagne from 1189. He was the author of the prose chronicle *La Conqueste de Constantinople*, an eyewitness account of the Fourth Crusade.

[29] Charles Mackay, *Extraordinary Popular Delusions and the Madness of Crowds* (New York: Farrar, Straus and Giroux, 1972), 412.

she consequently named her in honor of the Queen of Heaven.[30] (To differentiate between the two in this paper, I will refer to the Virgin as "Mary" and the
Countess as "Marie.") The identification of Marie with the Church is justified
on historical grounds, since in serving as a substitute for a male heir, she came to
resemble Bernard's "virile bride of Christ."[31] Our three authors identify Marie
with the Virgin in the latter's dual role as exemplary human being and *figura* of
the Church.

The crusader preacher Bernard exercised considerable influence on Marie
and her husband. When Marie was only one year old, her future husband Count
Henri participated in the Second Crusade as the representative of his father Thibaut II, son of another crusader count, Hugues de Champagne. In March 1146,
Count Henri, responding to the call made by Bernard of Clairvaux, took up
the cross, along with Marie's parents. Henri would be especially receptive to
Bernard's appeal since Bernard, his father's close associate, had been one of his
tutors.[32] Henri arrived at the imperial court of Manuel Komnenos with a letter
from the future St. Bernard asking the Byzantine ruler to dub "ce jeune homme
de grande noblesse, de lui faire prêter le serment de chevalier et de lui ceindre
l'épée contre les ennemis de la Croix" [this young man of great nobility, to have
him swear the vow of knight and to gird him with the sword against the enemies
of the Cross].[33] It is clear here that the sword, which will come up over and over
again in this study, is a symbol of the Church Militant.

To judge by the leanings of Marie's father, husband, and father-in-law, her
marriage was conceived of not only as a biological alliance, but also as a spiritual
one centered on the Crusades. The notion of higher chivalry, proposed to Henri
by Bernard and sanctified by the Byzantine emperor, could have its counterpart
in the notion of marriage based upon the Bernardian exposition of *Song* present
in the *Charrette*.[34] Marie could be expressing this higher form of love in the regencies she exercised on behalf of her husband and her son, which she assumed

---

[30] Marion Meade, *Eleanor of Aquitaine: A Biography* (London: Ted Smart, 1977),
66–67.

[31] See Shawn M. Krahmer, "Bernard's Virile Bride of Christ," *Church History* 69
(2000): 304–27, and Ann W. Astell, *The Song of Songs in the Middle Ages* (Ithaca: Cornell
University Press, 1990), 43–72. The chronicler of Tours suggests that Marie lived up to
this designation when he comments that she single-handedly governed Champagne for
over fifteen years "like a man": P. Stirnemann and T. Delcourt, "Biographies," in *Splendeurs*, 43–47, here 46.

[32] Stirnemann and Delcourt, "Biographies," 43.

[33] Henri d'Arbois de Jubainville, *Histoire des Ducs et des Comtes de Champagne*, 7 vols.
(Paris: Durand, 1861), 3: 15–18; Nicole Hany-Longuespé, "Les vestiges de Saint-Etienne
au trésor de la cathédrale de Troyes," in *Splendeurs*, 30–31. All the translations in this paper are my own unless indicated otherwise.

[34] For Bernard's influence on *Erec et Enide*, see Jeanne A. Nightingale, "Inscribing
the Breath of a Speaking Voice: *Vox Sponsae* in St. Bernard's Sermons on the Canticles

because of her devotion to the "heavenly bridegroom," Christ. And Henri could see in his marriage to Marie not only the responsibilities he had toward her and the lineage she bore him, but also an image of his greater duty to the Church.

It should be understood that I am not offering an orthodox Christian inter-pretation of the *Charrette* such as those advanced by Jacques Ribard[35] or D.W. Robertson. I instead consider the ways in which religious discourse and symbols, which were part of the dominant discourse of the time, were used ideologically, to form a human society dedicated to Christian ideals. Chrétien's approach in the *Charrette* is thus related to the exploitation, by France's "most Christian" monar-chy, of the devotional aspect of bridal mysticism present in omnipresent images such as those of the Annunciation, the Madonna and Child, and the Crucifixion. He gives his readers a hint that his approach will be ideological when in *Erec et Enide* he expresses the hope that his name will last as long as Christianity. His texts demonstrate the many possible permutations of "*conjointure*," whether they be textual, biological, sexual, or ideological. Accordingly, I argue that Chré-tien employs the union of Lancelot and Guinevere to symbolize devotion to the Church-State alliance of the nascent nation-state. Some of the most distinctive marks of that alliance were the nobility's crusading efforts.

These efforts received affirmation in *Les Grandes Chroniques de France* (here-after *GCF*),[36] the history of the royal house in which the ideology of the "most Christian" monarchy received its most definitive statement. The prologue of these vernacular dynastic chronicles includes a rendition of the *translatio stu-dii et imperii* motif remarkably similar to the one present in Chrétien's *Cligés*. In the prose context of the *GCF*, the motif implies that France will retain its stel-lar position only if it remains a staunch defender of the Church. France's on-going participation in the Crusades was one of the best ways for it to assert its supremacy in Christendom. The person who commissioned the *GCF*, Marie's great-nephew, Louis IX, illustrated this principle to the highest degree. In the 1240s he constructed the Sainte Chapelle to house two treasures brought back from the Holy Land, relics of the crown of thorns and the true cross. The con-summate crusader, Louis IX died a martyr to the cause. His title of "most Chris-tian" king derived (paradoxically) from his leadership of two failed Crusades.

---

and in Chrétien's *Erec et Enide*," in *Courtly Arts and the Art of Courtliness*, ed. Busby and Kleinhenz, 489–506.

[35] See, for example, *Chrétien de Troyes, Le* Chevalier de la Charrette*: essai d'interprétation symbolique* (Paris: Nizet, 1972). Bruckner, "That Obscure Object of De-sire," 147: "messianic reverberations effectively translate the extraordinary quality of Lancelot's secular heroism for a secular public." I signal, however, that the "secular pub-lic" was formed according to religious models, in order to create a community established "on earth as it is in heaven."

[36] Anne D. Hedeman, *The Royal Image: Illustrations of the 'Grandes Chroniques de France', 1274–1422* (Berkeley: University of California Press, 1991).

France's only canonized king, St. Louis was the ultimate model of the Christian King-as-new-Christ, whose present sufferings and defeats were seen as the sign of the eventual triumph of Christianity.

The *GCF* allied this eventual triumph with the reputation of its queens. In the words of these chronicles, France's destiny is to be a "dame renommée seur autres nations" [lady renowned over other nations]. Resorting once again to a female personification, the *GCF* aligned the image of the nation with that of the Church: "France comme loiaus fille secourt sa mere (i.e., l'Eglise) en touz besoinz" [France as a loyal daughter defends her mother (i.e., the Church) in her every need].[37] By personifying France as a lady of renown and a daughter of the Church, the *GCF* implicitly connected France's reputation with the good name of her queens and other great ladies. They were supposed to become virtual personifications of Wisdom and Virtue by molding themselves into images of humanity's teacher, the Church, the repository of Christ's wisdom. Their duty was to inculcate wisdom and virtue in their husbands and sons and inspire them to defend the Church. The *GCF*, for example, credits Marie's niece, Blanche de Castille, for her son's success because she had accomplished the task required of all Christian queens, to "bien endoctriner et enseigner" [indoctrinate well and teach] future monarchs.[38]

Besides having their husbands and sons live up to their responsibilities toward the Church, royal ladies likewise assured their country's reputation by assisting in the crusading ventures of their male relatives. The virtue of a noblewoman of Marie's line was in fact directly proportional to her participation in such activities. The encomium to Aliénor d'Aquitaine—Marie's mother and Blanche's grandmother—with which Wace opens his *Ascending Chronicle of the Dukes of Normandy* of ca. 1160 illustrates this point. It is revelatory that while its author praises Aliénor for being Henry's wife, he counts among her attributes her participation on a lengthy crusade to Jerusalem, where together with her first husband Louis VII she "suffered great pain and hardship."[39] Besides accompanying their husbands on Crusade, royal wives and mothers could also share in their husbands' and sons' hardships by tending to their lands and interests during their absence. Like her aunt Marie, Blanche de Castille assisted her son when he went on Crusade, serving as Louis IX's regent from 1257 to her death in 1252. Royal ladies also suffered when their menfolk were wounded, imprisoned, or killed

---

[37] *Les Grandes Chroniques de France*, ed. Jules Viard, 10 vols. (Paris: Champion, 1920–1953), 1: 4–5.

[38] *Les Grandes Chroniques de France*, 7: 34.

[39] Wace, *The Roman de Rou*, trans. Glyn S. Burgess, ed. Anthony J. Holden, annot. Glyn S. Burgess and Elisabeth van Houts (Jersey: Société Jersiaise, 2002), *Rou*, Part I, ll. 24–36.

while away. Marie de Champagne's example shows that women as well as men could be martyrs for the cross.[40]

The French monarchy adopted the lance or sword of compassion motif[41] as one of its primary symbols of the joining of men and women in all forms of Christian crusade. (Besides actually participating in a Crusade, these could include stamping out heresies, converting souls, or creating a more general change of heart in readers.) The motif expressed the idea that the Blessed Virgin, whose name the countess bore, became humanity's co-redeemer through the compassion she felt seeing her son suffer at the Passion and Crucifixion. Implicit in the motif is the idea that, at the very moment when Mary consented to become the fleshly vehicle of Christ's Incarnation at the Annunciation, she also knowingly agreed to suffer by witnessing her son's Passion and Crucifixion. While the lance of compassion motif could apply to all forms of male and female partnership, it had special application to the crusading mentality whose goal was to liberate Jerusalem, "queen of all cities" and symbol of a united Christendom. The lance was associated early on with the Crusades, since the first French Passion text was composed in Clermont, where Pope Urban II had, in 1095, presided over the council that called for the First Crusade. It was on this crusade that the lance that had pierced Christ's side was discovered. By securing the home front while their men were away in battle, women like Marie de Champagne and Blanche de Castille modeled themselves on the Virgin, who became her son's bride and partner by suffering along with him for the world's sins.[42] Paramount for my purposes in this paper is that in the *Charrette*, a text inspired by Marie, adultery and incest become symbolic of the spiritual relationship figured by the lance of compassion.

---

[40] It is a perfect illustration of how real-life situations could reflect the sword of compassion motif. The motif can in fact be seen both to reflect a psychological reality (the love of a mother for her son) and to structure human behavior (a mother's devotion to her son leading to her own self-annihilation at the time of his death). The scriptural model is of course Mary's suffering as an onlooker at the Crucifixion (John 19: 25) and its being earlier foreseen in Simeon's prophecy (Luke 2: 34–35). See below.

[41] In this paper I will refer to it most often as the "lance of compassion" in order to emphasize the echoes with Lancelot's name and to differentiate it from the symbolism of the sword used in the *Charrette*. The connections between the two motifs become evident in the Sword Bridge episode, to be discussed below. The motif has a direct biblical source in Luke 2:35. In this passage the prophet Simeon greets the Virgin bringing her son to the temple for his circumcision with the words: "And a sword will pierce your soul too, so that out of many, thoughts will be revealed." See William H. Gerdts, Jr., "The Sword of Sorrow," *Art Quarterly* 17 (1954): 213–29, here 213.

[42] Rachel Fulton, *From Judgment to Passion: Devotion to Christ and the Virgin Mary, 800–1200* (New York: Columbia University Press, 2002), 199.

## II. The presence of a crusading mentality in the *Charrette*, and its extension in Chrétien's *Conte du Graal* and its Continuations

This section begins with an overview of how the *Charrette* can be read allegorically as an expression of Christian devotion to a crusading ethic. The key term here is devotion. The narrative is structured by Lancelot's single-minded quest to rescue Guinevere. The protagonist's very name evokes the lance of compassion, suggesting that his connection to the queen is primarily spiritual in nature. The protagonist accepts his status as Christ-like social outcast and innocent victim when he freely consents to mount the cart of infamy that was traditionally reserved for criminals. Like Mary, Guinevere loves the "heavenly beloved" rather than her all-too-human husband. Guinevere is unjustly accused of adultery with the inept and verbally duplicitous Kay, symbolically the Church's unworthy defender. The charge of adultery leveled against her is reminiscent of Joseph's suspicions regarding Mary's pregnancy.[43] As the "knight of the cart" Lancelot is the pariah who in reality is superior to those who judge him; Guinevere is superior to those who would believe her to be a woman of easy virtue. Lancelot's exploit of traversing the Sword Bridge on his hands and knees symbolizes his prayerful service to a crusader mentality. In being marked by wounds similar to Christ's, he becomes a virtual prefiguration of Louis IX, whom Jacques Le Goff describes as assuming such austere devotional practices that he actually came to resemble the Man of Sorrows.[44]

The ideology to which I am referring here was governed by the transcendence of the passions of the flesh rather than their abnegation. In the *Charrette*'s Night of Love episode the highest earthly pleasures become symbols of the devotion that inspired someone like St. Louis,[45] and was supposed to inspire all

---

[43] In worldly terms they were well founded since he knew that he had not had sexual relations with her. If this interpretation seems far-fetched, let me cite the seven-hour Passion sermon ("Ad Deum vadit") in which the fifteenth-century theologian Jean Gerson elaborated on the gospel passage in which Joseph considers repudiating Mary when he finds her pregnant. The preacher stresses the idea that from the beginning, at the Annunciation, Mary had realized, and accepted, that her reputation would be tarnished in the eyes of the people of her own time.

[44] Jacques Le Goff, *Saint Louis* (Paris: Gallimard, 1996), in particular "Le roi souffrant, le roi Christ," 858–86, and "Portraits de Saint Louis," number 8. Sandra Hindman, *Sealed in Parchment: Rereadings of Knighthood in the Illuminated Manuscripts of Chrétien de Troyes* (Chicago: University of Chicago Press, 1994), 165, 168, 189, argues that certain *Conte du Graal* manuscripts recast Perceval on the model of St. Louis.

[45] For all his admiration of the mendicant ideal, Louis IX, the father of eleven children, was a good family man. He was represented as such in the royal abbey of St-Louis de Poissy, which was supposedly founded on the spot where his mother Blanche de Castille had given birth to him in the spirit as well as in the flesh. See Alain

the French. To outweigh the very real prospect of an excruciating death on a far-away battlefield (with nary a painkiller in sight), Chrétien opposes the enticing scene of a night of orgasmic pleasures with a beloved. The Night of Love episode is the narrative's high point, the culmination of a meditative process of ascent,[46] a mental pilgrimage enabling the practitioner to gain forgiveness for sins by imitating Christ's sacrifice. The depiction of ecstasy in the Night of Love episode functions as a call to total and unquestioning devotion to the crusader ideal. The highest testimony of that dedication would be death experienced for the cause.

With this overview in mind, let us now turn to the Night of Love episode. This is how Chrétien describes Lancelot's entry into Guinevere's chamber:

> Et puis vint au lit la reïne,
> Si l'aore et se li ancline,
> Car an nul cors saint ne croit tant,
> Et la reïne li estant
> Ses bras ancontre, si l'anbrace,
> Estroit pres de son piz le lace,
> Si l'a lez li an son lit tret . . . (4654–4657)[47]

[And then he came to the bed of the queen,
and bends down before her and adores her,
because in no saintly body does he have greater belief,
and the queen extends
her arms to him and embraces him,
tightly to her chest does she enlace him,
and draws him down on her bed next to her . . .]

The important verse is "Estroit pres de son piz le lace," which emphasizes that Lancelot and Guinevere become "joined at the heart." Such imagery became

---

Erlande-Brandenburg, "La Priorale Saint-Louis de Poissy," *Bulletin monumental* 129 (1971): 85–112.

[46] R. McMahon, *Understanding the Medieval Meditative Ascent: Augustine, Anselm, Boethius, and Dante* (Washington, DC: Catholic University Press, 2006). This quotation reveals the connection between meditative ascent and the crusader mentality: "All things were created by the Word, and Christ, as it were, initialed his work with the instrument of salvation, the cross" (41).

[47] In this paper I refer to the edition of the *Charrette* by Karl D. Uitti and Alfred Foulet (Paris: Garnier, 1989) because it is based upon BNF fr. 794 and to the transcription of this manuscript found on the Princeton *Charrette* website cited above. See also Lori J. Walters, "The King's Example: Arthur, Gauvain, and Lancelot in *Rigomer* and Chantilly, Musée Condé 472 (anc. 626)," in *"De sens rassis": Essays in Honor of Rupert T. Pickens*, ed. Keith Busby, Bernard Guidot, and Logan E. Whalen (Amsterdam: Rodopi, 2004), 675–93.

commonplace in later devotional texts,[48] where the sword or lance of compassion is in fact synonymous with the *"stimulus amoris"*[49] or "goad of love."[50] By pairing the lovers in this manner, Chrétien appears to express key Augustinian[51] and Bernardian ideas that were later developed by the pseudo-Bonaventure[52] and then translated into several vernaculars.[53]

Chrétien does not show any more of their lovemaking. He prefers to rhetorically "draw the curtain" around them, thus setting their physical relations in a secret place. He gives his readers assurances that the two lovers experienced the highest possible joy:

> ... il or avint sanz mantir
> Une joie et une mervoille
> Tel c'onques ancor sa paroille
> Ne fu oïe ne seüe (4676–4679)

> [... now without lying (I can say)
> that he experienced a joy and a marvel
> such that never yet its equal
> was heard of or known]

When Chrétien then proclaims that the greatest joys should be kept secret (4680–4681), he makes them analogous to the most sacred mysteries. The highest of those mysteries was the marriage of Christ and the Church (as the *Song of Songs* was interpreted as figuring), imagined as the joining of Christ and Mary in the sword of compassion motif.

---

[48] For example, in his fourteenth-century *Goad of Love*, a free translation of the *Stimulus Amoris* falsely attributed to St. Bonaventure (or to St. Bernard), Walter Hilton asks the Lord, "Why bindest thou me so goodly with the lace of love?": *The Goad of Love*, ed. Bonaventure Jacobus and Clare Kirchberger (London: Faber and Faber, 1952), 129; for the attribution, see 101, n.2. As with the *Charrette's* coupling of Lancelot and Guinevere, the sword or lance in the *Goad of Love* unites Christ and Mary in their sufferings and ultimate joy (80).

[49] Carol M. Schuler, "The Sword of Compassion: Images of the Sorrowing Virgin in Late Medieval and Renaissance Art" (Ph.D. diss., Columbia University, 1987), 99. See also Hans Belting, *L'Image et son public au Moyen Âge*, trans. Fortunato Israel (Paris: Gérard Monfort, 1998), 172–94.

[50] Kirchberger in Hilton, *Goad*, 15–17.

[51] The sword or lance of compassion motif is a direct outgrowth of *Civitas Dei* 17.16 and 22.17, where Augustine describes the Church as the mystical body of Christ.

[52] The sword or lance of compassion becomes in fact synonymous with the *"stimulus amoris"* or "goad of love." Kirchberger believes that the *Stimulus* author was the thirteenth-century Franciscan friar James of Milan: Hilton, *Goad*, 15.

[53] The Franciscan Simon de Courcy translated the *Stimulus* into French in 1406. Found in Paris, BNF fr. 926, the text is currently unedited.

Other details support this interpretation. Bloodstains replace more customary signs of passionate lovemaking. Lancelot is bleeding profusely from a gash in
his finger that he received while entering the queen's chamber. His hands, feet,
and knees have been slashed while crossing the Sword Bridge. This stigmata imagery is completed by the marking of Lancelot's heart, which had taken place in
the earlier episode of the Test of the Flaming Lance:

> Et li fers de la lance passe
> Au chevalier lez le costé
> Si qu'il a del cuir osté
> Un po, mes n'est mie bleciez. (524–527)

> [And the iron of the lance passes
> so close to the knight's side that it
> took off a little bit of the skin,
> but he was not wounded.]

In passing, the lance glances Lancelot's *costé*, a term in French that indicates the
region from the armpits to the hips. Although the lance attempts to sew him to
the bedsheets "par mi les flancs" [through his flanks; 517], it only succeeds in
leaving a scratch on his skin. Symbolically, this could mean that the ostensibly
carnal future adventure, i.e., the Night of Love episode, will actually be spiritual
in nature. Chrétien expresses the idea by saying that although Lancelot's body
must part from the queen after their coupling, his heart remains with her (4696).
The lance imagery that Chrétien liberally associates with the romance's protagonist is a fitting complement for the knight whose name is "Lancelot" (= "little
lance"). If Lancelot is the "knight of the cart," his name also proclaims him to be
the "knight of the lance." The organ of sexual consummation is, as it were, transformed into a symbol of his higher communion with Guinevere that has them
sharing "one heart."

To return to the scene of the lovers' coupling, we can now appreciate Chrétien's creation of an altogether striking image. The author implicitly likens Guinevere's welcome of Lancelot to her bed to the Virgin's embrace of her dead son's
scarred body (the visual image we call the 'Pietà'). If we interpret Guinevere's
bed as her final resting place, we can say that she appears to be inviting Lancelot
ever so seductively to share her metaphorical entombment with her. The image
brings to mind the *Passion de Clermont*, in which the Savior's mother comes to
represent the Church, whose first duty is to remember Christ's sacrifice in the
Eucharistic service. By extension, that text itself becomes a tomb of memory.[54]

---

[54] "La soa madre virge fu / et sen peched si portet lui. / sos munument fure toz nous,
/ anz lui noi jag unque nulz om" [His mother was a virgin / and bore him without sin. /
may she be the resting place for us all / no one will never rest in peace without her]; vv.
237–40. I translate the text rather freely in order to clarify its meaning.

Other texts, by authors like Chrétien, perpetuate this same "Christian" memory. That this original Passion text in French was preserved in Clermont, first in the cathedral treasury (until 1010) and then in the capitulary library,[55] residing there at the time Bernard preached the First Crusade to Louis VII and Queen Aliénor, is strong evidence that in his *Charrette* Chrétien was promoting the crusader ethic of Marie's extended family.[56]

We can by now, I hope, begin to see the night of love as a "holy adultery," an act more symbolic than real. The *Charrette* is especially symbolic. Rather than following a clear narrative development, events more often than not tell us about the lofty nature of Lancelot's quest to liberate all held prisoner by Meleagant, a quest motivated by his unfailing devotion to the queen. If the Future Cemetery episode reveals that Lancelot is the sole knight capable of accomplishing the superhuman feat of liberation, the episodes of the Immodest Damsel, the Tournament of Noauz, and the Sword Bridge all demonstrate that he will be able to do it only because of his extraordinary devotion to the queen. Other women, such as the immodest damsel and the seneschal's wife guarding him in prison, are forced to recognize that Lancelot's affections cannot be dislodged from their object.

We can add that the Night of Love is removed from everyday reality. We have seen that in entering her chamber, Lancelot venerates Guinevere as if she were a holy relic. That he genuflects in leaving her bed further brackets the scene as something occurring in another realm. We have a similar impression when we consider Guinevere's desire to sleep with Lancelot. The first time she entertains the thought is after hearing the erroneous report of his death. Crazed with guilt believing that her rejection of him was its cause, Guinevere expresses the desire to have given him pleasure before he died. At this time she envisions sexual consummation with Lancelot as a dream rather than as a reality. Nor does she believe their night together to be possible when she suggests that Lancelot meet her at her window, since the bars enclosing it appear too thick to be broken by human agency (4602–4606). Guinevere herself points out to Lancelot that sexual activity in her chamber would be out of the question since it would awaken Kay sleeping close nearby (4621–4623). Chrétien's comment that Lancelot experienced joy all night long (4686) would appear to indicate that their lovemaking was prolonged and exuberant, hardly something another occupant in the room could sleep through, especially one, who like Kay, was fully conscious the next morning. And not only does Lancelot remove the bars, he puts them back together exactly as they had been before (4714–4715). This is hardly possible in reality.

---

[55] G.D.P., "*Passion de Jésus-Christ*, dite *Passion de Clermont*," in *Dictionnaire des Lettres françaises (Le Moyen Âge)*, ed. Geneviève Hasenohr and Michel Zink, 2nd ed. (Paris: Fayard, 1992), 1100–1. The text is edited by G. Paris, *Romania* 2 (1873): 295–314.

[56] With this image Chrétien would symbolically "outdo" the double tomb motif of the Tristan and Iseut story, which was a persistent presence throughout his *œuvre*.

Lancelot is the man who can do the impossible, whether he is twisting iron bars, lifting the slab in the Future Cemetery, or crossing the Sword Bridge. In quotation that prefaces this study Bruckner calls the paradoxes surrounding the adulterous lovers "apparent impossibilities." One such impossibility cited in the text is the ability to return to the womb to be reborn (vv. 3071–3072). Like Lancelot who can accomplish seemingly impossible exploits, this feat can be realized when people decide to be reborn in the Church (cf. John 3: 4–5). Bernard spoke of just such a rebirth in his sermons on *Song*, a text that on the surface appears to be an erotic love song, but which churchmen like himself had long interpreted as an allegory of the love of Christ and his Church.[57] The Old Testament text speaks of the way the spiritual can spring from something that in appearance is the most carnal. If we apply this thinking to the Night of Love episode, we can see it announcing the birth of a spiritual partnership, one that unites Lancelot and Guinevere in a union that is superior to the one Guinevere has with her husband, who has to count on his best knight to rescue his abducted wife and to free those held prisoner by Meleagant. It is a bond entered into by free choice and decided by mutual consent.[58] Their relationship comes to approximate a union of people who have set "a seal upon their hearts," locking themselves together for all eternity in a love as "strong as death," as celebrated in *Song* 8: 6.

A criticism often made of *Song* can however also be raised about the *Charrette*. Readers can easily confuse its portrayal of sacred love with its profane equivalent.[59] Chrétien provides reflection upon both the sacred and the all-too-carnal qualities of Lancelot's and Guinevere's union through the imagery he employs in the Night of Love episode. No image is more paradoxical than the blood drops. On the one hand, they have a positive valence since they unite the two as lovers whose sufferings recall the conjoining of Mary and Christ in the lance or sword of compassion motif. On the other hand, the blood drops are negative in that they lead to the charge of adultery leveled against the queen. The charge suggests that the lovers' union is transgressive of the most sacred human bonds, one that joins the king and his queen and another that joins the king and his best knight.

Understanding these paradoxes begins with the realization that Chrétien encodes references to humanity's fall and eventual redemption into the Night of Love episode. The retelling begins when Lancelot gains access to the site of Guinevere's imprisonment by passing through a breach in the wall of an orchard (4590–4593). Lancelot's act of illegal entry (symbolic of his adultery as a whole)

---

[57] Fulton, *From Judgment to Passion*, 199, 289.

[58] Fulton, *From Judgment to Passion*, 445, discusses the fact that voluntary consent, whether of a man or woman to marriage or of an individual to the religious life, was a principal tenet of twelfth-century religious thought. Many monastic reformers argued that it was adult consent that made a man and woman husband and wife, and a man a monk or a woman a nun.

[59] Astell, *The Song of Songs*, 1, 27.

resonates with echoes of humanity's first sin. The story of the fall and redemption of the human race, begun in Eden, was continued in the Old Testament account of God's covenant with Abram. It stipulated that he and his descendants would rule the earth if they would sacrifice their carnal pleasures for spiritual ones. His transformation was indicated by the acquisition of a new name, "Abraham," meaning "father of many nations" (Gen. 17:5). In a transformation that will prove important for Marie de Champagne, his wife Sarai ("my Lady") became known as "Sarah," meaning "lady" in an absolute sense (Gen. 17:15). Abraham sealed the agreement with God by circumcising himself (Gen. 17:24).[60] As a result of this covenant with God, the couple was able to sire offspring despite Sarah's advanced age. The miraculous conceptions of her line looked forward not only to Christ, but also to Philippe II Auguste, called "Dieudonné" [God-given] in the *GCF*, and to Marie de Champagne, as we have seen previously. Abraham's act of self-mutilation marking his spiritual dedication is recalled in the wound to Lancelot's "premerainne jointe" [first joint, 4661]. His symbolic castration identifies him as a model guiding the reader's own pilgrimage towards self-sacrifice in the crusader cause.

Accordingly, we see that Lancelot's entrance into the garden evokes memory not only of the Fall, but also of the Annunciation, the "impossible" event[61] that marked the beginning of humanity's ultimate redemption by Christ. His access to the garden (compare also the "garden enclosed" of *Song* 4:12) recalls the Annunciation, in that it is a passing through a place where there should have been no entry. Lancelot does the impossible by entering the queen's chamber, which corresponds to the Annunciation's miraculous impregnation of a virgin. At that time Mary makes known her willingness to suffer a Passion commensurate with her son's. In proclaiming her "be it done to me according to thy word" (Luke 1:38) and singing her joyous "Magnificat" (Luke 1:46–55), Mary becomes a figure of all those who freely accept suffering in order to receive forgiveness for sin. To achieve redemption, they have to suffer along with Christ, as Mary did by witnessing his Passion. Mary thus functions as a mirror for the imitation of Christ, by serving both as a moral exemplar and as a guide to the contemplative processes that produce correct

---

[60] The text reads: "Abraham was ninety and nine years old, when he circumcised the flesh of his foreskin." The scene found its way into a Bible commissioned by Jean II le Bon (1319–1364), Paris, BNF fr. 15397, fol. 22v. Marcia Kupfer, ". . .*lectures. . .plus vrayes*: Hebrew Script and Jewish Witness in the *Mandeville* Manuscript of Charles V," *Speculum* 83 (2008): 58–111, here 108, describes the scene: "The seated patriarch, knees splayed and tunic split down the middle, grips his penis with his left hand as he cuts the tip with an impressive knife in his right." This miniature is proof of the significance of the episode for the centralizing monarchy of which the house of Champagne was a key player. In 1314, the last count of Champagne ascended the throne as Louis X (Blanche de Castille's great-great grandson), at which time Champagne officially became part of the kingdom.

[61] Luke 1:37: "Because no word shall be impossible with God."

imitation. People have to transform their carnal, Eve-like selves into figures approximating the ever-virtuous mother of Christ.[62] Lancelot and Guinevere function as textual models designed to induce meditative ascent in the readers of the text. Chrétien and Marie are also involved in that process, which is part of a larger process of societal purification and improvement.

The lessons encoded into the Night of Love episode provide reflection upon a human realm that still has a long way to go on its path to redemption. Lancelot's act of penetration into the queen's chamber, as we have said, has negative connotations as well as positive ones. His blood is symbolic of the imperfect nature of his mortal union with Guinevere as opposed to the holy nature of the Annunciation. If the New Testament gives humans the blueprint for regaining Eden, it remains for them to actually bring about the realization of the "city of God" in the here-and-now as a mirror of the heavenly order. The *Charrette* depicts a human realm in a serious state of disarray. Arthur's realm can hardly be described as a place of peace and justice for all. Unable to free his subjects held prisoner by an enemy, Arthur is likewise powerless to prevent the abduction of the queen, his wife. This is even more serious than it first appears, since Meleagant would have taken Guinevere by force had it not been for the intervention of his father Bademagus and for her eventual rescue by Lancelot.

The valiant Lancelot can be considered to be a "Christian soldier" who helps out King Arthur when he is unable to bring about peace and justice in his realm through his own efforts. Lancelot imitates Christ's Passion by enduring terrible physical trials on his quests to rescue the queen and liberate the prisoners. The seeming unreasonableness of many of the queen's demands, which has sparked a good deal of critical commentary, is, I believe, meant to elicit the total devotion required of any Crusader, who is asked to model his behavior on the treatment that Christ endured at the hands of his sadistic persecutors. It is undeniable that Lancelot's unquestioning devotion to Guinevere is at the root of everything that happens for the good in the *Charrette*. The queen's effect on Lancelot is analogous to Marie's effect on Chrétien. We can conjecture that Chrétien wishes his text to inspire a similar devotion on the part of his audience.

Devotion is the imperative word here. Rather than appealing to the intellect, this narrative appeals to the emotions, and most particularly to the emotions evoked when viewing an object the viewer considers to be sacred. Lancelot's extraordinary, indeed miraculous, powers have their source in his unquestioning devotion to Guinevere. That devotion also gives him the strength to break the bars separating him from her. Devotion also rules when Lancelot almost loses his life when he contemplates the queen riding along as Meleagant's captive, and when, lost in thoughts of her, he is oblivious to the warning of a knight guarding a ford. He is absorbed in just as passionate but less dangerous contemplative

---

[62] Lori J. Walters, "*Magnifying the Lord*: Prophetic Voice in *La Cité des Dames*," *Cahiers de Recherches médiévales* 13 (2006): 237–53, here 241.

reveries when he gazes upon strands of Guinevere's hair left in the teeth of an ivory comb or when he adores her bed and her body as if they were sacred relics. The narrator leads us to contemplate the scene of their conjoining, leaving readers with a devotional rather than an erotic image.

Let me summarize my argument to this point. Marie de Champagne asks a poet in her employ, one appropriately named "Chrétien," to retell the quintessential Christian narrative under the cover of a story of an adulterous love. He hides the story's higher meaning from the impious by covering it under a network of sacred imagery whose highest expression occurs in the Night of Love episode. The text's partially concealed message is intended to reinforce the ideology espoused by Marie's royal line, a line whose female members were becoming increasingly important to monarchical designs. The iconic image of Guinevere worshipped by Lancelot, which Chrétien places in a narrative requested from him by the crusader countess Marie de Champagne, is an image meant to encourage men and women to meditate upon it along with him and thereby become willing to accept the sacrifices needed to make the Crusades a success.

The unquestioning devotion asked of the *Charrette*'s readers may have been inspired by the best known of all allegorical interpretations, the city of Jerusalem represented as a figure of the Church[63] (which also makes Jerusalem a synecdoche of the Holy Land). Chrétien's depiction of Guinevere as a queen held prisoner and threatened with rape[64] accordingly becomes an image of the "queen of all cities" under Muslim rule. With this depiction Chrétien would be reminding his audience that parts of the Holy Land had been lost to Christians after their initial victory in the First Crusade (1099). The *Charrette*, I further argue, was intended to inspire the type of devotion required of a crusader, whose goal was to view relics in the Holy City. It was also meant to encourage devotion on the part of a crusader's wife or mother who either accompanied him on Crusade or remained back home tending their lands and family. In the *Charrette* Marie and Chrétien symbolically call upon Christian kings to endeavor to liberate the Holy Land from the infidel and for Christian queens to aid them in their charge. Queen Guinevere can thus be seen as an image of the Church Militant,[65] whose

---

[63] Minnis, *Theory of Authorship*, 34, gives the fourfold exposition of Jerusalem as set forth by Cassian and Guibert of Nogent: "Historically, it represents a specific city; in allegory it represents holy Church; tropologically or morally, it is the soul of every faithful man who longs for the vision of eternal peace; and anagogically it refers to the life of the heavenly citizens, who already see the God of Gods, revealed in all His glory in Sion" (the latter allusion is to Psalm 49: 1–2).

[64] In the Immodest Damsel episode Chrétien returns to the theme of Lancelot protecting a woman from rape.

[65] The spiritual marriage of Christ and the Church was also seen, as we know from psalters and books of hours, as an image of the Church Militant and Triumphant. A later example can be found on fol. 32v of *Les Très riches heures du duc de Berry*.

representatives mentally formulate ideas and carry them out in the many variet-
ies of Christian campaign mentioned above.[66] In this interpretation, Guinevere's
haughty ways are designed to elicit the unquestioning obedience asked by the
Church Militant, which called upon its followers to sacrifice their lives to free
the Holy Land from pagan dominion.[67]

We can now understand why Chrétien expresses the love of Lancelot and
Guinevere in a series of paradoxes. In the words of Caroline Walker Bynum, "Paradox is not, by definition, solvable; it can only be asserted, experienced, lived."[68]
Chrétien's narrative places readers in the position of Lancelot worshipping Guinevere's body as if it were a "cors saint" (4653), a body to which the observer is to
join him- or herself in ecstatic contemplation, a joy that passes all understanding. Chrétien locates the higher meaning of his text in the pleasures attendant
upon the contemplation of the highest mysteries.[69] If the *Charrette* has for so long
frustrated modern attempts to understand its paradoxes, it is, I believe, because
Chrétien consciously set about to confute those who were unwilling or unable to
read beyond the literal level of the text. Those medieval readers who did grasp its
higher meaning realized that the text was not complete unless they acted upon
its message, which was to imitate the Passion experienced conjointly by Christ
and Mary. Modern readers have even more trouble understanding the text than

---

[66] The Church Militant reflects the Church Triumphant in heaven, an idea often
rendered visually by the Virgin's crowning by Christ. Such an image appears in a psalter
realized for Marie's granddaughter, Jeanne de Flandre (see Stirnemann, "Bibliothèque,"
38, for a reproduction from this psalter). It is of interest that Jeanne was given a *Graal*
manuscript containing the First and Second Continuations (London, British Library,
Add. 36614) by Marie's daughter-in-law Blanche de Navarre (Blanche was married to
Marie's son, Thibaut III). On Jeanne de Flandre, see Lori Walters, "Jeanne and Marguerite de Flandre as Female Patrons," *Dalhousie French Studies* 28 (1994): 15–27.

[67] If it seems difficult to envision Lancelot as a defender of the Church, one has only
to cite the example of Pierre Salmon, who in his early fifteenth-century *Dialogues* urged
France's King Charles VI to defend and augment the Church as Charlemagne, St. Louis,
Alexander, Arthur, and Lancelot had in the past: Anne D. Hedeman, *Of Counselors and
Kings: The Three Versions of Pierre Salmon's Dialogues* (Urbana and Chicago: University
Press of Illinois, 2001), 34. Salmon's comment suggests that by the early fifteenth cen-
tury, people saw Lancelot as a defender of the Church in the line of other fictional char-
acters like Arthur and of real-life French kings like Charlemagne and St. Louis.

[68] Caroline Walker Bynum, "Patterns of Female Piety in the Later Middle Ages,"
in *Crown and Veil: Female Monasticism from the Fifth to the Fifteenth Centuries*, ed. Jeffrey
F. Hamburger and Susan Marti (New York: Columbia University Press, 2008), 172–90,
here 188.

[69] Chrétien's tale, which marries joy inextricably to pain, may be supposed to evoke
in its readers "a certain spiritual pleasure" that Augustine held was to be felt by the saints
when they contemplated the marriage of the King and Queen of the City of God (*Civitas Dei* 22. 20).

did medieval readers, for its message is not one that we are attuned to hearing, nor one (to add a personal note) that we particularly like when we understand it! But a message to undertake self-sacrifice, pain, and possible death for a cause, however holy, must have been unpalatable to many people even in those most Christian of times. Thus Marie enlisted Chrétien to help her couch her appeal to the audience's emotions. He did so by building upon techniques made famous in recent history by Bernard de Clairvaux, who was following in the line of prior founders of the Western Church like Paul and Augustine.

In his *Conte du Graal* (*Graal*, ca. 1185–1191),[70] Chrétien returns to many of the same issues he had treated in the *Charrette*. In the prologue he again takes up the idea of spiritual marriage as a reflection of the marriage of Christ and the Church, evoking St. Paul (1, 49),[71] as had Bernard in the opening lines of his first sermon on *Song*. Chrétien lauds Philippe de Flandre for being superior to all other knights because of his devotion to "Sainte Iglise" [Holy Church, 26]. The count had demonstrated this devotion by his participation in two crusades, the first a private one in 1177 in which he visited the tomb of his mother Sibylla, formerly queen of Jerusalem, the second in 1191, the Third Crusade, on which he died. McCash has noticed "intriguing parallels" between Philippe's family history and the Grail story: his mother was a member of a royal line in Jerusalem, where the leper king Baudouin had to be carried around in a litter like the Fisher King; his father Thierry d'Alsace had been rewarded for his service in the Second Crusade by a gift of a phial of the Holy Blood.[72] McCash adds that Philippe, an avid relic collector, would have been fascinated by accounts of the recovery of Longinus's lance at Antioch.[73] The count played a major part in promoting monarchical aims, serving as tutor to the future king of France Philippe II Auguste, carrying Charlemagne's sword at his former ward's coronation, and engineering the king's marriage to his niece Ysabel de Hainaut, which the *GCF* states he did expressly to return French kings to the line of the legendary crusader Charlemagne.[74] Philippe de Flandre is able to do great deeds, so says Chrétien, because

---

[70] I refer to Félix Lecoy's edition of the *Conte du Graal (Perceval)*, 2 vols. (Paris: Champion, 1972, 1975) because it is based upon BNF fr. 794.

[71] The first line echoes 2 Cor. 9: 6: "he who sows little, reaps little." For studies treating Chrétien's use of Paul, see Jean-Guy Gouttebroze, "'Sainz Pos le dit, et je le lui': Chrétien de Troyes lecteur," *Romania* 114 (1996): 524–35; and Luciano Rossi, "*Carestia, Tristan*, les troubadours et le modèle de saint Paul: encore sur *D'Amors qui m'a tolu a moi* (RS 1664)," in *Convergences médiévales: épopée, lyrique, roman: Mélanges Madeleine Tyssens* (Brussels: De Boeck Université, 2000), 403–19.

[72] William A. Nitze, "The Bleeding Lance and Philip of Flanders," *Speculum* 21 (1946): 303–11, here 306.

[73] McCash, "Chrétien's Patrons," 24–25.

[74] Hedeman, *Royal Image*, 22. On the treatment of Charlemagne in the *GCF* and his importance as a crusader king, see Lori J. Walters, "Christine de Pizan comme biographe royal," trans. Laurence Costa, in *Le passé à l'épreuve du present: Appropriations*

of the devotion present in the secrets of his heart (33–36). We have seen that the Night of Love, in which Lancelot and Guinevere experience supreme joy in the secret places of the heart, celebrates a similar union of a Christian knight and Holy Church.

But as in the *Charrette,* in the *Graal* true and lasting union is achieved only with difficulty. The text's protagonist Perceval has to learn proper adherence to the Church's precepts. This developmental process is expressed in terms of his relationship to his mother, who as a *figura* of Ecclesia instructs him in his duty to defend the Church and women in distress, and to revere him who "porta corone d'espines" [wore the crown of thorns, 589]. As in the *Charrette,* Chrétien associates blood drops with devotion. He imagines a now famous scene in which he represents Perceval leaning on his lance, lost in ecstatic contemplation before the "sanblance" [image, 4306] of three drops of blood displayed on freshly fallen snow. Left there by the wounding of a wild goose, the drops remind him of the face of his beloved Blanchefleur. From this first scene Chrétien moves to another, quite different one, this time staged in the interior space of the Grail Castle, where Perceval sees the mysterious grail, a bleeding lance, and a broken sword that must be mended. The drops of blood that perpetually flow from a lance are an obvious symbol of the sword of compassion; the broken lance, a symbol of the impetus to embark on crusade, that term to be understood, as I have discussed it above, either in its particular or more general manifestations.

The carnal associations of the blood drops are progressively purified over the course of the four *Graal* continuations, as the protagonist eventually learns to interpret the blood drops as the sign of his duty to the cross.[75] Wauchier de Denain, the author of the *Second Continuation* (ca. 1200), has Perceval promise to return to marry Blanchefleur after having found the Grail. In Gerbert de Montreuil's *Continuation* (interpolated, 1226–1230, between the *Second* and *Third Continuations*), Perceval weds Blanchefleur, but the two promise to observe a chaste marriage at least until he has completed the Grail quest. To judge by Gerbert's affirmation that Perceval's descendants would conquer Jerusalem, the couple seemed destined to reign together and give birth to a line of knights who would distinguish themselves in the Crusades. Manessier, the author of the *Third Continuation* (ca. 1225), has the hero leave Blanchefleur once and for all after a brief visit to defend her against aggression. Perceval becomes a priest and upon his death is assumed into heaven along with the grail and the lance. As Manessier brings the Grail saga to a close, he associates the drops' red and white color

---

*et usages du passé au Moyen Age et à la Renaissance,* ed. Pierre Chastang and Michel Zimmermann (Paris: Presses de l'Université Paris-Sorbonne, 2007), 223–36 + four accompanying plates.

[75] Armel Diverres, "The Grail and the Third Crusade: Thoughts on *Le Conte del Graal* by Chrétien de Troyes," *Arthurian Literature* 10 (1990): 13–104, suggests that the Continuations should be seen against the backdrop of the Crusades.

configuration with the crusader emblem of a red cross on a white field.[76] In having the Fisher King explain that the bleeding lance was the one used by Longinus to pierce Christ's side at the Crucifixion, he identifies it conclusively with the lance of compassion. Manessier composed this final continuation for Countess Jeanne de Flandre (1199/1200–1244), granddaughter to Marie de Champagne, and, like her, a "crusader queen."[77]

By Jeanne de Flandre's time, poets like Manessier were careful to dissociate a "crusader queen" from any association with an adulterous relationship, whether real or fictional. A similar movement can be discerned in the *Lancelot-Graal*, the compilation that amalgamated Chrétien's *Charrette* and *Graal*. Composed in prose, the language of truth and of historical writing like the *GCF*, the text envisions Lancelot and Guinevere's illicit love as the cause of the downfall of the Arthurian universe. A related impulse is likewise present in the texts of Adam de Perseigne and Evrat. Their dialogues with Marie were designed to impress upon her that a royal lady like herself should direct her thoughts away from literal expressions of adultery and in their place meditate upon "holy adulteries" and adapt her behavior to their dictates.

### III. The presence of a crusading mentality in two biblical adaptations done for Marie, the *Eructavit* and *Genesis*

Under Marie's direction, the Champagne court became an important center for the translation of Scripture from Latin into French. Such translations were among the earliest known. Marie's commissions of the *Eructavit* and *Genesis* testify to a growing spiritualization of her interests, whose origins can be traced to the *Charrette*. Adam de Perseigne's *Eructavit* is an extended gloss on Psalm 44 ("Eructavit cor meum verbum bonum," my heart uttered a good word) that is greatly indebted to Augustine's commentaries in his *City of God* 17.16 and his *Commentary on Psalms*.[78] Psalm 44 was well known: it was sung as part of the

---

[76] Lori J. Walters, "Female Figures in the Illustrated Manuscripts of *Le conte du Graal* and its *Continuations*: Ladies, Saints, Spectators, Mediators," in *Text and Image: Studies in the French Illustrated Book from the Middle Ages to the Present Day*, ed. David J. Adams and Adrian Armstrong, spec. iss. of *Bulletin of the John Rylands University Library of Manchester* 81.3 (Autumn 1999): 7–54, here 10–11.

[77] Jeanne was the daughter of Marie de Champagne's daughter Marie and Baudouin IX de Flandre (also referred to as Baudouin VI de Hainaut), who became the first Latin emperor of Constantinople after the Crusade of 1204. See Walters, "Jeanne and Marguerite de Flandre," 18, 22.

[78] Patricia Hollahan, "Daughter of Sion, Daughter of Babylon: Images of Woman in the Old English Psalms," *Essays in Medieval Studies* 2 (1985): 27–39. On 31 she rephrases

Christmas liturgy, as well as at the marriage ceremonies of French kings; several of its verses were incorporated into the coronation ceremonies of the kings of France and England;[79] and it figured in the Book of Hours.[80] The *Eructavit* is a divine epithalamium, "a sort of earthly reperformance of David's performance at the wedding of the King and Queen of Heaven."[81] As is usual in a sacred epithalamium, the lovers' conjoining takes place secretly, away from the sight of the earthly eye. In the opening lines we return to the *Charrette*'s initial image of the partnership between a royal figure and a writer who places himself in the role of simple scribe. Adam, Marie's confessor-poet, assumes the persona of the psalmist and repeats David's words from verse 1, "My tongue is like the pen of a ready scribe" as he addresses his "daughter," the Church, which also takes on the form of David's descendant Mary and Adam's own patroness Marie. Like Chrétien in the *Charrette*, Adam refers to Marie as "ma dame de Champaigne" [my lady of Champagne] and his work contains clear allusions to other Chrétien romances, particularly to *Erec et Enide*.[82] The *Eructavit* appears to consciously take up Chrétien's vocabulary in a more spiritual register, making it clear, for example, that "fin amors" comes from God (1445).

Adam celebrates Marie's status as a member of the royal line. McCash believes that he sought to flatter women of the royal house by his selection of a psalm that made reference to the "daughters of kings" who would give birth to sons who would become "princes of the earth" (*"Eructavit cor meum,"* 166–68).

---

Augustine's commentary as saying that every soul that has been born through the saints' preaching and evangelizing is a 'daughter of kings'; and that the psalmist, in addressing the queen, is addressing "each one of us, provided . . . we endeavor to belong to that body, and do belong to it in faith and hope, being united in the membership of Christ."

[79] McCash, *"Eructavit cor meum,"* 160.

[80] I quote from Roger Wieck's letter to me of 10 April 2007: "Psalm 44 occurs in the second nocturn of Matins' Hours of the Virgin. The long, ideal Matins has all three nocturns. Not all Books of Hours contain all three; some use the short version, which includes only the first nocturn. In those cases there will be no Psalm 44. When Psalm 44 does appear, it does so in its entirety in the Vulgate version." I extend my thanks to Wieck for supplying me with this information.

[81] Morgan Powell, "Translating Scripture for *Ma Dame de Champagne*: The Old French 'Paraphrase' of Psalm 44 (*Eructavit*)," in *The Vernacular Spirit: Essays on Medieval Religious Literature*, ed. R. Blumenfeld-Kosinski, D. Robertson, and N. Warren (New York: Palgrave, 2002), 83–103, here 85.

[82] Powell, "Translating Scripture," 92. Terms from Chrétien's romances, such as "joie de la cour" (joy of the court), "fin amors" (refined love), "s'oblier" (to forget oneself), and variants of "conjoïr" (to conjoin) appear frequently. Marie is described as a gem beyond compare (1323–1325) as she had been in the *Charrette*, although here we more easily recognize it as a reference to her virtue. This comparison was made famous by the onetime crusade advocate and advisor to Louis VI and Louis VII, Abbot Suger of Saint-Denis (1081–1151).

This praise follows a line of development stretching from Paul, Augustine, and Bernard. After all, it was Clairvaux's abbot who had seen in Mary the model for the royal lady: "the Virgin [. . .] is the royal way, by which the Saviour comes to us."[83] Bernard doubtless derived the terms of his encomium from the canticle's description of the Beloved, who is as lovely as Jerusalem, but as "terrible as an army set in array" (*Song* 6:9).[84] The queens celebrated by Adam go beyond their status as French royal ladies or ancestors of future kings to being symbols of the Church Militant and Triumphant.[85]

Adam proposes Marie's participation in the crusade effort as a way to wash away her sins. The divine bridegroom—Christ who spreads his arms on the cross to encircle his mother lamenting below him—will embrace her, Adam claims, even if her earthly husband rejects her for her sins (1570ff). Uniting his words to Marie's, Adam speaks of conquests made by means of God's voice and the true cross. Ending the work in a prayer to be pronounced by both himself and the countess, he asks that they be purified by the blood flowing from Christ's right flank: "Lavez moi, sire, par cele onde / Dont vos lavastes tot le monde" [Wash me, Lord, with this wave / With which you wash everyone; 2155–2156]. Adam associates Marie's royal status with the martyrdom he foresees for her through her participation in crusading activities. He draws out this association through the use of flower symbolism. Roses are for martyrs, who could represent actual crusaders who had died or would die in the future, such as Marie's husband and son; lilies, which are associated the French royal house, could represent Marie herself; and lastly, "violetes qui sont perses" [violets that are purple], which could represent Adam, since it contains a word play on the name of the abbey of Perseigne where he was first a monk and later abbot.[86] Martyrdom is a dominant motif in the passage, being symbolized by a "flaming ruby" (1882). First comparing the Church to a mother who saw her children martyred (alluding to the Slaughter of the Innocents in Matthew 2:16–18 with its quotation of Jeremiah 31:15), Adam extends the comparison to the countess. Like the Virgin her model, Marie becomes the human face of Holy Church, who, through her words and deeds, inspires her subjects to accept martyrdom by taking up the cross.

The second biblical adaptation commissioned by Marie de Champagne was a metrical translation of the Old Testament composed by Evrat, who was able to complete only the book of Genesis. He fills the text's 21,000 verses with extended

---

[83] Norman F. Cantor, *The Civilization of the Middle Ages* (New York: HarperCollins, 1993), 341: *Sermo* 2 on Advent, PL 183.43.

[84] Fulton, *From Judgment to Passion*, 341.

[85] St. Louis received his inspiration from his mother Blanche de Castille, who made sure her son had two Dominican and two Franciscan confessors, the latter being, along with the Cistercians, the primary propagators of the sword of compassion motif.

[86] This is one of the reasons for believing that the author of the *Eructavit* was Adam de Perseigne.

moralizing commentary and praise for the countess and her son. Evrat says he
is writing his book so that Marie, "Ki bien lo sout entendre et lire" [who knows
how to understand and read it well, 23], can take it out of her bookcase (*armaire*)
and benefit from the wisdom gained by reading its gloss of the Old Law by the
New.[87] *Genesis* associates Marie even more closely with her son's participation in
the Crusades than had the *Eructavit*. Evrat praises Henri II's work in the Holy
Land (143–145), which brings great honor to the county of Champagne, and comfort to the "prouz mere ki le porta" [valiant mother who bore him, 162]. Although,
as her confessor points out to her, Marie is often sad to be separated from her son,
she is comforted when she hears the great things said of him. Such a mother, Evrat
maintains, is worthy of having a great son. All living women should imitate her
example (174–175). Then he telescopes Marie and the Virgin, by saying that the
latter has removed blame from all women of the world (182–188), a reference to
the Virgin's redemption of Eve's sin. This reinforces his claim that women deserve
respect because of the eminent honor shown to the Virgin.[88]

A short excursus on the similarities among the dialogic structure of the *Eructavit*, the *Genesis*, and the *Charrette* will help clarify Chrétien's concept of "holy
adultery." Although it is not immediately apparent, the *Charrette* has a dialogic
structure. The initial conversations between Chrétien and Marie that gave rise to
the romance are continued throughout the narrative by the interactions between
Lancelot and Guinevere.[89] The dialogic form of the three works can be traced to
Augustine's *Soliloquies* and *Confessions*.[90] In the *Soliloquies*, a work whose importance

---

[87] This appears to have been Paris, BNF fr. 900, one of three surviving manuscripts
of the work: Boers, "La Genèse," 129.

[88] Boers, "La Genèse," 141.

[89] As is pointed out, by Bruckner, "That Obscure Object of Desire," 141, the verse
"come cil qui est suens entiers" [as one who is entirely hers], which Chrétien applies both
to his own devotion to Marie and Lancelot's dedication to Guinevere, clearly marks out
the analogy between the loyalty shown by the clerkly writer to his patroness and that
shown by the knightly lover to his queen. Metaphorically speaking, Marie gives birth to
the *Charrette* by supplying its subject matter and controlling idea, which Chrétien then
brings to fruition. The upshot is that Chrétien and Marie create a narrative through a
conjoined mental effort that is analogous to the conjoining of Lancelot and Guinevere, if
we interpret the latter as a divine epithalamium.

[90] This is not surprising, since Adam de Perseigne wrote a *Soliloquium* that was indebted not only to Augustine, but also to Bernard and to Guillaume de St. Thierry's *Letter to the Brothers of Mont-Dieu*, a sort of mini-commentary on the *Song of Songs*, which
at the time was believed to have been authored by Bernard. See G. Raciti, "Un opuscule
inédit d'Adam de Perseigne: le livre de l'amour mutuel," *Cîteaux* 31 (1980): 297–341,
here 300. In the entry on Adam de Perseigne in the *Dictionnaire des Lettres Françaises (Le
Moyen Âge)*, ed. Hasenohr and Zink (Paris: Le Livre de Poche, 1991), 13–14, J. Bouvet
and J. Longère discuss the controversy over whether Adam de Perseigne was the author
of *Eructavit*. A. Jenkins, H.R. Jauss, and M.R. Jung believe he was, whereas J. Benton

for poetic composition has long been overlooked, Augustine discusses the use of fables or lies to establish the truth. Grammar, he says, does not create falsehoods, but from them it teaches and presents a true system. Fables use something patently false used to teach something true.[91]Accordingly, although, he says, it is false that we are two people, we can divide ourselves mentally, and in this way find truth. Augustine applies this reasoning to the dialogic method he proposes and illustrates through the work's structure of a conversation between characters named "Augustine" and "Reason." These dialogues could also take place between two characters representing different "persons."[92] Adam's dialogues between two characters recall the *Charrette*'s opening dialogue between Marie and Chrétien, which is continued over the course of the narrative by means of the analogies established between this pair and Lancelot and Guinevere.

These three Old French works are also related to the *Confessions*, another dialogic text that Augustine composed about ten years after having written the *Soliloquies*.[93] The *Confessions* has been described as a meditative text that fosters ongoing personal transformation through dialogue. It grounds such transformation in Augustine's reading of Genesis 1 as the creation of the Church.[94] In the *Confessions* the future Church Father transforms the *Soliloquies'* figure of Reason into the figure of his mother Monnica, whom he holds responsible for bringing him to birth physically in her body and spiritually in her heart (*Confessions*

---

and J. Bouvet do not. Since the second paragraph of Adam's *Soliloquium* is a paraphrase of Ps. 44:11, the source text of *Eructavit*, it is likely that Adam was author of both. The play on the name "Perseigne" that I discuss above also implies that Adam was the author of the work.

[91] His commanding example is that "there could be no true fable about the flight of Daedalus, unless it were false that Daedalus had flown!" (11. 20 [77]).

[92] Adam's own *Soliloquium*, his treatise on the formation of a monk, for example, takes the form of conversations between a monk and Reason and a monk and his superior.

[93] It is important to realize that the French translation of the *Soliloquies* made for Charles V around 1373 was written through the optic of his later *Confessions* and began with a free rendition of the sword of compassion motif. See Geneviève Esnos (Hasenohr), "Les Traductions médiévales françaises et italiennes des *Soliloques* attribuées à Saint Augustin," *Mélanges d'archéologie et d'histoire* 79 (1967): 299–366. The *Soliloquies'* dialogue between "Augustine" and "Reason" becomes, in the French "translation," a prayer addressed by Augustine to God.

[94] McMahon, *Meditative Ascent*, 71, 101, 141–42. The texts considered by McMahon all enact a Platonic ascent. For a recent study of connections between the Platonic tradition and the *Charrette*, see K. Sarah-Jane Murray, *From Plato to Lancelot: A Preface to Chrétien de Troyes* (Syracuse: Syracuse University Press, 2008).

9. 8).[95] When Monnica dies, she becomes for her son a figure of the Church,[96] whose goal, as taught to mother and son by Paul, was to "edify" humanity (cf. Ephesians 4:12 and elsewhere). Augustine derives his identity as a spiritual being from Monnica, just as Lancelot will take his identity from Guinevere and Chrétien from Marie. Like Monnica, Guinevere and Marie are both *figurae* of the Church, which, together with all her loyal followers, has a duty to teach and give proper example to those in her care.[97] In his free adaptation of Genesis Evrat enters into a dialogue with Marie aimed at facilitating her ongoing transformation into a worthy representative of the Church.

The text gives insights into the way that Marie de Champagne could function as a model of virtuous words and deeds for Chrétien, her other subjects, and later readers of the *Charrette*. Evrat exploits the opposition of EVA and AVE (1020–1024) to say that women will be blamed if they follow Eve's example but praised if they abide by Mary's counterexample. God explains Eve's punishment for her sins by claiming that she was proud and insolent.[98] Whereas before sinning, she was free and a lady,[99] after sinning, she became a slave and a servant.[100] Evrat may be interpreting Genesis through *Confessions* 9.19 where Augustine explains that when Monnica's friends complained about the abuse they received at their husbands' hands, she replied that they should consider their marriage contracts to be legally binding documents by which they had become their husbands' servants. In Augustine's *Confessions* and Evrat's *Genesis,* marriage, given humanity's fallen state, is a sign of woman's subjection to her husband as punishment for her sins. Adultery accordingly becomes the paradoxical indication of a relationship based upon love and consent rather than upon constraint. However, it should be interpreted allegorically as a "holy adultery," one expressive of a woman's devotion to the Church or to the "heavenly bridegroom" rather than as the choice of a real-life lover.

Thus, when Chrétien, Adam, and Evrat refer to Marie as "ma dame de Champagne," they imply that she is trying to act like a true "lady" who, like

---

[95] This reference is recalled in the description of St. Louis's birth cited above.

[96] Kim Paffenroth, "Book Nine: The Emotional Heart of the *Confessions*," in *A Reader's Companion to Augustine's Confessions*, ed. idem (Louisville, KY: Westminster John Knox Press, 2003), 137–54, here 144.

[97] Patristic authors depicted her as "Holy Mother Church" who gives birth to her faithful children. Christine McWebb, "Female City Builders: Hildegard of Bingen's *Scivias* and Christine de Pizan's *Livre de la cité des dames*," *Magistra: A Journal of Women's Spirituality in History* 9 (2003): 52–71, here 60 depicts several of these images. See also Hugo Rahner, *Symbole der Kirche: Die Ekklesiologie der Väter* (Salzburg: Otto Müller Verlag, 1964).

[98] "orguilhouse et proterve," 1115.

[99] "franche," 1116 ; "dame," 1118.

[100] "serve," 1116; "baasse," 1118.

Sarah, Genesis's female *viator*, begins the spiritual pilgrimage of the human line[101] toward the proper imitation of models like Mary and Christ. Evrat specifically evokes memory of the biblical matriarch when he compares the tombs of Marie and her husband Count Henri to the double tombs of Abraham and his wife, located in Hebron (Gen. 23:19).[102] Evrat's *Genesis* continues the idea expressed in the *Eructavit* that Marie is a female ruler from whose line will come noteworthy "princes of the world." This prophecy was amply fulfilled in the birth of St. Louis from Marie's niece Blanche de Castille. Given that *Genesis* was a traditional subject of meditation before Easter, Marie may well have had Evrat's text read before her court during the Lenten season.[103] The *Charrette*, *Eructavit*, and *Genesis* are all dialogues designed to provoke a meditative process of self and societal improvement in their patrons, authors, and the audiences of the texts. In all three cases we are examining here these processes were inspired by Marie de Champagne, who evidently saw herself as a *viator* seeking to transform her imperfect self into a more exemplary one fashioned upon earlier models of the Church such as Monnica and Mary.

From what we know of her life, the Countess Marie was a model wife and mother. After being left, at the age of seven, with a stepmother[104] after her parents' divorce, she was the responsible elder sister of nearly a dozen royal children and grew up to be what one chronicler describes as "an honest and devoted" wife and mother of four.[105] In speaking of her final resting place, Evrat renders a last homage to Marie by representing her as a loyal patron of the Church: "A Meaz regist la gentils dame / Ki l'eglise a si maintenue. . ." [In Meaux reigns the noble lady, who supported the Church so well].[106] At the end of the twelfth century in the county of Champagne, upholding the Church and its laws implied supporting the Crusades. As Augustine proposed, identifying with the crucified Christ was a solution to mankind's fallen state. The Church Father's realization has been stated in the following way:

> Wisdom is not to be found by ascending to a godlike eminence that enables one to look down on the rest of humanity as so many fools, but rather

---

[101] This is shown by the scene in which Abraham is prevented from sacrificing his son Isaac, who thereby becomes a prefiguration of Christ as a Christian ruler.

[102] Boers, "La Genèse," 98–100.

[103] Boers, "La Genèse," 143.

[104] This was Louis VII's second wife, Constance de Castille.

[105] Jane Frances Anne Henderson, "A Critical Edition of Evrat's *Genesis*: Creation to the Flood" (Ph.D. diss., University of Toronto, 1977), 34.

[106] Quéruel, "Une cour intellectuelle," 18.

to humbly identifying oneself with the crucified Christ, the foolishness of God that is wiser than human wisdom. [107]

Following this reasoning, Lancelot's "adulterous" devotion to Guinevere is part of his godlike foolishness that goes beyond human reason and wisdom. He exhibits the type of devotion that led Crusaders to shed their blood in the hope of gaining forgiveness of their sins.

### IV. The presence of a crusading mentality in Paris, BNF fr. 794 and in a moralized Bible, New York, Pierpont Morgan 240, commissioned by Marie's niece, Blanche de Castille

Through Guiot, BNF fr. 794 has connections to Chrétien's patroness and to her family of illustrious crusaders. The portrait of Marie de Champagne, found in an initial capital that heads the *Charrette* in BNF fr. 794 (Figure 4.1), conforms to the view of her as a personification of the Church. It reflects the spiritualization of her interests and the royal character of her biological lineage, each conforming to consistent family patterns. In this picture, the sole illustration in the compilation, Marie represents *grosso modo* the Church Militant seeking to inspire allegiance to its crusading efforts through the alliance of the pen and the sword as described in Psalm 44 and perpetuated by French monarchical theorists. [108] It conforms to Chrétien's tacit view of her in the *Charrette* as a maternal figure capable of generating both royal lineage and a spiritual or intellectual lineage of exemplary texts and manuscript books.

BNF fr. 794 provides evidence of Marie's desire to inspire a continuation of her spiritual leadership that had appeared not only in the *Charrette*, but also in the *Eructavit* and *Genesis*. The manuscript, which was produced around 1230 in the circles around Marie, includes the most complete copies of all five of Chrétien's romances plus four other texts. The scribe who copied all three units names himself "Guiot" in a colophon at the end of *Yvain*. [109] The present order, different

---

[107] Eric Plumer, "Book Six: Major Characters and Memorable Events," in *A Reader's Companion to Augustine's Confessions*, ed. Paffenroth, 89–105, here 101. The final allusion is to 1 Cor. 1:25.

[108] From Charlemagne's time they adopted Augustine as their primary authority after the Bible, as was reported by Charlemagne's first biographer, Einhard. See Walters, "Biographe royale."

[109] Lori Walters, "Le rôle du scribe dans l'organisation des manuscrits des romans de Chrétien de Troyes," *Romania* 106 (1985): 303–25; and eadem, "The King's Example." BNF fr. 794 contains three units: (i) Chrétien's *Erec et Enide, Charrette, Cligés*, and *Yvain*; (ii) *Athis et Prophilias*; (iii) the *Roman de Troie* by Benoît de Sainte-Maure, Wace's *Brut*, Calendre's *Empereurs de Rome*, Chrétien's *Graal*, its First Continuation, and a fragment

**Figure 4.1.** Portrait of Marie de Champagne. MS BNF fr. 794 fol. 27r.

Photographic credit: The Bibliothèque Nationale de France, Paris.

from the original one, was established by the second half of the thirteenth century, when a verse table of contents was added to the front flyleaf.[110] Beginning, then, from around the middle of the thirteenth century, viewers opened the 433-folio manuscript book to *Erec et Enide*. As they read on to the next text, the *Charrette*, they came upon its initial letter "P" on fol. 27, which displayed a small but brilliantly colored image of a noblewoman. The image presumably depicts Countess Marie de Champagne, whose gestures suggest that she is dictating her wishes to Chrétien. This initial, the only picture of any sort in the entire compilation, is a type of "author or authorizing portrait" that complements Chrétien's avowal that he composed the work by closely following the dictates of his patroness.[111]

Marie's portrait establishes Chrétien as a vital link in a line of vernacular authority emanating from her court in Troyes in Champagne, beginning with Chrétien de Troyes and ending with the second compiler of BNF fr. 794. The colophon localizes activity of the scribe and probable first compiler, Guiot de Provins, to the collegiate house of Notre-Dame-du-Val in Provins, which Marie de Champagne founded in 1196.[112] Since she endowed the church with thirty-eight prebends, and was entitled to award nineteen to clerics of her choice, it is likely that Guiot was a canon at Notre-Dame-du-Val who owed his living to Marie.[113] Some time around 1230 Guiot worked in accordance with the pronounced religious interests Marie de Champagne had exhibited toward the end of her life. It is plausible that the person who re-ordered the compilation around the turn of the century was, like Chrétien and Guiot before him, inspired by the exemplary image Marie had communicated to posterity thanks to those writing for her.

The image of Marie in Paris, BNF fr. 794 is overwhelmingly positive. Stirnemann and Hasenohr emphasize the authority emanating from the manuscript. It has bookmarks sewn into the beginning of each text, a practice otherwise exclusive to liturgical texts in other early collections in the Romance languages.[114] The book's quasi-religious character would go along with the ideological promo-

---

of the Second Continuation. Based upon the typical placement of a colophon at the end of a scribe's transcription of a text, it is reasonable to believe that the scribe Guiot was the compiler of the first ordering, and that another compiler re-ordered the collection several decades after Guiot's work.

[110] Terry Nixon, "Catalogue of Manuscripts, " in *Les Manuscrits de Chrétien de Troyes*, 2: 1–85, here 29.

[111] Sylvia Huot, "The Manuscript Context of Medieval Romance," in *The Cambridge Companion to Medieval Romance*, ed. Roberta L. Kruger (Cambridge: Cambridge University Press, 2000), 60–77, here 69.

[112] Mario Roques, "Le Manuscrit fr. 794 de la Bibl. Nat. et le scribe Guiot," *Romania* 73 (1952): 177–99, here 189–90.

[113] Putter, "Knights and Clerics at the Court of Champagne," 251.

[114] Patricia Stirnemann and Geneviève Hasenohr, "Description of BNF fr. 794," in *Splendeurs*, 66.

tion of the Church-State alliance discussed above. In the context of BNF fr. 794, Marie becomes associated with the saintly woman whose name she bears.[115] As a female ruler, the countess is assimilated above all to the Queen of Heaven. Chrétien's rhetorical question, "vaut la contesse de reïnes?" [does the countess eclipse queens in worth?, 18], appears on fol. 27, not far from her picture. If this question likens her textually to a queen, visual elements equate her with the Queen of Heaven. As she sits ensconced in the *Charrette*'s initial letter, Marie assumes the "seat of wisdom" pose typical of heaven's queen.[116] In the Guiot manuscript Marie can thus be seen as a maternal figure presiding over a line of authors who compose works for the benefit of future kings, queens, and other royals. This representation of her coincides with the way that Adam de Perseigne portrays her in the *Eructavit* and in that text's principal source, Augustine's commentaries on Psalm 44.

A crusader mentality is implicit in the manuscript's two orderings.[117] The first ordering, established around 1230, traces the movement of the *translatio studii et imperii* as found in *Cligés* and in the *GCF* prologue. The idea expressed by the latter is that France would lose its cultural, political, and moral supremacy if it did not defend the Church, which meant upholding the proper teaching of its doctrines and supporting it on crusade. The second ordering, which was established ca. 1250, around the middle of St. Louis's forty-four-year reign, places the image of Marie near the book's opening. Even more than in the original placement, in this position she appears to be the quintessential Christian ruler who leads by her deeds, words, and impeccable reputation. According to the criteria established in the *GCF* commissioned by her great-nephew, the reigning king of France, Marie was thus fit to represent the country.[118] The second ordering is also noteworthy because it substitutes a fragment of the Second *Graal* Continuation for *Yvain* and the closed ending of the ordering.[119] In so doing, it provides a new ending to the cycle. In the second (and permanent) ordering, the incomplete *Graal* narrative issues an implicit invitation to writers and warriors to continue to

---

[115] There may also be an implied comparison between Marie and Mary Magdalen, thought of at the time as the reformed adulteress.

[116] The *sedes sapientiae* is related to the *sedes Salomonis*, whose pictorial development reached a peak during the reign of Louis IX: Allan Dean McKenzie, "The Virgin Mary as the Throne of Solomon in Medieval Art," 2 vols. (Ph.D. diss., New York University, 1965), 1: 10. Forsyth, *The Throne of Wisdom* (Princeton: Princeton University Press, 1972).

[117] See Richard and Mary Rouse, "The Crusade as Context: The Manuscripts of *Athis et Prophilias*," in *Courtly Arts*, ed. Busby and Kleinhenz, 49–104. *Athis et Prophilias* was the lead text in the original ordering. It occupied the middle position in the second ordering.

[118] Ideologically speaking, Marie repudiated her mother's choice of England over France.

[119] That ending is closed even more securely in BNF fr. 794 than elsewhere because it is followed by Guiot's colophon.

defend Christendom, and France's stellar position within it, through all means known to pen and sword.

Marie's image in BNF fr. 794 is recalled in the picture of Blanche de Castille found on fol. 8 of New York, Pierpont Morgan 240 (Figure 4.2). John Lowden concludes that Blanche commissioned the manuscript in the later 1220s as a gift for her son Louis IX,[120] and that she probably gave it to him to celebrate his wedding to Marguerite de Provence in May 1234.[121] This picture of Blanche is the final image in what was a monumental three-volume moralized Bible, the majority of which is today housed in the library of Spain's Toledo Cathedral. It is important to note that Blanche commissioned the Bible for her son Louis during the time she was queen regent. Like her aunt Marie, she assured regencies for her son. The first time was from 1226, when Louis ascended the throne at the age of eleven, until 1234. She again acted as Louis's regent from 1248 to 1257 when he participated in the Seventh Crusade. Even though Morgan 240 was completed before Louis went on Crusade, it depicts Blanche as a powerful maternal pedagogue. Her instruction undoubtedly had an influence on Louis's view, which was expressed in the *GCF* that he commissioned ca. 1250, that France had a duty to live up to its image as Christianity's staunchest defender.

Blanche de Castille's hand gestures in this Bible illustration are similar to Marie's in BNF fr. 794. In the large, elaborately drawn portrait, it is clear that Blanche's right hand is open with the thumb and fingers poised. Although the sketch of Marie is too roughly drawn to make out the exact details of her right hand, her gestures appear to be the same as Blanche's. The similarities are brought out by the description of those gestures given by Stirnemann and Hasenohr:

> La comtesse y esquisse de sa main droite un geste d'ordre qu'elle nuance par le geste accueillant de la main gauche (paume ouverte). Cette attitude renvoie aux vers 24–7 du roman: "Del chevalier de la charrete / Comance Crestïens son livre / Matiere et san li done et livre / la comtesse. . ."[122]

> [There the Countess sketches with her right hand a gesture of command that she nuances by the welcoming gesture of her left hand (open palm). This attitude refers to verses 24–7 of the romance: "Of the Knight of the Cart / Chrétien begins his book / Subject matter and controlling idea / the Countess gives and delivers to him. . .."]

In the top register of Figure 2 Blanche raises her hand toward her son, depicted as a young man, in gestures that have been described as being ones of

---

[120] John Lowden, *The Making of the 'Bibles moralisées'*, 2 vols. (University Park: Penn State University Press, 2000), 1: 132, first says of the image that it "undoubtedly represents at a generic level the power and majesty of the king and queen of France."

[121] Lowden, *The Making of the 'Bibles moralisées'*, 1: 9.

[122] Stirnemann and Hasenohr, "Description of BNF fr. 794," in *Splendeurs*, 66.

**Figure 4.2.** Leaf from a moralized Bible showing Blanche de Castile (upper left). Pierpont Morgan MS M. 240 fol 8r.

Photographic Credit: The Pierpont Morgan Library, New York.

"admonition and instruction."[123] Thus, in both images, the hands of Marie and Blanche are seen to be signaling a combination of stern and gentle gestures, of command and/or admonition with one hand and of gracious invitation with the other. The similarities between the two figures suggest analogies between Marie and Blanche. Did Marie influence the piety of her niece, a French queen whose wise instruction formed the greatest king in Christendom?[124] The relationship between the two women of royal blood would seem to bear out the promise of Psalm 44, which speaks of a line of female rulers giving birth to a line of future princes (verse 16).

In this Bible Blanche is related pictorially to an author figure, which again brings to mind Marie's image in the Guiot manuscript. On the left-hand side of the bottom register of the miniature in Figure 2 is a cleric who composes or selects the texts and moralizations and directs the artists; on the right, a lay craftsman carries out the cleric's wishes. The leaf on which the craftsman works shows the layout of a typical page in the book, consisting of two columns of medallions and accompanied by narrow columns of text.[125] By analogy, Blanche is placed in the role of the person composing the moralization. She seems to be a bona fide composer, since her throne, like that of her son Louis, has elements recalling those in the depiction of the Creator's throne appearing in the picture on folio iv.[126] This depiction is consonant with the fact that queens, especially Blanche, played a major role in the making of the *Bibles moralisées*.[127] In helping create

---

[123] Pierpont Morgan Library, *In August Company: The Collections of the Pierpont Morgan Library* (New York: The Library, 1993), 90.

[124] It may be significant that Aliénor left one Louis, Louis VII, to become England's queen, whereas her granddaughter Blanche married Louis VIII and produced a king who was the envy of both England and France. For a study of how the rivalry between France and England was played out through the actions of its queens, see Lori J. Walters, "Reconfiguring Wace's Round Table: Walewein and the Rise of the National Vernaculars," *Arthuriana* 15.2 (Summer 2005): 39–58.

[125] *In August Company*, 90.

[126] Lowden, *The Making of the 'Bibles moralisées'*, 1: 127–28. Lowden's description of the architectural elements surrounding Blanche also tends to confirm my observation above that queens were being viewed as incarnations of the Heavenly Jerusalem. He claims that the architectural design of the image in the upper register is "strongly reminiscent of the Heavenly Jerusalem seen in the preceding folios of the Apocalypse." He adds that "the composition is immediately reminiscent of that used for images of Christ and his mother (the Coronation of the Virgin) or Christ and Ecclesia (the Church as Bride of Christ)."

[127] Lowden, *The Making of the 'Bibles moralisées'*, 1: 9 makes several points about these Bibles that are especially relevant. First, Blanche played a major role in the making of the moralized Bibles. She probably commissioned for her own use the first moralized Bible (Vienna 2554), a picture book with captions in French. Second, these Bibles had dynastic significance, with French queens playing a major role in their making. Lowden

biblical texts in French, Blanche resembles her aunt Marie who had commissioned moralized vernacular adaptations of Holy Scripture.

The way that the *Bible moralisée* miniature is drawn implies that Queen Blanche creates the book out of her physical presence and her conceptual abilities, actualizing the metaphor of Christ as Incarnate Word proceeding from the Virgin's womb. The picture recalls visually what Chrétien describes textually in the *Charrette*, where he insists upon Marie's "authorship" and his own assumption of the role of obedient scribe carrying out her wishes. These two examples, both products of the same time period, are alike in portraying two noblewomen, close blood relatives, each of whom was instrumental in producing French versions of biblical texts and in providing sagacious teaching to male rulers and writers. This finding reinforces my claim that the *Charrette* was designed to perpetuate a positive image of the countess and of her textual analogue Guinevere. Chrétien's portrait of Marie de Champagne reflected her role as the inspirer of edifying texts designed to unite the house of Champagne ever more securely to the royal family through women's participation in their husbands' and sons' Christian projects, chief among them their crusading efforts.

### V. Conclusions: "Holy Adultery" and Crusader Queens

To judge by the examples examined in this paper, the *Charrette* would fit into a Pauline, Augustinian, and Bernardine worldview, in which humanity progresses by transforming its carnal desires into more spiritual ones.[128] In dialogic works like the *Soliloquies* and *Confessions*, Augustine advised writers to use the *Verbum* as a tool to accomplish this transformation, which would then provide a pattern for further transformations by others. A woman could enter into this dialogic system by choosing to play the role of "Reason," "Monnica," "Mary," or, more generally, the Church, the institution supposed to edify humanity (in the double sense of instructing and building). Marie's example, as presented by Chrétien, Adam, Evrat, and the compilers of BNF fr. 794, implies that spiritualization of both biological and intellectual lineage takes place when women choose to act like "*dames*" [ladies] and when men are inspired by this stance. The *Charrette* celebrates public over private morality, for Guinevere is not deemed adulterous as long as her love remains secret. The romance upholds the lesson of Chrétien's *Cligés* that the public image of the queen must be maintained. Although this idea may seem hypocritical to modern eyes, it was a product of the medieval belief

---

thinks that the queens may have even provided an area in which specially chosen teams created and assembled the manuscripts.

[128] In *City of God* 22. 21, Augustine, in a gloss on 1 Cor. 15: 44, says: "It is sown an animal body, it will rise a spiritual body" (*Ep.* 147. 19, PL 33. 617; *CD* 13. 20, PL 41. 393).

that the carnal was inherently sinful. Humans are by nature "adulterous," if this term is viewed in a larger sense of a tendency to commit illicit acts, or to simply to "love the creature more than the creator," as Augustine put it. The goal proposed by the Church Father, following Paul, was to transform our animal impulses into more spiritual ones,[129] and, by creating permanent artifacts, to pass on the memory of that exemplary self as an inspiration to others to do the same.

That is what is conveyed by the image of Countess Marie de Champagne in BNF fr. 794. When she addresses the reader with gestures of admonition and instruction in the *Charrette*'s initial letter "P," she has become Paul's "living letter,"[130] a life transformed into a text that encourages others to transform their carnal desires into "holy adulteries." Like the animal symbols of three of the four evangelists, the image of Marie bears Chrétien's association of her with the love of Lancelot and Guinevere as a mark of her transcendence of any and all of its possible negative connotations, standing for all eternity as a foretaste of the heavenly glory she will know as reward for a virtuous life well lived. So too, the prefiguration of eternal glory encoded into Marie's image in BNF fr. 794 received temporal realization in the figure of her niece Blanche, whose instruction, surely patterned upon earlier female models like her aunt Marie, helped transform her young son into the "most Christian" of all rulers. Part of this transformation involved Louis's authoritative incorporation of the ideal of the crusader king into the royal persona. The previously quoted line from the *GCF* implies that the impetus for this transformation came from Blanche. It seems logical to suppose that the team executing the *Bible moralisée* eternalized the queen's image as one who inspires both men and book production in order to guide the development of the nascent nation-state of France. Certainly, France would take a giant step forward during the reign of her son Louis IX. The image seems to say that it takes a saintly queen mother to produce a saintly king.[131]

But I emphasize that the image left by Marie de Champagne in BNF fr. 794 is not static. It succeeds in being exemplary only if generations to come perpetuate the alliance the bookmaker has forged between the virtuous royal lady and writers inspired by her example. The question becomes whether the book can shape a glorious future for the kingdom of France out of the never-ending

---

[129] Walters, "The King's Example," 705; eadem, "*Magnifying the Lord*," 274.

[130] 2 Cor. 3: 2–3: "You are our letter, written not with ink but with the spirit of the living God, not on tablets of stone but on the fleshly tablets of the heart." The fact that it is a letter "P" would perhaps be appreciated for its ability to bring the Pauline text more readily to mind. This evocation of Paul is reinforced by Chrétien's mention of him in the *Graal* prologue.

[131] Christine de Pizan would phrase it similarly in her *Epistre au Dieu d'amours*: "Aux meres bien ressemblent les fieulz," Sons certainly resemble their mothers (758): Christine de Pizan, *L'Epistre au Dieu d'amours*, in *Œuvres poétiques*, ed. Maurice Roy, 3 vols. (Paris: Firmin Didot, 1886), 2: 1–27.

struggle of the carnal human body and the monarchy governing it to rise to a more spiritual state. That is why the topic of how Guinevere's virtue, or lack thereof, affects the kingdom would continue to be reformulated by later writers and bookmakers, most notably in prose, the form chosen by the future St. Louis to present the "defense and illustration" of dynastic genealogy in the *GCF*. As the language of truth, prose must condemn adultery, with its ever-present potential to pervert lineage. Poetry, however, as Augustine explains in his *Soliloquies*, is a beautiful lie that can expound a higher truth. Chrétien, I believe, builds upon the higher truths about love set forth by David in Psalm 44, by Solomon in *Song*, and by Augustine and Bernard in glosses on these and other sapiential texts, to produce in his *Charrette* a poetic statement about the glories, drawbacks, and responsibilities of "holy adultery." For if the latter in fact represents a coalition of writer and patroness in an alliance perpetuated by the power of the pen, it implies that the application of the significance of such fictional *conjointures* to actual persons and situations unfolds from a reflection that remains ongoing. To borrow the term employed by Bruckner in my opening quotation, adultery would remain a "conundrum" whose wisdom each and every generation would have to harvest in its own particular way.

# Chrétien's Lancelot Rewritten: From the *Charrette* to *Rigomer* in Manuscript and Narrative Cycles[1]

Douglas Kelly
University of Wisconsin

L'interférence de matières narratives est visiblement une sorte d'*adunaton* puisqu'elle consiste à fusionner deux univers littéraires, régis par des lois spécifiques et *a priori* incompatibles entre elles.[2]

Both verse and prose romances of the twelfth and thirteenth centuries offer divergent readings of their principal characters, notably of Gauvain, Perceval, Tristan, and Lancelot. Such divergences are most striking in manuscript anthologies. The subject of this volume, Lancelot in manuscripts that include Chrétien de Troyes's *Chevalier de la charrette*, is an instance of such divergence in the romances that follow Chrétien's. I propose to examine the ways the knight Marie de Champagne and Chrétien invented was rewritten in subsequent romances, especially in thirteenth-century verse romances whose Lancelot has not been studied as intently as he has been in the prose romances. In conformity with the context of this volume on the *Charrette Project*, I shall give special attention to the manuscript environments in which the rewritten Lancelot finds himself.

Richard Trachsler's observation, quoted in the epigraph, on the fusion of two literary universes that are on the surface incompatible offers an opening to our subject. When scribes collect works into a manuscript anthology, seemingly

---

[1] An earlier version of this paper was read at the University of Western Michigan Medieval Conference, Kalamazoo, 4–7 May 2006.

[2] Richard Trachsler, *Disjointures–conjointures: étude sur l'interférence des matières narratives dans la littérature française du Moyen Âge*, Romanica Helvetica 120 (Tübingen: Francke, 2000), 45; cf. Alexandru N. Cizek, Imitatio et tractatio: *die literarisch-rhetorischen Grundlagen in Antike und Mittelalter*, Rhetorik-Forschungen 7 (Tübingen: Niemeyer, 1994), 78–107. On figural devices in rhetorical ornamentation applied to narrative structure, see Douglas Kelly, *The Art of Medieval French Romance* (Madison: University of Wisconsin Press, 1992), 282–90.

Gina L. Greco and Ellen M. Thorington, eds., *Dame Philology's Charrette: Approaching Medieval Textuality through Crétien's 'Lancelot': Essays in Memory of Karl D. Uitti.* MRTS 408. Tempe: ACMRS, 2012. [ISBN 978-0-86698-456-0]

incompatible juxtapositions may occur. Take Gauvain. Scholars have noted the prominence of Arthur's nephew in several anthologies and in post-Chrétien verse romance in general; they have recognized too that his person and conduct may vary from romance to romance.[3] Lauded for his courtesy in Chrétien, he becomes more a figure of farce in narratives like the *Chevalier à l'épée*, the *Mule sans frein*, and the *Vengeance Raguidel*; typically a knight rewarded with facile erotic adventures, in two romances, *Beaudous* and *Floriant et Florete*, he actually marries. The knight who never refuses to name himself in Chrétien and elsewhere loses his name in the *Atre périlleux*. Other knights may undergo similar recycling. Kay, Arthur's acerbic, headstrong seneschal and a true villain in *Yder*, becomes a sterling knight in *Escanor* after love enters his heart.

When such anomalies, or *adunata* in Trachsler's sense, in depictions of prominent Arthurian knights occur in manuscript anthologies, they raise a number of interpretative issues, including the *san* (in Chrétien's sense of the word in the *Charrette*) of the first author and the *antancion* of the scribe compiling a given manuscript or of the person who requested it; these issues frequently relate to the art of rewriting and authorial and scribal performance practices. Here we shall look at some of these issues in the light of the *Charrette Project*. How does Lancelot appear in codex and context?[4]

## Simultaneity, Parallel Universes, and Romance Interlace

Trachsler's observation recalls a useful metaphor for this inquiry: that of parallel or multiple universes. I shall explain how I understand this term and then relate it to romance composition, rewriting, and anthologizing, with special attention to Lancelot.

---

[3] Beate Schmolke-Hasselmann, *Der arthurische Versroman von Chrestien bis Froissart: zur Geschichte einer Gattung*, Beihefte zur Zeitschrift für romanische philologie 177 (Tübingen: Niemeyer, 1980), chap. 1, 4; Keith Busby, *Gauvain in Old French Literature*, Degré Second 2 (Amsterdam: Rodopi, 1980); idem, "Diverging Traditions of Gauvain in Some of the Later Old French Verse Romances," in *The Legacy of Chrétien de Troyes*, ed. Norris J. Lacy, Douglas Kelly, and idem, Faux Titre 37 (Amsterdam: Rodopi, 1988), 93–109; Lori Walters, "The Formation of a Gauvain Cycle in Chantilly Manuscript 472," *Neophilologus* 78 (1994): 29–43.

[4] I borrow the terms codex and context from Keith Busby's recent in-depth study of the phenomena. His *Codex and Context* is essential reading on the subject, a point reiterated by Boyd and Murray in the Afterword to this volume. See *Codex and Context: Reading Old French Verse Narrative in Manuscript*, Faux Titre 221–222, 2 vols. (Amsterdam: Rodopi, 2002).

A parallel universe has been defined as "a universe [that] exists 'right now' somewhere that differs from our own" in one or more ways. According to this view, "If a universe can be imagined, it exists."[5] M. R. Franks provides several examples that illustrate the phenomenon. "Another universe exists in which the earth has two natural moons. Another universe exists in which there is no planet earth. Another exists in which Elizabeth Taylor has brown eyes. Another exists in which George Washington has a wart on his nose." Taking parallel universe as a metaphor, we may ask what relation this modern scientific hypothesis has to the romances of Chrétien de Troyes and the epigonal romances he influenced, when we confront what Trachsler calls "l'interférence de matières narratives," where two parallel, but incompatible universes confront us in medieval manuscripts—for example, when Gauvain is an eternal bachelor in one romance and a husband in another.

We must distinguish parallel universes from simultaneous narratives. The latter are chronologically parallel, contemporary developments that are interlaced in medieval narratives. In Chrétien's *Erec et Enide*, Arthur and the Knights of the Round Table hunt the White Stag while Erec escorts Arthur's queen and encounters quite different adventures that, however, lead back to and complete the White Stag hunt when Arthur bestows the customary kiss on Enide as the most beautiful woman at court. These two narrative strands are not incompatible with one another. For this reason Chrétien can call his romance a *bele conjointure*.[6] Simultaneous narratives are found in Chrétien's other romances. *Cligés* relates the rebellion of Angrés and the capture of his castle at Windsor; parallel to this narrative line, but largely independent of it, Chrétien relates the *gradus amoris* of Alexandre and Soredamors. The *Charrette* too depicts parallel but separate quests by Lancelot and Gauvain to liberate Guenevere from Gorre. These are simultaneous quests, spatially separated and requiring, therefore, interlaced plots; they are not parallel universes because they are not incompatible even though they raise issues such as the relative worth of love and knightly prowess.

---

[5] My use of this definition is based not on the scientific validity of Franks's definition and examples, which I am not qualified to judge, but on the apposite metaphor they provide for discussing medieval rewriting and manuscript compilation: M. R. Franks, *The Universe and Multiple Reality* (New York: iUniverse, 2003). One might compare the modern notion of parallel universes with the medieval belief that God could create more than one universe. For example, "Dieu pourroit faire, sy ly plaisoit, le monde assez plus grant ou pluseurs autres mondes s'il vouloit" [God could, if he wished, make the world much bigger or several other worlds if he wanted]: Evrart de Conty, *Le Livre des Eschez amoureux moralisés*, ed. Françoise Guichard-Tesson and Bruno Roy, Bibliothèque du moyen français 2 (Montreal: CERES, 1993), 215. Using the model according to which Nature imitates God and the artist imitates both, one might say that medieval adapters were inventing various possible worlds.

[6] Kelly, *Art*, 26–31.

A different adaptation of such "simultaneity" is found in *Yvain*'s links to the *Charrette*. Gauvain's absence from and return to court are explained by his activities in the *Charrette* quest for Guenevere at three junctures in the *Yvain* plot.[7] This simultaneous sequence is readily comprehensible within the spatial and temporal coordinates of the two plots. Indeed, the links between the plots of the *Charrette* and *Yvain* are such that Barbara Nelson Sargent-Baur has argued that the two narratives conjoin as a single romance and that this *conjointure* was Chrétien's intention when he linked them using Gauvain.[8]

But then there is *Perceval*. Does not this romance, in its second part, illustrate virtually parallel universes as Franks defines the term and "interférences" like those referred to by Trachsler (see epigraph)? During Gauvain's quest for the Bleeding Lance, he meets Arthur's mother (*Perceval* 8733) and his own mother (*Perceval* 8749–8753), both of whom he believes to be dead for decades, as well as his sister who, given her age, must have been born after her mother's presumed death and maybe her father's (*Perceval* 8758–8763).[9] But there is an important difference. Unlike the stark separation of worlds that obtains according to the parallel universe hypothesis, one can easily pass back and forth between the mothers' Otherworld and the Arthurian world of King Arthur. Gauvain does so when he comes to the castle Roche de Canguin in which his mother resides. Arthur and Guenevere are preparing to do so when the romance abruptly stops, incomplete, after a valet has gone from Roche Canguin to Orquenie, where he invites them to come to that castle to witness a duel between Gauvain and Guiromelant.

Anonymous lays offer similar examples of seeming incompatibilities. Like time out of joint, or out of *conjointure* as it were,[10] in the Roche de Canguin episode

---

[7] Chrétien de Troyes, *Le Chevalier au Lion ou le Roman d'Yvain*, ed. David F. Hult, Lettres Gothiques (Paris: Librairie Générale Française, 1994), 429 n. 1.

[8] Barbara Nelson Sargent-Baur, "The Missing Prologue of Chrétien's *Chevalier au Lion*," *French Studies* 41 (1987): 385–94.

[9] On the presumed death of mothers in *Perceval*, see Matilda Bruckner, "Rewriting Chrétien's *Conte du Graal*—Mothers and Sons: Questions, Contradictions, and Connections," in *The Medieval "Opus": Imitations, Rewriting, and Transmission in the French Tradition. Proceedings of the Symposium Held at the Institute for Research in Humanities, October 5–7 1995, The University of Wisconsin-Madison*, ed. Douglas Kelly, Faux Titre 116 (Amsterdam: Rodopi, 1996), 213–44. Gauvain believes his mother and Arthur's are dead, although Guiromelant says they actually came to their castle when their husbands passed away. Their disappearance and proximity to Arthur, suggested by the invitation sent to him to join them in their castle, evoke the Otherworld of narrative lays rather than the savage forest of Perceval's own mother. But the incomplete state of this romance points as well to a narrative *adunaton*, a direction that, as I suggest below, seems to have inspired analogous features in the Perceval Continuations.

[10] Laurence Harf-Lancner, *Les Fées au Moyen Âge: Morgane et Mélusine. La Naissance des fées*, Nouvelle Bibliothèque du Moyen Âge 8 (Paris: Champion, 1984), 243–61. On the analogous relation to tales deriving from folklore, see Marie-Luce Chênerie,

in *Perceval*, fairy world time is not experienced in the same way as in the real world. In several narrative lays, a knight passes from his own world into an otherworld, or a virtual parallel universe. In *Guingamour*, for example, the hero remains young while in a fairy otherworld for three hundred years. His wish to visit his original world is granted and all goes well, despite the time change. But when he breaks a pact with his fay by eating three apples, he immediately becomes a decrepit old man no longer free to reintegrate the fay's otherworld. The Celtic background and its supernatural realm can therefore be described in terms of parallel universes as parallel otherworlds. On the other hand, the *Perceval* is incomplete and, therefore, we cannot know how Chrétien intended bringing his "universes" together into a *bele conjointure* like that he put together in *Erec et Enide*.

However, the *Perceval* anomalies raise another, more philological issue in the manuscript tradition of Chrétien's romances. I shall illustrate this problem by the example of *Rigomer*,[11] a thirteenth-century verse romance that survives incomplete in two manuscripts. Lancelot has an important, but strikingly new role in this work. It is also a noticeable revision of the Lancelot-Gauvain hierarchy found in the *Charrette*.

## Parallel Universes in Manuscripts and Cycles

Chantilly 472 contains most of *Rigomer*.[12] The manuscript has seemed to some to be more rag-tag than cyclic. Did readers view the Chantilly manuscript as a potpourri, an anthology, or a cycle? Walters states that "the collection seems to have been assembled in a rather bizarre fashion."[13] It begins with the incomplete *Rigomer* and the anonymous *Atre périlleux*, then adds Chrétien's *Erec et Enide* and Guillaume le Clerc's *Fergus*, followed by an incomplete *Hunbaut*; then come, in succession, the *Bel Inconnu*, also incomplete, the *Vengeance Raguidel*, Chrétien's *Yvain* and *Charrette* (incomplete), and—finally—*Perlesvaus* (incomplete) and a

---

"Un recueil arthurien de contes populaires au XIII^e siècle? *Les Merveilles de Rigomer*," in *Réception et identification du conte depuis le Moyen Âge: actes du colloque de Toulouse, janvier 1986*, ed. Michel Zink and Xavier Ravier, Travaux de l'Université de Toulouse-Le Mirail A41 (Toulouse: Service de Publications UTM, 1987), 39–49.

[11] I refer to Jehan, *Mervelles*, as *Rigomer* (*Les Merveilles de Rigomer*, ed. Wendelin Foerster and Hermann Breuer, Gesellschaft für romanische Literatur 19, 39, 2 vols. [Dresden: Gesellschaft für romanische Literatur, 1908–1915]); on this title see Francesco Carapezza, "Le Fragment de Turin du *Rigomer*: nouvelles perspectives," *Romania* 119 (2001): 76–112.

[12] Turin L IV 33, the only other manuscript that contains part of *Rigomer*, is a fragment that was severely damaged in the Turin library fire of 1904. It is known today principally through copies that are defective and not in agreement with each other (Carapezza, "Le Fragment de Turin"; Busby, *Codex*, 87–93).

[13] Walters, "Formation," 29.

*Roman de Renart*.[14] How might audiences or readers have reacted to Chrétien's *Charrette*, coming as it does after *Rigomer*?

This manuscript collects many romances into what Karl Uitti termed a "super romance" and Lori Walters has also called a cycle.[15] Cycle connotes a kind of *conjointure* that gives a fuller and more complete version of the numerous narrative threads illustrated by the romances copied into the manuscript. They may or may not be complete, just as some of Chrétien's romances have been considered incomplete. The *Charrette* does not relate a full biography of Lancelot but only an episode in his life, not the continuation of his affair with Geunevere. *Yvain* is incomplete without the *Charrette*. *Perceval* is incomplete because Chrétien apparently died before finishing it. Several other romances in Chantilly 472 are incomplete.[16] The Chantilly manuscript foregrounds Gauvain[17] and, by dint of the anthology format, conforms to the principle of multiple quests;[18] the manuscript includes the multiple quest romance *Rigomer*, juxtaposing it to other romances that also contain one or more quests. But "rather than following a narrative line from beginning to end, in MS 472 we encounter a 'cluster work'"[19] or manuscript, each branch of which features Gauvain or his son, or analogous branching, as in its *Perlesvaus* and *Renard* "branches." The whole constitutes a cycle.

The definition of the term cycle is a problem. Medieval writers might have known the term in the pejorative sense found in Horace's *Art of Poetry* (*Ad Pisones*), a poem that was commented on and glossed from late antiquity well into the twelfth century. This commenting and glossing influenced the twelfth- and thirteenth-century arts of poetry and prose.[20] For Horace a cycle was an epic poem that continually digressed, lacked unity, and failed to achieve a denouement.[21]

---

[14] Keith Busby, Terry Nixon, Alison Stones, and Lori Walters, eds., *Les Manuscrits de Chrétien de Troyes–The Manuscripts of Chrétien de Troyes*, Faux Titre 71–72, 2 vols. (Amsterdam: Rodopi, 1993), 2:39–41.

[15] Lori Walters, "The Creation of a 'Super Romance': Paris, Bibliothèque Nationale, fonds français, MS 1433," *Arthurian Yearbook* 1 (1991): 3–25, here 31; and eadem, "Formation."

[16] Busby, *Codex*, 405–9. Chantilly 472 also deleted Godefroy de Lagny's continuation (Walters, "Formation," 37–38).

[17] Walters, "Formation." This permits a distinction between the manuscript anthology like Chantilly 472 and the manuscript miscellany that evinces no organizing or shared feature.

[18] On this term, see Douglas Kelly, "Multiple Quests in French Verse Romance: *Mervelles de Rigomer* and *Claris et Laris*," *L'Esprit créateur* 9 (1969): 257–66.

[19] Walters, "Formation," 40.

[20] Karsten Friis-Jensen, "The *Ars Poetica* in Twelfth-Century France: The Horace of Matthew of Vendôme, Geoffrey of Vinsauf, and John of Garland," *Cahiers de l'Institut du Moyen Âge grec et latin, Université de Copenhague* 60 (1990): 364–67.

[21] David Staines, "The Medieval Cycle: Mapping a Trope," in *Transtextualities: Of Cycles and Cyclicity in Medieval French Literature*, ed. Sara Sturm-Maddox and Donald

But there is another feature of Horace's art that is important here. Rewriting should be original, not follow well-worn paths or plots. Horace believed, for example, that the Trojan War should be retold in a new, original way.[22] The Middle Ages knew these lines, but gave its own interpretation to them.[23]

Cycle has other, less pejorative meanings today.[24] It has been used to describe narrative that may well be complex, but that nonetheless is coherent and achieves a satisfactory denouement. For example, in an important study of narrative composition in the *Lancelot en prose*, Annie Combes defines cycle as follows: "un *cycle* est formé d'une série d'œuvres autonomes reliées par une unité thématique et une successivité chronologique."[25] The definition fits the *Lancelot en prose*, a romance that expands Chrétien's *Charrette* into a complete biography of Lancelot, from birth to death.[26] It is a cycle different from those Horace condemns because, despite its length, it offers a coherent narrative that focuses on Lancelot and a moral evaluation of his career and his love for Guenevere. In effect, Lancelot dominates this prose cycle just as Gauvain does Chantilly 472.

---

Maddox, MRTS 149 (Binghamton, NY: Medieval and Renaissance Texts and Studies, 1996), 15–37, here 23–24; Cizek, Imitatio et tractatio, 103–7.

[22] Rita Copeland, *Rhetoric, Hermeneutics, and Translation in the Middle Ages: Academic Traditions and Vernacular Texts*, Cambridge Studies in Medieval Literature 11 (Cambridge: Cambridge University Press, 1991), 158–78; Cizek, Imitatio et tractatio, 87; Douglas Kelly, "The *Fidus Interpres*: Aid or Impediment to Modern Translation and *Translatio*?" in *Translation Theory and Practice in the Middle Ages*, ed. Jeanette Beer, Studies in Medieval Culture 38 (Kalamazoo: Medieval Institute Publications, 1997), 47–58.

[23] See Friis-Jensen, "The *Ars Poetica*," 354 ¶136 for the glosses on cycle in an influential, widely known twelfth-century commentary.

[24] See *Cyclification: The Development of Narrative Cycles in the Chansons de Geste and the Arthurian Romances*, ed. Bart Besamusca, Willem P. Gerritsen, Cory Hogetoorn, and Orlanda S. H. Lie, Koninklijke Nederlandse Akademie van Wetenschappen: Verhandelingen, Afdeeling Letterkunde N. R. 159 (Amsterdam: North-Holland, 1994) and *Transtextualities*, ed. Sturm-Maddox and Maddox.

[25] Annie Combes, *Les Voies de l'aventure: réécriture et composition romanesque dans le "Lancelot" en prose*, Nouvelle Bibliothèque du moyen âge 59 (Paris: Champion, 2001), 55 (her emphasis). Cf. Emmanuèle Baumgartner, "Robert de Boron et l'imaginaire du livre du Graal," in *Arturus Rex, Vol. II: Acta Conventus Lovaniensis 1987*, ed. Willy Van Hoecke, Gilbert Tournay, and Werner Verbeke, Mediaevalia Lovaniensia, ser. 1: Studia 17 (Leuven: Leuven University Press, 1991), 259–68; and Mireille Séguy, *Les Romans du Graal ou le signe imaginé*, Nouvelle Bibliothèque du moyen âge 58 (Paris: Champion, 2001), 386–87.

[26] Matilda Bruckner, "Intertextuality," in *The Legacy of Chrétien de Troyes*, ed. Norris J. Lacy, Douglas Kelly, and Keith Busby, Faux Titre 37 (Amsterdam: Rodopi, 1987), 1: 223–65, here 225; Elspeth Kennedy, "The Making of the *Lancelot-Grail Cycle*," in *A Companion to the "Lancelot-Grail Cycle,"* ed. Carol Dover, Arthurian Studies 54 (Cambridge: Brewer, 2003), 13–22; and Douglas Kelly, "Interlace and the Cyclic Imagination," in *A Companion to the "Lancelot-Grail Cycle,"* 55–64.

But there is a major distinction to be made regarding the cyclic *Lancelot-Graal* that is crucial in understanding cyclicity. There is, according to Elspeth Kennedy, a non-cyclic *Lancelot*.[27] This prose romance derives its coherence by reference to antecedent verse romances that present Perceval as the knight who achieves the Grail quest; moreover, it offers a less harsh evaluation of Lancelot's love. This is analogous to the *conjointure* postulated by Sargent-Baur for the *Charrette* and *Yvain*. By contrast, since Hartmann von Aue wrote no *Karrenritter*, he was obliged to summarize Chrétien's *Charrette* in his adaptation of *Yvain* in order to explain the references to Gauvain's absence at court while on the quest to liberate Guenevere in the *Charrette*.

Chantilly 472 includes a parallel, but incomplete, analogue in the *Perlesvaus* that is copied towards the end of the romance.[28] But Chantilly 472 can be seen as self-sufficient, unlike the non-cyclic *Lancelot* that uses cross-references that are meaningless unless the audience knows or has access to the Perceval romances it refers to. Both *Perlesvaus* and the non-cyclic *Lancelot* show how a prominent figure like Lancelot or Gauvain can be rewritten in new contexts. This is a feature they share with Chantilly 472, the cluster cycle as defined by Walters.

## Lancelot in Centripetal, Centrifugal, and Cluster Cycles

We now have three different definitions and, therefore, kinds of cycle: Horace's that stresses digression and incompletion; Walters's that extrapolates from the use of branch in the prose romances the notion of cluster in manuscript anthologies that emphasize a person, motif, or structural feature; and Combes's that, while admitting narrative complexity and branching as well as featuring a prominent personage, evinces a broad coherence from beginning to end. In short, each interpretation of cycle identifies a species of the more general term cycle as a composite narrative.

Matilda Bruckner provides terms that permit us to define more precisely our three kinds of cycle. The cycle Horace describes angles away from closure while the other (the kind Combes defines for the *Lancelot-Graal*) leads to closure.[29]

---

[27] Elspeth Kennedy, *Lancelot and the Grail: A Study of the Prose "Lancelot"* (Oxford: Clarendon Press, 1986).

[28] On the similarity between the non-cyclic *Lancelot* and the *Perlesvaus*, see Douglas Kelly, *Medieval French Romance,* Twayne's World Authors Series 838 (New York: Twayne, 1993), 36–38. Cf. Richard Trachsler, *Clôtures du cycle arthurien: étude et textes,* Publications romanes et françaises 215 (Geneva: Droz, 1996), 67–68. In Chantilly 472 *Perlesvaus* is further truncated, like the *Charrette* (Walters, "Formation," 38; Busby, *Codex,* 405–6).

[29] On closure, see Trachsler, *Clôtures.*

First, Bruckner distinguishes between what she terms centripetal intertextuality that characterizes the bond between Chrétien's *Charrette* and the Prose *Lancelot* and centrifugal intertextuality that one finds in his *Conte du graal* and its Continuations.[30] The centripetal species makes the *Charrette* a model and a center out from which the prose romance flows, as it were, and to which it returns in search of new material. The open-ended feature of many of the adventures in Chrétien's *Charrette* illustrates this. Examples are the episodic maidens Lancelot encounters on his quest. In one instance, both Lancelot and Gauvain promise a boon to the maiden who shows them the two routes into Gorre, a boon each is obliged to grant whenever she asks (*Charrette* 708–713). She never does. In the next episode, the maiden at the ford Lancelot falls into before defeating her *ami* does not want him to recognize her, but Chrétien does not tell us why (*Charrette* 936–937). Yet he could complete such episodes, as we see when the maiden who requests an arrogant knight's head in Lancelot's last adventure before the Sword Bridge returns later as Meleagant's sister to free him from the tower (*Charrette* 6592–6601). Unlike the *Charrette* that relates an episode in Lancelot's life — Meleagant's abduction of Guenevere and her return to Arthur — the *Lancelot-Graal* relates Lancelot's life in a complete and ultimately coherent cycle as Combes describes it, that is, as a biography from birth to death. In the context of this paper we can also note that parallel moralities, but not universes, are evident in the quests of Gauvain, Lancelot, Boort, Perceval, and Galaad in the *Queste*. The overall pattern conforms to a basic Christian conception of sin as lust. This conception provides a coherent reading and evaluation of all these quests and, by reflection, on all that precedes and that follows the *Queste* in the prose cycle.[31] Gauvain's chivalric and courtly morality centers on Arthur's court, Lancelot's amorous morality on that court's queen, and Boort's, Perceval's, and Galaad's religious morality on the Grail.

 In Chrétien's *Conte du graal,* Bruckner identifies a centrifugal intertextuality that allows for the centrifugal cycle. We observe this in Chrétien's romance in the episodes discussed above and in the Continuations that it inspires. The composite plot moves away from its narrative, emotional, and psychological contexts into virtually parallel universes that do not interact coherently or realistically by standards of realism even for the romance's medieval audiences. They constitute *adunata.* How can Gauvain's mother and Arthur's mother still be alive if they

---

[30] Bruckner, "Intertextuality," 225–26, 237, 251–52; eadem, *Chrétien Continued: A Study of the* Conte du Graal *and its Verse Continuations* (Oxford: Oxford University Press, 2009). Cf. Trachsler, *Clôtures*; idem, *Disjointures*; Paul Vincent Rockwell, "'Je ne suiz mie soffisanz': Insufficiency and Cyclicity in the Lancelot-Grail Cycle," in *Transtextualities*, ed. Sturm-Maddox and Maddox, 71–91; and Donald Maddox, "Cyclicity, Transtextual Coherence, and the Romances of Chrétien de Troyes," in *Transtextualities*, 39–52.

[31] Kelly, "Interlace."

have been dead for, respectively, twenty and sixty years? Chrétien's failure to complete this romance leaves the question open and the model patent.

The centrifugal features of the *Conte du graal* permeate its narrative. Perceval sets himself different goals or is preoccupied with different concerns as he wanders through the romance's first part. The travel to Arthur's court to become a knight is completed. Perceval's projected return to his mother as he promised her is abruptly terminated when he learns that she has died. He does not keep his promise to return to Blancheflor. These multiple, sequentially replaced or unachieved goals recall the meandering Horace faulted in cycles he knew.[32] This is the centrifugal cycle. When Perceval actually undertakes a real quest for the Grail castle, more than five years pass before anything worthy of being related happens (*Perceval* 6217–6243); that is, we have over five years of adventures that, Chrétien explains, are unworthy of being related because Perceval forgets God. The one adventure deemed worthy of being told is the Easter after the fifth year when Perceval remembers God and spends the holy days at his uncle's hermitage. While there, he learns the answer to the question about whom the Grail serves, one of the two questions he failed to ask earlier, a failure that prevented him from achieving the grail adventure (*Perceval* 6409–6419).

The centrifugal tendency of the romance's plot is also evident in Gauvain's plot. After vowing to relieve the siege of the Demoiselle de Montesclaire's castle, with the *Espee as Estranges renges* as reward for success (*Perceval* 4701–4720), Gauvain quickly sets this task aside when Guingambresil accuses Arthur's nephew of murdering his lord, the king of Escavalon (*Perceval* 4755–4796). Arriving at the deceased king's court to defend himself against the accusation, and following a passionate but foreshortened encounter with the dead king's daughter, Gauvain is granted a reprieve in conformity with the customs of hospitality (*Perceval* 6078–6080). He also finds another way to escape blame, by agreeing to look for the Bleeding Lance and bring it to Escavalon; this lance is destined to destroy his uncle's kingdom of Logres (*Perceval* 6158–6203). That quest no sooner begins than it disappears from the plot. Soon, after Gauvain encounters several adventures whose narrative significance is obscure, he meets his mother and sister as well as Arthur's mother. Gauvain's centrifugal plot, like Perceval's wanderings, recalls Horace's digressive cycles too. Centrifugal is an appropriate metaphor for such narrative.

Centrifugal composition in *Perceval* became a model for its Continuations.[33] Unlike the *Lancelot-Graal*, this cycle seems to swing out like a parabola, never coming round to its goal of returning to the Grail Castle. Its readers or audiences may well have felt as if they wonder as knights wander through virtually parallel universes in which demands and explanations of the one realm are replaced by new demands and explanations in another world. Major figures disappear and

---

[32] Kelly, "Interlace," 55–56.
[33] Bruckner, "Intertextuality," 250–51.

return, then disappear again. Even virginities are lost and restored; I am referring to the ambiguous nights Perceval spends with Blancheflor in the *Conte du
graal*, his consummated affair with the Chessboard Maiden in the *Second Perceval Continuation*, and his and Blancheflor's chaste and virgin marriage in the
*Fourth Continuation* by Gerbert de Montreuil. In these three instances we have
truly parallel universes bound up in single manuscripts in which one passes easily
from the one world to the other. As Bruckner aptly summarizes these centripetal
and centrifugal narratives, "While Chrétien's *Lancelot* is absorbed at the center of
the *Prose Lancelot* and exerts its centripetal intertextuality through the Vulgate's
widening circles of narrative, the *Perceval* and its Continuations form a different spatial configuration, propelled by the centrifugal textuality of the *Conte du
graal*."[34] The Middle Ages has, therefore, two distinct conceptions of the cycle to
choose from: the centrifugal cycle like that Horace condemns and the centripetal
cycle that we find best exemplified in the *Lancelot en prose*. But what of the cluster
cycle in manuscript anthologies?

Bruckner describes a third (in her case first) kind of intertextual adaptation
in the verse romance tradition. In these romances "the romancer consciously re-
invents and combines features from a number of different romances giving himself wide latitude in the intertextual play."[35] She then illustrates such play in
several verse romances in both the Arthurian tradition (*Bel Inconnu, Meraugis
de Portlesguez*) and outside of it (*Partonopeu de Blois*). Such intertextual 'reinven-
tions' illustrate the writer's art of adaptation; they also define reception by those
who know Chrétien's romances while reading or hearing later works modeled
on or deriving from them—assuming they noted such parallels. One step more
brings us to the manuscript that collects such rewritten romances into the cycle
as cluster. Multifarious audience reception results from what each person recalls
while hearing or reading these romances.[36] The manuscript anthology makes
more likely the awareness of the cluster principle. Let me illustrate this by focusing now on Lancelot in post-Chrétien verse romances. He is there, but in worlds
rather different from those we know from the *Charrette* and the prose romances.
These romances reinvent his person, sometimes making him so different from
previous descriptions that he might be perceived as existing in parallel universes,
each exploiting a possible Lancelot.

---

[34] Bruckner, "Intertextuality," 264.

[35] Bruckner, "Intertextuality," 225. Cf. Maddox, "Cyclicity," on such invention in
Chrétien's romances.

[36] Douglas Kelly, "How Did Guiolete Come to Court? Or, the Sometimes Inscrutable Paths of Tradition," in *"De sens rassis": Essays in Honor of Rupert T. Pickens*, ed. Keith
Busby, Bernard Guidot, and Logan E. Whalen, Faux Titre 259 (Amsterdam: Rodopi,
2005), 309–23.

## Lancelot and the Cluster Cycle
## in Medieval Manuscripts

Lancelot, or his name, appears in many post-Chrétien romances,[37] including romances outside the Arthurian tradition and the *Matière de Bretagne*. For example, Adenet le Roi's *Cleomadés* compares Cleomadés to Tristan, Gauvain, Lancelot, and Perceval (8258–8268).[38] Although these knights do not belong to his tale, Cleomadés stakes out a third place among all these, the best knights who ever lived—"ce set on bien par verité" (8268) [this is a well-known truth].[39] Although Lancelot is among them, he is merely one in a catalogue that ranks knights; he has no clearly defined features like the moralities or his love for Guenevere that distinguish him elsewhere. In Adenet le Roi's romance, Lancelot is ranked in fourth place in valor after the insertion of Cleomadés in his former third-place position (8265). In this context, then, Lancelot in post-Chrétien verse romances seems less an adaptation of the *Charrette* Lancelot than his namesake in *Erec et Enide* and *Cligés*.

In the former romance Chrétien ranks Lancelot third after Gauvain and Erec (1679–1682). The valor Adenet le Roi emphasizes shows more clearly in *Cligés*, Chrétien's next romance, but not to Lancelot's advantage. Success in tournaments determines hierarchies in many medieval romances. In the Oxford tournament Cligés defeats, or unhorses, Sagremor, Lancelot, and Perceval, a succession that adumbrates a hierarchy analogous to that in the *Erec* catalogue. On the last day he fights to a draw (4931–4941)[40] Gauvain, "cil a cui nus ne se prant" (4907) [he who has no peer]. These two relatives—Soredamors, Cligés's mother, is Gauvain's sister and therefore Gauvain is the young knight's uncle—achieve an equality that enhances Cligés's renown. Cligés is superior to Lancelot, as in

---

[37] Louis-Fernand Flutre, *Table des noms propres avec toutes leurs variantes figurant dans les romans du moyen âge écrits en français ou en provençal et actuellement publiés ou analysés* (Poitiers: Centre d'Etudes Supérieures de civilisation médiévale, 1962), 118; G. D. West, *An Index of Proper Names in French Arthurian Prose Romances*, University of Toronto Romance Series 35 (Toronto: University of Toronto Press, 1978), 187–88; idem, *An Index of Proper Names in French Arthurian Verse Romances 1150–1350*, University of Toronto Romance Series 15 ([Toronto]: University of Toronto Press, 1969), 99. On the significance of the naming *topos* and other descriptive features in verse romances, see Norris J. Lacy, "*Les Merveilles de Rigomer* and the Esthetics of 'Post-Chrétien' Arthurian Romance," *Arthurian Yearbook* 3 (1993): 77–90.

[38] Adenet le Roi, *Cleomadés*, vol. 5 of *Les Œuvres d'Adenet le Roi*, ed. Albert Henry, Université Libre de Bruxelles: Travaux de la Faculté de philosophie et lettres 46 (Brussels: Éditions de l'Université de Bruxelles, 1971).

[39] Adenet le Roi has in mind the prose romances because the four knights he compares to "en l'enqueste dou Graal / firent plusours proueces grans" (8260–8261).

[40] Chrétien de Troyes, *Cligés*, ed. Stewart Gregory and Claude Luttrell, Arthurian Studies 28 (Cambridge: Brewer, 1993).

*Cleomadés*; there is no mention of Lancelot's love for Guenevere, as the *Charrette* has not yet been written. When Chrétien has written it readers confront the problem of multiple Lancelots in the romance tradition.

In Chantilly Condé 472, there are three Lancelots. First comes the figure-head I have just described who appears in Chantilly 472's *Erec et Enide*. This is the Lancelot who is an important, but otherwise undistinguished Round Table knight. He is a stock Round Table figure, recognizable as a name in catalogues. Second, *Perlesvaus* conforms to the prose romance tradition by identifying Lancelot as a failure in the Grail quest because of his love for Guenevere. Like the *Prose Lancelot*, the anonymous author of *Perlesvaus* builds on, but does not radically alter or ignore, the *Charrette* world; rather, he brings it into the Grail world with its own plot and a moral hierarchy analogous to that in the *Queste*.

The third Lancelot appears in *Rigomer*. He is quite different from his name-sake in the *Charrette*.[41] Readers of the Chantilly manuscript would have known the *Charrette* because it is found in the manuscript after *Rigomer*. Their memory would have been jogged when his name came up in other romances, albeit, as I said, more in the context of *Erec* and *Yvain*, both of which are found in the manuscript after *Rigomer* but before the *Charrette*. For those who did not know the *Charrette*, the subordinate role of Lancelot in *Rigomer* would have confirmed the *Erec* ranking of Round Table knights, where Lancelot is placed third after Gauvain and Erec. *Rigomer* shows this, although in a way that might have pre-cluded Lancelot's reappearance in any ranked list of top Round Table knights. The *Charrette* cross-references in *Yvain* link these two coherently; they are found together in the Chantilly manuscript, although the *Charrette* is placed after the *Chevalier au lion*, a fact that might raise problems for those not familiar with Chrétien's Lancelot romance when they heard the cross-references to it in *Yvain* before coming to the *Charrette*. It is, then, Chrétien's version of Lancelot that might have seemed to stand in stark contrast to *Rigomer*. This brings us back into the "parallel universes" motif of the *Conte du graal*. That is, the different Lance-lots exist together in the manuscript, but in worlds that are quite different and rather incompatible with one another. The divergent romances are virtually par-allel universes that form a cluster in the anthology.

But the cluster cycle differs from the centrifugal cycle. For those in the man-uscript's audiences accustomed to centrifugal romances like the *Conte du graal* and its Continuations, the manuscript juxtaposition of *Rigomer* and the *Charrette* may have been intriguing. However, the narrative line is no longer continuous, but digressive and even fractured such that, as separate branches, the manuscript becomes a cluster of separate plots, viz. romances. The emphasis on Gauvain as different post-Chrétien romances describe him, including Chantilly 472, would

---

[41] Schmolke-Hasselmann, *Der arthurische Versroman*, 12.

have formed the taste for and appreciation of such divergence. How many different ways can one identify or describe a Round Table knight?

## Troping in Chantilly 472

To answer this question, we must introduce another term: trope. David Staines noted that the cycle was a trope for the movements of heavenly spheres.[42] However, the centrifugal cycle is not circular, as with the spheres, but parabolic such that what goes around does not come around. Keith Busby has shown that those who collect manuscript anthologies, or cluster cycles, were attentive to the ways in which one narrative "tropes" another so that the reader of such a manuscript—he includes Chantilly 472 among them—examines "sequences of texts rather than . . . individual texts themselves. In a sequence of several texts, the first may state a theme explored or 'troped' in later ones, or suggest a particular reading of them; later parts of the sequence may also cast retrospective light on earlier ones."[43] In the context of this paper, it is important that, as Busby notes, Chantilly 472 "opens with . . . *Rigomer.*"[44] We may therefore see how *Rigomer*'s representation of Lancelot "tropes" the *Charrette* itself as well as other romances in Chantilly 472. Such troping is analogous to what Bruckner calls "intertextual play" and, indeed, Horace's admonition not to conform to sources when rewriting antecedent matter.

We see this in the way *Rigomer* rewrites *Charrette* matter.[45] The goal of each romance is to liberate a lady constrained against her will by a malevolent custom. In the *Charrette* Guenevere needs a knight (a lover?) to free her. The cemetery episode identifies Lancelot as the knight predestined by mysterious powers to achieve the goal of liberating Guenevere from Gorre because he can lift the stone covering the tomb in which he will be buried (*Charrette* 1912–1915). In *Rigomer*, Dionise, lady of Rigomer, wants a husband, but can find one only when a knight overcomes the enchantments of Rigomer after achieving the quest for Rigomer castle.

In this mid-thirteenth-century romance, Lancelot fails, as Gauvain does in the *Charrette*; and like Gauvain in the *Charrette*, he is saved from disaster by the predestined knight, Gauvain himself. Lancelot's is a single-knight quest, unlike the double-knight quest in Chrétien. However, he is not the knight mysteriously predestined to achieve the quest.

---

[42] Staines, "The Medieval Cycle," 16–21.

[43] Busby, *Codex*, 367.

[44] Busby, *Codex*, 409.

[45] Cf. Richard Trachsler, *Les Romans arthuriens en vers après Chrétien de Troyes*, Bibliographie des écrivains français 11 (Paris: Memini, 1997), 189: *Rigomer* "se nourrit . . . d'une profonde connaissance des romans arthuriens en prose, dont certains techniques et éléments sont ostensiblement repris au second degré."

Cil venra,
Qui saiges ert et biax sera
Et avera en sa baillie
La flor de la chevalerie
Sor tous les chevaliers del mont,
Qui dont erent ne qui or sunt. (1109–1114)

[A prudent and handsome man who holds the flower of chivalry
over all the knights in the world who have lived or who exist now.]

That knight is Gauvain.[46]

Gauvain starts out after Lancelot's failure with fifty-seven others, some of
whose aborted quests are related.[47] Gauvain succeeds in breaking the Rigomer
spells and freeing Dionise, but (like Lancelot and, usually, Gauvain himself) he
does not marry her because he is already committed to a fay named Lorie.[48] Gauvain finds another knight, Midomidas, to become her husband. Troping Lancelot's feat in liberating Guenevere and the other prisoners in Gorre, Gauvain frees
prisoners held in bondage by the custom of Rigomer castle as well as Dionise so
that she can marry.

Other adventures Lancelot encounters in *Rigomer* rewrite *Charrette* episodes. For example, a damsel asks Lancelot to bed with her in exchange for hospitality in her castle; Lancelot does so while remaining faithful to Guenevere.
In an analogous *Rigomer* episode Lancelot is immodest, although he is still the
queen's lover.[49] The Maiden becomes pregnant (4586), but Lancelot leaves her
and she has no further role in the plot[50] — for example, she does not accompany
Lancelot on part of his quest as her counterpart does in the *Charrette*. In an earlier episode, a father offers his daughter to Lancelot as wife or concubine (1064)
if he will abandon his quest after defeating a robber knight who tried to force

---

[46] Harf-Lancner, *Les Fées*, 30–31. Perhaps because of his royal pedigree, as Chênerie has suggested (Marie-Luce Chênerie, *Le Chevalier errant dans les romans arthuriens en
vers des XII<sup>e</sup> et XIII<sup>e</sup> siècles*, Publications romanes et françaises 172 [Geneva: Droz, 1986];
and eadem, "Recueil," 44–45).

[47] Kelly, "Multiple Quests," 260–61.

[48] Peter S. Noble, "The Role of Lorie in *Les Merveilles de Rigomer*," *Bibliographical
Bulletin of the International Arthurian Society* 48 (1996): 283–90.

[49] There is some uncertainty on this matter. I accept it in the context of Chantilly
472, a point supported by two pieces of evidence. One, Lancelot asks the queen's permission to undertake his quest (229–255). Two, he sends defeated opponents to the queen
(1805–1808, 2236–2240, 3256–3261, 3783–3789, 3909–3910, 5963–5970).

[50] An analogous episode occurs in the *Gauvain* Continuations.

the father to give him his daughter by force to serve as his concubine; Lancelot refuses this offer.[51]

Lancelot's quest in *Rigomer* is successful, but he ultimately fails to escape the malevolent magic of Rigomer castle. Enchantment makes him an impotent knight and as dumb as a beast. He becomes a scullion in the Rigomer castle kitchen (unlike his imprisonment in the *Charrette* or at Morgain's castle in the prose *Lancelot*).

> Dont fu Lanselos si sopris,
> Ne li menbre de nule rien,
> D'armes porter ne d'autre bien,
> Ains fu ausi comm'une beste.
> Contreval encline le tieste
> Si comme chil qui rien ne set,
> Ne bien n'aime ne mal ne het.
> Lors est tournés a desepline:
> Cele le maine a le cuisine,
> Commande li buise taillier
> Et le mangier aparillier,
> Et commande, que c'on li die,
> Que nule cose n'escondie.
> Il li respont que bien fera
> Tot çou c'on li commandera. (*Rigomer* 6328–6342)

[Lancelot was so struck that he could remember nothing, how to bear arms or any other worthy thing. Rather he became like a beast. He lets drop his head like an ignorant man, nor does he long for what is good or hate evil. Now he is reduced to servitude. She leads him into the kitchen, ordering him to cut logs and prepare meals. She orders him not to refuse doing whatever he is told to do. He answers that he will indeed do everything he is ordered to do.]

One can see how *Rigomer* tropes both Lancelot's ecstatic immobility before Guenevere in the *Charrette* and, conversely, the fate of those prisoners in Rigomer

---

[51] Perhaps we have here a variant of the Harpin de la Montagne episode in *Yvain*. See Chênerie, *Chevalier errant*, 570. On these and other examples of troping in *Rigomer*, see Busby, *Codex*, 405–13; Carapezza, "Le Fragment de Turin," 106–10; Isabelle Arseneau, "Lancelot échevelé: la parodie dans *Les Merveilles de Rigomer*," in *La Chevelure dans la littérature et l'art du moyen âge: actes du 28ᵉ Colloque du CUER MA, 20, 21 et 22 février 2003*, ed. Chantal Connochie-Bourgne, Senefiance 50 (Aix-en-Provence: Publications de l'Université de Provence, 2004), 9–21. Lacy terms such analogies "doublets": "*Les Merveilles de Rigomer*," 80–81.

forced to do menial labor like the Pesme Aventure maidens in *Yvain*.[52] The magic ring given by a fairy that assists him in identifying and avoiding such spells in the *Charrette* and the *Prose Lancelot* is now a ring that produces the benumbing spell that demotes him to scullion (*Rigomer* 6325–6326). There is a concomitant decline in his character and physique. As scullion he grows lazy and paunchy while gorging himself on the scraps he finds in an obviously well-stocked kitchen. "Mais tot i estoit bestïaus / Et ausi fols comme une bieste" (*Rigomer* 14002–14003) [But he was absolutely bestial, and as dumb as a beast]. This is how Gauvain discovers him upon achieving the quest and unspelling the Rigomer magic. It is therefore Gauvain who liberates Lancelot, not an avatar of Meleagant's sister.

When Gauvain recognizes Lancelot in the kitchen, he first laughs at the sight, but then bursts into tears: "ore rit et ore pleure" (*Rigomer* 14060) [he alternately laughs and weeps]. *Rigomer* emphasizes the tears. Never before is Gauvain known to have wept no matter how great the misfortune or difficulty he encountered.

> Mais por Lanselot a ploré
> Por qu'il le vit dessëuré.
> Qui tout le monde li donast
> Et tout l'avoir abandonast,
> Mien essïent ne se tenist,
> Que li larme de l'uel n'isist. (*Rigomer* 14067–14072)[53]

[But he wept for Lancelot because he saw him dimwitted. Were one to give him the whole world and offer all that it contained, I am sure that he would not have refrained from shedding tears.]

The decline into such a bestial ("biestial," 14015, 14121) state for a knight like Lancelot is a lamentable misfortune. As laughable as the great knight may appear at first glance,[54] the impression is not strong enough to preclude the sorrow that overwhelms Arthur's nephew.[55]

Analogous scenes in other verse and prose romances found in Chantilly 472 reinforce this reading of Gauvain's sorrow. Yvain's madness is an obvious

---

[52] For example, a number must weave while Lancelot keeps to the kitchen (*Rigomer* 14178–14184); cf. Jean-Charles Payen, *Le Motif du repentir dans la littérature française médiévale (des origines à 1230)*, Publications romanes et françaises 98 (Geneva: Droz, 1968), 388 and n. 38, 462 n. 17.

[53] See Chênerie, *Chevalier errant*, 646–47.

[54] Cf. Richard Trachsler, "Lancelot aux fourneaux: des éléments de parodie dans les *Merveilles de Rigomer*?" *Vox Romanica* 52 (1993): 180–93; Peter S. Noble, "Le Comique dans *Les Merveilles de Rigomer* et *Hunbaut*," *Arthurian Literature* 19 (2003): 77–86; Arseneau, "Lancelot échevelé."

[55] Philippe Ménard, *Le Rire et le sourire dans le roman courtois en France au moyen âge (1150–1250)*, Publications romanes et françaises 105 (Geneva: Droz, 1969), 310–11.

example. The maiden that finds him asleep in the woods weeps when she recognizes him (*Chevalier au lion* 2916–2921). In the *Charrette*, emprisoned in Meleagant's tower and fully conscious of his misfortune, the Knight of the Cart abandons himself to tears and despair, lamenting the unfortunate turn of Fortune's Wheel, Gauvain's alleged failure to seek him out, and Meleagant's treachery, the true cause of his predicament. Lancelot's liberation requires time to restore his noble features and strength, as his imprisonment has left him "roigneus" and "esgeünez" (*Charrette* 6693) [scabby, famished],[56] unlike the paunchy Lancelot of the Rigomer kitchen.

After being released from the magic spell that reduced Lancelot to a scullion, he is eager to become again his former self. "Onqes tex chevaliers ne fui / Con jou seroie et con jou sui" (14149–14150) [never was I such a knight as I would be and now am], he vows. He sets out in quest of adventures and combat, disappearing for a year and a half (14785).[57] But we learn nothing about his adventures during these *errances*, a ploy analogous to both Gauvain's unrelated adventures in the *Charrette* and Perceval's in the *Conte du graal*, presumably because they are of no significance. Yet so arduous are these encounters that, when Lancelot reappears, he is hardly recognizable, not because of sloth and fattening, but because his travails have been so great and numerous. Indeed, he has again become "bestial." No one recognizes him at first, and all mock the unsightly Lancelot with his great "hure" [bristly head of hair] like that of a wild boar.[58] He is not the handsome and handsomely decked-out knight who, in the denouement to Chrétien's *Charrette*, comes to court to confront Meleagant. In *Rigomer*, mockery turns to amazement when all learn the identity of the unsightly Lancelot. The *Rigomer* world is a universe, parallel in the Chantilly cluster, but distinct from that in the *Charrette* it tropes.

------

[56] On the prison motif, see Trachsler, "Lancelot," 182–90.

[57] For two and a half years according to 15371–15373. There are obvious chronological problems with each time.

[58] Chênerie, *Chevalier errant*, 158; Arseneau, "Lancelot échevelé." See the description of Lancelot's person, dress, and horse, *Rigomer* 15546–15634. *Rigomer* appears to trope Chrétien's description of Gauvain in the *Charrette*, where Arthur's nephew "molt avoit sofferz travauz, / Et mainz perils et mainz asauz / Avoit trespassez et vaincuz" (*Charrette* 5139–5141) [had endured much travail, as well as having gone through and overcome many perils and attacks]. On armor as a defining feature in *Rigomer*, see Lacy, "*Les Merveilles de Rigomer*," 82–83. That armor makes a knight be himself while identifying his status to others is apparent in Beroul's *Tristran* when Tristan begs for his armor before being banished from court: "N'en merré armes ne cheval / Ne compaignon for Governal. / Ha! Dex, d'ome desatorné! / Petit fait om de lui cherté" (241–244) [I will take with me neither arms nor horse nor a companion apart from Governal. Oh lord! Woe be a man bereft of all—others will have little esteem for him]. A knight without armor is "naked," and "Hom nu n'a nul leu de parler" (248) [A man unarmed has no right to speak].

Of course, the Middle Ages did not know any more about parallel universes than people today did a few years ago. How then did medieval authors and audiences understand the anomalies we have been discussing in *Rigomer* in its manuscript cluster and, indeed, appreciate them in the French sense of the word? First and foremost, did they perceive them as anomalies and, if they did not, why do we treat them as such? Apart from audiences who may or may not have sought consistency when the same figure reappears, there was a medieval notion of rewriting that allowed for our metaphorical universes. It finds expression in the glosses on Horace's *Art of Poetry* on original rewriting that is evident in countless imitations and emulations of sources.

Let me begin with sources. By and large, I think scholars still understand this word in the traditional way. A source is an earlier work that a subsequent author retells more or less faithfully. Earlier source scholarship valued the earlier versions, especially lost ones, and was critical of works that modified them. Referring to "the inconsequences and absurdities in his [Chrétien's] four poems,"[59] Roger Sherman Loomis attempted to excuse them by suggesting that Chrétien himself did not properly understand the Celtic tradition on which he drew: "If the result is to deprive the poet of any claim to vast inventive powers, to the creation of a new genre largely by the exercise of a fertile imagination, it will also relieve him of responsibility for the faults of construction and the lapses in coherence to which otherwise he would have to plead guilty."[60] Loomis and scholars of his persuasion obviously wanted Chrétien to repeat or explain his sources, not rewrite them as something new. They expected Chrétien to be a *fidus interpres*, a role Horace rejected. My point is not to correct Loomis's evaluation of Chrétien's achievement—it is obviously no longer tenable—but, rather, to ask whether we are not applying the same standards to Chrétien's epigones that Loomis did to Chrétien himself. Is the *Rigomer* Lancelot an example of "inconsequences and absurdities" or an original version of this Round Table knight? Is Lancelot as an overfed, unkempt scullion an absurdity?

Medieval tradition, inherited though various channels of transmission, accustomed writers to invent new versions of old matter.[61] The *Rigomer*'s rewriting of Lancelot material found in the *Charrette* does this just as much as the prose romances do, but differently and according to different standards. Audiences, like authors, may well have enjoyed discovering how a familiar character could be seen in different lights, or in different worlds, or in different romances. After all, to conclude by returning to Franks's book on parallel universes, if in another universe Elizabeth Taylor can have brown eyes and George Washington a wart on his nose, could not Lancelot, the best knight in the world in one romance because

---

[59] Roger Sherman Loomis, *Arthurian Tradition and Chrétien de Troyes* (New York: Columbia University Press, 1949), 4.

[60] Loomis, *Arthurian Tradition*, 6.

[61] See Boyd and Murray, in this volume, for additional discussion of the use of sources.

he loves the queen, become a sinner for the same reason in another, and a scullion in still a third? The frequency of incomplete romances in Chantilly 472 suggests that its audiences did not expect a denouement, as in the centrifugal cycles Horace condemned, but did like to consider variety and alternatives.[62]

In this paper I have suggested new ways to appreciate the achievements of medieval romances. Three kinds of cycle, centripetal, centrifugal, and cluster, characterize not only the composition of specific works but also the assemblage of works in cyclic manuscripts. Troping one work by another suggests how rewriting might avoid repetition while raising issues of emphasis, verisimilitude, and incompatibility for medieval audiences.[63] Chrétien's Lancelot as he passed from one romance to another and from one manuscript to another was troped in these diverse ways, as were many other so-called stock figures in the multiple worlds of medieval romance.

---

[62] This recalls an issue occasionally raised in *Charrette* scholarship: is the romance incomplete because it does not bring Lancelot and Guenevere back to bed together? Apart from the possibility that the romance may be principally about the liberation of the prisoners in Gorre, one may wonder why it needed to add another tryst. Implicitly, the resolution of that issue is the *Lancelot-Graal*, where every tryst presupposes another, however distant in time that may be.

[63] An electronic archive built around the codex, as proposed by Boyd and Murray, provided with features that allow for visualization of rhetorical devices and, in particular, their association with characters, as described by Alvarado (also in this volume), might prove useful in the tracing and analysis of such troping.

# CROSSED SWORDS: *LE CHEVALIER DE LA CHARRETTE* AND *LA QUESTE DEL SAINT GRAAL*

GRACE MORGAN ARMSTRONG
BRYN MAWR COLLEGE

The legacy of Chrétien de Troyes's *Le Chevalier de la Charrette* (c.1177–1181)[1] is both rich and varied in the five romances that constitute the thirteenth-century Vulgate Cycle. One of the most interesting and ideologically marked of these heirs is *La Queste del Saint Graal* (c. 1225).[2] Three scenes from Chrétien's romance—Lancelot's heroic support of the citizens of Logres in a combat in Gorre, his deliberately uneven performance at the tournament at Noauz, and his crossing of the Pont de l'Epée despite his sighting of lions at the other end—are echoed in two scenes of the *Queste*. The *Charrette* reads the first two battles, in which Lancelot's prowess eventually triumphs, as proof of his total submission to the dictates of love and, therefore, of his exceptional heroism. In contrast, the *Queste*, which conflates both battles in the first combat that Lancelot encounters after undertaking the Grail quest, reads his powers and intentions pejoratively. His espousal of "chevalerie terriane" (*Queste* 143:8) can lead only to defeat under the cosmic, spiritual redefinition of chivalric heroism that the prose romance proposes. The reversal of Lancelot's fortunes is even more striking when the *Queste* rewrites the hero's crossing of the Sword Bridge, repositions it as the first movement of his final adventure, and thereby problematizes his access to an unknown and—to him unknowable—world. What the *Charrette* had presented in Gorre as a hell-like land of no return[3] and the ultimate arena to test Lancelot's heroism

---

[1] Chrétien de Troyes, *Le Chevalier de la Charrette (Lancelot)*, ed. Alfred Foulet and Karl D. Uitti, Classiques Garnier (Paris: Bordas, 1989).

[2] *La Queste del Saint Graal*, ed. A. Pauphilet, CFMA (Paris: Champion, 1978).

[3] Jacques Ribard, *Chrétien de Troyes, Le* Chevalier de la Charrette*: essai d'interprétation symbolique* (Paris: Nizet, 1972), 43–45. Despite the fact that he claims Gorre to be "non pas le royaume des morts, mais le monde des esprits" (43), Ribard goes on to demonstrate that "les captifs de Gorre représentent les hommes qui ont vécu et sont morts avant la venue du Christ-Lancelot" (45). While I agree that Lancelot's passage into Gorre—and specifically his passage du Pont de l'Epée—are resonant with parallels

in the service of love becomes the Grail's refuge of Corbenic, to which Lancelot accedes only temporarily when his heroic impulses fail the test and thereby brand him as unfit for the permanent company of the elect. Comparison of these textual borrowings can afford us insight into the complex process of rewriting, whereby a prose romance reworks wellknown *peripeteiae* from metric material, ascribes new values to them, and calls attention to the contrasting meaning they now signify.[4] By thus proclaiming its indebtedness to the intertext, the prose romance builds its textual authority and advertises its interpretive difference.[5]

## Battles

Lancelot's participation in a combat following his passage into Chrétien's Land of Gorre both demonstrates his remarkable fighting abilities and contributes to the growing certainty among witnesses that he will rescue Guenièvre and liberate the citizens of Logres from their imprisonment. The beginning of Chrétien's scene is marked by the offer of hospitality. This *topos* presents an interesting play on the generalized scorn with which the Chevalier de la Charrette was

---

between Lancelot and Christ, I will argue, unlike Ribard, that Chrétien places Lancelot's martyrdom purely in the context of Amors. This religion of love claims his entire devotion, as is clear from the episode of the Demoiselle Impudique, when he is compared to "un convers" (1230), a lay brother, who resists her sexual display as strongly as if he were on his pallet in the monastery. I agree with Baumgartner that various elements of the *Charrette* "limitent... les tentations d'une interprétation trop exclusivement allégorique": Emmanuèle Baumgartner, *Chrétien de Troyes: Yvain, Lancelot, la charrette et le lion* (Paris: PUF, 1992), 72.

[4] Kelly, Greco, and Boyd and Murray also explore this process in this volume.

[5] The importance of the *Charrette* as an intertext for the *Queste* has for obvious reasons attracted much less critical attention than its relationship with the *Lancelot en prose* which precedes the *Queste* in the five romances that comprise the Vulgate Cycle. Kelly briefly notes that Lancelot's sinfulness prevents him from accomplishing the Quest for the Grail but does "not diminish his stature as a knight" in a reading that this essay sees as problematic: Douglas Kelly, Sens *and* Conjointure *in the Chevalier de la Charrette* (The Hague: Mouton, 1966), 25. In referring to the scene in the cemetery, Baumgartner concludes in *Chrétien de Troyes*: "Lancelot ne peut manquer d'évoquer pour un lecteur médiéval ou moderne l'image du Christ triomphant de la mort et libérant de l'enfer les âmes des Justes. Aussi bien cette lecture est celle que fera l'auteur de la *Quête du Saint Graal*, en élaborant le personnage et les aventures de Galaad, le fils de Lancelot" (72), as I also argued in "Father and Son in the *Queste del Saint Graal*," *Romance Philology* 21 (1977): 1–16. In her 1981 study, *L'Arbre et le pain*, Baumgartner notes that "récriture" [*sic*] in the *Queste* is characterized by "l'obstination avec laquelle l'auteur surimpose un sens nouveau à un motif traditionnel, sans chercher pourtant à en oblitérer le sens originel": *L'Arbre et le pain: essai sur la* Queste del Saint Graal (Paris: SEDES, 1981), 68.

greeted while still in Logres: in the same way that Gorre is a phonetic inversion and anagram of Logres, the rivalry exhibited when citizens of Logres now imprisoned in Gorre vie for the privilege of hosting Lancelot completely reverses the critical fingerpointing of which he was the object in the first 1700 lines of the poem. In this scene, an unidentified man, who we later learn is a citizen of Gorre (2314), offers lodging to Lancelot and his two companions, the sons of his most recent host, and the three follow him. A squire gallops up, tells the putative host that the prisoners from Logres have revolted against the people of Gorre, and announces that a knight who has overcome all opposition along his way is now thought by all to be the one who "les deliverra toz / et metra les noz au desoz" (2313–2314) [. . . will soon free them (all) / And defeat our people, 2301–2302].[6] At this point, the host gallops off to a nearby fortress, followed closely by Lancelot and his two young companions, who are energized by the news of their compatriots' revolt. Immediately after they enter the fortress, a portcullis comes down, barring their way back, and once the "host" exits, another portcullis falls before they can follow him. Lancelot consults his magic ring to determine whether they are the victims of an enchantment (they are not), and happily the three prisoners find a barred postern which they destroy, thus escaping to see before them "l'estor / Aval les prez, molt grant et fier, / Et furent bien mil chevalier" (2374–2376) [the battle raging / Great and fierce down in the meadows, / With a full thousand knights, 2362–2364]. The elder of his two companions wisely offers to find out which side is that of the men of Logres, Lancelot agrees, and the youth swiftly returns to announce that their compatriots are right in front of them. Lancelot joins the battle, kills an enemy in the eye, and the elder of the two youths captures and dons the dead man's armor. Lancelot's prowess is such against his adversaries from Gorre that "Nes garantist ne fuz ne fers / Cui il ataint, qu'il ne l'afolt / Ou morz jus del cheval ne volt" (2414–2416) [Neither wood nor iron served as defense / To those he attacked, as he knocked them / Dead or wounded from their steeds, 2402–2404]. The narrator credits him alone with overcoming all the enemy, this to the great surprise of the compatriots from Logres who do not recognize him ("nel conuissent," 2422) and throng the two young companions to find out his identity. It is then that the youths announce that Lancelot will be their liberator:

> Seignor, ce est cil
> Qui nos gitera toz d'essil
> Et de la grant maleürté
> Ou nos avons lonc tans esté;
> Se li devons grant enor feire
> Qant, por nos fors de prison treire,

---

[6] All English translations of the *Charrette* are from *Lancelot or, The Knight of the Cart*, ed. and trans. William W. Kibler (New York: Garland, 1981).

> A tant perilleus leus passez
> et passera ancor assez;
> Molt a a feire et molt a fait. (2425–2433)

[Lords, this is he / Who will lead us out of exile / And free us from the great misery / We have been in for so long, / We should honor him highly / Since, to set us free, / He has crossed many a treacherous pass / And will cross more to come./ He has much yet to do, and has already done much. 2413–2421]

Energized by this news, the captives kill even more of the enemy before vying with each other to host Lancelot personally, even going so far as to seize his horse's reins and almost coming to blows with each other. Combining harsh words about their *folie* with a *captatio benevolentiae* that assures all the knights of his eternal gratitude for their proposed hospitality, Lancelot eventually restores order and spends the night with a knight furthest along his way.

The tournament at Noauz, some three thousand lines later (5525 ff.), is a reprise of this scene as well as a specular inversion of it. For the purposes of our comparison with the *Queste*, the repetition of the prophetic tone, this time with the herald's mysterious and eventually misplaced announcement (or so it soon seems), "Or est venuz qui l'aunera" (5583) [The one is come who will take their measure, 5563], is particularly striking. Equally important is the fact that the prophecy depends upon the herald's secret knowledge of Lancelot's identity, as is adumbrated in his visual recognition of Lancelot ("et puis qu'il le vit / Le conut, et si s'an seigna," 5568–5569; "and as soon as he saw him, / He recognized him and crossed himself," 5548–5549) and his pledge of fidelity to Lancelot's command not to reveal it (5571–5580). Lancelot's initial and final performances at the tournament are, of course, as spectacular in their prowess as his feats in the earlier battle against the men of Gorre, and the result (general concern at not recognizing him, 5652–5653) emphasizes again the importance of his concealed — or unknown — identity. The inversion of this noble behavior, sandwiched between Guenièvre's messages to him to perform "au noauz" [do your worst, 5654] both at the end of the first day (5665, 5674) and at the beginning of the second (5862, 5873), makes Lancelot the object of hilarity, then scorn and humiliation, when witnesses turn around the herald's prophecy to decry: "Tant a auné c'or est brisiee / S'aune que tant nos as prisiee" (5703–5704). [He's measured so much that he's broken it, / That measuring stick you bragged so about! 5683–5684.] Similarly, the glee with which the news of Lancelot's arrival in the first battle was greeted by the prisoners from Logres is reversed and becomes a scornful quest for news of the "cowardly knight": "Ou est des chevaliers li pire / Et li noauz, et li despiz? /. . ./ Qu'el monde n'a rien si malveise (5756–5757, 5763). [Where is the worst, the lowliest / And the most despicable of knights? /. . . / That there cannot be another so lowly in the world, 5736–5737, 5743.] This abasement of Lancelot's reputation reprises the rude welcome he had received in Logres on two occasions toward the beginning of the romance when the news of his climbing aboard the cart rapidly preceded him. It is precisely his humiliation in this second tournament, rather than his eventual victory once Guenièvre releases him from her order to joust "au noauz," that the *Queste* will develop with alacrity. Thus, while the *Charrette* views this repeated abasement positively as proof of the totality of Lancelot's love for the queen (even to sacrificing his reputation), the *Queste* reworks it to emphasize the social and moral degradation that his adulterous love has wrought on him.

The *Queste* conflates the poem's two battle scenes in a short interlude between Lancelot's visit to a third hermitage and his consultation of a recluse. The interlude is situated after the midpoint of the romance and in the second sequence dealing with his adventures. The battle itself is embedded in repeated acts of hospitality, here accompanied by exegetical discourse that constitutes the fundamental structural paradigm in the interlaced adventures of all the questing knights. Nonetheless, since Lancelot and Perceval are the principal recipients of didactic and allegorical readings of their visions and actions, it seems legitimate to construe this structural and thematic use of hospitality as an echo of the *Charrette*. Furthermore, the *Queste* appears to take the *Charrette*'s global opposition between inhospitable greetings in Logres and excessive offers of hospitality in Gorre and to incorporate that opposition into *each* of Lancelot's visits to a *Queste* exegete. Thus, the night before the tournament at issue here, a weary Lancelot happens upon a hermit whose hospitality he requests (in an interesting reversal of Chrétien's Lancelot who *shuns* hospitality as often as he accepts it), and who offers him lodging and spiritual comfort, including vespers and confession. Such hospitality is, however, always accompanied in the *Queste*, unlike the *Charrette*, by reminders of Lancelot's humiliating fall from the great promise which was his birthright. While the third hermit is gentler than the second who excoriated him "Einsi te perdi Nostres Sires, qui t'avoit norri et escreu et garni de toutes bones vertuz" (126:12 ff.) [Thus were you lost to Our Lord, who had nurtured and enhanced you and equipped you with every virtue, 143],[7] nonetheless Lancelot's voyage from lodging to lodging is constantly punctuated by reminders of his ignoble fall from excellence. The news of it precedes him as effectively as his mounting the cart had in Chrétien. For example, in this second sequence a valet castigates him between visits to the hospitable, if severe, hermits: "ne vos merveilliez pas se honte vos en avient en ceste Queste . . . mout poez avoir grant duel, qui soliez estre tenu au meillor chevalier dou monde, or estes tenuz au plus mauvés et au plus desloial" (117: 33–118:4). [Be not surprised if, in the course of this Queste . . . dishonour follow fast on your demur . . . you have good cause to grieve, you who were once held to be the best knight in the world and now are

---

[7] All English translations of the *Queste* are from Pauline Matarasso, *The Quest of the Holy Grail* (London: Penguin, 1969).

shown the worst and most disloyal! 136.] The intimate knowledge that this valet, only a secondary figure, and the more important hermit-hosts-exegetes have
of Lancelot's personal behavior as well of his glorious antecedents echo thematic
elements of the *Charrette*: specifically the mysterious knowledge that the herald
has of Lancelot prior to making his prophecy, that the two young squires reveal
when they forecast his liberation of the prisoners from Logres, or, indeed, that
the monk at the cemetery of the future dead makes public when he predicts that
this knight has performed such a miracle in removing the top from the sepulchre
that "il vet rescorre la reïne, / et il la rescorra sanz dote, / Et avoec li l'autre gent
tote" (1984–1986). [He is going to rescue the queen / And no doubt will—and
will rescue / All the other people along with her, 1972–1974.]

Against this backdrop so reminiscent of the *Charrette's* interlaced motifs of
hospitality, humiliation, fast-moving news, and predictions, the *Queste's* Lancelot happens upon a clearing in front of a castle where five hundred knights, some
in white armor, the rest in black, are engaged in a tournament. In the *Charrette*,
Lancelot waited to learn from his companion which side was that of the prisoners from Logres. Similarly, the *Queste* Lancelot, now, however, unaccompanied,
observes the battle before joining in. Judging that the black knights, of whom
there are already many victims, are losing even though more numerous, he decides to lend them his aid even though he does not know who they are. Such a
decision is perfectly consonant with the rules of chivalry. His performance is as
heroic as in the *Charrette's* two battles, with temporarily the same result: an individual exhibition of prowess at arms that outshines all the others and on which
everyone's attention is riveted: "si fet tant en poi d'ore que tuit cil qui le voient li
donent le los et le pris del tornoiement" (141: 27–28) [wreaking such damage in so
short a space that all who saw him there accorded him the palm and guerdon of
the tournament, 156]. But the resemblance stops here, and so clear an echoing of
the two *Charrette* scenes up to this point only makes the new twist added by the
*Queste* more striking to an audience already familiar with the Lancelot tradition.
Now, even when "il fiert sus aus et maille ausi come il feist sus une piece de fust"
(140:31) [He slashed and struck at them as he might upon a log, 156],[8] Lancelot
cannot get the upper hand since his adversaries seem not even to feel his blows,
but instead keep advancing, and force him, exhausted, to retreat. His humiliation is complete when he is seized bodily and deposited in a nearby forest by his
captors, who liberate him on condition that he promise to do their will. It is as if
the *Queste* had decided to leave Lancelot in the shameful position he temporarily occupied after the first day of the tournament at Noauz. Chrétien's Lancelot
had willingly agreed ("molt volantiers," 5675; "very gladly," 5655) to perform at
his worst when Guenièvre asked him to do so. The *Queste's* Lancelot, however,
wills himself to perform his best. Yet, as the narrator notes, for the first time in

---

[8] The choice of vocabulary recalls the *Charrette's* description of the first combat:
"Nes garantist ne fuz ne fers, / cui il ataint, qu'il ne l'afolt" (2402–2403).

his career he fails to win a tournament and is taken prisoner; and Lancelot's reaction is devastation when he interprets his defeat as yet another confirmation of his fall from grace: "si comence a fere trop grant duel et dit que or voit il bien qu'il est plus pechierres que nus autres" (141: 16–17). [These thoughts brought bitter chagrin in their train, and made him recognize that he was deeper sunk in sin than any other, 157.]

While it would be incorrect to suggest that the *Charrette* lacks religious imagery, as we will see in the next section of this essay, the vocabulary of sin is absent from it. The *Queste's* rewriting of this scene makes Lancelot both a participant and a retrospective observer, whose hermeneutic abilities, honed as they are by his three recent conversations with hermits, immediately come into play as he reflects ("se porpense de ce," 141: 16; "he reflected," 157) upon his humiliating turn of fortune and ascribes it ("or voit il bien," 141:17; "made him recognize," 157) to his sinfulness.[9] "Or voit il bien" suggests that the following interpretation is his own,[10] in what would then be an example of *style indirect libre*, a hypothesis all the more convincing because the fourth exegete (the recluse) is not yet present and the *Queste's* anonymous diegetic narrator does not indulge in spiritual readings:

> Car ses pechiez et sa male aventure li a tolue la veue des eulz et le pooir dou cors. De la veue des elz est il bien esproveee chose de la venue dou Saint Graal qu'il ne pooit voir [in the first sequence]. Del pooir del cors a il bien esté esprové, car il ne fu onques mes entre tant de gent come il a esté a cest tornoiement, qu'il poïst estre lassez ne traveilliez, ains les fesoit toz foïr de place, ou il vousissent ou non. (141: 19–24)

> [. . . for his crimes and his ill-fortune had robbed him of both sight and strength. His loss of sight had been made clear in his failure to discern the Holy Grail, when in its presence. And now the loss of physical strength was well and truly proved, for until this tournament, however great the crush that pressed around him, he had never been fatigued or jaded, but had driven his rivals willy-nilly from the field. 157]

The *Queste's* emphasis on Lancelot's interiority, and specifically on his progress in learning to read the spiritual meaning of his actions, marks a very clear departure from the equally heroic but more successful *Charrette* Lancelot, whose sensitivity and moments of reflectivity are catalyzed by love. The *Queste's* Lancelot, having internalized his exegetes' spiritual lessons, is well on the way to understanding

---

[9] Matarasso similarly interprets Lancelot's understanding of the *senefiance* of his failure: Pauline Matarasso, *The Redemption of Chivalry* (Geneva: Droz, 1979), 129–30.

[10] This example of Lancelot's growing sensitivity to the spiritual meaning of his adventures is an early example of the full-fledged hermeneutic ability that he shows, as Baumgartner notes (*L'Arbre*, 80), when he interprets his twenty-four-day coma at Corbenic as figuring his twenty-four years of sin.

his fate, whereas the *Charrette's* Lancelot depends on the cemetery monk to confirm prospectively his future liberation of the Logres prisoners.

Lancelot's intellectualization of his experience is not yet, however, at the point that the *Queste* lets him skip an informed reading from one more religious interlocutor, this time a recluse. Her discourse is further motivated by the fact that although Lancelot clearly understands his crushing defeat as the sign of his sinfulness, he does not understand all the implications of a vision he saw right after the disastrous tournament. A figure descended from the sky to berate him in terms alluding to Matthew 6:30 (and many other gospel passages) and Revelation 9:1–2 (and elsewhere): "Hé, hom de male foi et de povre creance, por quoi est ta volenté si legierement changiee vers ton anemi mortel? Se tu ne t'i gardes il te fera chaoir ou parfont puis dont nus ne retorne" (142: 1–4). [Ah! Man of little faith and most infirm belief, why is thy will so easily bent toward thy mortal foe? If thou dost not take heed he will plummet thee down into the bottomless pit whence none return, 157.] While Lancelot cannot yet read all the details of the vision and his humiliating and inexplicable defeat preceding it, he again shows his developing adeptness at spiritual interpretation when he notes that his failure to see the recluse's chapel the night before is a sign of his eyes being blinded by sin. Possessing the same limitless knowledge of his past as the male exegetes but more economical in interlacing her reading of his past and her predictions of his future, the recluse explains those details which Lancelot cannot, however correct his global interpretation is. She is really the first figure to state clearly that he has crossed the threshold between "chevalerie terriane" and "chevalerie celestiel" (143:8 and 10). She also avers that the first combat — "sanz faillance nule et sanz point de decevement" (143:14–15) [without any question or deception, 158] — was a real battle between earthly knights but that it was embedded in a spiritual Christian context of which the participants themselves were even unaware: "car assez i avoit greignor senefiance qu'il meismes n'i entendoient" (143: 16–17) [who themselves were far from realizing its full significance, 158]. The white knights following the son of King Pellés would have beaten the black-clothed knights of King Herlen's son, whether Lancelot had helped the latter or not and whether they had had more champions on their side. The reason revealed in the recluse's reading is that the tournament is none other than a figure of the Quest itself, a metatest as it were, undertaken by sinless knights armed in white and by sinful knights, like Lancelot, whose heart and eyes are blinded by earthly cares, like the black clothes they wear. Lancelot's error — inevitable since he is still a sinner, in spite of the numerous confessions and hard penance he has performed at the hands of his three hermits — was to help the sinners because they were losing. In other words, his reading of the progress of the tournament was perverted by interpreting events according to the code of terrestrial chivalry, which demands support of the losing side. Lancelot further endangered his son Galaad, who, along with Perceval on the side of the white knights, then killed Lancelot's horse. The good men who, in the recluse's reading could as easily be

Galaad and other white knights in the actual battle *or* the hospitable exegetes in the allegorical metadiegesis, took Lancelot into the forest "en la voie Nostre Seignor, qui est pleine de vie et de verdor ausi come la forest estoit" (144: 19–20) [upon the path of Jesus Christ, which quickens with life and greenness like the forest, 159]. In her retrospective interpretation, Lancelot had made spiritual progress up until the tournament when his terrestrial chivalric instincts, with their values of vainglory and reputation, kicked in, compelled him to support the wrong side, and then made him despair at his humiliating defeat. Hence the divine figure berated him in a vision and held out the possibility of defeat at the hands of the devil. The recluse adds that Lancelot is poised to go in either direction. This important sequence ends when Lancelot confirms his understanding that if he were now to fall into mortal sin, it would be his own fault and will. Her parallel response is an offer of nourishment, presumably to strengthen the body as her hospitality and discourse have reinforced his soul. A final event, reminiscent of the numerous occasions in the *Charrette* when Lancelot is unhorsed or needs to borrow another's mount, as he seems often to prefer, brings the sequence to its conclusion: a black-armed knight astride a black stallion materializes from the dark Eau Marcoise, kills Lancelot's mount from under him, and leaves him in an inhospitable impasse, hemmed in on three sides by the forest, the water, and the rocks.

## Lions

Lancelot's heroic crossing of the Pont de l'Epée to King Bademagu's castle in the *Charrette* is the dramatic prelude to his first combat with Meleagant in his quest to liberate Guenièvre from her captivity in Gorre. In the *Queste*, Lancelot's arrival by boat at King Pellés' castle initiates his final adventure in the quest for the Grail, which he finally sees from a threshold in answer to his prayers, as a divine voice makes clear: "Lancelot, is de cele nef et entre en cest chastel, ou tu troveras grant partie de ce que tu quierz et que tu tant as desirré a veoir" (253: 12–14). [Lancelot, leave the boat and enter this castle, where thou shalt find in part the object of thy search and of thy deepest longings, 260.] What the two scenes have in common, in addition to their structural function of introducing the climactic fulfillment of the hero's two quests, is the presence of lions. While the similarity of structural function is undoubtedly more important, the lions' role in the *merveille* is nonetheless a striking sign that the *Queste* scene, however different it may be from the *Charrette* passage, clearly echoes the crossing of the Sword Bridge.[11]

Chrétien's scene describes in substantial detail the dangerous and virtually impossible task Lancelot assumes without hesitation under the impetus of Love (3019–3155).[12] The water underneath is "felenesse" [treacherous], as frightening as if it were "li fluns au deable" (3026) [As if it were the Devil's river, 3012], the bridge itself a polished and acutely sharp sword. Particularly important to the impression of dread it elicits is the reaction of Lancelot's two young companions who are especially discomfited by the presence at the bridge's other end of two lions or leopards. In direct discourse uncharacteristically long and rhetorical for secondary characters and thereby all the more striking, they rehearse the impossibility of overcoming the bridge's challenge, especially that posed by the lions:

> Pöez vos savoir et cuidier
> Que cil dui lÿon forsené,
> Qui de la sont anchaené,
> Que il ne vos tüent et sucent
> Le sanc des voinnes et manjucent
> La char et puis rungent les os?
> [. . .]
> Se de vos ne prenez regart,
> Ils vos ocirront, ce sachiez;
> Molt tost ronpuz et arachiez
> Les manbres del cors vos avront,
> Que merci avoir n'an savront. (3074–3086)

[(If you do get across,) could you believe and be sure / That those two wild lions, / Which are chained over there, / Would not kill you and suck / The blood from your veins and eat / Your flesh and then gnaw upon your bones?/ . . . / If you do not take care, / I assure you, they will slay you: / They will break and tear / The members from your body / And show no mercy. 3060–3072]

Laughing goodheartedly at their fear, Lancelot places his faith in God who will save him, removes his armor, crosses the bridge which cuts him at the knees, the hands, and the feet, and, totally submissive to *Amors*, suffers pain as if it were sweetness. Arriving at the end of the bridge, he remembers the lions he thought he had seen from the other side, but "there was not so much as a lizard" (3136,

---

[11] Matarasso sees the presence of the two lions only as an allusion to the two lions flanking Solomon's throne in 3 Kings 10:19, which one medieval commentator, Rupert of Deutz, read as "typifying the majesty of the Last Judgment" (*Redemption*, 137) (PL 169.915C).

[12] For a substantially different reading of this passage, see Ribard, *Le* Chevalier de la Charrette, 103–7.

3122). As with the enchantment he had thought operative in the battle scene we discussed earlier, he looks through his magic ring at the current scene and ascertains that he was the victim of an illusion since no living creature menaces him at the end of the Sword Bridge. His heroism having impelled him into the land where Guenièvre and the other citizens of Logres are imprisoned, Lancelot now readies himself for the climactic battle with Meleagant to liberate her—and Arthur's subjects—from their exile. Thus Lancelot's successful passage sets in motion the immediate liberation of the queen and the citizens of Logres and, although slightly postponed, the joyful night of love.[13]

While the *Queste* episode serves the same function of introducing the climactic scene of Lancelot's search for and discovery of the Grail, it is quite understated and short. No sword bridge tests the hero's mettle: he simply arrives at King Pellés' castle in the same boat in which he had voyaged with his son Galaad and the body of Perceval's sister. In fact, in the redefined chivalry of the *Queste*, Lancelot's immobilization in a boat that he does not control and in the presence of these two saintly figures is itself proof of his spiritual "mettle." The only reminiscence of Chrétien's scene is the presence of two lions that guard the entrance to the castle. And unlike Chrétien's lions that were only an illusion intended to test the courage of Lancelot, these are quite real and test not his bravery but his faith in God. Thus, when a divine voice commands Lancelot to disembark and find "grant partie de ce que tu quierz et que tu as tant desirré a veoir" (253:13–15) [in (great) part the object of thy search and of thy deepest longings, 260], he assembles his arms, thinking that he must battle with the beasts in order to proceed to his reward. Not surpisingly for those characters and readers who have learned the *Queste's* new code of spiritual "chevalerie," a fiery hand knocks the sword from his grasp and a voice berates him for putting more faith in his armor than in the Lord. The astonished Lancelot falls to the ground, thanks God for the reprimand since, as he astutely argues, the blow indicates that God has not yet given up on him (253: 32), returns his sword to its scabbard, and faces the lions with the sign of the cross. He passes between them without their making a movement in his direction. He then ascends through the castle to the threshold of a room whose door opens in response to his prayer and reveals the Grail whence issues "une si grant clarté come se li soleux feist laienz son estage" (255: 3–4) [a great light flooding through the opening, as if the sun had its abode within, 262]. The *Queste's* reprise of the *Charrette's* lions guarding the entrance to Lancelot's final adventure in his new quest is something of a master stroke. With great economy, it indicates the high seriousness of the ensuing acts, but it does so by inverting the very illusion or *merveille* that had been the hallmark of Lancelot's career in

---

[13] In the next essay of this volume, Thorington demonstrates the significance of this episode in Chrétien's text, marked by the romance's highest incidence of rich rhyme which peaks with the rhyme of "freor" and "peor" describing the terror inspired by the lions.

Chrétien's romance. Whereas the lions at the end of the Sword Bridge are the elements of illusion that test the hero's bravery and materiality, their reality in the *Queste* gives substance to a new order of ineffable truth, God's, which is stronger and stranger than the fiction of Arthurian verse romance.[14] That they are real and that, in this new spiritual order, a knight is required to place greater faith in God's protection than in his own skill at arms involves a considerable leap of faith and an inversion of the chivalric ethic of the late twelfth century.

From a purely narrative point of view, it is important to note that the thematic elements apparently sacrificed by the *Queste* from its much more detailed verse model are not really jettisoned, but rather repositioned. For example, the difficulty and danger posed by the shining, highly polished sword are to be found thirty lines later when, in response to Lancelot's prayer, the door of the Grail room opens and reveals a brightness whose dangerous seductiveness could lead to as mortal a danger as a fall from the Sword Bridge. And, indeed, this is the case when the *Queste*, on two occasions, depicts Lancelot as tempted to cross the threshold into the Grail room, transgressing the command when he believes that the officiating priest is about to let the Grail fall. The mutilation that his body suffers in crossing Chrétien's bridge, thus announcing Lancelot's new role as a martyr[15] in the religion of Love, prefigures the loss of his finger joint prior to his union with Guenièvre, a mutilation of which he is unaware until the end of this ecstatic experience. The *Queste*'s rewriting of the suffering/non-suffering body involves a twenty-four-day suspension of Lancelot's bodily functions, as he lies inert, unseeing and unspeaking once he is struck down for transgressing the divine commandment and his body is removed to the other side of the threshold. His body is, then, as much of a witness in the *Queste* as in the *Charrette* to the life-changing consequences of Amors in the latter and of spiritual love in the former. The "martyre d'Amour" in Chrétien, translated by Lancelot's ectasy and adoration of the queen as he leaves her bedchamber unaware of the new stigma his body has suffered, differs only in register from the martyrdom he experiences in the *Queste*. The twenty-four days of suspended animation in which he lives after stepping over the Grail room's threshold are similarly marked by an ambiguity between punishment and ecstasy.[16] The punishment is clear from the onset of his "lifelessness" in direct consequence of transgressing the divine commandment not to enter the Grail room; but ecstasy is equally evident when he

---

[14] The shift to clear and simple prose is further highlighted by the contrast with the richness of rhyme in Chrétien's romance. See Thorington, this volume.

[15] See also Baumgartner, *Chrétien de Troyes*, 60, 74.

[16] See G. Armstrong, "Father and Son in the *Queste del Saint Graal*," *Romance Philology* 21 (1977): 1–16 for a detailed analysis of the promise partially fulfilled and yet incomplete in Lancelot's crossing the threshold of the Grail Room and his subsequent cataleptic "punishment" which is also the means of his accession (albeit temporary) to divine truths.

bewails awakening from his twenty-four-day trance ("Ha! Diex, por quoi m'avez si tost esveillié? Tant je estoie ore plus aeise que je ne seré hui mes!" 257: 31–33; "Ah! God, why didst Thou waken me so soon? I was far happier now than ever I shall be again!" 264). Despite his "regarz pechierres" (258: 3) [sinful sight, 264], Lancelot can use Pauline terminology (cf. 1 Cor. 2:9, 2 Cor. 12:4) to approximate the inexpressible marvels and ecstasy to which his twenty-four day punishment has given him access: "Je ai, fet il, veu si granz merveilles et si granz beneurtez que ma langue nel vos porroit mie descovrir, ne mes cuers meismes nel porroit mie penser . . ." (258: 6–8). [I have seen such glories and felicity that my tongue could never reveal their magnitude, nor could my heart conceive it, 264.] The parallel with Lancelot's and Guenièvre's "joie et . . . mervoille / Tel c'onques encore sa paroille / Ne fu oïe ne seüe" (4695–4697 [a joy and wonder, / The equal of which had never / Yet been heard or known, 4677–4679] is inescapable, the only difference being that Chrétien's narrator rather than Lancelot gives voice to the experience. Whereas the lovers' joy in the *Charrette* may find new opportunities for expression even after their return to Logres, Lancelot's vision of divine truths during his twenty-four-day coma is finite, and, by his own admission when he regrets being awakened from it, imperfect because incomplete.[17]

Equally inescapable is the conclusion that the *Queste* repositions and remotivates elements from the *Charrette* in such a way that Lancelot's desire—and quest—for Guenièvre in the former is replaced by his desire—and quest—for the Grail in the latter. But the narrative grammar that allowed him to reach the queen and liberate her from Gorre in the former no longer works with the new syntax imposed by the religious figures and exegetes who control physical and spiritual access to the Grail in the latter. Hence it is precisely because Lancelot has desired Guenièvre and satisfied that desire in the inner sanctum whose threshold he crossed by tearing out the window grill in the *Charrette* that he will see only "grant partie" of "what he so desired to see" in the *Queste* when he is repelled from across the threshold of the Grail's inner sanctum by a wind as hot as fire, the fire, I would add, of passion. It is perhaps ironic, but perfectly justified, that a chastised and now emasculated Lancelot in the *Queste* should accede to his final adventure not by a sword bridge but by humbling himself before real lions which could tear him to shreds as easily as his hermit exegetes have laid bare the stains of his sinful soul.

---

[17] See Matarasso, *Redemption*, 137: "Lancelot too has his vision of the Trinity, but translated into human terms and thus a limited and partial vision."

# Part III.

## Weighing Words:
## The Language of the *Charrette*

# Rhyme, Reason, and Poetic Technique in Chrétien's *Chevalier de la Charrette (Lancelot)*

Ellen M. Thorington
Ball State University

## I. Introduction

The octosyllabic rhyming couplets employed by Chrétien and other Old French poets have a rhythm and a cadence that is almost musical in nature. A major part of this musicality results from the rhyme, fashioned at its simplest from two paired vowels or, in more complex forms, from paired sounds that can extend to encompass the entirety of the verse line. Rhyme, particularly rich rhyme, pleases the ear, serves as a device for word play, aids in memorization, and generally adds a greater dimension to the text (and the performance) it ornaments.[1] In the hands of a master storyteller like Chrétien, it becomes a tool employed for emphasis and to deepen meaning.

Scholars have long been interested in the ways in which Chrétien employs rhyme; J.C. Laidlaw, in his 1983 article on rhyme in *Erec and Enide*, argues convincingly that Chrétien's use of rhyme constitutes a departure from that of his immediate predecessors, that he in fact is one of the first to combine rhyme and

---

[1] See Benoît de Cornulier's discussion of the use of rich rhyme in "Rime 'riche' et fonction de la rime: Le développement de la rime 'riche' chez les romantiques," *Voix et figure du poème* 59 (1985): 115–25. For further discussion of the use of rich rhyme, see idem, "La rime n'est pas une marque de la fin de vers," *Poétique* 46 (1981): 246–56, as well as Jean Molino and Joëlle Tamine's response to it in "Des rimes, et quelques raisons . . .," *Poétique* 52 (1982): 487–98 and de Cornulier's rebuttal in "La cause de la rime: Réponse à Jean Molino et Joëlle Tamine," *Poétique* 52 (1982): 498–508. For a discussion of the musicality of rhyme, see also Kenneth Burke, "On Musicality in Verse," in *The Philosophy of Literary Form: Studies in Symbolic Action*, 2nd ed. (Baton Rouge: Louisiana State University Press, 1967), 369–78.

Gina L. Greco and Ellen M. Thorington, eds., *Dame Philology's Charrette: Approaching Medieval Textuality through Chrétien's 'Lancelot': Essays in Memory of Karl D. Uitti.* MRTS 408. Tempe: ACMRS, 2012. [ISBN 978-0-86698-456-0]

other traditional poetic techniques to "consistent effect."[2] Chrétien himself states clearly in the prologue to *Guillaume d'Angleterre* that he composes and fashions this story through rhymes both rich and simple:

> Chrestiiens se veut entremetre,
> Sans nient oster et sans nient metre,
> De *conter un conte par rime*,
> U *consonont u lionime*,
> Ausi come par ci le me taille.
> (*Guillaume d'Angleterre* 1–5 [emphasis mine])

[Without leaving anything out or adding anything in, Chrétien wants to undertake to tell a story in rhyme, either simple or rich, to shape it just so.][3]

Moreover, anyone who can begin a story—as Chrétien does—with a beautiful *rime cloisonnée*:[4] "Des que ma dame de **Chanpaigne** / Vialt que romans a feire **anpraigne**..." (*Charrette* 1–2)[5] that links the name of his patroness to the undertaking of his literary endeavor, reveals rich training in the arts of poetry and prose.

The following paper represents the results of part two of a literary-statistical study of Chrétien's use of rhyme—specifically rich or ornate rhyme—in the *Charrette*. Accordingly, in addition to exploring the central question of how Chrétien employs rich rhyme as a poetic technique, I examine a number of issues that arose from the preliminary results published in 2002.[6] As the 2002 study showed, an analysis of the distribution of rich rhymes in the portion of the *Charrette* attributed to Chrétien reveals that he chose to highlight pivotal sections of the text through the absence or presence of this poetic ornament. First, therefore, this essay examines the sword bridge episode, which demonstrates one of

---

[2] J. C. Laidlaw, "Rhyme, Reason and Repetition in *Erec et Enide*," in *The Legend of Arthur in the Middle Ages: Studies Presented to A. H. Diverres by Colleagues, Pupils, and Friends*, ed. P.B. Grout, Arthurian Studies 7 (Cambridge: Brewer, 1983), 129–37, here 131.

[3] Text cited from "Guillaume d'Angleterre," trad. Anne Berthelot, in the Pléiade edition of Chrétien's works: *Œuvres complètes*, gen. ed. Daniel Poirion, Bibliothèque de la Pléiade (Paris: Gallimard, 1994), 955–1036. English translation mine.

[4] Alfred Foulet termed these the "rimes cloisonnées" (our RR2). These are multisyllable rhymes with slightly differing phonemes in the consonantal pivot point of the syllable. See Karl D. Uitti, "Autant en emporte *li funs*: Remarques sur le Prologue du *Chevalier de la Charrette* de Chrétien de Troyes," *Romania* 105 (1984): 270–91, here 280 n.2. For definitions of rich rhyme types, see n.12 below. A more detailed discussion of rich rhyme types is available in E. M. Thorington, "'De conter un conte par rime': Rimes riches dans *Le Chevalier de la Charrette (Lancelot)*," *Œuvres et Critiques* 27 (2002): 132–54.

[5] References to the *Chevalier de la Charrette* are from the Foulet-Uitti edition: *Le Chevalier de la Charrette (Lancelot)*, ed. Alfred Foulet and Karl D. Uitti, Classiques Garnier (Paris: Bordas, 1989).

[6] For these results, see Thorington, "'De conter un conte par rime'," 134–37.

the highest concentrations of rich rhyme in the entire *Charrette*, in order to show most precisely how Chrétien employs rich rhyme throughout the text, and how he interweaves it with other poetic figures such as *adnominatio* and *oratio recta* to make his point. Secondly, new analysis both reinforces and refines the previous findings: certain types of rich rhyme appear more statistically significant than others, and hence serve as better indicators of Chrétien's technique. Not coincidentally, an analysis of their form indicates that these particular types of rhymes are those that are most obviously recognized through oral/aural means.

## II. The Sword Bridge Episode (14)

In both an overall distribution of rich rhyme throughout the text (Figure 2) and in the distribution of the more visible multisyllabic and homonym rich rhyme types (Figure 3), episode 14 (2956–3155),[7] the moment when Lancelot, empowered by love, crosses the sword bridge, is marked by the highest incidence of rich rhyme within Chrétien's section of the text. As Daniel Poirion notes in his introduction to the Foulet-Uitti edition, it is this episode, situated at the numerical midpoint of the portion of the text attributed to Chrétien and marked by a narrative intervention, which serves to bridge the two parts of the romance.[8] Accordingly, at this high point of the tale, it is not surprising to find a high incidence of rich rhyme. This technique, which can also be viewed as a kind of "bridge" between verses, is most certainly employed here to draw attention to this pivotal episode.

But how does Chrétien use rich rhyme within the episode itself? A look at the distribution of rich rhymes can give a general idea of their ebb and flow throughout the section (Figure 1).[9] Here, the percentage of rich rhymes was charted using a moving average at thirty-line intervals; this provides a detailed image of the text.[10]

The incidence of rich rhyme peaks and plummets at three distinct points in the episode (Figure 1). This pattern of high and low incidence of rich rhyme

---

[7] See Foulet and Uitti's division of the text into episodes: *Le Chevalier de la Charrette*, xlv–il.

[8] Daniel Poirion, "Avant-Propos," in *Le Chevalier de la Charrette*, ed. Foulet and Uitti, viii.

[9] The work in this article is based on the data collected by Deborah Long and the present author; this data is presented in Figura, the rhetorico-poetic database constructed by Rafael Alvarado and available to the public at the *Charrette Project 2* website (www.lancelot.baylor.edu). I am most grateful to James A. Jones, Assistant Director for Research and Design at Ball State University, for assistance with the statistical analysis.

[10] Figures 2 and 3, in contrast, were charted using a moving average at fourteen- and eleven-line intervals, which provide a better global picture of the distribution of rhymes within the text.

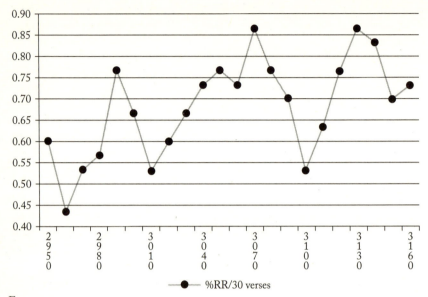

FIGURE 1

follows the narrative structure of the episode closely: episode 14 consists of three "mini-episodes" that each includes narrative and arrives at some kind of high point. The three peaks shown in Figure 1 at vv. 2990, 3070, and 3130, respectively, correspond almost exactly to the central moment of the mini-episode; the troughs at vv. 2960, 3010, and 3100, in contrast, tend to occur during simple narration.

To illustrate this precise correspondence, a review of the episode of the sword bridge is in order. As it begins, Lancelot—as yet unnamed—has just bested an arrogant knight. He and the two knights with him are courteously received by the people of the town and a dinner is prepared. This narrative section appears as the first trough (Figure 1) and has a frequency of about 40% rich rhyme, which is the absolute lowest in an episode that normally runs much higher ($\bar{x}$ .6876, $\sigma$ .21939, s.e. .05863). This frequency is also noticeably lower than Chrétien's overall mean ($\bar{x}$ .5507) and represents a contrast to the dinner, in which the Vavasseur welcomes Lancelot and his entourage courteously, and Lancelot replies briefly but in kind.[11] Here, the incidence of rich rhyme begins to mount—there

---

[11] The different pictures given by bisecting the text in 14-line and 30-line segments, along moving averages, have roughly the same standard of error regardless of the segmentation size. They are therefore easily comparable in this study.

appears to be a correspondence between *oratio recta* and rich rhyme. I have yet to find a passage of *oratio recta* in the *Charrette* that is not abundantly ornamented with this poetic figure.

This section then reaches its peak between vv. 2979 and 2994, when the Vavasseur's son adds his welcome to that of his father, and courteously offers to supply Lancelot with a horse and anything else he might require:

Et dist: "Sire, an vostre servise
Devrïens toz noz pooirs *metre* RR7[12]
Et doner einçois que pro*metre*; RR7
Se mestier avïez del <u>prendre</u>, RR8
Nos ne devrïens mie a<u>tendre</u> RR8
Tant que vos demandé *l'aiez*. RR3
Sire, ja ne vos es*maiez* RR3
De vostre cheval s'il est <u>morz</u>, RR8

---

[12] Deborah Long and I identified by hand nine different types of rich rhyme and labeled them RR1-RR9. RR1 through RR6 contain the multi-syllable and homonym rich rhymes, RR7 through RR9 are primarily single-syllable rich rhymes. The various types are defined as follows:

RR1 rhymes encompass two or more completely identical syllables and may be composed of one or more words. They follow Morier's definition of *rimes leonines*. See Henri Morier, "Rime," in idem, *Dictionnaire de poétique et de rhétorique* (Paris: PUF, 1961), 349–56.

RR2 rhymes, Foulet's *rimes cloisonnées* (see n.4 above), contain a supporting vowel prior to the rhyming syllable. Often the consonant that separates the syllables shares one or more phonologic characteristics with its counterpart in the second segment.

RR3 are multi-syllabic rich rhymes that differ only in the first phoneme of the first syllable.

RR4 are homophonic rhymes that may encompass one or more syllables. The two words that form the rhyming pair never perform the same grammatical or semantic function in the sentence.

RR5 are rich rhymes that encompass more than half of the verse line.

RR6 is a very rare form that appears only twice in the *Charrette* (vv. 5583–5584 and 5637–5638), in which the entire verse line is repeated.

RR7 rhymes are single-syllable feminine rhymes that begin with the same supporting consonant and contain at least three rhyming phonemes.

RR8 rhymes are single-syllable rhymes without an identical supporting consonant but including at least three identical rhyming phonemes.

RR9 are masculine rhymes formed by an identical supporting consonant that precedes the accented vowel and a final consonant that is pronounced.

For a detailed discussion of these rhyme types, their definitions, and how they were derived, see Thorington, "'De conter un conte par rime'," 134–37.

Car ceanz a chevax bien <u>forz</u>; RR8
Tant voel que vos aiez *del nostre*: RR2
Tot le meillor an leu *del vostre* RR2
En manroiz, qu'il vos est mestiers." (2982–2993 [emphasis mine])

[We should put all our resources in your service and offer you more than promises. If you have need of our help, we should not wait until you ask for it before we give it. Sir, do not worry that your horse is dead, for there are many more strong horses here. I want you to have whatever you need of what we might be able to give you: since you need it, you will ride off on our best horse to replace your own.][13]

This speech is remarkable for its rhymes: virtually every verse, except for the first and last, contains a rich rhyme. Although these are not, perhaps, the most exciting of the rich rhymes Chrétien employs (they are almost all single-syllable rich rhymes), they fit the eager young man who attempts to speak courteously and with gracious ornament, but who is still young and perhaps less adept at the flourishes of courtly speech.

The section ends with a brief narrative passage that describes how the entire party went off to bed:

A tant font les liz *atorner*, ADN RR2
Si se couchent. A l'*ajorner* ADN RR2
Lievent matin et *si s'atornent*. ADN RR5
*Atorné* sont, puis *si s'an tornent*. ADN RR5 (2995–2998 [emphasis mine])

[With that, they had the beds prepared and went to sleep. They arose early the next morning, outfitted themselves, and were soon ready to be off. 244]

While Chrétien usually does not ornament narrative passages as much as he does speech, he is always ready to surprise his audience with delightful exceptions such as this, in which he couples extremely ornate rich rhymes with *adnominatio* to create a word play on the idea of turning down (i.e., preparing) the beds at night and turning oneself out (i.e., getting up and dressed) in the morning at daybreak.

Following this description, the frequency of rich rhymes drops throughout the narrative passage that tells of the knights' preparations for their departure. It begins to rise again only at the beginning of the second mini-episode, when Lancelot and his entourage go to the sword bridge and see the perils it represents.

---

[13] Chrétien de Troyes, *The Knight of the Cart (Lancelot)*, in William W. Kibler, trans., *Chrétien de Troyes: Arthurian Romances* (London: Penguin, 1991), 244. All translations of the *Charrette* will be from Kibler. Here, however, Kibler's version differs slightly from the OF presented in Foulet and Uitti: "I want you to have all the best of what is ours in place of yours; take what you need" (2991–2993), translation mine.

Chrétien carefully describes the water and the bridge (3021–3045), creating a narrative tension as detail is layered on detail. His use of rich rhyme increases here, as does the pace of the whole passage:

> Einz ne fu, qui voir m'an re*quiert*, RR8
> Si max ponz ne si male <u>planche</u>: RR8
> D'une espee forbie et <u>blanche</u> RR8
> Estoit li ponz sor l'eve *froide*, RR9
> Mes l'espee estoit forz et *roide* RR9
> Et avoit deus lances de lonc (3034–3039 [emphasis mine])

[I'd say, were you to ask me for the truth, that there has never been such a treacherous bridge and unstable crossing. The bridge across the cold waters was a sharp and gleaming sword—but the sword was strong and stiff and as long as two lances. 244–45]

Short but rich rhymes such as planche/blanche; froide/roide add an almost rhythmic beat which makes Lancelot's intended crossing appear all the more inevitable.

The crowning terror of the bridge comes in the form of the two lions that appear to guard the other side. As the pinnacle of the horrors the bridge represents, which corresponds to the first peak of rich rhyme use in this passage (Figure 1), these lions ornament both the bridge and the textual description. Chrétien evokes the fear they inspire in the knights through a rich rhyme "freor/peor"—a use of rich rhyme that emphasizes the idea through repetition of sound and semantic meaning:

> Que dui lyon ou dui lie*part* RR9
> Au chief del pont de l'autre *part* RR9
> Fussent lïé a un perron.
> L'eve et li ponz et li lyon
> Les metent an itel <u>freor</u> RR3
> Qu'il tranblent andui de <u>peor</u> RR3 (3047–3054 [emphasis mine])

[(The two knights . . . were convinced) that there were two lions or two leopards, tethered to a large rock at the other end of the bridge. The water and the bridge and the lions put such fear into them that they trembled. 245]

The terrifying sight of the lions is thus the last straw that causes the two terrified knights to beg Lancelot not to try to cross the bridge.

Moreover, their relatively lengthy plea, as with other examples of *oratio recta*, is peppered with rich rhyme as they address Lancelot with all the courtly flourishes and rhetorical persuasiveness they can muster. Not surprisingly, the frequency of rich rhymes during this section reaches a new height at approximately v. 3070 (Figure 1), and the rhymes themselves are among the most beautiful within the entire *Charrette*:

> Or soit c'outre soiez *passez* RR3
> Ne por rien ne puet <u>avenir</u>, RR3
> Ne que les vanz pöez <u>tenir</u> RR3
> Ne desfandre *qu'il ne vantassent*, RR5
> Et as oisiax *qu'il ne chantassent* RR5
> Ne qu'il n'osassent mes <u>chanter</u>, RR2
> Ne que li hom porroit <u>antrer</u> RR2
> El vantre sa mere et re<u>nestre</u>, RR8
> Mes ce seroit qui ne peut *estre*, RR8
> Ne qu'an porroit la mer <u>vuidier</u> RR3 (3064–3073 [emphasis mine])

[Suppose you could get across—but that could never happen, any more than you could contain the winds or forbid them to blow or prevent the birds from singing their songs; any more than a man could re-enter his mother's womb and be born again (clearly impossible; alluding to John 3:4), or any more than one could drain the oceans . . . 245]

For example, the RR5, which appears in vv. 3067–3068 and covers more than half of the verse line, is of extraordinary quality and advances the semantic meaning of the text. The knight tells Lancelot here that even were he to manage to reach the other side—which appears more difficult than mastering the winds and forbidding them to blow, or than keeping the birds from singing (*qu'il ne ventassent / qu'il ne chantassent*), etc., he still would not be able to pass by the lions. The sibilant sounds he employs here suggest that even Chrétien cannot keep the wind from blowing or the birds from singing in his own poem—they sing out through the means of rich rhyme, proving the semantic point by their sound.

As the passage continues, Chrétien continues to use rich rhyme as a means to reinforce how terrible the lions seem to the knights:

> Pöez vos savoir et <u>cuidier</u> RR3
> Que cil dui l on forsené,
> Qui de la sont anchaené,
> Que il ne vos tüent et sucent
> Le sanc des voinnes et manjucent
> La char et puis rungent *les os*? RR4
> Molt sui hardiz quant je *les os* RR4
> Veoir et quant je les <u>esgart</u>. RR2
> Se de vos ne prenez <u>regart</u>, RR2
> Il vos ocirront, ce *sachiez*; RR3
> Molt tost ronpuz et *arachiez* RR3
> Les manbres del cors vo<u>s avront</u>, RR1
> Que merci avoir n'an <u>savront</u>. RR1 (3074–3086 [emphasis mine])

[(. . . yet, if you should get across,) couldn't you be sure that those two wild lions that are chained over there would kill you and suck the blood from your veins, eat your flesh, and then gnaw upon your bones? It takes all my courage just to look at them! (. . .)[14] I assure you they'll kill you: they'll break and tear the limbs from your body and show you no mercy. 245]

In vv. 3079–3080, for example, "les os" for bones is equated by means of a homonym rhyme with "les os" for courage, thereby creating a word- and sound-play illustrating the idea that even to look upon such terrifying beasts who are capable of gnawing on human bones requires almost more courage than the knights possess. A similar technique linking sound and meaning follows in vv. 3085–3086, where the knights are certain that the lions will kill Lancelot. This "knowing" (*savront*) is again emphasized by means of rich rhyme, as is the fact that lions have no knowledge of mercy. Here again, Chrétien ornaments the ornament, making the lions appear even more terrible through the addition of rich rhyme.

After this extremely ornate passage, which concludes the second "mini-episode" (Figure 1), the final section recounts Lancelot's preparations for crossing the bridge and then the deed itself. Similarly to other descriptive passages seen here, the initial narrative, where Lancelot removes his gauntlets and footwear in order to keep from slipping off the bridge, is again marked by a lesser frequency of rich rhyme. Although of course important—as it sets the stage for the greater feat—it is not of as much concern as the passage that will follow, hence a corresponding decrease in ornamentation is to be expected. However, when Chrétien begins to describe the crossing, the frequency of rich rhymes again begins to rise.

Once more, important details are outlined through extremely ornamental rhyme, particularly types 2 and 3:

De ce gueres ne s'es*maioit* RR3
S'es mains et es piez se *plaioit*: RR3
Mialz se voloit il ma<u>haignier</u> RR3
Que cheoir del pont et <u>baignier</u> RR3
An l'eve don ja mes *n'issist*. RR3
A grant dolor si con *li sist* RR3
S'an passe outre et a grant <u>destrece</u>: RR2
Mains et genolz et piez <u>se blece</u>, RR2
Mes tot le rasoage *et sainne* RR2
Amors qui le conduist *et mainne*, RR2
Si li estoit a sofrir <u>dolz</u>. RR8
A mains, a piez et a ge<u>nolz</u> RR8
Fet tant que de l'autre part vient. (3119–3131 [emphasis mine])

[It did not matter to him that he might injure his hands and feet: he would rather maim himself than fall from the bridge into the water from which

---

[14]  Section not contained in the OF text from Foulet and Uitti.

there was no escape. He crossed in great pain and distress, wounding his hands, knees, and feet. But Love, who guided him, comforted and healed him at once and turned his suffering to pleasure. He managed to get to the other side on hands, feet, and knees. 246]

The rich rhymes here give the poem a merciless beat that emphasizes the assault on Lancelot's body. One is not to be astonished (*esmaoioit*) that his hands and feet split (*se plaioit*): this mutilation (*mahaignier*) is better than falling from the bridge to bathe (*baigner*) in water that is impossible to escape (*issist*). Lancelot's distress (*destrece*) is linked to his hurts (*se blesce*). Chrétien links all these details through the sounds of rich rhyme, emphasizing the relentless nature of the assault on Lancelot's body and spirit, and setting the stage for the important narrative intrusion about to come.

For it is at this pivotal point in the text—at the moment when Lancelot endures such terrible suffering—that love enters the picture once again. It is love that sustains him, that makes his suffering sweet. This is illustrated, once more, through the means of rich rhyme—he is both healed (*et sainne*) and led (*et mainne*) by Love. The soft, nasal rhyme contrasts with the earlier harsh sibilants of "blece" and "destrece" or "sist" and "issist" to provide a warmer and longer rhyme that even sounds like a balm for wounds.

After this third and final peak (Figure 1), the episode winds down slowly. The lions, it turns out, were just an enchantment; and nothing remains in Lancelot's way to prevent the end of his crossing. His companions, who remained on the other side, are joyful to see him alive, although they do not know how badly he is wounded. But being Lancelot, he staunches his wounds, prepares to go on, and is rewarded for his valor with his first sight of the tower in the Kingdom of Gorre.

From examining both the frequency of rich rhyme and the uses to which Chrétien puts this ornament in this important episode, it is possible to draw some general conclusions. Starting on the most basic level of the verse line, he employs rich rhyme to emphasize meaning and create word play. This often occurs, as in the bed scene, in conjunction with *adnominatio*. Secondly, Chrétien is obviously conscious of the oral impact of his text—of its performance and how that performance and the sound correspondences therein can enhance meaning. Rich rhymes extend the sound, and hence its ability to add meaning either through onomatopoeia (as with the example of the wind and the birdsong) or through a kind of word painting (as, for example, with the soothing quality of love), or through rhythm and musicality. At crucial moments in the story (such as the suffering of Lancelot on the bridge), rich rhymes come thick and fast, adding to the rhythmic quality and excitement of the text, and likely serving to increase the tempo of performance.

Thirdly, the rhymes Chrétien uses tend to match the importance of the situation or, in cases of *oratio recta*, of the character who speaks. The son of the Vavasseur, for example, speaks in rich rhyme, but this rhyme is less complicated than that of the two knights who attempt to persuade Lancelot not to cross the sword bridge. It is possible to see a metaphor here—or a type of characterization—where knights more experienced in the courtly world can make more ornate speeches than the younger, less experienced, and lower ranked man. It is also possible that the more ornate speech of the knights is particularly elaborate chiefly because they are employing all possible rhetorical techniques in their attempt to dissuade Lancelot from his dangerous undertaking.

Hence, from the very basic level of the verse line, the effect of rich rhyme stretches outwards, helping to delineate sections and even episodes. Chrétien obviously employs rich rhyme to emphasize important passages. Less important narrative—with some exceptions—contains correspondingly fewer rich rhymes. *Oratio recta*, on the other hand, appears to be linked quite closely to rich rhyme and the ideals of ornamented courtly speech. Until recently, however, it has been extremely difficult to look at Chrétien's use of rhyme in a systematic way throughout a text. The *Charrette*, for example, contains 7134 verses, and hence some 3567 rhyming pairs, making this type of study extremely time-consuming. Technological developments, however, have made systematic analysis of rhyme or other poetic techniques not only feasible but also eminently doable.

## III. Distribution of Rich Rhyme, significance of types, and their importance for the poem

As an analysis of the Sword Bridge episode has shown, a systematic overview of a rhetorical figure, such as rich rhyme, can provide a new and different way of reading the text, one that has much to offer the philologist and the literary historian. Having looked at one episode in particular, it would be useful to turn now to the overall image of rich rhyme in the poem. Using the poetic database from the *Charrette Project*, it is relatively easy to come up with a distribution of rich rhymes throughout the text (Figure 2).

This figure represents the mean distributions of rich rhymes (all types RR1–RR9) per episode throughout the text. To arrive at these means, each episode, as defined by Foulet and Uitti, was divided into segments of fourteen lines; the means were calculated using moving averages. Since the sections are not equal, a harmonic mean sample size of 12.379 was used. For the purposes of these calculations, the Epilogue, which contains only fourteen verses and hence only one measurable segment, was disregarded as containing too small a sample size.

Figure 2 contains the total rich rhyme distribution throughout the entire *Charrette*, including—with the exception of the Epilogue (27)—both the sections attributed to Chrétien (Episodes 1–22) and those attributed to Godefroi (23–26). Chrétien's section of the narrative demonstrates a regular use of rich rhyme ($\bar{x}$ .5507, $\sigma$ .21689). Those episodes which contain a relatively higher or lower incidence of rich rhyme are significant, particularly when equal variances

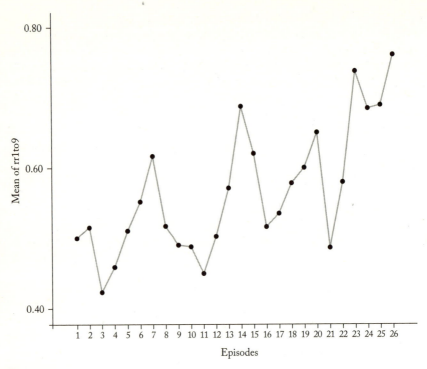

FIGURE 2

are assumed (F=.577, df=493, 91.366, P< .001), and occur at pivotal moments in the story. For example, episode 3 ($\bar{x}$.4233), which contains the lowest incidence of rich rhyme in the entire romance, recounts the disappearance of the queen, suggesting the delightful metaphor that a court deprived of its queen is like a text deprived of its rich rhyme.[15] While not as dramatic, Lancelot's disappearance corresponds to a similar dip in episode 21 ($\bar{x}$.4870). The high points that occur during the episodes of the immodest damsel (7) and the crossing of the sword bridge (14) ($\bar{x}$.6171 and $\bar{x}$.6876 respectively) would seem to indicate that Chrétien employs more rich rhyme here in these very significant episodes, to illustrate, first, Lancelot's faithfulness and courtesy in the face of a temptress, and secondly, one of his greatest achievements in the romance.

The way in which Chrétien employs rhyme to highlight these episodes becomes even more apparent with an analysis of the significance of different rich rhyme types. Where one might expect the different types of rich rhyme to be used with some regularity, this is not the case. As noted in the first part of this

---

[15] Thorington, "'De conter un conte par rime,'" 145, n.24.

study, RR6 (repetition of the entire verse line) occurs only twice in the entire poem.[16] An Analysis of Variance (ANOVA) test of the frequencies of rich rhyme types shows the presence or absence of RR1, RR3, RR4, RR5, RR7 to be particularly significant (Table 1).

| Table 1 | |
|---|---|
| RR1 | F = 2.58, df=25, 469, P < .001 |
| RR3 | F = 1.075, df=25, 469, P < .01 |
| RR4 | F = 6.15, df=25, 469, P < .001 |
| RR5 | F = 1.778, df=25, 469, P < .05 |
| RR7 | F = 2.225, df=25, 469, P = .001 |

This was not the case for the other forms (RR2, RR6, RR8, and RR9), which suggests a number of possibilities about Chrétien's use of and even his concept of what constitutes rich rhyme. As discussed in the earlier study, the question of when a rhyme can be defined as "rich" is a complex one. The multisyllabic rich rhymes (RR1–3, RR5) and the homonym rhymes (RR4) are fairly easy to distinguish, and we can argue with some certainty that Chrétien recognized these as particularly "rich." This would seem to be borne out by the above data, for all of the rhyme types with statistic significance are particularly easy to identify orally. Only the RR2 rhymes, or *rimes cloisonnées*, appear not to fit this pattern. However, as they vary over a number of phonemes, they are more complex to distinguish, and possibly more difficult to compose. In re-considering the rhyme types as defined in the previous study, the RR2s may also fit together with RR5 to form a larger class of more complex multi-syllabic rhymes. RR8 and RR9 are perhaps the least of the single-syllable rich rhymes, and may in fact not have been considered by Chrétien as particularly "rich": RR9 consists of one-syllable masculine rhymes, and although RR8 rhymes are feminine and consequently ring longer in the ear, they differ in the first phoneme and so do not constitute a complete rhymed syllable. As noted above, RR6 is a case unto itself, occurring only in two couplets.

With these considerations in mind, it would be useful to look at the distribution of multisyllabic and homonym rhymes (Figure 3).

Here it becomes very clear that episodes 3 and 21 represent some of the lowest incidences and episode 14 represents one of the highest incidences of rich rhyme in Chrétien's section of the poem. What also becomes even more striking in Figure 2 is the difference between the two sections of the poem, episodes 1–22 attributed to Chrétien ($\bar{x}$ .5507, σ .21689, s.e. .01046) and episodes 22–26 (27 is too brief to be statistically significant) attributed to Godefroi ($\bar{x}$ .7187, σ .18935,

---

[16] Thorington, "'De conter un conte par rime'," 136.

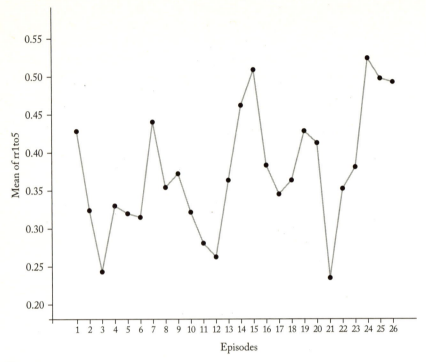

FIGURE 3

s.e. .02349). Indeed, the use of rhyme differs so significantly in these two parts of the poem that dual authorship of the *Charrette* is a virtual certainty.[17]

Chrétien thus appears to shape his work through the use of rich rhyme, drawing attention to important passages through the means of the presence or absence of these rich ornaments. Accordingly, the overall patterns of rich rhyme throughout Chrétien's portion of the *Charrette* follow the highs and lows of the tale itself. Use of technology provides the philologist and the literary historian with new tools and new ways of reading the text. As seen in the above systematic analysis of rich rhyme patterns, and closer look at an individual passage, they reveal Chrétien's craft in all its glory, and show how he employs this important poetic device to shape his tale and its performance.

---

[17] The 2002 study discusses the differences between these two sections of text in detail. See Thorington, "'De conter un conte par rime'," 147–51.

# THE DEVELOPMENT OF THE DEMONSTRATIVE DETERMINER CE IN THE MANUSCRIPTS OF CHRÉTIEN DE TROYES' *LANCELOT* OR *LE CHEVALIER DE LA CHARRETTE*

CHRISTIANE MARCHELLO-NIZIA,
ENS LETTRES ET SCIENCES HUMAINES, UMR 5191 'ICAR', LYON

ALEXEI LAVRENTIEV,
ENS LETTRES ET SCIENCES HUMAINES, LYON

TRANSLATED BY DOROTHY STEGMAN,
BALL STATE UNIVERSITY

## 1. The Evolution of Demonstratives and the Development of the Determiner *ce*

In the present analysis of the *Charrette* manuscripts, we will study the determiner *ce*, a new form that appeared in French around 1200. Over the course of the twentieth century, there have been ongoing studies of both the forms and meanings of the demonstrative adjective. Our current research is based on two series of findings: the first deals with the forms of the demonstrative, the second with its meaning in Old French (OF).

To begin, the demonstrative determiners CES and CE do not derive from the paradigm CIST (as some grammars have claimed). The form CES derives both from *cez* (from the paradigm CIST) and from *cels* (from the paradigm CIL)[1] while CE is an analogical creation modeled on the definite article *les*: *le* :: *ces*: X, with X = *ce*. A number of questions remain regarding the appearance of this form which occurs around 1200. First, what factors favor its development? Also, in what kinds of texts, in what semantic and syntactic contexts, and in what region does the determiner first appear? Furthermore, an interpretation of determiners

---

[1] Anthonij Dees, *Étude sur l'évolution des démonstratifs en ancien et moyen français* (Groningen: Wolters-Nordhoff, 1971), chap. 3.

Gina L. Greco and Ellen M. Thorington, eds., *Dame Philology's Charrette: Approaching Medieval Textuality through Crétien's 'Lancelot': Essays in Memory of Karl D. Uitti.* MRTS 408. Tempe: ACMRS, 2012. [ISBN 978-0-86698-456-0]

in OF based solely on placement is insufficient and controversial. Georges Kleiber has shown that the situation was complex due to the fact that the paradigm CIST not only was characterized by the required referent in its immediate context (situational or contextual), but that it had CIL as a complementary (extra-situational or extra-contextual) and unmarked form which corresponds to Modern French *celui-là, ce N là* designating a present element.[2] However, this value is found only from the thirteenth century onward. There were still several uses which Kleiber's study did not cover,[3] namely, those dealing with the passage of values of Latin demonstratives into OF. A careful diachronic study of texts from the ninth to the thirteenth centuries has shown that these values underwent a profound modification at about the same time period,[4] moving from a subjective value, for the most part carried over from the Latin, to a spatial value.[5]

Within this general framework, the question at hand is whether one can discover factors which favored the appearance of the atonal form of the determiner *ce* in OF. This development is of primary importance. *Ce* along with *ces* will constitute a paradigm of determiners that ruptures the well-ordered structure of the two paradigms CIL and CIST and will transform the system of demonstratives in French. This occurs in no other Romance language. Thus our specific objective is to determine if this change is linked to certain semantic contexts or syntactic constructions.

The broad scope of the *Charrette Project* provides an extensively rich corpus in which to study this phenomenon. It is unique among existing OF texts in that it allows us to examine the Foulet-Uitti edition (FU) along with the C manuscript which was the basis for this edition. At the same time, if we take into

---

[2] See, for example, Georges Kleiber, "L'opposition CIST/CIL en ancien français, ou comment analyser les démonstratifs?" *Revue de Linguistique Romane* 51 (1987): 5–35.

[3] Christiane Marchello-Nizia, "'Se voz de ceste ne voz poéz oster, Je voz ferai celle teste coper.'(*Ami et Amile* 753): La sphère du locuteur et la déixis en ancien français," in *Mémoire en temps advenir: hommage à Theo Venckeleer*, ed. A. Vanneste, P. De Wilde, S. Kindt, and J. Vlemings (Louvain-la-Neuve: Peeters, 2003), 413–27.

[4] See Christiane Marchello-Nizia, "Deixis and Subjectivity: The Semantics of Demonstratives in Old French (9th–12th century)," *Journal of Pragmatics* 37 (2004): 43–68, http://authors.elsevier.com/sd/article/S0378216604000864; eadem, "La sémantique des démonstratifs en français: une neutralisation en progrès? " in *Le Français parmi les langues romanes*, ed. Mario Barra Jover, spec. no. of *Langue française* 141 (2004): 69–84; eadem, "Du subjectif au spatial: l'évolution sémantique des démonstratifs en français," in *Le Démonstratif en français*, ed. Céline Guillot, spec. no. of *Langue française* 152 (2006): 114–26; eadem, "From Personal Deixis to Spatial Deixis: The Semantic Evolution of Demonstratives from Latin to French," in *Space in Languages*, ed. M. Hickman and Stéphane Robert (Amsterdam and New York: John Benjamins, 2006), 103–20.

[5] Georges Kleiber, "Sur la sémantique des descriptions démonstratives," *Lingvisticae Investigationes: Revue Internationale de Linguistique Française et de Linguistique Générale* 8 (1984): 63–85.

consideration some adjustments and adaptations, we can compare MS C to each of the other seven manuscripts containing all or part of Chrétien's romance. Because of the careful transcription of the manuscripts and morphological tagging in the FU edition in the Figura browser, we are able to compare the use of determiners by the various copyists of the text. Thus the tendency to substitute the forms of the paradigms CIST and CIL can be explored via the use of data from both the critical edition and the manuscripts. This allows for a clearer idea of the evolution of the system of determiners in medieval French.

In order to answer the particular questions of this study, we first needed to ascertain which manuscripts employ the new form of the determiner *ce*. We could then examine whether the uses of *ce* belonged to Chrétien's language or had been added by the various copiers of the text. These cases were then subjected to a contextual comparison between manuscripts. Returning to the evolution of the phenomenon, we examined the question of whether the demonstrative system of those manuscripts containing the new form *ce* reflects the older subjective value or the new spatial value. To begin, we present the search protocols used for the Figura browser which make possible the procedures and analysis presented above.

## 2. Search Methods for the Figura Browser

The *Charrette Project* website, with its careful transcriptions in XML-TEI and color images, allows us to examine the entire manuscript tradition of Chrétien's romance in conjunction with a new corrected version of the FU edition. All of the project's resources are available online through the Figura browser (created by R. Alvarado of Princeton) found at http://lancelot.baylor.edu[6] (tab "Charrette db").

At present, the critical edition based on the scribe Guiot's manuscript (referred to as C by W. Foerster)[7] is the most advanced both linguistically and electronically. The text is lemmatized and tagged morphologically. Both direct

---

[6] Since January 2006, the *Charrette Project 2* website offers the updated version of the project. Due to copyrights, the manuscript images are available only on the project's original site at Princeton: http://www.princeton.edu/~lancelot. All citations of the manuscripts are from either actual observations or from the *Charrette Project* images. All other citations are from the corrected Foulet-Uitti edition as presented on the website. As line numbers differ slightly, references have also been given to Mario Roques' edition: Chrétien de Troyes, *Le Chevalier de la Charrete*, ed. Mario Roques (Paris: Champion, 1958).

[7] Alexandre Micha presents a good summary of Chrétien's manuscripts and their designations: *La Tradition manuscrite des romans de Chrétien de Troyes* (Paris: Droz, 1966 [1st ed. 1939]). The designations vary for nearly every romance; Micha explains the variants: "Foerster change les sigles des mss. collectifs d'un roman à l'autre, parfois dans l'intention d'honorer la mémoire des philologues qui les ont partiellement édités" (18). As for the currently known manuscripts of the *Charrette*, see chaps. 3 and 4.

and indirect discourse and figures of speech such as chiasmus and enjambment are also marked in the database.

The manuscript transcriptions can be examined in two ways. First, by means of the tab "pages" in the Figura browser, a page of the manuscript can be selected and the image and transcription will appear side by side. Second, from the tab "Charrette (txt)" on the homepage, one can select lines from one or two manuscripts from the critical edition or from the modern French version. In both cases, in order to search for an occurrence in a transcription, one can effect a "basic search" from the web browser, but it is necessary to know the passage of the particular occurrence in advance.

We found that the most efficient way of using the manuscript transcriptions is to take the occurrence which was of interest to us from the tagged FU edition and then to search for the corresponding examples from the various manuscripts. This is easily done because the numbering of the lines in the transcriptions and the FU edition is the same.

Thus, we searched the instances of the lemmas CE (ICE), CEL (ICEL), and CEST (ICEST) labeled "adjective" in the Figura browser. A simple search in the lexical module (tab "word") gave the index of the forms and the references of the occurrences. By clicking on each occurrence, a passage of five lines appeared (the line with the occurrence and the two preceding and two following lines). In order to access a larger context (50 lines), it is necessary to click on the number of the verse in the description of the occurrence. In our search, we found 120 occurrences of the determiner CEST, 67 of CEL, and 14 of CE.

For the purposes of this study, the five-line context seemed sufficient for morphological analysis and for the first steps of the semantic analysis. The limited contexts were thus placed in a table by simply cutting and pasting—a rather time-consuming method. However, as will be seen, in a certain number of cases it was necessary to examine a larger context and to proceed "by hand" in order to obtain a correct semantic and contextual interpretation. We then searched for corresponding occurrences in the eight manuscripts and placed them in the same table (one column for each manuscript and one line for each occurrence and its corresponding instances). Finding the occurrences was not difficult, but took a considerable amount of time.[8] The table provided a synthesis which made it possible to locate all

---

[8] One can view the transcriptions of the manuscripts from the tab "Charrette txt" on the website by specifying the manuscript and the desired line numbers. The accuracy of the transcription can thus be verified by comparison with the photo of the folio for the corresponding manuscript. In doing so, we noted several transcription errors (*cest* → *ceste* in line 4888 of MS A) and errors or editorial interventions which were difficult to explain in the FU edition (*ceste* → *cest* in lines 22, 1113, 1134, and 4938). These few errors, inevitable in an edition of a text of such proportions, do not lessen the scholarly value of the edition, all the more so because the *Charrette Project* allows one to consult the pictures of the manuscripts if a question arises.

the instances where the manuscripts agreed in the choice of the demonstrative and also where they varied. The variants were of primary interest because we were able to clarify "in real time" the modification of the demonstrative system.

## 3. Analysis of the Occurrences of Demonstrative Determiners in the Eight Manuscripts of the *Charrette*

### 3.1. Method

It should be noted that Chrétien's romance comes to us in eight manuscripts, six of which were known to Foerster and Micha. These are MSS A (Chantilly 472: missing the first thirty lines and the end after line 5873 according to Foerster's edition), C (BnF fr.794: complete), E (Escurial: missing the end after line 5763), F (BnF fr. 1450), T (BnF fr. 12560: complete), V (Vatican: Biblioteca Vaticana, Regina 1725: missing the first 861 lines) and two others included in the FU edition and the Figura browser. These two manuscripts are G (Princeton, Firestone Library, Garrett 125: very fragmented) and I (Paris, Bibliothèque de l'Institut de France 6138: two short fragments). Only C and T give the entire text.

Our analysis will treat in turn the following points in section 3:

• The search and analysis of all the occurrences of the determiner ("adjective" *ce*) in the eight manuscripts of *Charrette*. As we observe in 3.2, only three of them offer this form.

• From the preliminary results, we will formulate a hypothesis that the presence of CE is a result of the copyists' choice and that the determiner is apparently not a part of Chrétien's own language.

• We will then find which factors led three of the eight copyists to use *ce* where, in view of the other manuscripts, Chrétien used *cest*, *cel*, or another determiner (be it demonstrative or not).

• We will begin by examining the cases where Guiot, the copyist of C and the most "modern" (he uses *ce* 15 times), and the copyist of T brought about this modification; we will then compare their usage with that of the other manuscripts, in particular those which do not use *ce*. We will then attempt to clarify the system in which *ce* is used.

• We will finish by noting the concurrence of *ce*, *ces*, and *cel* in MS C.

In section 4, we will present an explanatory hypothesis for the following questions: does the new spatial system of demonstratives permit the expansion of *ce* and thus broaden the new paradigm CE?; or is it the case that the old system of subjective value allows for this expansion?

### · 3.2. The Determiner *ce* in Three of the Manuscripts of the *Charrette*: Comparison with the Other Manuscripts

Only three of the eight manuscripts contain the new form of the demonstrative determiner *ce*, namely manuscripts C, T, and V (in the nomenclature proposed by Foerster and used in the *Charrette Project*). The Guiot copy (MS C, BnF fr. 794), which served as the base manuscript for both the FU edition and Roques' edition, offers the largest number of occurrences, fifteen in all. We find fourteen in MS T, four of which are also found in Guiot (*En ce tans* + Impft in lines 327, 2823, 3445, 6630). One of these occurs as well in MS V (Vatican 1725).

Table 3.2 shows all the occurrences of the determiner *ce* in the manuscripts of the *Charrette*. There are twenty passages where one of the three manuscripts, C, T, and V (and often C and T together), use *ce*. This form corresponds to:

• *cel* most often in occurrences 1, 4, 5, 6, 10, 11, 14, 16, 17;

• *cest* less often in occurrences 2, 18, 19 (where only T gives *ce*) and 20 (where only V has *ce* in the masculine NS);

• either *cest* or *cel*, depending on the manuscript, in occurrences 3, 8, 12, and 13; note that there is no homogeneity in the choice;

• *ciz* in occurrence 15 where it could be that *ciz* in the masculine NS is the equivalent of *cist* or, if not NS, the equivalent of *ce*,[9] although a rare form of *ce* in V would seem to support the first interpretation, thus linking *ciz* to the paradigm CIST;

• *ce* in occurrences 7 and 9 where only MS C gives *ce*; the reading of 7 is difficult and, in 9, all the other manuscripts have *le*.

---

[9] Christiane Marchello-Nizia, *L'Évolution du français: Ordre des mots, démonstratifs, accent tonique* (Paris: Armand Colin, 1995), 145.

TABLE 3.2. CE IN THE MANUSCRIPTS OF THE CHARRETTE

| FU – MR | C | A | T | V | E | F | G | I |
|---|---|---|---|---|---|---|---|---|
| (1) FU 75 – MR 73<br>"... Que la reïne li osasses<br>Baillier por mener an ce bois<br>Aprés moi, la ou je m'an vois ..." | ce bois | encel bois | ence bois | --- | entel bois | --- | cel bois | --- |
| (2) FU 956 – MR 946<br>"... Einsi le vos ofre et presant."<br>Plusor sont qui de ce presant<br>Li randissent .v.c. merciz, | ce presant | cest p'sent | cest p'sent | cest p'sent | tel present | --- | --- | --- |
| (3) FU 2263 – MR 2251<br>Ne ja mes ne s'an partira<br>De ce chevalier, tant qu'il l'ait<br>Adobé.... | ce ch'r | decel ch'r | de tel ch'r | cel ch'r | cest ch'r | --- | --- | --- |
| (4) FU 2835 – MR 2821<br>"... mes je vos pri<br>Que vos aiez de moi merci<br>Por ce Deu qui est filz et pere ..." | ce deu | cel diu | Porce deu | cel dieu | --- | --- | cel dieu | --- |
| (5) FU 2839 – MR 2825<br>"Ha! Chevaliers, fet la pucele,<br>Ne croire pas ce traitor ..." | ce traitor | cel t'itor | ce t'itor | cel traitor | tel traito R | --- | le traitor | --- |
| (6) FU 3669 – MR 3653<br>"Dame, ... vos requier, ...<br>Que le non a ce chevalier ...<br>Me dites ..." | ce ch'r | acel ch'r | ce ch'r | cel ch'r | acel ch'r | --- | cel ch'r | --- |

| FU – MR | C | A | T | V | E | F | G | I |
|---|---|---|---|---|---|---|---|---|
| (7) FU 4400 – MR 4382 "S'ai fet ce geu don an me blasme" | ce geu | S o't fait eue je de mõ blame | S i ont fet ce cuit. de lor blame | S ont fet ce de qoi len me blasme | C onfait ceu giev ce-mensembl | --- | --- | --- |
| (8) FU 4800 – MR 4780 ". . . Ce sanc que an mes dras regart Onques ne l'i aporta Ques," | C esanc | C est sanc | C e sanc | C el sanc | ~ cis sans | --- | --- | C est sanc |
| (9) FU 5554 – MR 5534 Lanceloz trestoz desarmez S'estoit sor ce lit acostez. | sor ce lit | sor le lit | sor le lit | sor le lit | sor le lit | --- | --- | --- |
| (10) FU 5662 – MR 5642 ". . . Jus de ces loges avalez, A ce chevalier m'an alez Qui porte cel escu vermoil . . ." | ce ch'r | cel ch'r | ce ch'r | cel ch'r | cel ch'r | cel ch'r | --- | --- |
| (11) FU 6254 – MR 6234 Ce jor tenoit cort molt joieuse Li rois a Bade sa cité. | Ce ior | --- | C e ior | C el ior | --- | L e ior | --- | --- |
| (12) et (13) FU 6599 – MR 6579 "Por ce don et por ce servise Me sui an ceste poinne mise . . ." | ce don<br>ce seruise | ---<br>--- | ce don<br>cel seruise | cest don<br>cest seruise | ---<br>--- | cel don<br>cel ser-uise | ---<br>--- | ---<br>--- |
| (14) FU 6752 – MR 6730 Car cil Meleaganz meïsmes Qu'il menace et tient ja si cort Estoit ce jor venuz a cort . . . | ce ior | --- | ce ior | cel ior | --- | ~ ia | --- | --- |

| FU – MR | C | A | T | V | E | F | G | I |
|---|---|---|---|---|---|---|---|---|
| (15) FU 6865 – MR 6843<br>. . . Et se Reisons ne li tolsist<br>Ce fol panser et cele rage, . . . | Ce fol | --- | C e fol | C iz pensers | --- | L or fol | --- | --- |
| (16) FU 327 – MR 325<br>N'en avoit a **cel** tans que une | a **cel** tans | acel tans | En ce tans | --- | acil tens | --- | --- | --- |
| (17) FU 2823 – MR 2808<br>"Ce est li chiés<br>De **cest** chevalier que tu as<br>Conquis. . ." | de **cest** ch'r | decel ch'r | de ce ch'r q-tu as | decel ch'r | De cel ch' | --- | Decel ch' | --- |
| (18) FU 3445 – MR 3429<br>"Biax flz, car t'acorde<br>A **cest** chevalier sanz conbatre!" | A **cest** ch'r | A cest ch'r | a ce ch'r. | A ce ch'r | A cest ch' | --- | --- | --- |
| (19) FU 6630 – MR 6610<br>"Aucun engin, se je le truis<br>Don puissiez croistre **cest** pertuis" | cest pertuis | --- | ce *partuis* | cest *partuis* | --- | **ceste** *partus* | --- | --- |
| (20) FU 2321 – MR<br>"Sire, öez que dit **cist** sergenz." | cist sergenz | cis sergans | cist s'ianz | ce seriant | cis serianz | --- | cis sergans | --- |

## 3.3. Analysis of Factors Linked to the Use of *ce*

The variety of equivalents for *ce* makes it impossible to attribute the substitutions we have just noted to a simple cause. Thus, we will first see whether the instances of *ce* in C and T have specific characteristics.

The first noticeable trait is that, in the majority of the cases (11 out of 18), *ce* is used in direct discourse; this occurs in 1, 4, 5, 6, 7, 8, 10, 12, 13, 17, and 18; in 3 we find indirect discourse. The determiner *ce* appears in narration only in occurrences 2, 9, 14, 15, and 16. Interestingly, occurrence 2 marks the return to the narration and acts as a discourse deictic word.[10] One should also note that in four cases some manuscripts have *cest*, others *cel*, and that the fluctuation between these two forms occurs in direct discourse.

Thus, in passage 8, the manuscripts disagree:

". . . Ce sanc que an mes dras regart
Onques ne l'i aporta Ques," (FU 4800–MR 4780)

[This blood you see on my sheets / never came from Kay. 4780–4781][11]

Manuscripts A and I give *cest* and V *cel*. This example is significant in that it allows us to distinguish between two grammatical and two semantic systems for demonstratives. In V, we would thus have the grammar used in OF derived from Latin where the opposition between the paradigms CIST and CIL is subjective. CIST is used by the speaker to designate what is placed within a personal "sphere" or what belongs to that particular speaker, and CIL is complementary.[12] So, in V, Guenièvre establishes a distance between herself and the blood visible on her sheets when she uses *cel sanc*. In A and I (and possibly in G with *ciz*?), however, *cest* refers to an element which is present in the situation of the enunciation—the protagonists examine the blood on the sheets.

One could attribute the use of *ce* in manuscripts C and T to the various copyists' hesitation between the forms (or to one copyist taking up the form another

---

[10] Nikolaus P. Himmelmann, "Demonstratives in Narrative Discourse: A Taxonomy of Universal Uses," in *Studies in Anaphora*, ed. Barbara Fox (Amsterdam and Philadelphia: John Benjamins Publishing Company, 1996), 205–54; Holger Diessel, *Demonstratives: Form, Function, and Grammaticalization* (Amsterdam and Philadelphia: John Benjamins Publishing Company, 1999); Céline Guillot, "Démonstratifs et déixis discursive: Analyse comparée d'un corpus écrit de français médiéval et d'un corpus oral de français contemporain," *Langue française* 152 (2006): 56–69.

[11] All English translations of the *Charrette* are from *Lancelot, or, The Knight of the Cart*, ed. and trans. William W. Kibler (New York: Garland, 1981).

[12] Marchello-Nizia, "'Se voz de ceste ne voz poéz oster'," 425–26, and eadem, "La sémantique des démonstratifs en français," 115–20.

copyist had chosen). In direct discourse, *ce* refers to the present situation without further clarifying the relation between the designated element and the speaker. As one can see, the meaning of the demonstrative is thus rendered neutral.

In occurrence 3, the same type of grammatical difference distinguishes manuscripts E, A, and V, this time in indirect discourse. In E, the demonstrative relates the knight in question to the speaker (*cest*, i.e., this knight who interests me), whereas V and A give *cel* because indirect discourse is used in narration.

In 12 and 13, V has *cest* because the speaker links the gift and the service to himself. We find, however, that F and T (in 13) are examples of the new grammar in which CIL refers to what is not or is no longer present; the text evokes a past action. It can thus be proposed that the change to *ce* is the result of indecisiveness at a particular moment in the development of the determiner; both distinctive grammatical choices coexisted and competed with each other. The question is, does the deixis refer to the speaker's sphere or to the place of the words spoken? The form *ce*, induced by analogy (le / les) from *ces*, allows the opposition to be subsumed. The determiner is less precise and can be used in a more neutral manner.

## 3.4 The Uses of the Demonstratives CIL and CIST in Manuscript C

Is the above hypothesis confirmed by the use of demonstrative determiners in manuscript C? If we examine all of the uses of the paradigm CIL and CIST (there are 49 occurrences of CIL and 120 of CIST), we can affirm that the new grammar is already in place in C. Out of 120 cases, 105 are in direct discourse, 100 are situational deictic expressions, and 5 are discursive deictic expressions. Discursive deictic expressions are attested in the *Chanson de Roland* and are thus not examples of the use of the two grammars. Similarly, when CIST in direct discourse designates an element which is both present and belonging to the speaker or the person concerned, it cannot be used as a proof. Nevertheless, there are some occurrences of CIST where one would have expected the older deictic expression CIL. Let us examine three of these, the first of which is v. FU 283–MR 282:

> "Et je cuit que **cist** dui destrier
> sont vostre ; or si vos prieroie . . .
> . . . que vos, ou a prest ou a don,
> le quel que soit, me baillessiez."

> [(And) I believe these two war-horses / are yours; Now I would pray you /
> . . . / (that you) give me one or the other at your choice, / either as a loan or
> gift. 283–287]

In the old grammar, CIST would have been incompatible with "vostre" because it could designate only an element belonging to the speaker. In the quotation above, this would have meant using *cil dui destrier*, as one finds in manuscripts A and G. However, T and C give *cist*, CIST referring henceforth to an element present in the enunciation: "ces deux chevaux ici présents", and E has *chi dui* (did the copyist have difficulty choosing?); the passage is missing in F, I, and V.

The second occurrence is v. FU 2823–MR 2808:

> Et cele dit: "Ce est li chiés
> De **cest** chevalier que tu as
> Conquis; et, voir, einz ne trovas
> Si felon ne si desleal."

[She said: "I ask for the head / of this knight you have just / defeated; in truth, you have never encountered / a more base and faithless knight." 2808–2811][13]

Here, in MS T, one finds *ce*; the others have *cel*.

In the third example, C uses *cist*; however A and E, the only other manuscripts containing the passage, give *cil* despite the fact that the knight is present—seemingly to indicate that he hates Gauvain:

> Li nains dit: "Se tu tant te hez
> Con **cist** chevaliers qui ci siet," (FU 389–MR 385)

[The dwarf said: "If you think so little of yourself / as this knight sitting here . . ." 384–385]

Other similar passages confirm these results (FU 443, or 1593, or 4987). Thus C and T, both of which use the new grammar, lie in contrast to the more archaic A, E, and G (and also to the heterogeneous V, which uses both the old and the new). F and I, which are very fragmented, do not provide enough context to permit us to draw conclusions.

---

[13] The first line of this citation, which responds to the Knight's question ". . . Dites moi / Que vos volez . . ." (FU 2818–2820) [Tell me. . . / what you desire, 2804–2805], may be more literally translated as: And she said, "This (referring to the desire) is the head / of the knight. . ." Modified translation, E. Thorington.

## 3.5. The Cases of Concurrence Between *ce, cel,* and *cest* in Manuscript C

We will now look more closely at cases of actual concurrence, notably the case where *ce* can be used as a masculine Oblique Case. MS C has the following number of demonstrative determiners in the masculine singular Oblique Case: 49 *cest*, 10 *cel*, and 15 *ce*.

As we have shown, *ce* is almost always in direct discourse; the same holds true for *cest* and *cel* in the majority of the occurrences. The frequency of the number of cases where this occurs makes it clear that *ce* could have replaced either *cest* or *cel*. This happens in nearly all instances of direct discourse when the resolution of a situational or resumptive deictic expression is found in the context. The form gives the minimum amount of information and becomes less clear in relation to *cel* or *cest*.

## 4. Two Hypotheses

## 4.1. C, T, and V: Related Manuscripts?

The fact that only three out of eight manuscripts contain the new form makes it possible to deduce that, as we have seen, this form did not belong to Chrétien's language; it was introduced by mainly two copyists.

According to Micha's description, generally, "une première certitude acquise, c'est qu'aucun de ces six mss.[14] n'est copié sur l'autre, puisque chacun d'eux a des lacunes qu'on ne retrouve pas dans les autres." ('the first item we can be certain of is that none of the six manuscripts is copied from the others, as each one has lacunae that we do not find in the others.')[15] Nevertheless, for him, C, T, and V are not particularly related; he noted three families: 1) C, 2) T and F, 3) V, E, and A. However, C, finished around 1230, and T, dating simply from the thirteenth century, both contain traits which mark them as *champenois*.[16] On the basis of the use of the new determiner, a re-examination of the relationship between C and T would be in order. It is hardly likely that the two copyists, independently of one another, changed a *cest* or a *cel* in exactly the same ten passages. MS T has ten out of fourteen occurrences in common with C. Thus it is necessary to see if there is a factor which could have motivated the use of the two forms of the determiner *ce* in V, independently of any relationship with C and T or with either one or the other of them.

---

[14]  Micha did not know of G and I.
[15]  Micha, *La Tradition manuscrite*, 128.
[16]  Micha, *La Tradition manuscrite*, 39.

## 4.2 An Explanatory Hypothesis: is the New Paradigm CE (*ce/ces*) Compatible with the Old Subjective Value System or did it develop in the New Semantic Field?

We have shown that a factor could have come into play, namely that the new form is found almost exclusively in direct discourse. However, the fact that the two older forms *cel* and *cest* are also found mostly in direct discourse prevents us from claiming this as a distinguishing factor in the use of *ce*.

Because no clear correlation can be found between the appearance of *ce* and the prior existence of either *cel* or *cest* by themselves, we cannot establish a link between the new form and one of the old forms. We are left with one possible explanation: the development of *ce* could have been facilitated by the change in meaning of demonstratives as they passed through the various stages,[17] moving from a subjective value to a spatial value. Since we have noted that the two manuscripts which offer nearly all the uses of *ce*, C and T, are also the ones which do indeed use the new grammar for demonstratives, and also that three of those which follow the old grammar (A, E, and G) do not have the determiner *ce*, we can connect the two elements. There remains a small restriction that one cannot explain for the moment: V, which still has the old demonstrative grammar, contains two uses of *ce*.

How can one explain the correlation between *ce* and the new meanings for the demonstrative? We propose that it is not a cause and effect relationship, but rather two results of the same evolution toward a deictic system which is no longer subjective. What the new form and the new value of demonstratives have in common is the absence of a trait referring to the speaker.

---

[17] Marchello-Nizia, "Du subjectif au spatial," 121–41, and eadem, "From Personal Deixis to Spatial Deixis," 115–18.

# Part IV:

# Historical Perspectives on Digital Philology

# THE 'EAST PYNE CONSORTIUM' IN THE DAYS
## BEFORE THE *CHARRETTE PROJECT*:
## A BRIEF MEMOIR

ROBERT HOLLANDER
PRINCETON UNIVERSITY

This is an attempt to reconstruct the beginnings of the Dartmouth Dante Project.[1] It will be coupled with some observations concerning the origins of what was then commonly referred to as "Humanities Computing" in the Department of Romance Languages and Literatures at Princeton University, in which activity both Karl Uitti and I were involved. I had taught a course on Dante at Dartmouth College in the summer of 1979. Until then, despite the urgings of both my brothers-in-law (a physicist and a mathematician) and of a friend, Reinhardt Kuhn (a professor of French at Brown, who had a very large apparatus in his home that was somehow wired to the mainframe at the university and that included what resembled the teletype machine one found in brokerage houses bringing the good or bad news to investors), I thought the advocates of "humanities computing" were deluded, beguiled by their own technology-for-technology's-sake enthusiasms.

In fact (and in an attempt at self-defense), I must admit that I had not even heard of Roberto Busa, who had begun development of his monumental *Corpus Thomisticum* (www.corpusthomisticum.org) in collaboration with IBM in 1946. Nor did I know that the son of one of the two founders of the Hewlett-Packard Company, David Packard, a Harvard PhD in classics, was bringing about a revolution in his field with a project (the *Thesaurus Linguae Graecae*[2]) that would eventually have so profound an effect on how American humanists (and then others around the world) pursued their scholarship. Packard himself led in the

---

[1] In October 1993 the DDP was selected as an exemplary project by FARNET, one of the "51 Reasons to Build the National Information Infrastructure."

[2] Comparanda are the Duke Data Bank of Documentary Papyri (DDBDP) and the Advanced Papyrological Information System (APIS); also the Patrologia Latina Database (PLD).

Gina L. Greco and Ellen M. Thorington, eds., *Dame Philology's Charrette: Approaching Medieval Textuality through Crétien's 'Lancelot': Essays in Memory of Karl D. Uitti.* MRTS 408. Tempe: ACMRS, 2012. [ISBN 978-0-86698-456-0]

development of what was then the fastest small computer in the world, known as Ibycus, its output issuing only in Greek character font. However, in 1979 a visiting professor at Dartmouth would have had to be even more cautious about the Brave New World of humanities computing than was I (and I was extremely cautious) not to have realized that something of real interest was happening or, for most of us, was about to happen. John Kemeny's presidency had already had the effect of making Dartmouth (along with Carnegie-Mellon and very few other institutions) a center for the development of the computational aspects of information retrieval and dissemination in a number of non-quantitative fields of study. I remember attending several presentations tailored to the interests of social scientists and humanists given by personnel of the Kiewit Computation Center at Dartmouth. I had a harder time understanding what this all might mean to me than did my son, then several months shy of his tenth birthday. It seems unfair to have to report that Buzz (who within three years was designing his own computer games on a tiny Sinclair computer with a memory not much larger than that of a jelly doughnut) was just one of the people with whom I spent time during that period who saw the implications of the "new technology" for my professional development far more clearly than I. Indeed, like God, in the title of a Tolstoy short story, if I saw the truth, I waited.

In 1982, I returned to Dartmouth for a second Dante summer. One afternoon in our living room, only a few days into the term, I had what may be considered an obvious idea, but which at the time seemed an epiphany to its thinker. I had been considering the plight of my Dartmouth colleagues (Nancy Vickers, Kevin Brownlee, Stephen Nichols) who were involved in medieval romance literatures (and thus, at least from time to time, in talking about Dante). How, in light of Dartmouth's relatively undeveloped library resources in this field, could they possibly do the sort of preparation in which I believed so strongly, based in examination of the single most ample commentary tradition devoted to any Western secular work? And in that moment the obvious answer to my question overwhelmed me. The Dartmouth Dante Project, an assemblage of all the most important commentaries of the last seven centuries in easily consultable form, seemed a necessary adjunct to our field of study. Since I have recounted the narrative of how this idea was realized several times,[3] I shall not do it here. How-

---

[3] Robert Hollander, "Il *Dartmouth Dante Project*," in *Letteratura italiana e arti figurative*, ed. A. Franceschetti (Florence: Olschki, 1988), 1: 277–85; idem, "The *Dartmouth Dante Project*," *Quaderni d'italianistica* 10 (1989): 287–98; idem, "Il *Dartmouth Dante Project*: i commenti danteschi consultabili via Internet," in *Macchine per leggere: tradizioni e nuove tecnologie per comprendere i testi (Atti del Convegno di studio della Fondazione Ezio Franceschini e della Fondazione IBM Italia)*, ed. C. Leonardi, M. Morelli, and F. Santi (Spoleto: Centro italiano di studi sull'alto medioevo, 1994), 83–90; and idem and Stephen Campbell, "The Dartmouth Dante Project," *Computational Lexicology and Lexicography: Linguistica Computazionale* 6 (1992): 1: 163–79.

ever, I do want to underline two aspects of that narrative. The project probably could not have been accomplished without the support of the National Endowment for the Humanities, and that support was almost not forthcoming because of several reviewers whose backgrounds apparently allowed them only inadequate understandings of the proposal.

Projects in the humanities in those days (the early 1980s) did not often involve even elements of computing technology. With the magnificent exception of Packard's *Thesaurus*, the Endowment was not involved in "humanities computing" and gave little hint of an interest in ever becoming so. Thus an application for a major project in this area was a long shot; however, not applying was not an option, because other foundations, having basically given over large "hard-edged" humanities projects to the sole stewardship of the NEH, could be expected to fund a proposal only on a matching basis, i.e., to lend support after the Endowment had given its *imprimatur*. When I later read the (on balance) so-so responses of the anonymous reviewers, as applicants were entitled to do, I was amazed that we had been funded. While several of these reviewers obviously did not grasp the design and scope of the project because they were unfamiliar with the technology involved, one of them was obtuse enough (and I allow myself to hope that he or she will read these words, feeling the nettle of remorse) to wonder why the computer was the proper vehicle for this project and whether it could not be accomplished well enough through the use of microfiches. Credit probably belongs to the then-director of Research Programs at NEH, Harold Cannon, who had both the vision and the courage to support funding and obviously steered our application past some dangerous shoals. Eventually the Endowment put up, in two separate grants, more than $600,000 (basic computing costs in those days, even in relatively uninflated dollars, were much higher than they are today); Dartmouth and Princeton themselves, along with several private foundations, ended up contributing roughly two-thirds of that amount. With the award letter for its second grant, the Endowment sent notice that it was treating us as a bellwether: the success or failure of future similar requests from other institutions would be influenced by our ability to provide, in an effective and timely way, what we had promised. Knowing that (and hardly welcoming the resultant necessary sense of responsibility), I decided to open the project to public use well in advance of when we wanted to (i.e., after more work had been completed), with only a dozen or so commentaries consultable, on 8 October 1988. That was slightly more than six years after the idea found me in our living room in Hanover. And it would be another ten years before the launch of a second and larger enterprise, the Princeton Dante Project (www.princeton.edu/dante).

Ray Neff, then director of Humanities Computing at Kiewit, was the first person in a position to help who gave the project effective support. Dartmouth was interested in encouraging its faculty to envision major projects in the humanities, and the DDP fit this bill. Ray left for another institution just as the grant kicked in, and I left Dartmouth to return to Princeton in September 1983.

It was our extremely good fortune that the young Jeffrey Schnapp had just arrived (from Stanford) in Hanover as an assistant professor; he was not only far
more "computer-literate" than I, but he saw the possibilities of the project and
was willing to take over supervision of the Dartmouth end of the operation, over
the next three years, during the nine months that I was in Princeton. However,
the single decision from which we benefited most was Neff's choice of Stephen
Campbell to serve as manager of the project. Steve has been serving in one version or another of that capacity on and off for more than twenty years now, most
recently in collaborating with Kirt Johnson, both of them reporting to Malcolm
Brown (Dartmouth's Director of Academic Computing), in redesigning the old
Telnet interface for the Web in 2005. (The database [www.dante.dartmouth.edu]
currently contains seventy-two commentaries, completed between Dante's death
and the present, that are searchable in various ways.)

Those years (the 1980s) also saw the formation at Princeton of the East Pyne
Consortium. J. Arthur Hanson (a Latinist [whose wife was Ann Ellis Hanson,
the papyrologist] and friend of David Packard) and I had an earnest talk about
what the two of us could do to increase awareness among our colleagues of the
computer's resources for humanistic inquiry. At that time IBM, with the Prince-
ton-IBM Project Pegasus, was making the new PCs available to departments or
programs that were willing to develop projects involving the use of computers in
teaching. Art and I were able to convince the Dean of the College at Princeton
that several of the language-literature departments clustered in East Pyne Hall,
including our own (Comparative Literature, Romance Languages, and Classics),
should move into the twentieth century before it was over. Such a polyglot lot
was gathered under that imposing (or so Hanson and I hoped) name, the East
Pyne Consortium. IBM made roughly a dozen and a half PCs available for distribution to colleagues who were willing to involve computers in just about any
way in developing their courses. It is hard to imagine anyone today *not* using a
computer for such tasks, but (and this was only twenty years ago) we had a difficult time giving away all of those machines for only a pledge to make them
useful in designing and conducting one's courses. And the cost of the equipment
that IBM was donating was considerable: I myself had spent more than $6,000
(in 1982 dollars; I was fifty years old, my wife and I had two young children, and
that left under $2,000 in our savings account) to purchase my own PC, printer,
and modem in January 1983.

Karl Uitti was one of the colleagues who was a member of the EPC. I remember Karl being skeptical, as I had been, about the usefulness of computers
to humanists. The next thing I knew, he was deeply interested and involved with
his students in developing the *Charrette Project*. I am glad to be able to say that
Karl's first computer was furnished by the EPC.

Looking back on that experience from the vantage point of today, I find myself harboring the following thoughts. Karl, like many of us who develop such
projects for the benefit of our own work and that of our students and colleagues

and disciplines, spent his energy and intellectual resources gladly and without desire for financial gain from his activity. It was part of his contribution to the Romance philology he had loved all his professional life. And that is—in the opinions of many—as it should be. There are others who want to be remunerated for such efforts, as is also completely understandable. On the other hand, to make what seems to me to be a defensible and even a necessary distinction, those who have benefited from the largess of the American public, i.e., who have accepted taxpayers' money in the form of a federal or local grant, ought not to be able to profit from their labor until they have put back, for at least the potential use of others, what they have taken away. This, I believe, at least resembles NEH policy today, but for many years the government only insisted that one could not receive income from a project while it was still being funded. The instant the funding stopped, one could turn on the meter, and not return a cent to the taxpayers—a misuse, in my opinion, of the taxpayers' good will.

To conclude, I should like to address, in the name of all who have created databases that are available for use without charge, a related issue, the right of a private enterprise to make work available to all users of the Internet without asking permission or paying royalties to the owner of the intellectual property that is being redistributed. This is so obviously and absurdly wrong that one wonders why the participants in the controversy have allowed it to continue as long as it has. Theft is theft, and probably unnecessary for most academic work, as most scholars would only gladly make their books and articles available without fee. However, it is as wrong to take my work without my permission as to write another's name on it in place of mine, a sin the discovery of which used to place under a cloud the reputation of its perpetrator in any institution worthy of respect. *Ach, die schönen alten Zeiten!*

# A *CONJOINTURE* OF PHILOLOGY AND LITERARY THEORY: EARLY VISIONS OF THE *CHARRETTE PROJECT*

## GINA L. GRECO
## PORTLAND STATE UNIVERSITY

Chrétien de Troyes's *Le Chevalier de la Charrette*, a text recast and reinterpreted within a generation of its composition, has long been at the center of critical debates regarding such diverse issues as Lancelot's worthiness as a hero, the author's position on courtly love, and the role of the editor in textual transmission. It is thus not surprising that the romance became the focal point for one of the first major electronic projects devoted to an Old French text, the *Princeton Charrette Project*.[1] While previous publications have presented the *Charrette Project* in its various stages of development,[2] this essay revisits specifically the guiding principles that the team assumed at the very beginning of its endeavor.[3] In doing so, it raises the following questions: what is, and more significantly what should be, the relationship between methodology and technology in medieval studies? In other words, in the age of electronic technologies, how do we balance between,

---

[1] *The Princeton Charrette Project*, 24 August 2006, The Trustees of Princeton University, 15 October 2006 http://www.princeton.edu/~lancelot/ss. The project archive presents an electronic edition of the text, images and electronic transcriptions of the entire manuscript tradition, and extensive annotation of grammatical information and rhetorico-poetic figures. Web-based applications allow the reader to search and manipulate the material, and to move logically from one element of the archive to another.

[2] See the bibliography on the Publications page of the *Princeton Charrette Project* website for publications devoted to various aspects of the *Charrette Project*, its history and rationale, including essays by Greco, Long, Murray, Robinson, Shoemaker, Thorington, Paff, Pignatelli, Uitti, Witt, and Zarankin. Complete references to these works are also included in the bibliography to this volume.

[3] For a complete history of project participants and listing of contributors, see the Authors page on the *Princeton Charrette Project* website. For the period of time covered by most of this essay, team leaders were Toby Paff, Peter Shoemaker, and myself, working under the direction of Karl Uitti.

Gina L. Greco and Ellen M. Thorington, eds., *Dame Philology's Charrette: Approaching Medieval Textuality through Crétien's 'Lancelot': Essays in Memory of Karl D. Uitti*. MRTS 408. Tempe: ACMRS, 2012. [ISBN 978-0-86698-456-0]

on the one hand, putting the cart before the horse and, on the other, failing (like Perceval) to ask the question that has been served before us? The original *Charrette* team's guiding principles offer a useful entry into such a discussion, since it is due largely to these ideas that the project has withstood so well the march of time: it has been more than two decades and many generations of computers since we began work in a pre-Windows and pre-Internet environment.

In 1989, the year that saw the publication of both the Foulet-Uitti edition of *Le Chevalier de la Charrette*[4] and Bernard Cerquiglini's *Eloge de la variante*,[5] Professor Karl Uitti put several of his graduate students at Princeton University to work making electronic transcriptions of the *Charrette* manuscripts. By 1991, a committed core team, of which this author was a member, emerged with a conception of what would one day be the *Charrette Project*. The two generations, advisor and students, developed a vision based on an exploration of matters related to editing Old French texts and an understanding of the relationship between a static modern edition and a variable manuscript tradition, and of the relationships between authors and scribes. But while we shared these common concerns, we approached them from different angles: the students were initially more motivated by the theoretical writings of the moment, and aimed to prepare a new type of edition—or, rather, presentation of the text—that would reflect those theories and allow textual scholarship to respond to the theoretical discussion underway. Karl Uitti, on the other hand, was motivated more by his intimate knowledge of the poem's manuscript tradition and variations, the result of his recent work on the edition for the Classiques Garnier series and a strong long-term interest in scribal poetics.

Despite these varied perspectives, we sought to bring together theory and practice and to study relationships between authors and scribes. These same questions had already gained critical momentum with Paul Zumthor's concept of *mouvance* (1972),[6] integral to his theories of intertextuality. Cerquiglini's subsequent use of the notion *variance*[7] coincided with the beginning of our work. Zumthor and Cerquiglini were not the first to recognize the movement inherent in manuscript culture, nor were they the first to note the parallels between that

---

[4] Chrétien de Troyes, *Le Chevalier de la charrette (Lancelot)*, ed. Alfred Foulet and Karl D. Uitti (Paris: Bordas, 1989).

[5] Bernard Cerquiglini, *Eloge de la variante: histoire critique de la philologie* (Paris: Seuil, 1989).

[6] Paul Zumthor, *Essai de poétique médiévale* (Paris: Seuil, 1972).

[7] For more on the influence of these notions on our work, see Gina Greco and Peter Shoemaker, "Intertextuality and Large Corpora: A Medievalist Approach," *Computers and the Humanities* 27 (1993): 349–55. See also Zumthor, *Essai*, and idem, "Intertextualité et Mouvance," *Littérature* 41 (1981): 8–16, and Jean Rychner, *Contributions à l'étude des fabliaux: variantes, remaniements, dégradations*, 2 vols. (Neuchâtel: Faculté des lettres; Geneva: Droz, 1960).

movement introduced by scribes into a manuscript tradition and the recastings of texts performed by medieval authors. Indeed, as is well recognized, writing as rewriting was a technique of which the authors themselves were quite aware, one that they participated in consciously and spoke of frequently in their prologues or elsewhere in their texts.[8] Traces of authors' awareness and even mistrust of scribal interventions also survive, such as the *Estoire del Saint Graal*'s admonition to future copiers not to tamper with the text.[9] Scholars are equally aware of the similar *remaniements* effected by the scribes of certain codices, including the transformations performed on Chrétien's romances by the scribe of B.N. fr. 1450 and Guiot in B.N. fr. 794, each in an apparent attempt to build a coherent codex.[10] Karl Uitti, among others, wrote eloquently about these textual matters, grounding his analysis in a material study of the manuscripts, an approach that also informed work on the electronic archive.

Likewise, in the present volume, Douglas Kelly examines the juxtaposition in manuscript Chantilly 472 of divergent versions of the character Lancelot, arguing for a new way to appreciate not only the rewriting practiced by medieval authors and scribes, but also (and especially) the openness of the medieval reader, who accepted and enjoyed difference in a way that we medievalists have taken several generations to recognize. In doing so, he cites the importance of Keith Busby's work on the codex, as do Boyd and Murray in their call in the Afterword for an extension of the *Charrette Project* to include complete codices. Indeed, the Digby 23 Project that they describe is another, more recent, example of electronic scholarship informed first and foremost by philological principles.

These same kinds of philological principles informed the original student members of the *Charrette* team. Inspired by Roland Barthes's notion of the

---

[8] See for example the prologue to the *Lais* attributed to Marie de France and Chrétien's *Cligés.*

[9] "Car ce tesmoigne li contes ensi com vous orres conter cha auant que toutes les auentures del saint graal ne seront seues par homme mortel anchois en couient asses trespasser . mais en la sainte escripture qui fu enuoie en terre par la bouce ihesu crist en celui ne uerra on ia vn seul mot de fausete . Car cil seroit trop fel hardement plains qui oseroit adiouster menchoigne en si haute cose com est la sainte estoire uraie que li urais crucefies escrist de sa propre main": *The Vulgate Version of the Arthurian Romances*, ed. H. O. Sommer, vol. 1, *Lestoire del Saint Graal* (Washington, DC: Carnegie Institute, 1909), 1: 119.

[10] In particular, see Lori Walters, "The Creation of a 'Super Romance': Paris, Bibliothèque Nationale, fonds français, MS 1433," *Arthurian Yearbook* 1 (1991): 3–25, and eadem, "Le Rôle du scribe dans l'organisation des manuscrits des romans de Chrétien de Troyes," *Romania* 106 (1985): 303–25. Keith Busby's *Codex and Context*—cited by a number of essays in this collection—argues most cogently for the importance of reading any medieval text within its manuscript context. See *Codex and Context: Reading Old French Verse Narrative in Manuscript*, Faux Titre 221–222, 2 vols. (Amsterdam: Rodopi, 2002).

"writerly" text,[11] we sought to explore a new way to "read" the complexities of a romance's manuscript tradition, one that requires the reader to participate actively in the production of meaning. Yet we understood that Barthes's theoretical paradigm was useful for the project only because it provided a model for representing the medieval process of textual production, a process which inspired Karl Uitti more directly. Both students and advisor felt that the print medium did not facilitate a scholar's active engagement with manuscript tradition and, furthermore, that the electronic medium could best represent the *mouvance* inherent in manuscript culture.

The *Charrette Project*, then, represents the team's response to contemporary discussions in our discipline. In exploring these theoretical notions concretely within a text, this response acknowledges the roles of both author and scribe in textual production, and recognizes the value both of a good edition and of access to a complete manuscript tradition. To avoid the dangers of an inability to see beyond the printed page of the modern edition or of an uncritical valorization of any and all variation, we chose, from the beginning, to anchor the archive to a modern critical edition, while at the same time providing complete transcriptions and images of the extant manuscript tradition. In this way, the archive offers a central role to Chrétien's voice and text, as best established by philologists, while also including the complete testimonies of each scribe. The user is better able to appreciate the notion of an edition as a series of judgments based on a set of principles and can simultaneously explore a medieval textual tradition through searchable transcriptions and actual images. The project therefore has two main goals that are both scholarly and pedagogical: to offer literary scholars a representation of the text that allows for a consideration of the work of scribes as well as of authors; and to acquaint students with manuscript culture and train them to put textual theory into concrete practice.[12]

Of course, the *Charrette Project* was not the first to forge this idea of the edition of Old French texts grounded in an appreciation for the reality of the medieval text and its participation in a process of reproduction and recreation.

---

[11] In *S/Z* (Paris: Seuil, 1970), Barthes establishes a distinction between what he terms the "readerly" (*lisible*) and "writerly" (*scriptible*) text. See also idem, "De l'œuvre au texte," *Revue d'esthétique* 3 (1971): 225–32; trans. Stephen Heath, "From Work to Text," in *Image-Music-Text* (New York: Hill and Wang, 1977), 155–64.

[12] Indeed, as the references throughout the essay to advisor and student interactions show, the pedagogical value of the project was exploited by Karl and appreciated by all team members from the very beginning. Furthermore, scholars who, as graduate students, participated on *Charrette Project* teams were deeply influenced by the work. As can be seen in the essays contributed to this volume by Katherine Brown and Juliet O'Brien, the experience contributed not only to their understanding of Chrétien's poem, but more significantly, to their ways of reading medieval texts more generally and to the types of questions they formulate and explore.

To cite one important example, Rupert T. Pickens's 1978 edition of the *Songs of Jaufré Rudel* follows similar principles, providing all variants of the author's seven songs.[13] This and other similar editions served as inspiration to Karl and other team members in the project's early stages. But such a version of Chrétien's romance could not be offered in a printed edition, at least not in a user-friendly way, a realization which led us to consider the computer's strengths as a medium. We recognized that the computer would allow us to recreate and offer to scholars the manuscript tradition of Chrétien's *Lancelot* in a form that would be preferable to the printed book because it facilitates both the manipulation of data and the ability to compare variants instantaneously. At the time we were working with WordPerfect 4.0, a simple DOS-based word processing program, in a pre-Internet and pre-hypertext world. Yet, thanks to excellent advice from humanities computing specialists at Princeton's Office of Information Technology we did not let technology govern our perspective; rather, we had a vision about what technology could eventually do for us and, more specifically, what we wanted it to do for us. When hypertext became a possibility, we were ready for it.

It is important to keep in mind the fact that the *Charrette Project* was conceived using very elementary computers and operating systems. Yet, despite the limitations of the technology at our disposal, the project—as is attested by its current state—was not ultimately limited by those initial constraints, precisely because we focused from the beginning on the philological and theoretical interests of medievalists, and not on the capabilities of the available technology. We directed our attention to Chrétien's poem, as both poetic and historic object, to its manuscript tradition, and to the representation of that material in a new type of edition, which we came to term more aptly an electronic archive. Furthermore, we realized from the start that each choice we would face—and there were many involved in developing such a project—should be resolved in a way that would not preclude the pursuit of future avenues of research. Conscious of the fact that we can never escape our own value-judgments, we embraced ours in the project's guiding principles. Interest in manuscripts is therefore betrayed by the early architecture of the project. Later, the editorial grid Albert Foulet and Karl Uitti used to prepare their edition of the *Charrette* for the Classiques Garnier series served as the starting point for the database of rhetorico-poetic figures.

It would of course be naïve to say that we were not influenced by new technologies: after all, we were embracing that technology as the medium of our enterprise at a time when few humanities scholars were doing so, and the final product was as technologically innovative as philologically motivated. But our

---

[13] Jaufré Rudel, *The Songs of Jaufré Rudel*, ed. Rupert T. Pickens (Toronto: Pontifical Institute of Medieval Studies, 1978). See also Mary B. Speer, "Editing Old French Texts in the Eighties: Theory and Practice," *Romance Philology* 35 (1991): 7–43, and eadem, "Wrestling with Change: Old French Textual Criticism and *Mouvance*," *Olifant* 7 (1980): 311–26.

vision of the computer's potential for the medieval textual scholar remained a global one, inspired by the computer's strengths, particularly its ability to organize and manipulate complex material. We did not let any individual electronic tools or functions guide our work.[14]

As medievalists, the issue for us was thus the data, and the benefit of conserving all their details was immediately apparent. The transportation of the project files to various computer platforms and their manipulation with the electronic tools that became available would be an ongoing process; but data collection and preservation could proceed with even the simplest technology. Since our approach was grounded in respect for both the value of a good critical edition and the significance of a medieval manuscript tradition, we sought to preserve each of those entities, edition and manuscript, in their specific and actual states. Yet we intended to present them in an electronic medium that would allow the scholar to view, manipulate, and eventually examine the material in new ways.

As Cinzia Pignatelli demonstrates in the following essay, some of the data we chose to preserve and encode — such as short and long $s$ — proved not to be particularly meaningful, and the resulting markup is cumbersome and distracting. But our philosophy as we were starting out was that we should encode everything from the beginning — first, because it is always easier to remove information than to add it, but primarily because we wondered what information initially deemed useless might reveal itself significant. Were we to start afresh on a new text — or codex, as has Murray with Digby 23 — there are certainly decisions that we would revisit, and Pignatelli's guidelines would serve as an excellent guide in that process; nonetheless, there are some controversial choices that we would probably maintain.

For example, because manuscript transcriptions are provided in the archive as representations of steps in a process of textual production, they are offered without any editorial intervention. Currently, users of the archive often ask why we chose not to resolve abbreviations, and why we chose to respect the word spacing as it appears in the manuscript rather than as it would appear in a dictionary or edition. The first reason is that we were interested in presenting the medieval text as it really existed, in all of its uniqueness, in response to our respect for each manuscript's role in the process of textual production and contemporary discus-

---

[14] In this essay I will focus on our team's interests in medieval poetics and philology. But I must add that we could never have allowed ourselves to focus so exclusively on such issues, without concern for the specifics of technology, were it not for the support and, more importantly, the participation as full team members of several humanities computers from Princeton's Office of Information Technology. Our first colleague from OIT, Toby Paff, encouraged us to think beyond the technology's specific capacities and limitations, and to focus globally on what we as medievalists would like to do. Of course, such a course was productive only because of the ability of our colleagues from OIT to translate our vision into technological reality.

sion of the role of variants in medieval textuality and poetics. Second, we did not wish to make editorial decisions on the manuscript transcriptions that would result in the loss of data that a future researcher might need. The variants, diacritical marks, and early punctuation marks are of interest to linguists, text editors, and literary scholars. Moreover, we offer the transcriptions with direct links to a modern edition, which provides the user with a more accessible version of the poem. Furthermore, it was always our intention to provide various display choices to the user, including, for example, a display with abbreviations resolved, and yet another with abbreviations represented visually rather than by codes. But it was our goal to encode all manuscript details in the first and primary transcriptions so that these data would be part of the archive and could later be presented in a more readable fashion.

The first step of the original project was thus to establish a protocol for transcribing handwritten documents. This required creating both a set of codes to replace the manuscript abbreviations and symbols not found in modern character sets, and a way to encode information such as the presence and size of miniatures. As an example, let us examine the case of abbreviations. We first began with user-friendly choices, using word-processing programs to create codes that physically resembled the abbreviations on the manuscript, such as a WordPerfect superscript "a" to represent a superscript "a" on the manuscript. This proved unwieldy, so we quickly switched, in some cases reluctantly, to a more uniform, albeit less aesthetically pleasing, encoding system using Standard General Markup Language (SGML):

| User-friendly representation (ms abbreviation of quant) | SGML code |
|---|---|
| q$^a$nt | q&nt-alpha; |

Some might counter that the adoption of the often unreadable codes of SGML at an early stage in the project contradicts the claim not to let technology govern our vision; but, rather, this adoption points to an understanding of the computer not only as an ideal *medium* for recreating, representing, and manipulating a complete manuscript tradition, but also as a useful *tool* for studying and analyzing the data. Thanks to the help of Toby Paff, our humanities computing colleague, we realized that the visually satisfying representations made with a word-processing program were not useful for storing data. While we valued the computer's ability to present a manuscript tradition to the user, we valued equally the ability to search for items, and recognized SGML as a way at that time to ensure, first, that the files would be searchable and second, that we would not lose information over the long term.

The focus on preserving data was rooted in a goal of providing a complete, searchable record of the manuscript tradition so that future scholars could not only view the information, but also make queries on topics of their own choice.

It is a simple fact that it is easier to remove details than to add them. So, while the SGML tags were often unreadable—and at the time we began using them they provoked a strong negative reaction among many of our colleagues—we never intended for these files to be the only version available to the user. Rather, they were intended as searchable files, containing the details that could one day be the topic of a scholar's research, files sitting behind a more user-friendly version that would appear on the screen. Indeed, we imagined two different user-friendly versions—one with visual reproductions of the abbreviations, the other with abbreviations resolved, word spacing standardized, and punctuation added. We assumed that the resolution of abbreviations could be accomplished relatively quickly, in a semi-automated way. Owing to the immensity of the project, in particular the markup of linguistic and rhetorico-poetic annotations, those user-friendly versions of the transcriptions have not yet been realized. However, even if the conversion step has not been as clean and fast as we imagined, resolving and removing abbreviations from a file is certainly much faster than starting with a file in which abbreviations were resolved during the transcription, and adding back the occurrence of abbreviations by consulting the manuscript images. This was the logic that convinced us to strive to conserve every element of the data on the manuscript pages, and to do so in a way that the computer could recognize and retrieve the information.[15]

While the project's original principles dictated perfect fidelity to the manuscript, there were moments when this was not possible. Moreover, we recognized that transcribers needed to make judgments in the course of their work, for example, in passages where the actual word spacing is not clear. In theory, we tried to minimize those judgments by asking transcribers to choose a photographic solution by reproducing exactly what they saw on the manuscripts.[16] Since the work was prepared by many different generations of students, the judgments were not always made consistently. Nonetheless, the transcriptions as they exist

---

[15] We do nonetheless recognize that more user-friendly displays would facilitate the non-initiated user's manipulation of the archive, and thus developing character display is the top priority for the project's new generation, *Charrette Project 2* (CP2). Work on this step is currently underway, undertaken by Baylor University graduate student Stephen Bush under the supervision of CP2 Co-Director K. Sarah-Jane Murray.

[16] Since the transcribing was all done by students, over a period of many years and thus representing a succession of cohorts, there are errors and inconsistencies in their work. Manuscripts are handwritten documents and the legibility of human handwriting varies. As Cinzia Pignatelli points out in her essay in this volume, an inexperienced eye is not always equipped to "see" what the scribe "wrote." Pignatelli has carefully classified the types of errors transcribers made, which will help the CP2 team to proofread the transcriptions, but more importantly, her analysis of the *Charrette Project* transcriptions provides a theory of transcription that can be used fruitfully by future teams undertaking similar electronic archive projects.

have already proved useful to linguists, as demonstrated by Marchello-Nizia and Lavrentiev's essay in this same volume.

At first, the original *Charrette* team members attempted to annotate rhetorical and poetic figures during the manuscript transcription process, for the poetics of scribal practice was of great interest to us. But it soon became apparent that we could not make adequate progress if we tried to do everything at once, so we chose to focus on the manuscript transcriptions as phase one of the project. Beginning in 1997, once that first phase had been realized, members of the second generation of "charrettistes" turned their energy to an exhaustive study of linguistic and rhetorico-poetic properties of the romance.[17] Guided by the same respect for the medieval process of textual production and the same need to preserve all data for the use of future archive readers embraced by the first generation, they commenced the annotation of the words and figures of the romance. Due to issues of time, they undertook initially only to mark up the Foulet-Uitti edition, rather than every manuscript version of the poem. Nonetheless, since the archive allows for such easy comparison between edition and manuscript versions, scholars can efficiently take manuscript variations into account when doing quantitative studies.

In consonance with the project's initial goals, both the linguistic and poetic teams strove to encode the text with as much detail and nuance as possible, using categories that reflect the actual words and structures of the edition. For the linguistic team, which tagged each occurrence of each word for 23 possible properties (such as lemma, part of speech, line position, case for nouns, tense for verbs, etc.) this respect for the materiality of the word meant, for example, tagging according to a word's function in context, rather than according to its form. The linguistic team soon realized that, as much as their work was facilitated by electronic tools such as an interface that allowed for some automation, each word still needed to be analyzed in context, in its material reality.

The rhetorico-poetic team set out to map Chrétien's use of five key figures, chiasmus, enjambement, rich rhyme, *oratio*, and *adnominatio*, in order to analyze his poetic practice. While they limited their work to these five figures, they approached each one with a keen eye for detail, distinguishing, defining and tagging, for example, nine different types of rich rhyme and six categories of chiasmus. Obviously, the team responsible for the markup of these figures had to work directly with the text, line by line and word by word, as computers are unable to

---

[17] Their work is now available through the *Figura* database of the *Princeton Charrette Project*. For a complete listing of team leaders and members during this phase of the project, in which this author did not participate, see the Author's page of the project website. See Rafael Alvarado's essay in this volume for a discussion of the *Figura* database. A special volume of *Œuvres & Critiques* (vol. 27.1) devoted to Chrétien's *Charrette* includes essays, listed in this volume's bibliography, that demonstrate literary analysis performed using the database (by Long, Murray, Robinson, Thorington, Witt, and Zarankin).

recognize rhetorical figures unless there is a clearly-defined searchable aspect. That said, the manipulation of the text while under analysis, the organization and storage of the data found, their presentation and manipulation for searches and queries, all take advantage of the particular strengths of the computer. Moreover, they allow for a more rapid and comprehensive markup of the text (through tagging and searching) than can be accomplished without electronic tools.

At different stages in the work, new technologies emerged that allowed us to configure the data in the archive in ways that increasingly corresponded to our original vision. Most significantly, we collaborated with Princeton's humanities computing specialists who, themselves inspired by the project's principles and objectives, wrote applications to adapt emerging technologies to the project's needs. Indeed, such collaboration between literary scholars and humanities computing specialists provides one answer to the original challenge of balancing the relationship between methodology and technology in medieval studies. While it may seem counterintuitive, a literary scholar or philologist cannot create an effective merger of poetics and technology without working intimately, from step one, with a computing specialist, aside from the exceptional case of a scholar with deep expertise in both domains. It is only through such a collaborative and interdisciplinary process that technology can be brought to serve the medievalist's goals since it allows for the development of electronic tools and applications that are driven by the scholar's concerns. Yet creating an electronic project that responds to theoretical interests of the medievalist is only the first step. The next step is for scholars, who now have access to a growing number of electronic tools, to ask new questions of the texts, questions that take advantage of the particular strengths of these new media. Many of the essays in the present volume benefit from this marriage of technology and philology; they represent the potential of this new stage in a continuing *translatio*.

# Philological Perspectives on the Textual Corpus of the *Charrette Project*: A Rereading of the Transcriptions

Cinzia Pignatelli
Université de Poitiers, Centre d'études supérieures
de Civilisation médiévale de Poitiers

Translated by Gina L. Greco,
Portland State University

## 0. Point of Departure

Following the 1989 publication of his critical edition of Chrétien de Troyes's *Le Chevalier de la Charrette*, completed with Alfred Foulet, Karl Uitti decided to put his graduate students at Princeton University to work transcribing the extant manuscript tradition of the same poem. A pedagogical objective, central to the project, consisted in providing students with linguistic training in Old French through direct contact with the texts. This objective was coupled with a second noble ambition, that of intellectual cooperation and exchange beyond institutional and political boundaries. Karl was fond of championing this goal, realized through the creation of a textual archive available to all scholars via the Web. The archive provided the possibility—quite new at the time—of consulting and comparing the eight versions of the poem, all conserved in thirteenth-century manuscripts, through a few simple clicks of the mouse.

The pioneering nature of the project required the consideration of a series of questions concerning the presentation of the transcriptions: which computer language to use; how to number the lines to facilitate comparisons between different versions; what system(s) to use for the encoding of abbreviations, punctuation, and other diacritical marks too often ignored even in diplomatic editions; and finally, what significance to accord to the description of the material state of the manuscript or the size and forms of letters.

The intention was to propose for each manuscript a diplomatic, non-interventionist transcription. This is to say, a transcription that respected the material

Gina L. Greco and Ellen M. Thorington, eds., *Dame Philology's Charrette: Approaching Medieval Textuality through Crétien's 'Lancelot': Essays in Memory of Karl D. Uitti.* MRTS 408. Tempe: ACMRS, 2012. [ISBN 978-0-86698-456-0]

reality of the work of the medieval copyist, which makes each copy both a unique text, different from all the others, and yet one variant among many of an original work that the philologist tries to recapture.[1]

The textual archive thus elaborated is impressive for the modernity of its conception, the extent of its corpus (approximately 36000 lines), and the facility with which the user navigates from one file to the next. On the other hand, the extensive coding systems necessary to portray both the characters, abbreviations, and other signs that do not figure in modern character sets, as well as other physical elements of the manuscript page,[2] makes reading the transcriptions a rather daunting task. For that reason, few users have taken full advantage of the possibility of comparing the transcriptions with the scanned reproduction of the manuscript images available on the site. While the *Charrette* team was obliged to make many decisions early in the process, hindsight combined with the experience of scholars who have consulted the archive for their research suggest that some of those initial choices merit reconsideration.

Within the context of a research project financed by the French CNRS in 2002–2003, we undertook a 'transcodage' of the data so that it could be studied using the software Phoenix.[3] The process provided the occasion for a systematic review of the first 2200 lines of the transcriptions, approximately one-third of the corpus, and more selective verifications of the rest of the text.

This article provides both our suggestions for emending the archive's coding system and a summary of the corrections that we made to the original transcriptions after comparing them with the digitized images of the corresponding manuscript folios. Our formulation of a typology of errors made by transcribers in reading, interpreting, and inputting the data, and set of suggested emendations for improving the system of codes, should be useful to the members of

---

[1] On the reasoning for the inclusion in the archive of the entire *Charrette* manuscript tradition, see Karl D. Uitti, "Informatique et textualité médiévale: l'exemple du 'Projet Charrette'," *Le Médiéviste et l'Ordinateur* 37 (1998): 25–36, http://lemo.irht.cnrs.fr; and Gina L. Greco, "L'édition électronique de textes médiévaux: théorie et pratique," in *L'Épopée romane, Actes du XVe Congrès International Rencesvals (Poitiers, 21–27 août 2000)*, ed. G. Bianciotto et C. Galderisi (Poitiers: Université de Poitiers, 2002), 2:1045–50.

[2] Documented by an archive page titled *Transcription Key*, the codes follow the TEI (*Text Encoding Initiative)* directives which at that time recommended the use of *Standard General Markup Language* (SGML) for the preparation and exchange of electronic texts for scholarly research.

[3] The transcriptions of the eight manuscripts in clear form (with abbreviations resolved, modern word separation, and suppression of paleographical notes not relevant to linguistic analysis) were translated to neutral XML, considered today more reliable than SGML, so that they could be analyzed using Phoenix software, which allows for precise and effective philological querying. Phoenix was programmed with TUSTEP by Martin Glessgen (professor, University of Zurich) and Matthias Kopp (engineer, University of Tübingen).

*Charrette Project 2*, represented in this volume, who are reshaping the content of the archive to make it more readable and visually attractive.[4] We offer them in the same spirit of collegial collaboration that motivated Karl Uitti to create the *Charrette Project*. This essay stands as an homage to him, in recognition of the colossal enterprise that he initiated, as well as a contribution to the improvements he had envisioned and would certainly have accomplished himself had his time not been cut short.

# 1. Disconcerting Spaces:

## Word Separation

In medieval manuscripts, words are separated according to criteria that we often have trouble understanding, as our idea of the written word was formed essentially from practices established with the advent of print. This conceptual difficulty is magnified by the dense writing styles common in thirteenth-century manuscripts, which makes it difficult for the reader to distinguish the blank spaces of word separation within a sequence of characters. We thus have at our disposal few arguments for challenging the presence or absence of a space following an abbreviation sign, or for invalidating the reading of an unresolved continuous chain of graphemes proposed by the Princeton transcriptions.[5]

However, studies published since the completion of the transcriptions invite us to revisit some of the initial choices made. In particular, recent studies have demonstrated that when two lexical elements are joined graphically, there is sometimes doubling of either the initial consonant of the second element (if that which precedes ends with a vowel) or the final of the first (if the second begins with a vowel), in which case there is never a blank space.[6] These doubled

---

[4] Recognizing that all users do not need the same level of detail in the transcriptions, and moreover that nonspecialists, philologists, and paleographers have different interests, the project has transcoded the transcriptions into XML and plans to make these files available in different forms, with varying levels of markup. The user will be able to select from a range of formats and displays of codes and editorial interventions. Cf. K. Sarah-Jane Murray, "Informatique et textualité médiévale: l'exemple du *Projet Charrette*," *Cahiers de Civilisation Médiévale* 48 (2005): 219–26, here 221, and the archive page *Charrette-XML.doc* (http://www.princeton.edu/~lancelot/ss/media/docs).

[5] In the interest of readability, the next phase of the project could offer "critical editions" of the transcriptions, adding signs such as apostrophes or hyphens to indicate the separation or unification of graphemes into recognizable lexemes.

[6] Claude Buridant, *Grammaire nouvelle de l'ancien français* (Paris: SEDES, 2000), 462; cf. N. Andrieux-Reix, "Transcription, lisibilité, transgression: quelques problèmes posés par les éditions de textes médiévaux," in *Le Moyen Français: le traitement du texte (édition, apparat critique, glossaire, traitement électronique). Actes du IX<sup>e</sup> colloque international*

consonants, which could only belong to the same "word," serve to indicate that, despite the graphical agglutination, there are two clearly distinct lexical elements in which the one with a doubled consonant is a marked variant of the lexical form with single consonant. From this we deduce that, in a case where a pair of identical consonants appears at the junction of two elements, they *cannot* have a separator between them — a blank space would be redundant. Thus, for example, "*V t tos lib(ien)s del mont serra*" (A 5470, abbreviations resolved within parentheses) reads in MS E as "*V ttos . . .*" (literally, 'where all the good of the world will be'). In "*V q(ue) ces soit en ceste terre*" (F 6628) and "*(Et) as ses euz et as sabouche*" (E 1476) the final *s* of *ces* and *as* is attributed to the following word, thus the continuous sequences should be interpreted as "*V q(ue) ce-ssoit . . .*" ('où que ce soit . . .', wherever it be . . .), and "*a-sses euz et a-ssa-bouche*" ('à ses yeux et à sa bouche', 'to his eyes and to his mouth'), the dashes indicating the deglutination of forms that possess lexical status according to modern typographical standards.

The profusion of this phenomenon in MS E clarifies several readings that Alexandre Micha considered inexplicable or faulty.[7] Uitti's team, following Micha,[8] reads line 1145 as "*Kellsovillor espees fichierent*": the first sequence of characters, once interpreted correctly, contains two "words" with doubled initial consonants, which allow us to read the sequence without any ambiguity: "*Ke-lli-dui-llor espees fichierent*" ('que les deux enfoncèrent leurs épées', 'that they both thrust their swords'). The Princeton team reads line 1098 correctly, "*Mais aurescore iert illoz*," a line which Micha considered useless, interpreting it as a corrupted reading of: "*Mes au rescorre en ert li los*" (MS V, 'il sera louable de la secourir' 'there will be honor in the rescue').[9] If *illoz* is recognized as a variant of the pronoun *il* with the final consonant doubled, then the predicative adjective *os* ('daring') emerges,[10] which makes sense in the context of the dangerous situation Lancelot faces in the passage (cf. "*Ker al'entree, auoit portiers / Trestouz armez .ii. cheualiers / Qui espees nuez tenoient / Apres quatre serianz estoient / Si-tenoit cescuns vne hache . . .*" 1100 ff.

---

*sur le moyen français, Strasbourg, 29–31 mai 1997*, ed. Claude Buridant (Strasbourg: Presses Universitaires de Strasbourg, 2000), 55–63; S. Monsonégo and M. Henin, "Le traitement des groupements variables de morphèmes: Aspects lexicaux," also in *Le Moyen Français: le traitement du texte (édition, apparat critique, glossaire, traitement électronique)*, 149–64, and their bibliography.

[7] A. Micha, *La Tradition manuscrite des romans de Chrétien de Troyes* (Paris: Droz, 1966 [1st ed. 1939]).

[8] Micha, *La Tradition manuscrite*, 382.

[9] Micha, *La Tradition manuscrite*, 129.

[10] This solution, which offers a hypometric line, nonetheless seems preferable to the repetitive reading of C (*Si n'en iert mie talentos / Ne tant ne quant n'an ert jalos* 'he felt no desire at all, he was not one bit jealous'), as well as that of T, chosen by Foulet and Uitti for their edition (*Si n'en ert il mie jalos / Ne ja de lui ne sera cos* 'he was not jealous at all, and did not feel cuckolded'), which is not very courtly despite the justification given by the editors.

'Furthermore, doormen guarded the entrance: / two well-armed knights / with drawn swords; / behind them [there were] four men-at-arms, / each holding an axe . . .' [1088–1091][11]).

## Punctuation

The punctuation system used by the eight scribes to indicate syntactic or prosodic units is particularly sparse; it is limited to the period—placed mid-height in the line in MS T, but found at the foot of the last letter of the word, aligned with the bottom of the line in the other MSS—and a sign which looks like a modern colon or an upside-down semi-colon, forms which seem to have been considered equivalent in medieval writing.[12] These two punctuation marks are named respectively *colon* and *comma* in medieval treatises (for example, Papias, Jean de Gênes, Thomas de Capoue), the first prescribed to mark a medium pause, and the second a weak pause.[13]

The identification of these two signs is sometimes inexact in the archive's transcriptions: while researching the transmission of punctuation in the *Charrette* manuscript tradition,[14] we realized that the upside-down semi-colon, as well as its variant, which resembles the modern colon, was not always recognized as such and thus did not receive the SGML code (&puncl; or &punc2;) used for symbols not found in modern character sets; for example, it is treated as a simple period in A 1402, A 1974, A 2725, A 2880, A 3079, A 3531, E 1805, E 3428, and G 3881.

---

[11] All English translations of the *Charrette* are from *Lancelot, or, The Knight of the Cart*, ed. and trans. William W. Kibler (New York: Garland, 1981).

[12] Other dots used by scribes, to underline superfluous characters, will be discussed separately.

[13] The eight scribes do not seem to share similar understandings of the relationships between different graphic signs and oral pauses presented in contemporary rhetorical treatises: for example, use of the upside-down semi-colon is limited in most manuscripts to Discourse (to indicate the change in intonation required when *oratio recta* is read aloud), yet in MSS A (with only two exceptions) and F, the *comma* fills all punctuation needs as opposed to MS I whose scribe seems to use only the period, even in the rare passages of Discourse that we can identify with certainty (of course, the manuscript's fragmentary nature precludes significant analysis). Finally, the rate of punctuation is highly variable from one copy to another, which seems to indicate that the eight scribes have rather different views regarding the oral performance of the poem.

[14] The results are presented in Cinzia Pignatelli, "Présence et fréquence de la ponctuation dans les manuscrits en vers du XIIIe siècle: les huit manuscrits du *Chevalier de la Charrette* au banc d'essai," in *Systèmes graphiques de manuscrits médiévaux et incunables français: ponctuation, segmentation, graphies*, Actes de la Journée d'étude de Lyon, ENS LSH, 6 juin 2005, ed. Alexei Lavrentiev (Chambéry: Université de Savoie, 2007), 85–105.

Furthermore, in A 1525, A 3531, and E 1805, the punctuation sign was attached by the modern transcribers to the word that follows (for example, "*li-rois .tantost on-li amai(n)ne*" A 3531). This was done despite the notable difficulty of evaluating spacing in this set of manuscripts, and in spite of the medieval habit of drawing contiguous signs in a chain of writing with a single pen stroke whether or not they belong to the same lexeme. In the cases cited above, the punctuation mark does not appear to us any closer to the item that it follows than to that which it precedes. Opting for the first solution thus seems to us a choice which perturbs the reader, inviting him to consult the manuscript superfluously.

To resolve these issues, we believe that a global decision should be made to abandon the ambition of attempting to satisfy every potential reader, from the specialist to the amateur. Taking into account the most frequent placement of punctuation marks in thirteenth-century verse manuscripts, and statistical evaluation of each scribe's tendencies, it would seem acceptable to restore all punctuation marks to the base of the last letter of the preceding word, where the scribe surely intended to place them. Codicological notes would suffice to indicate any unusual placement of the signs, particularly since the archive also allows the user to view the manuscript images at a relatively good resolution. A linguist studying the history of graphic systems and punctuation, or a paleographer interested in the habits of an individual scribe, would not work solely from transcriptions, but would always return to the manuscripts. [15]

## Sequences of Minims

In the rapid writing common to thirteenth-century manuscripts, the scribes themselves did not distinguish clearly the *ductus* of an *n* from that of a *u*, and *m* could easily be confused with the sequences *ui/iu/ni/in*, likewise *n* with *ri*, especially if the *i* is not dotted. In such cases, the Princeton transcribers too often opted for "photographic" solutions, without trying to understand the scribe's intention. For example, in line 184 of MS E, transcribed as "*Mais irriez et main lefist*," the reading *main* is unacceptable from grammatical, semantic, and metrical perspectives. Without doing any violence to the material text, the sequence of minims could be interpreted as *marri* ('vexed, distressed,' TL 5, 1198), a reading which solves all of these problems. In line 237 of the same manuscript, the archive presents another visually faithful reading, "*Que uos apres euz n'allissons*," in which the pronoun *uos* cannot be the subject of the subsequent verb. Why then imagine the use of an agrammatical sequence on the part of the copyist, in the

---

[15] In light of the systematic use of long *s* in the thirteenth century, it is superfluous to encode it in SGML or XML. A single note would suffice to present the systematic exceptions (i.e. round *s* in final position in certain manuscripts, such as E and G, approximately 1 case per 100 lines), with additional notes identifying the episodic appearance of round *s* elsewhere.

case of what must simply be an imprecise realization of the form *nos*? Similarly, in the passage

> *Deuz liz furent aparoillie*
> *Enmi la-sale haut et lonc*
> *Et enmout vn autre selonc*
> *Plus beaux des-autres et-pl(us)-riche* (464–467)

Two long, high beds / were prepared in the hall; / alongside these was a third bed, / more resplendent than the others (corresponding to Kibler 460–464)

the "photographic" reading *enmout* of line 466 does not make sense. Yet experience with the relaxed hand of MS E's scribe, coupled with his habit of doubling the initial or final consonant in cases of graphic agglutination, allows us to piece together the reading *"enn-i-out,"* ('il y en avait', 'there was').

In this same manuscript, a trickier case is presented by certain forms of demonstratives and personal pronouns. In line 1769, the neuter demonstrative is interpreted correctly as *ce(n)* (tilde above the *e*). The same form certainly occurs in lines 2229, 4506, and 5308, in which the second minim of the *n* is elongated, yet the Princeton team reads *ceu/cheu*, as the scribe's writing would justify elsewhere (for example, lines 113, 158, 315, etc.). In lines 710, 2388, and 2951, either *geu* or *gen* could be read for the first-person singular subject pronoun, even though the strong predominance of the form *gen* in the manuscript might favor its generalization. The spellings in *-n*, formerly noticed by Foerster who was the first to connect them with the nasalized Lorraine *amin*,[16] are well attested in Normandy: Eggert finds *cen, chen,* and *icen* in documents from the Norman archives and indicates the survival of the form *chen* in the contemporary dialect of Jersey Island.[17] Meyer first recognized a form *cen*,[18] frequent in the north, which he then noted in Normandy.[19] Dees identifies it with high frequency in Normandy, and less in the Somme, Haute-Marne, and the Vosges.[20] Rydberg cites *jen* only in

---

[16] Wendelin Foerster, "Zur altfranzösischen Uebersetzung der Isidorschen Synonyma," *Zeitschrift für romanische Philologie* 1 (1877): 397–402, here 402.

[17] B. Eggert, "Entwicklung der normandischen Mundart im Département de la Manche und auf den Inseln Guernesey und Jersey," *Zeitschrift für Romanische Philologie* 13 (1889): 353–403, here 396.

[18] Paul Meyer, "Maître Pierre Cudrifin, horloger, et la ville de Romans (1422–1431)," *Romania* 21 (1892): 39–52, here 40, n.1.

[19] Paul Meyer, "Recettes médicales en français, publ. d'après le Ms. B. N. Lat. 8654 B," *Romania* 37 (1908): 358–61, here 361.

[20] Anthonij Dees, *Atlas des formes linguistiques des textes littéraires de l'ancien français* (Tübingen: Niemeyer, 1987), 10.

Normandy.[21] Subsequent to these studies, linguistic manuals definitively localize to Normandy the forms in *-n* (although the forms identified in the past suggest a more varied diatopic distribution).[22] And we are not the first to have recognized a clearly Norman coloring in MS E, in addition to a Walloon layer that would testify to the text's passage through the north at some moment during its transmission.[23] As for the variants in *-u*, they would be forms from the east: *jeu* is known in the northeast;[24] as for *ceu*, Zink[25] and Buridant[26] consider it also an eastern form, after Rydberg,[27] as well as Dees,[28] had noticed it in the west (Charente, Yonne, Deux-Sèvres, etc.) but also along the eastern frontier.[29]

---

[21] G. Rydberg, *Geschichte des französischen ə* (Uppsala: Almqvist & Wiksells Buchdruckerei, 1907), 636.

[22] For example, Gérard Moignet, *Grammaire de l'ancien français* (Paris: Klincksieck, 1988), 43; Gaston Zink, *Morphologie du français médiéval* (Paris: PUF, 1997), 80; Buridant, *Grammaire nouvelle*, 124.

[23] Micha (*La Tradition manuscrite*, 60) speaks of a Norman-Picard dialect (cf. Wendelin Foerster, ed., *Der Karrenritter (Lancelot)*, in *Sämtliche Erhaltene Werke nach allen bekannten Handschriften* [Halle: Niemeyer, 1899], 4:iii). A Norman redaction would explain the elevated percentage in this text not only of the neuter demonstrative forms *cen* and *chen* (Anthonij Dees, *Atlas des formes et des constructions des chartes françaises du XIII^e siècle* [Tübingen: Niemeyer, 1980], n° 27 and 33), but also the use of the spelling *-eit-* instead of *-et-* (n° 164) and the almost exclusive use of the variant *ker* of the conjunction *car* (Dees, *Atlas des formes linguistiques des textes littéraires*, n° 478). However, the intervention of a Walloon hand at some point in the text's transmission explains the use of initial *wa-* for *gua-* (Dees, *Atlas des formes et des constructions des chartes françaises*, n° 251) and *vau-* for *vou-* in the forms of the verb *vouloir* (Dees, *Atlas des formes linguistiques des textes littéraires*, n° 411). The rather frequent (and confusing) use of the form *il* in place of the subject pronoun *ele* (E 614, 2063, 4123, 5393) also seems characteristic of Northern dialects (Buridant, *Grammaire nouvelle*, 417). The frequency of such phenomena in this manuscript, compared to that in charters and literary texts definitively localized to Normandy by Dees (*Atlas des formes et des constructions des chartes françaises* and *Atlas des formes linguistiques des textes littéraires*), compels us to recognize its 'Norman-ness' (cf. Cinzia Pignatelli, "Une approche de la tradition textuelle du *Chevalier de la Charrette*: la quantification des phénomènes régionaux," in *Cinquante années d'études médiévales: À la confluence de nos disciplines, Actes du Colloque organisé à l'occasion du cinquantenaire du CESCM (Poitiers 1er-4 septembre 2003)*, ed. C. Arrignon, M.-H. Debiès, C. Galderisi, and E. Palazzo [Turnhout: Brepols, 2006], 741–52, here 751).

[24] Rydberg, *Geschichte des französischen ə*, 633; cf. Moignet, *Grammaire*, 38.

[25] Zink, *Morphologie*, 80.

[26] Buridant, *Grammaire nouvelle*, 124.

[27] Rydberg, *Geschichte des französischen ə*, 772–80.

[28] Dees, *Atlas des formes linguistiques des textes littéraires*, 9.

[29] Curiously, only Moignet (*Grammaire*, 43), cites it among the Anglo-Norman forms; although Eggert ("Entwicklung der normandischen Mundart," 396) finds an

## Similar Graphemes

The confusions induced by the juxtaposition of minims are not the only ones to have interfered with transcription of the eight manuscripts. They frequently combine with resemblances between letters with rounded forms, such as *c, t, e, s,* and *r,* or letters with an ascender, such as *f, l,* and long *s,* to create readings such as *\*liet* for *uet* E 1038, *\*volloit* for *valoit* E 5136, *\*tren* for *trai* E 5194, *\*eissez* for *eissir* E 5548, *\*tiede* for *ne de* A 1211, and *\*cuident* for *cuidoit* A 3133. Of all the graphemes confused by transcribers, these exchanges represent the source of the most numerous errors.

Most of the time, deciphering difficulties lead to readings that either do not make sense or are unacceptable from a lexical, grammatical, or metrical standpoint. Certainly, the students assigned the task of transcribing, and who thus familiarized themselves with Old French *in vivo,* through practice, did not have an easy task. Nevertheless, it would have been useful for the students to verify doubtful readings with an *auctoritas* in order to evaluate the possibilities of alternate combinations. It would also be helpful, now that the students' work has been placed at the disposition of the public, to signal the project's pedagogical nature to that public.

The following list of errors represents the kinds of pitfalls that the novice reader of Old French manuscripts may encounter, and is provided—in recognition of the centrality of Karl Uitti's pedagogical goal—as a sample for those who are first-time transcribers or who are teaching first-time transcribers.

Remaining with MS E, in line 546 *\*ais* is not a preposition that could introduce *la charete,* rather, it should be read as *ens;* in line 374, the parallel with the syntagma *en-la-bouche* should have raised suspicions regarding the form *\*eleuer,* which should be read *el-cuer* ('dans le coeur', 'in the heart'). Likewise, in line 1265 the possessive *ma [compagnie]* could have facilitated the interpretation of the form, in the same line, preceding *solax: mis* (with long *s*) rather than *\*mil* ('my pleasure'); and in line 2504 why not question the initial photographic reading of the article *\*une,* unacceptable with *chevaliers,* and which should be interpreted as *uns?* In MS V, *\*locil* is impossible at the end of line 5096, not only because it would make the line hypermetric, but also because of the rhyme with *voeil* of the preceding line (thus, the sequence should be *l'oeil*). In line 5125, the reading *le pont soz \*lenc* ignores the sense of the text, in which it has been a question of the *pont soz l'eue* (the 'Pont-sous-l'Eau') that Lancelot must cross. In MS F, the form *li-\*cuiu(er)tj* of line 6635 should have invited reinterpretation since the sequence *tj* is unlikely at the end of a word in Old French (especially as an ending in the masculine subjective case). Furthermore, the grapheme *z* is always elongated underneath the line in medieval writing, thus the reading *li-cuiu(er)z* ('the villains').

---

example of *ceu* in a thirteenth-century tale written in Normandy (specifically, the south of la Manche), which he compares to the form *chu* of the contemporary Guernsey dialect.

In T 96, the reading *(Et) q(ua)nt il respondre *il pot* offers a doubly questionable subject pronoun: is *il* for *li* an error of reading, an exchange of similar graphemes, or is it a typo produced at the moment of data entry?

Sometimes abbreviation signs are not recognized, and are instead interpreted as an alphabetic character. Such is the case, for example, with *ogie (V 5066) which should be transcribed in SGML as *&com;gie* ('*congié*'); the apostrophe of *ml't* (F 6595) should have been encoded, as elsewhere, as *ml&apost;t* ; and the abbreviated form for *Lanc(elot)* is transcribed photographically as *Laut* (E 3797), and leads to three errors (confusion of *n/u*, exchange of *c/t*, and disregard for the abbreviation sign which should be encoded as *&apost;*). The encoding of the form *ue&n-nine* (F 5883 or 6273) references an abbreviation in the form of a superscript 9 at the end of a word which, borrowed from Latin script, replaces the ending *us* (*venus*). Yet, in the same syntactic context and in the same manuscript, in lines 6119 and 6132, we find the form coded as *ue&n-u*, which corresponds to *venu*. As such a twist away from a two-case declination has never been established in this Picard manuscript, the error must not be from the medieval scribe but from the modern transcriber, who has either misread the abbreviation in the form of a superscript 9 as an *n*, or mistranscribed the code.

## Additions, Omissions, and Inversions

Of course, not all of the incoherencies in the text are the work of the modern transcribers. Even when the philologist chooses to respect *variance*, he is obliged to recognize that negligence and distraction can generate unacceptable forms in the quill of the medieval copyist. Grapheme confusion, for example, was widespread among medieval scribes who did not always understand what they were reading.[30] (The latter often show that they acknowledge their own errors by crossing out words or writing a correction directly over an error.) Although using another, more sophisticated medium of both writing and correcting, the modern transcriber is subject to the same inattentions as the thirteenth-century copyist; his incomprehension of the source text is further aggravated by the distance between the two linguistic systems.

Hurried data entry may be responsible for inversions of characters (i.e., *veniot* for *venoit* V 2796, *bein* for *bien* V 5136), skipped letters (i.e., *Nse* for *Ne se* V 3692, *Ssen* for *Si s'en* V 4128), or the omission of entire words[31] (notably, the skipping of rhyme words in v. 1017–1020 of MS C: *atendre/a-descendre/descendue/atandue*), types of errors of which the medieval scribe was responsible (i.e., *S* in-

[30] For example, *Est ce songes *ouous relles* for *Est ce songes ou-uos reues* F 6363 (cf. C *Est ce songes ou vos resvez*); *p(ar) mes *cels n'i ara garde* for *par mes oels n'i ara garde* G 1194 (cf. C *p(ar) mes ialz vos n'avrez garde*).

[31] By way of example, we note an average of two graphemes omitted every 1000 lines in the transcriptions of MS T, and 3 to 4 in MS V.

stead of *Si* in F 5825, *\*hu* for *hui* in A 1815, *\*l uenoison* in place of *la uenoison* in T 2560, *\*tiraz* in T 207 which should have been written *tira(n)z*, as the rhyme with *soupirant* in the following verse would suggest) and which he sometimes indicated with intra-linear insertions (i.e., a superscript *t* after *atan* to complete the adverbial form in T 4651, and the sequence *q(u'i)l* added supralinearly in E 4105).

When he adds inexistent elements, the transcriber—ancient as well as modern—often seems less guided by his eyes than by his expectations. As a result, attention to the textual reality decreases. If a doubling of letters is common in the manuscripts after an initial capital (i.e., *\*A a grant tropiax . . .* F 7000–7001 for *A grant tropiax . . .*, *\*Ddes qu'il uos plest* T 2007 for *Des qu'il . . .*), the transcriptions also offer "rich" readings, for which the motivation is easily understood: *\*de soz* for *soz* V 4562, *\*ia la laissast* for *la laissast* T 223au,[32] *\*fra&h-bar;ncoise* T 42 (where the *n* is only represented in the manuscript by the tilde over the *a*). In rendering the lines 223ao *si com ele. espoire* ('just as she hopes') and 223dg *facent une letiere. seure* ('make a safe litter'), the transcriber lets himself be led by the abundant punctuation that the scribe of MS T adopts even in this long digression of which he is probably the author. Assigned according to precise criteria (to emphasize a coordination or subordination, a parallelism in the line, the end of an enjambment, the opening or closing of direct discourse, or to separate a verb from its prepositional complement),[33] the punctuation mark nonetheless does not appear in any case between a verb and its subject or between a substantive and its attribute.

Finally, in these diplomatic transcriptions, the reader sometimes finds modern diacritical marks, such as quotation marks to open and close direct discourse in the first sections of MS E (i.e., E 72–81, 89–94, 134–143, etc.), with an occasional neglect of symmetry (i.e., E 242–?, 836–?, 910?). The isolation of this practice to one section of one manuscript suggests a lack of coordination between the different teams who produced the work.

## Capital Letter Usage

In medieval scripts, the use of capital letters, insofar as they can be distinguished from the lowercase form, does not necessarily follow the same criteria as in modern typography, which itself varies from language to language and across time periods. The scribe of MS T uses a capital R rather often, but not systematically, to accentuate the first letter of the nouns *Roi* et *Roine*, perhaps out of respect for their rank. The Princeton archive takes into account this atypical usage.

MS E, which has two columns of text per folio, presents a particularly remarkable use of capitals for the last letter of each line in the second column. These capi-

---

[32] As this interpolation, inserted after verse 223, is unique to MS T, the lines containing it are numbered alphabetically.

[33] Cf. Pignatelli, "Présence et fréquence."

tals are set off from the rest of the text, forming a vertical line that accentuates the right-hand margin of the folio. The first letter of each line in both columns is also set off from the rest of the line, creating another set of vertical rows down the left-hand margin and center of each folio, resulting in an elegant layout.

The transcriptions of this manuscript treat the *j* as upper case, for instance, in the initial position of the words: *j-va* 131, *justice* 717, *jure* 755, and *jre* 173. However, in the manuscript, the *j* is only used as a positional variant of *i*. This occurs when it falls in the initial position, following a large initial and at the end of a line; the latter case occurs only in column *b* of the folio, in which the final letter is separated from the rest of the text.[34] Furthermore, even if its format is always rather imposing, nothing in its *ductus* allows us to discern whether it really is a capital letter except when it is placed in initial line position and final line position in the right-hand column. Although this was a decision made at the initial stages of the project, ostensibly to recognize the manuscript's creative use of vertical columns of capital letters, in our view the attribution of a capital *j* seems redundant: its different nature is already marked by its position. For these reasons, we suggest simplifying both transcription and reading by marking as capital letters only those located in initial and, in column *b*, final positions in the line.[35]

One of the transcribers of MS A uses the sign $, which could be interpreted as a code for a capital form, for the *s* in the following words: *vius* v. 2624, *cuers* v. 2943, *rois* v. 3531, *escus* v. 3605, *vos* v. 3848, *son* v. 5245, *tost* v. 5659. In fact, these signs correspond to examples of the long *s* found so frequently throughout the archive, and in medieval scripts in general, that we have argued against encoding them.[36] In any case, the isolated use of the symbol *$* brings us back to the problem of a modern transcriber adopting different conventions to represent identical signs within the manuscripts, and more fundamentally, the lack of justification for such an initiative.

---

[34] For example, the *i* of the words *moi* (v. 4187) or *merchi* (v. 4519), placed at the end of a line, is not drawn like a *j* because these lines appear in the left-hand column of the folio, whereas these same words are written with a final *j* (in upper case) at the end of lines 137 et 144, which lie in the right-hand column.

[35] We must, however, mention the uppercase L, R, and V used readily by this scribe in initial position and after a large capital. We are presently unable to understand the criteria for this use. For some analogies, see G. François, "L'émergence de la majuscule dans la *Chanson de Roland*," *Revue de Linguistique Romane* 70 (2006): 41–52.

[36] In T 6180, the final letter of the word *Cels* is not a capital, as the transcription might lead us to believe (*\*Cel&S1;*). On the other hand, in F 6729, the code *&s-e;* is inadequate for representing an *e* written over a long *s*, the superimposition of a diacritical sign on any letter meriting an SGML code in addition to the one used to represent the long *s* (see the archive page, *Transcription Key*).

## The Conventions of Medieval Script

Medieval scribes' use of certain alphabetic characters and diacritical marks placed above, below, and in the margin of the lines of text were meant to indicate supplementary readings to all who would manipulate the manuscript, beginning with the other tradesmen responsible for its creation (corrector, rubricator, binder, etc.), to those meant to use it, and to the future scribes called upon to recopy it. It is thus important, prior to retranscribing them, to understand the significance attributed to the position of signs set around the lines of text, and also to review the set of codes with an eye to reflecting better a sign's meaning through its code.

As a general rule, it seems that it would be better to take account of any superscript or subscript signs *after* transcribing the principal character, which is most often modified by the intralinear elements. In MSS A, C, and T, for example, the *c* superposed above *v* fills a role of multiplier, which in French—Old as in modern—is expressed by a lexeme placed after the number to which it refers (i.e., five hundred). Therefore, to facilitate reading and comprehension of these superscripts, and to accentuate their modifying role in relation to the head of the syntagma, we would prefer that the modern transcription present the superscript number after the principal number: *v[add place=supralinear]c[/add]* rather than *[add place=supralinear]c[/add]v.* Yet in a case such as this one, where the superscript sign should not be considered as a copyist's second thought, but rather as a diacritical mark modifying the principal character, a more elegant solution would consist of adopting a complex substitution code, such as those in the archive used to represent a tilde or a small superscript *a* through the SGML sequences *&xx-til;* and *&xx-a;* (in which *xx* represents the letter or sequence of the principal characters, while the sequence following the hyphen describes the type of diacritical sign used for the abbreviation of a letter or syllable). In this case, we could imagine the code *&c-v;,* while the marker *[add]* would be reserved for corrections introduced by scribes *a posteriori.*

Another very common practice in medieval manuscripts is expunctuation, which consists of adding a dot or dots below a single or group of characters written in error, to indicate that they should be ignored. We find an example in G 2643 below an isolated *s* in front of *et.* The copyist, whether distracted or rushed, had begun too early to write the form *soef,* which is found after the conjunction. Other examples are found in the series of dots below *millor* in G 3797, *donoit* in T 5866, and *tuit* in T 5950. Our use of the archive indicates that it would be preferable for the modern transcription to indicate the expunctuation *after* the form that the medieval scribe rejected, for example *tuit[add place=infralinear]. . .[/add]* rather than *[add place=infralinear]. . .[/add]tuit.* In F 6001, it is the sequence *ne-saille* which is expunctuated by the four subscript dots, yet the encoding used in the modern transcription encodes a single dot under *ne,* and then three successive ones below *saille*, as if the three dots referred only to *saille*.[37] The reader's confusion would be alleviated if an editorial apparatus described and justified the encoding of special characters and the order followed for the transcription of intralinear elements.

## 2. Some Consequences: Phantom Lexemes

As Project Co-Director Sarah-Jane Murray has stated, "Certains choix élémentaires se sont imposés dans la transcription: par exemple, là où trois lignes verticales pouvaient représenter un 'u' suivi d'un 'i' ou un 'm', etc. nous avons opté pour le choix évident et nécessaire pour obtenir un mot en ancien français."[38] Despite this principle, the student transcribers inadvertently coined many lexemes new to Old French. We think it would be helpful to future proofreaders of the archive, as well as to scholars contemplating a similar project, to present the types of errors that generated these mistaken readings:

• confusion of similar letter pairs:

*o* for *e*, i.e., *\*auors* T 1503 > *avers*, and *\*sousouffre* E 1833 > *seu-souffre*; *b* for *h*, i.e., *\*bors* V 4981 > *hors*; *r* for *t*, i.e., *se \*guere* V 1228 > *se guete*.

• minim confusion:

*\*aleme* A 317 > *aleüre*; *\*canrine* A 5552 > *caunue* (?); *\*chimer* E 4309 > *clinner*; and *\*gingue* G 269 > *gingne* (variant of the verb *guignier*) 'to wink'.

Our second example proposes an unattested, yet plausible, variant of *chanvre/chanve*, for which the forms *canve/canvie/camvene*[39] and *canvne*[40] are attested (the second *u* in our reading would have a consonantal value). The rhyme with *tenue/tenvre* in the preceding verse, additional evidence for a bisyllabic form here,

---

[37] In MS T, the copyist makes abundant use of erasures, expunctuations, and intralinear additions; in trying to account for all these interventions, the modern transcription becomes unreadable, as in 6980 which notes the supralinear addition, but neglects to encode for an erasure in the same line: *Bien [add place=supralinear]sai[/add]serai touz serai desm(em)brez.*

[38] Murray, "Informatique et textualité," 220.

[39] A. Tobler and E. Lommatzsch, *Altfranzösisches Wörterbuch* (Berlin and Wiesbaden: Franz Steiner Verlag, 1915–2002), 2:233.

[40] Frédéric Godefroy, *Dictionnaire de l'ancienne langue française et de tous ses dialectes du XI$^e$ au XV$^e$ siècle* (Paris: Bouillon, 1880–1902), 9:41. Cf. W. von Wartburg, *Französisches Etymologisches Wörterbuch* (Bonn: F. Klopp, 1928–2003), 2:210.

is also used by Chrétien in the *Roman de Perceval*[41] and appears again in the thirteenth century in the *Miracles de Nostre Dame* and the le *Roman de la Rose*);[42]

- inversion of graphemes:

*\*lature* in *Siuoit l'un lature apie requerre* E 2712 > *Si-uoit* [= *vet*] *l'un l'autre a-pie requerre*, a correction which would also fix the line's meter.

- deciphering difficult forms

*\*cheuer* E 4817 > *chaier*, from CADERE; the metaplasm in *–ir*, characteristic of Picard, but which also appears in many Old French literary texts,[43] is complicated by the spelling *ie* for *i*, frequent in Normand.[44] MS A, heavily Picardized,[45] offers *cair* (cf. *cheoir/chaer/chaoir* in the other manuscripts).

*\*coue* E 4844 > *corte* (?); we read this form as a variant of *coute* (cf. C, I, T *coute*, A *kiute*, V *coite*), to be corrected perhaps to *coite*, the latter matching a spelling the same manuscript uses later, in line 5551. The word does, however, invite other possibilities, for example, from our corpus, line 1211, A *coce*, G *colte*; see also *cote/coste/couste/cutre*,[46] *coulte*,[47] *coite/coutre/kurte*.[48]

## 3. Some Suggestions by way of a Conclusion

After proposing a typology of errors in the transcriptions, and illustrating the potential results of inattention and inexperience, we can arrive at some basic principles for the benefit, first, of our colleagues who are undertaking the revision of this important component of the *Charrette Project*.[49] This revision is essential, for the transcriptions of the manuscript tradition of Chrétien's romance add significant value to the archive. Yet the value of these principles is not limited to

---

[41] See *Le Roman de Perceval*, ed. William Roach (Geneva: Droz, 1959), 1165–1166.

[42] Cf. Tobler and Lommatzsch, *Altfranzösisches Wörterbuch*, 2:233.

[43] Cf. Dees, *Atlas des formes linguistiques des textes littéraires*, c. 264.

[44] Cf. Carl Theodor Gossen, *Grammaire de l'ancien picard* (Paris: Klincksieck, 1970), § 10. On the Norman coloring of MS E, see above, n. 23.

[45] Cf. Pignatelli, "Une approche de la tradition textuelle," 749.

[46] Godefroy, *Dictionnaire de l'ancienne langue française*, 9:232.

[47] Godefroy, *Dictionnaire de l'ancienne langue française*, 2:333.

[48] Tobler and Lommatzsch, *Altfranzösisches Wörterbuch*, 2:967–68. Cf. also Wartburg, *Französisches Etymologisches Wörterbuch*, 2:1492–93.

[49] This ambitious revision is being undertaken under the direction of Gina Greco, professor at Portland State University, and K. Sarah-Jane Murray, professor at Baylor University, with a team of young scholars possessing the necessary linguistic knowledge. The new transcripts will be published on the *Charrette Project 2* site.

the *Charrette Project*: we anticipate that these suggestions could prove useful to others who would like to initiate a similar textual transcription project.

## What Transcription?

The decisions regarding what information is made available need to be reconsidered, taking into account the intended public. Even if the team chooses to encode descriptions of all aspects of the text and its medium, such information can be relegated to a critical apparatus that the non-specialist can ignore. The use of long *s* and the position of periods (as immediately following the last letter of the preceding word) could be assumed, thus requiring markup only for significant diversions from the established rule. As for the description of the different forms of the letter *r*, or of a particular abbreviation sign, as well as each scribe's calligraphic variants, these subtleties require such a level of technical competence that the degree of fidelity to the material manuscript risks being insufficient for the needs of a paleographer, who will need to refer to the manuscript itself, or its image.

## Reading

• Taking into account the above suggestions for reassessing the type of transcription desired, transcribers can focus on developing sensitivity to the pitfalls of medieval script and a solid understanding of its conventions (value of abbreviations, modes of punctuation, use of diacritical marks, etc.), instead of on rare paleographic skills.

• We believe that transcribers also should not focus solely on producing a "photographic" reproduction of the text. Rather, their interpretation of what they see should be informed by existing descriptions and studies of the manuscript's hand and language. This approach would help them to recognize scribal particularities such as the doubling of initial consonants in MS E and the placement of punctuation in MS T.

## Interpretation

• There now exist simple computer programs that allow the user to juxtapose parallel versions of the same line. These tools could be used by the transcribers to compare different manuscripts, a process which can often clarify a reading that seems incomprehensible in one manuscript.

• Automated query software, designed specifically for philologists, can easily flag low-frequency forms, thus alerting the scholar to check the item.

• A philological rather than paleographical approach would also use metrical consistency and syntagmatic coherence to detect omissions and insertions.

• We believe that complete mastery of Old French and its regional variations should be a *condicio sine qua non* for future endeavors of this kind. Most of the forms that the Princeton students did not recognize were simply rare lexemes or regionalisms, poorly documented in textbooks, but exceptions appear in any standard language, including Old French. And in the thirteenth century, the period during which all the archive's manuscripts were produced, the written Francien *koiné* was not yet widespread and the vitality of regional systems was such that the language of our manuscripts is always marked at some point in their transmission by the region in which they were copied. The competencies enumerated here are not in contradiction with the project's pedagogical goals; rather, they support them by outlining learning objectives for the student participants.

## Publication

• Transcription conventions should be the same throughout the archive: the same sign, or group of calligraphic variations of a sign, must be assigned a single code.

• All conventions need to be described in a protocol accessible to the public, so that users understand the editorial choices made and future archive authors can consult them for their transcriptions.

• There should at least be a single person responsible for supervising all transcriptions, checking both their fidelity to the material manuscript and respect of the editorial grid.

These recommendations result from the observation of the workings of a series of electronic textual archives developed in the tradition of the project launched by Karl Uitti, including for example the Project 'MENOTA,'[50] which

---

[50] A large electronic archive of Nordic manuscripts undertaken by a Scandinavian consortium: http://www.menota.org/. Longer-standing projects are cited by René Pellen, "Les textes sur Internet d'après Ménestrel: lacunes et problèmes," *Le Médiéviste et l'Ordinateur* 37 (1998): 7–10, http://lemo.irht.cnrs.fr; "Conclusion: Internet, une situation contrastée et ambiguë," *Le Médiéviste et l'Ordinateur* 37 (1998): 42–45, http://lemo.irht.cnrs.fr;

made a concerted effort to make explicit its norms of coding and markup.[51] In autumn 2006, the Consortium International pour les Corpus de Français Médiéval (CCFM, contact: ccfm@cru.fr) met to discuss standards for the digitization of medieval textual corpora and put forward propositions for the labeling of texts, for the elaboration of metadata descriptors, and for the enrichment of textual databases. We are certain that Karl Uitti would have wished to participate actively in these discussions, in the spirit of sharing and cooperation that was his. His project, which gave rise to so many emulations and exchanges between international research centers, deserves to benefit now from the suggestions that come in return. With our proposed updates, the project will endure as a collaborative endeavor and remain a point of reference in the evolving domain of electronic editions. Indeed, the *Charrette Project* has always considered itself, in addition to a specific philological enterprise, as also a space where questions about electronic editions are posed and explored.[52] We hope that our most recent observations concerning his transcription files will continue this process of collaborative reflection and also aid in the ongoing amelioration of the archive.

---

and "L'édition critique à l'âge d'Internet," in *L'Épopée romane: Actes du XV^e Congrès International Rencesvals (Poitiers, 21–27 août 2000)*, ed. G. Bianciotto and C. Galderisi (Poitiers: Université de Poitiers, 2002), 2:1059–68; for Old and Middle French, see Pierre Kunstmann, "Ancien et moyen français sur le Web: textes et bases de données," *Revue de Linguistique Romane* 64 (2000): 17–42.

[51] An initiative to standardize the codes for "special medieval characters" has resulted in a formal proposal to the Unicode consortium (C. Marchello-Nizia, *Projet 'Graal'. Edition en ligne de textes médiévaux*, Dossier CIBLE 2006, communication personnelle).

[52] For example, within the archive itself, the XML transcriptions tested by Alexei Lavrentev represent the result of advanced reflection on this question. See http://www.princeton.edu/~lancelot/ss.

# PART V:

## DIGITAL POETICS:
## THE *CHARRETTE PROJECT* AND BEYOND

# Figuring the Data in a Database of Figures

Rafael C. Alvarado
University of Virginia

## A Problem of Representation

A significant problem of representation faced by the text encoders of the *Charrette Project* is known in the field of humanities computing as "overlap," a term that "describes cases where some markup structures do not nest neatly into others, such as when a quotation starts in the middle of one paragraph and ends in the middle of the next."[1] Overlapping structures are particularly problematic for text encoders who seek to represent the poetic, rhetorical, and grammatical data associated with a given text, as in the case of the *Charrette* poem, since these dimensions of description and interpretation are complex and do not comprise a simple, unitary hierarchical structure. One must continually open and close tags, and stitch them together by providing common attributes. It is a tedious, time-consuming, and error-prone business, and one that cannot be taught easily to non-expert editors. If the resultant encoded text is difficult to read, it is also difficult to decode and transform into displayable form to readers, using formatting techniques such as variations in font color, type, size, and style. One may with relative ease devise an interactive text, which would allow the reader to turn layers of markup on and off, but that would still not solve the problem of simultaneous representation, in effect missing the point of encoding multiple hierarchies in the first place. As for machine processing, non-nesting structures are much more complex to manipulate than nesting ones, and may lead to undecidable encodings. Finally, whereas most texts contain at least two layers of markup—one for the physical structure of the vehicle that contains the text (e.g., manuscript folios and columns), one for the so-called logical structure of the text into chunks (e.g., chapters, sections, paragraphs)—the *Charrette Project* has five others: one

---

[1] Steven DeRose, "Markup Overlap: A Review and a Horse," in *Proceedings of Extreme Markup Languages 2004,* Montreal, Québec, 2–6 August 2004, 1, http://conferences.ideal-liance.org/extreme/html/2004/DeRose01/EML2004DeRose01.html.

Gina L. Greco and Ellen M. Thorington, eds., *Dame Philology's Charrette: Approaching Medieval Textuality through Crétien's 'Lancelot': Essays in Memory of Karl D. Uitti.* MRTS 408. Tempe: ACMRS, 2012. [ISBN 978-0-86698-456-0]

for each of the figures of chiasmus, *adnominatio*, enjambment, rich rhyme, and *oratio*. Moreover, in some cases, the figural instances of a given kind themselves may overlap.

In addition to overlap, the *Charrette Project* faced the problem of managing the considerable number of students who contributed to the digital encoding of the textual material over time. Because traditional markup and word processing solutions are document-centric, they have the problem of integrating the work of multiple contributors. Two solutions are generally available, neither of which is satisfactory: one may work in series, having one person edit the text and then pass it on to the next, or one may work in parallel, either chopping the text up into smaller parts (which may then be worked on serially) or having copies of the text worked on separately and then synchronized. The first is time-consuming, and misses the windows of opportunity that open and shut for a grant-funded project, while the second poses enormous challenges and may lead to data loss. One could, of course, use a versioning tool such as CVS or Subversion, but, again, there is the problem of training and sustainability—such tools are de-signed for software engineers who manage relatively large code bases.

Beyond these issues, there is a third, less recognized one that will eventually have to be solved if the *Charrette Project* is to succeed in making a contribution not simply at the level of philology, but of digital philology as well. It is an issue that I think applies to the great majority of projects in the digital humanities where, in the process of pursuing what might be called a statistical criticism, they produce "thick documents,"[2] critical editions top-heavy with interpretive and critical information stuffed into the tags that describe the structure of a given text. After a certain point, the information contained in these documents cannot be visualized in any ordinary sense of the term, so that no scheme relying on altering the format of a text to represent the logical layers of information would ever succeed in laying bare any of the patterns that the encoders of text surely seek to discover. The problem is how to represent multidimensional structures in such a way that implicit patterns may be revealed, the discovery of which will contribute to the production of rich interpretations of the texts at hand.

Given these issues, it was clear that traditional markup methods and tools would not meet our needs, even as we recognized the intrinsic value of using SGML/XML and the Text Encoding Initiative's DTD[3] for the representation of both our primary sources and the final critical edition we expected to produce. The approach I suggested, and which Professor Uitti adopted, marked a

---

[2] Willard McCarty, "Depth, Markup and Modelling," in *Proceedings of the ACH-ALLC 2004 International Humanities Computing Conference. Athens, GA. 30 May 2003*, http://www.digitalstudies.org/ojs/index.php/digital_studies/article/viewArticle/67.

[3] Michael Sperberg-McQueen and Lou Burnard, "The Design of the TEI Encoding Scheme," in *Text Encoding Initiative: Background and Context*, ed. Nancy Ide and Jean Veronis (Berlin: Springer, 1995), 17–40.

radical departure: rather than marking up the text directly, or using some form of "stand-off" markup that would work in conjunction with an index of the text, we chose to convert the entire Foulet-Uitti edition itself into a set of database tables, and to invert the traditional figure/ground relationship between text and index. In our case, the index itself became the text. This method proved both robust and flexible.

## The data model explained

The suite of web-based applications I wrote for the *Charrette Project* I called *Figura*, a play on the core content of the project as well as a tongue-in-cheek reference to the further evolution of the word and concept to which Auerbach devoted his famous essay. Here I want to describe the representation of the concepts of text and figure in the database back-end of those web applications, in order to provide the scholar with a more or less realistic understanding of what one is working with when "reading" *Figura*. For the relationship between it and the Foulet-Uitti edition on which it is based is not direct. Indeed, no database is ever an objective repository of zero-degree information, waiting passively to be converted into the stuff of interpretation. A database, or more precisely a data model, is a transformation of information from one form into another, and therefore filters out some differences at the expense of others, and may even add others, for better or for worse. Here as much as anywhere applies Bateson's rule that "information is any difference that makes a difference," by which he meant any difference that survives between acts of copying that are never transparent.

Before I describe the data model of *Figura*, it's worth describing my rationale for using a relational database in the first place, given the view of some that the relational model of Codd[4] has now been superseded by the hierarchical data models of XML and object-oriented programming.[5] From a purely practical standpoint, relational databases are mature technologies, with tools that are cheap, robust, well documented, and adapted to a variety of application programming frameworks. Throughout the course of our work, our data moved between Microsoft Access 97, Oracle 9, and finally MySQL 4. At each stage of the process, data transfer was trivial, as we had adopted, for the most part, ANSI-compliant SQL as our data language (as opposed to proprietary extensions provided by each of

---

[4] E.F. Codd, "A Relational Model of Data for Large Shared Data Banks," *Communications of the ACM* 13 (1970): 377–87, http://doi.acm.org/10.1145/362384.362685.

[5] Rafael C. Alvarado, "Of Media, Data and Documents: An Argument for the Importance of Relational Technology to the Project of Humanities Computing," in *Proceedings of the ACH-ALLC 1999 International Humanities Computing Conference. Charlottesville, VA. 10 June 1999*, http://www.iath2.virginia.edu/ach-allc.99/proceedings/alvarado.html.

these products). Additionally, these back-ends integrated seamlessly with our application frameworks, which evolved from Perl, ModPerl, and Embperl, to Java and Cocoon, and finally to PHP. Moreover, we were able to solve the problem of collaboration by building on the concurrent editing architecture built into these database products, along with the use of the web as our client-server environment. But beyond these immediately practical reasons, the relational model has its foundations in set theory, and remains the most theoretically grounded data model available today. The rise of such promising tools as XSchema, native XML databases, and XQuery has not changed this fact. For although these provide very powerful tools for working with XML, they remain both theoretically and practically complex. More importantly, none of these tool sets possess the statistical functions and operations built into SQL—a fact that will prove useful in addressing the issue of visualization mentioned in the previous section.

I should emphasize that our use of a relational database to replace the direct use of XML (and an indexing engine) as our framework for constructing the new critical edition, was never intended to replace the use of XML (and the TEI) altogether. On the contrary, *Figura* is designed to mediate between source material, which can be encoded in XML, and a final product, which can also be in XML. Indeed, the entire contents of *Figura* are now available as a single XML document (see the FAUX Charrette).[6]

Now for the data model: I said that a database is a construction, an artifact based on subjective assumptions. Here are some of the assumptions I made concerning the representation of text and figure in *Figura*. Essentially, I followed four simple rules:

1. A <u>text</u> is just a series of word instances.

2. A word instance, or <u>token</u>, is just a string of characters delimited by an arbitrary pattern of characters.[7] These delimiting characters are normally known as punctuation marks. A token is just an instance of a word, which defines the character pattern associated with the token, which is in turn classified as a variant of a "dictionary form" (or "dform").

3. A <u>segment</u> is just a series of contiguous word instances with an optional name associated with it. (A word may belong to more than one segment, and the same contiguous set of words may belong to more than one segment.)

4. A <u>figure</u> is just a collection of word segments, classified by a figure type.

---

[6] The FAUX Charrette. *The Princeton Charrette Project.* 24 August 2006, 1 October 2006, http://www.princeton.edu/~lancelot/ss/materials.shtml#faux.

[7] By "pattern of characters" I mean, technically, a regular expression of the kind implemented by Perl 5 and developed originally by Henry Spencer.

Following these rules, the representation of a text in *Figura* is just a table of tokens. Each record in the text table has, in addition to the character string for the
token (TOKEN_STR), the following information: a unique identifier for the token
(TOKEN_ID),[8] an identifier for the text itself, so that it can store more than one text
(TEXT_ID), a number to describe the line number that contains the token (LINE_
NUM), a number to describe the position of the token on the line (TOKEN_NUM), and
a string to define the delimiting character pattern associated with the token, expressed as Unicode XML entities (PUNC). Here is a selection of the first two lines
of the Foulet-Uitti edition from the table:

| TOKEN_ID | TEXT_ID | LINE_NUM | TOKEN_NUM | TOKEN_STR | PUNC |
|----------|---------|----------|-----------|-----------|------|
| 89769 | 1 | 1 | 1 | Des |   |
| 89770 | 1 | 1 | 2 | Que |   |
| 89771 | 1 | 1 | 3 | Ma |   |
| 89772 | 1 | 1 | 4 | Dame |   |
| 89773 | 1 | 1 | 5 | De |   |
| 89774 | 1 | 1 | 6 | Chanpaigne | *NULL* |
| 89775 | 1 | 2 | 1 | Vialt |   |
| 89776 | 1 | 2 | 2 | Que |   |
| 89777 | 1 | 2 | 3 | romans |   |
| 89778 | 1 | 2 | 4 | A |   |
| 89779 | 1 | 2 | 5 | feire |   |
| 89780 | 1 | 2 | 6 | anpraigne | ,  |

TABLE 1: SAMPLE DATA FROM TEXT_TOKEN

The fact that each word instance (TOKEN_STR) is paired with a punctuational
string is an artifact of the process by which the text was parsed in the first place.
As mentioned above, a word instance (in this context) is a string delimited by an
arbitrary character pattern. In our case, we chose to parse the text into a series
of alternating segments of alphabetic characters, and nonalphabetic characters
(e.g., periods, commas, apostrophes, quote marks, angle brackets, etc.), a word
instance being a contiguous series of alphabetic characters. Thus, the table reflects the alternating series as a series of token + punctuation pairs that comprise
the text.

One consequence of this decision is that contractions are represented as two
tokens, with the apostrophe associated with the first but not the second. Another
is that individual punctuation marks are not parsed with the precision required if

---

[8] Database developers will notice our use of a unique identifier in addition to the
natural key formed by the tuple (TEXT_ID, LINE_NUM, TOKEN_NUM). This is mainly
a matter of database design style and convenience, and does not prevent the natural key
from being used in joins.

the encoded text were of paleographic importance; multiple punctuation marks are lumped together into what are in effect meaningless lumps, although, of course, individual marks remain usefully identified. Another consequence to this approach to text representation is that it interestingly blurs the distinction between the text and the index of the text, as both are but variant queries from the same table. In SQL, the two constructs can be expressed as respectively as follows:

```
Text: "select LINE_NUM, TOKEN_NUM, TOKEN_STR, PUNC from TEXT_
TOKEN order by LINE_NUM, TOKEN_NUM"

Index: "select distinct LINE_NUM, TOKEN_STR from TEXT_TOKEN
order by TOKEN_STR, LINE_NUM"
```

Turning now to figures, as our rules imply, these are represented in the most general manner possible. Rather than having a model for each of the particular structures associated with each figure type (and subtype)—for example, a chiasmus has four parts (A1, B1, B2, A2), rich rhyme two (call them A and B), etc.—in *Figura* all figures are represented as an arbitrary collection of segments, where a segment is just a set of contiguous tokens (with their punctuational partners) with a name, and a figure is just a set of segments. So, for example, a chiasmus would be represented thus:[9]

| GENUS | SPECIES | FIGURE_ TOKEN_ID | TITLE | LINE_START | TOKEN_START | LINE_END | TOKEN_END |
|-------|---------|------------------|-------|------------|-------------|----------|-----------|
| CH | 2 | 351 | A1 | 4 | 1 | 6 | 6 |
| CH | 2 | 351 | B1 | 7 | 1 | 9 | 5 |
| CH | 2 | 351 | piv | 9 | 5 | 9 | 5 |
| CH | 2 | 351 | B2 | 10 | 1 | 12 | 7 |
| CH | 2 | 351 | A2 | 13 | 1 | 15 | 5 |

TABLE 2: SAMPLE DATA FROM FIGURE_SEGMENT

Obviously, this is an extremely flexible model—some might say too flexible. But to those in favor of a more sclerotic model that would constrain the database to store only instances of figures that matched a particular understanding of figure structures, let me suggest that such a model would not only impose an unnecessary hurdle to the process of data entry, it would also put the structural cart before the observational horse. An important benefit of our model is that it allowed us to learn something empirically about the structure of figure types as the data were being entered, even if these structures were already understood at a general level. One such finding has been to regard the structure of rhetorical figures as

---

[9] The two tables shown here are actually views of a "normalized" collection of tables. For a full account of the data model, download the database itself from the *Princeton Charrette Project* website (see The *Figura* Database).

precisely analogous (that is, homologous) to the structures of annotation graphs used by discourse analysts,[10] providing a useful methodological bridge between the two apparently disparate fields of traditional (indeed ancient) philology, poetics, and rhetoric on the one hand, and contemporary discourse analysis, pragmatics, and natural language processing on the other.[11]

It is worth emphasizing that the rules I followed in creating the preceding data model are decidedly not the rules that we, as human beings and scholars, would use to define the terms text and figure in a non-digital, more properly discursive context. They are practical rules that conform to the representational constraints of the digital technologies at hand. Certainly, the data model is not an ontological representation of textuality *per se*, although it may, as my reference to annotation graphs implies, support one. It is rather the result of a kind of *bricolage*, a making do with the tools at hand in order to produce technological results that might be useful to scholars as they pursue the implications of the digital regime in which we find ourselves. They have been crafted with the sober recognition that there remains a very wide gap between cognition and computing, between language as it is spoken and written by people and as it is represented and transmitted by electronic communication devices such as the computer. Other ways of defining these terms either avoid or clumsily stumble across this divide. It is better, in our view, to recognize the gap and work with it.

In any case, the validity of this model should be measured by the degree to which it solves the three problems I describe in the Introduction. It clearly solves the first two. As for the third, the problem of visualization, that is to be seen. In the following section I produce an example, for methodological purposes only, which should provide the beginning of an answer to this question.

---

[10] Stephen Bird and M. Liberman, "Annotation Graphs as a Framework for Multidimensional Linguistic Data Analysis," in *Proceedings of the Workshop Towards Standards and Tools for Discourse Tagging* (Somerset, NJ: Association for Computational Linguistics, 1999), 1–10, http://papers.ldc.upenn.edu/DTAG1999/dtag.pdf.

[11] I submit that the mathematical structure of the annotation graph provides a much better foundation for the study of text than that of the hierarchical model of text—the so-called Ordered Hierarchy of Content Objects (OHCO) model—associated with such projects as the TEI. The latter is hampered by a desire to locate ontology-in-text, a project bedeviled by a conflation of message and signal, to use the language of information theory. A text per se is only a signal, not a message, and the work of markup ought to begin with this premise, as does Bird and Liberman's approach. Deep markup, on the other hand, should apply to the decoded message in the signal.

## A Brief Example

Let us take as our point of departure the constitutive opposition between form and content, *lexis* and *logos*. Can the data encoded in *Figura* help us answer questions regarding the relationship between these two general dimensions of rhetoric, recognized since Aristotle? To pursue this larger question, we must rephrase the question so as to comply with our data model. That is, we must perform a higher-order classification on the set of categories and relations that comprise our data model.

What will count as form in our experiment? Here I would place all of our figural data, in the sense that the presence or absence of a figure in a given part of a poem has no necessary connection to the presence or absence of any of the contents of that part. Figures are independently variable with respect to the *matière* of the story.[12] This is not to say that the two dimensions may not covary—indeed, this is what we are looking for (see below). But such covariation will be "accidental" at the level of *langue* and "achieved," in the language of ethnomethodology, at the level of *parole*.

Under the category of content, we are restricted to a much smaller set of data, as the database does not encode anything directly significant about character, plot, or theme. (Of course, our data model is sufficiently general to encode this sort of thing: we could easily add annotation graphs that describe content, using the coding techniques of qualitative data analysis employed by sociologists in the study of spoken discourse.) As it stands, our only "hooks" into the content of the story are the appearances of proper nouns, every instance of which has been classified in our table of grammatical data. So we will let these data stand in for our notion of content.

Finally, let us also assume that the two dimensions, although orthogonal and independently variable, are nonetheless meaningfully related, in the sense that, if an author were not to pay attention to their covariation, he or she would be passing up on an effective device in the art of storytelling. Indeed, without control of this relationship, we can easily imagine that the story would quickly leave the control of the storyteller. It is at the level of pragmatics that they are related.

Given these assumptions, we can produce an operational question on this general topic: *Is there a non-random correlation between the use of particular figure types (form) and the appearance of certain characters (content) in the story?* It turns out that this is a question that the database can support quite easily. But, before we pursue it, we need to simplify our task, since, on the one hand, there are 82 proper nouns (most of them characters) in the *Charrette* story, while, on the other, there are 42 distinct types of figure that have been discovered in it. Clearly, 3444

---

12 Karl D. Uitti, *Chrétien de Troyes Revisited* (New York: Twayne Publishers, 1995), 11.

combinations are not manageable, especially in this context, where the point is to illustrate a method and not reach final conclusions. To simplify our task, we shall reduce the number of figure types by considering only their genus, and disregard variations at the level of species. Furthermore, we shall consider the properly poetic devices of *adnominatio*, chiasmus, rich rhyme, and enjambment, leaving to one side both forms of *oratio*. For sake of brevity, I shall also refer to these four figure types as AD, CH, RR, and EN respectively. This still leaves us with a large number of proper nouns, but our number of combinations is reduced by an order of magnitude. At this point we may let the data speak for themselves.

The following is a "cross-tabulation" generated from the database which shows the appearance of each of the text's proper nouns as members of segments associated with the four figure types described above. The rule is simple: if a noun appears as a member of the word set of a particular figure, then it is counted toward the genus of the figure. The rule is not perfect: it does not, for example, include proper nouns that appear on the same line as an enjambment or a rich rhyme, but which are not included in the actual figure segments, nor does it include nouns that appear between the framing segments of a chiasmus. These appearances may or may not be significant. Of course, at some point, it would be worthwhile to produce a result set based on those assumptions, but for the purposes of the current exercise I have kept to a minimalist premise. In any case, the value of generating a cross-tabulation of this kind is that it allows us to visualize the opposition between form and content as a matrix, the vertical and horizontal axes representing our operationalized notions of form and content respectively.

| Name | Appearances | Figures | AD | CH | EN | RR |
|------|-------------|---------|----|----|----|----|
| LANCELOT | 138 | 77 | | 45 | 16 | 16 |
| MELEAGANT | 61 | 39 | 11 | 10 | 15 | 3 |
| DEU | 106 | 24 | 4 | 4 | 6 | 10 |
| GAUVAIN | 53 | 21 | | 13 | 4 | 4 |
| KEU | 46 | 15 | | 11 | 4 | |
| BADEMAGU | 7 | 7 | | 4 | 1 | 2 |
| LOGRES | 8 | 5 | | 2 | | 3 |
| ARTU | 15 | 5 | | 3 | 2 | |
| EVE | 7 | 4 | | 1 | 3 | |
| Name | Appearances | Figures | AD | CH | EN | RR |
| IRLANDE | 5 | 4 | 1 | | 1 | 2 |
| PERE | 2 | 3 | 1 | | | 2 |
| CRESTIIEN | 3 | 3 | | 2 | 1 | |
| FORTUNE | 3 | 3 | | 2 | 1 | |
| ABEL | 1 | 2 | | 1 | | 1 |

| Name | Appearances | Figures | AD | CH | EN | RR |
|------|-------------|---------|----|----|----|----|
| MARTIN | 1 | 2 | | 1 | | 1 |
| JAQUE | 1 | 2 | | 1 | | 1 |
| ESPAINGNE | 2 | 2 | | 1 | | 1 |
| DONBES | 1 | 2 | | 1 | | 1 |
| GUENIEVRE | 2 | 2 | | 1 | | 1 |
| REISON | 3 | 2 | | 2 | | |
| NOAUZ | 3 | 2 | | | | 2 |
| SELVESTRE | 1 | 2 | | | 1 | 1 |
| SARRAZIN | 1 | 2 | 1 | 1 | | |
| AMIENS | 1 | 1 | | | | 1 |
| ANGLETERRE | 1 | 1 | | | 1 | |
| ARRAGON | 1 | 1 | | | | 1 |
| CRIATOR | 1 | 1 | | | | 1 |
| GANT | 1 | 1 | | | | 1 |
| GODEFROI | 1 | 1 | | 1 | | |
| BREIBANÇON | 1 | 1 | | | | 1 |
| ESPERIT | 1 | 1 | | | | 1 |
| BUCIFAL | 1 | 1 | | 1 | | |
| CARLION | 1 | 1 | | | | 1 |
| CHANPAIGNE | 1 | 1 | | | | 1 |
| ASCANSION | 1 | 1 | | | | 1 |
| PANPELUNE | 1 | 1 | | 1 | | |
| YSORE | 1 | 1 | | | | 1 |
| TOLOSE | 1 | 1 | | | | 1 |
| TESSAILE | 1 | 1 | | 1 | | |
| TAULAS DE LA DESERTE | 1 | 1 | | | | 1 |
| ROSNE | 1 | 1 | | | | 1 |
| ROBERDIC | 1 | 1 | | | | 1 |
| **Name** | **Appearances** | **Figures** | **AD** | **CH** | **EN** | **RR** |
| PIRAMUS | 1 | 1 | | 1 | | |
| PILADES | 1 | 1 | | | | 1 |
| KEU D'ESTRAUS | 1 | 1 | | | | 1 |
| PANTECOSTE | 1 | 1 | | 1 | | |
| GORRE | 2 | 1 | | | | 1 |

| | | | | | |
|---|---|---|---|---|---|
| NOEL | 1 | 1 | | 1 | |
| MARIES, LES TROIS | 1 | 1 | | | 1 |
| LOOYS | 1 | 1 | | | 1 |
| LONDRES | 1 | 1 | | | 1 |
| LIMOGES | 1 | 1 | | | 1 |
| LEIGNI | 1 | 1 | | 1 | |
| LANDI | 1 | 1 | | | 1 |
| YVAIN | 1 | 1 | | | 1 |
| LAC | 2 | 1 | | 1 | |
| PEITIERS | 1 | 1 | | | 1 |

TABLE 3: COVARIATION OF PROPER NOUN AND FIGURE GENUS IN THE *CHARRETTE*

The first column after the name shows the total number of appearances of the proper noun in the text, whereas the next shows the total number of figure instances in which the word appears. Note that the latter can be greater than the former because the same word can participate in more than one figure. The final four columns represent the number of figures by type.

Now, although our sample is relatively small, let us venture to draw some conclusions—points of departure for more conclusive work. I will focus on one fact that emerges rather strongly, namely, that Lancelot is overwhelmingly correlated with CH, whereas Méléagant is strongly correlated with AD. In each case our character has a kind of monopoly over the figure, with Lancelot's ratio far exceeding that which can be accounted for simply by his greater overall appearance on the text. And Méléagant's association with AD is equally interesting: he is the only major character associated with the figure, unless we count Deu (whose association makes an interesting side note). Only three other nouns (one of them Irelande) participate in this figure type, but only once each—an order of magnitude less than Méléagant. It is possible that Méléagant's strong association with this figure is an artifact of the ease with which the name itself lends itself to wordplay in Old French, but it is hard to imagine that our author would not have had the resources to submit the other characters' names to this particular device if he had wanted to do so. We must assume that the correlation has a point. Let us cast this theory in the form of a proportion:

Lancelot : Méléagant :: CH : AD

The question now is, before we can begin to assess the truth value of this proposition, what possible sense does it make? For we are comparing orthogonal dimensions, the equivalent of saying something like "5:00 PM = New York, NY." But this is not such an absurd operation after all; from the point of view of an individual life, times very often map onto places, as in "If it's Tuesday, this must be Belgium." Such a proposition becomes sensible to the degree that one's life is choreographed by a schedule or a rhythm or any other pragmatic device for linking these dimensions, emergent or contrived. Applying the metaphor to our case, we need to ask, to what degree is the *Charrette* poem grounded in an implicit structural armature—again, emergent or contrived—that would link the independently variable dimensions of form and content into something like a schedule, or perhaps nearer to our target, what Bakhtin called a chronotope, a form-content matrix?

Such a matrix, I submit, would allow us to make significant progress toward resolving the problem of visualization, and I believe that *Figura* is ideally suited to generating information that would lead us to answer this question. But I of course cannot answer it here. I leave it to anyone interested in pursuing what I will characterize as a neostructuralist project with the aid of a deep knowledge of Old French, a project enhanced by the methodological possibilities opened up by the digitization of source materials as provided by the *Charrette Project* and *Figura*.[13] However, I will submit the following thesis regarding a possible structural relationship among the four figure types that may make a contribution toward an answer to the question I have posed, namely, to describe the form-content matrix within which the proposition submitted above would make sense.

It turns out that our four figure types—AD, CH, EN, and RR—may be distinguished according to two simple dimensions: (1) whether the device is applicable to exactly a single pair of lines, or else to an arbitrary span of lines, and (2) whether it may be regarded as "resonant" or "dissonant," pleasant in its linguistic and cognitive effect, or else ambivalent. Regarding the first dimension, it is immediately obvious that both rich rhyme and enjambment apply to pairs of lines, and that both chiasmus and *adnominatio* apply to arbitrary spans of lines. Indeed, regarding the latter, Professor Uitti felt compelled to specify an upper limit on the number of lines an instance of *adnominatio* could span, whereas chiasmus has been known to span the entire poem.[14] Less obvious, and more problematic from an objective point of view, are the assignments of what I have chosen to call resonance and dissonance. But these are not as controversial as they may seem.

On the side of resonance, it is clear that rich rhyme produces a pleasant effect, given that a rhyme is, literally, a kind of resonance (echo) in itself. Regarding chiasmus, I will simply refer to the obvious symmetry and closure it introduces, the general arc of "there and back again," as well as the delightful cognitive side effects produced by grasping the juxtaposition of inverse pairs of terms, at the level of grammar, meaning or sound. In both cases, the principles of symmetry and repetition are at play.

---

[13]   *The Princeton Charrette Project*, ed. Karl D. Uitti, 1994, Trustees of Princeton University, 2006, Dept. of French and Italian, Princeton University, 3 April 2007, http://www.princeton.edu/~lancelot.

[14]   K. Sarah-Jane Murray, personal communication.

On the side of dissonance, the effect of enjambment is surely that of a breaking, however slight, a separation of something that the mind would rather grasp as
a whole. Against the grain of a steady stream of verse lines lining up with clauses,
enjambment forces a crossing—a tiny transgression—of the semantic over the formal. Finally, with *adnominatio*—although Professor Uitti carefully distinguished
this device from pure folk etymology and punning—we have, none the less, a form
of paronomasia that participates in raising to the level of awareness the sometimes
subversive, but always destabilizing rhizomic network of meanings that underlie
discourse. As Frederick Ahl has argued, both Latin and Celtic writers—the major
influences on Chrétien—were not unfamiliar with the deconstructionists' device
of choice, and many employed the effects of wordplay for a variety of artful or clan-
destine purposes, even political ones.[15] In this connection, it is interesting to note
the predominantly negative connotations of the words with which Méléagant is
joined in his eleven examples of *adnominatio*: *mal, maudire, maufe, mautalant, mau-
vestie, mescreance, mesprisier,* and *mesprison.* The last word in this set in particular
seems appropriate to the understanding of this figure type that I wish to convey
here, given that one modern derivate of the word, *misprision,* has, in our time, been
famously appropriated by Harold Bloom to signify the entire practice of playful
and creative misreading that *adnominatio,* in this view, seems to encourage. Flip-
ping the relation on its head, we may also note that among the four instances of the
word *mesprison* in the poem, each of them participates in at least one *adnominatio.*
This may be coincidental, but nonetheless the prospect of a form/content rupture
here should attract our attention.

Finally, because the CH and AD may span a greater number of lines, while
RR and EN span a small number of lines each (2), I classify the former pair as
the "major" figures and the latter as the "minor" ones. The following matrix summarizes the preceding remarks:

|       | Resonant (+)              | Dissonant ( - )                   |
|-------|---------------------------|-----------------------------------|
| Major | Chiasmus (CH) *Lancelot*  | Adnominatio (AD) *Méléagant*      |
| Minor | Rich Rhyme (RR)           | Enjambment (EN)                   |

FIGURE 1: STRUCTURAL MATRIX OF THE FOUR MAIN FIGURE TYPES

---

[15] Frederick Ahl, *Metaformations: Soundplay and Wordplay in Ovid and Other Classical Poets* (Ithaca: Cornell University Press, 1985). Regarding the resonant/dissonant
distinction, I should point out that, at some risk of misunderstanding, I have intention-
ally reduced this to what I hope are readily intelligible psychological terms. A more satisfying approach would be to characterize the opposition as one between structure and
anti-structure, evoking the pragmatic structuralism of Victor Turner. However, to do so
would require creating a bridge between poetics proper and the anthropology of ritual
behavior, a task which, although already begun by Turner, would exceed the bounds of
this essay.

Reversing our tack and taking this matrix as our starting point, we may inquire as to the nature of the relationship between Lancelot and Méléagant on the one hand, and the minor figures on the other. In the case of RR, it turns out that, again, Lancelot has a monopoly, participating in anywhere from 4 to 16 times the number of such figures when compared to the other proper nouns, and over 5 times greater than Méléagant, who appears to have the average allotment for a major character. This is in contrast to Méléagant's association with EN which is quite strong, belonging to more instances of the figure than any other character (besides Lancelot), and 5 times more frequently than RR. So, the following proportion would seem to follow, which echoes our first:

Lancelot : Mélégant :: RR : EN

However, a problem with this proportion is that Lancelot is equally likely to appear in EN as in RR, and that he also participates in the most EN instances. We do not want to dismiss this anomaly as insignificant. In fact, it is likely to be evidence for some other variable at work, the details of which would be revealed in a more finely grained study of the data. For example, it is possible that at the level of the minor figures, we must also consider the play of minor characters, not because they are both "minor," but simply because a consideration of the other characters will fill out our representation of the story. Additionally, we may detect here evidence of a difference of function between the major and minor figures: the latter may reflect more on the action of the story, whereas the former may reflect on the categories of character that underlie the story.


## Conclusion

I believe I have gone about as far as I may reasonably go — actually, much farther — as an outsider to the field of Old French. In my defense, I repeat that my point has been largely methodological, in order to make sense of the *kinds* of things that may be asked of the database, and not to make any substantive conclusions about the Charrette poem per se. On that count, I propose that the four-part matrix introduced above is part of a more comprehensive form-content structure that provides an armature for Chrétien's work. This matrix is a figure in its own right — a chiasmus — that structures the data produced by a query (that is, a reading) of the database of poetic figures. My hope is that it gives us a glimpse of how we might approach the problem of visualization that I described at the beginning of this essay, and which will help us make sense of the material Professor Uitti worked so long and hard to compile. There are entire regions of scholarship open to us if we recognize that a database such as *Figura* produces its own figures, derivatives of the first level of figures found in the text, which require their own interpretation, and which may be folded back into the process of primary interpretation.

# Reading (and) Courtly Love in *Flamenca*, *via* the *Charrette*

## Juliet O'Brien
### The University of British Columbia

Courtly love, a topic Karl Uitti wrote upon at length, has been associated with Chrétien de Troyes's *Chevalier de la Charrette* since Gaston Paris's 1883 *Romania* article.[1] Paris's terminology has been called into question as the words "courtly" and "love" never appear in the same line, let alone within the same syntactic unit, in Chrétien's romance. However, as Joan Ferrante's re-evaluation of the material evidence for courtly love has demonstrated, "'Courtly love' is not a figment of a nineteenth-century imagination, nor simply a useful term which we choose to preserve, but a perfectly valid medieval concept."[2] Ferrante finds an instance of *amor cortes* in the thirteenth-century Occitan *Romance of Flamenca* (1197), and the *amor* and *cortes* lexemes in close proximity (albeit not in the same phrase) in twelfth-century Occitan lyric (Cercamon, Bernart de Ventadorn, Marcabru, and Peire d'Alvernhe), the *Charrette* and *Yvain*, *Hueline et Aiglentine*, and some later texts (Dante, Petrarch, Cino da Pistoia, and Chiaro Davanzati). She examines how "courtly" is used in connection with "love" elsewhere in Occitan lyric materials (Bernart de Ventadorn, Raimbaut d'Aurenga, and the *vidas*), then moves on to the uses of *cortesie* in French romance (*Brut*, Chrétien's romances, Marie de France, and the *Roman de la Rose*) and Italian lyric.

In the present essay, I show how *Flamenca* uses the notion of courtly love, *amor cortesa*, in juxtaposition with another form of love, *amor coral*, "love of the heart." The examination of the evidence, its analysis, and the development of ideas about courtly love in *Flamenca* all came about through the use of electronic texts and tools devised specially for this project. As a further investigation into the existence of *amour courtois* in medieval Romance literature, this essay hopes

---

[1] Gaston Paris, "Études sur les romans de la Table Ronde: *Lancelot*," *Romania* 12 (1883): 459–534.

[2] Joan M. Ferrante, "*Cortes' Amor* in Medieval Texts," *Speculum* 55 (1980): 686–95, here 695.

Gina L. Greco and Ellen M. Thorington, eds., *Dame Philology's Charrette: Approaching Medieval Textuality through Crétien's 'Lancelot': Essays in Memory of Karl D. Uitti.* MRTS 408. Tempe: ACMRS, 2012. [ISBN 978-0-86698-456-0]

to add a footnote to the 120-odd years' courtly love debate[3] in support of Uitti's stance on courtly love and his argument for a more subtle and sophisticated reading of Paris and of medieval Romance literature.

## Amor *Coral*

*Amor coral* is, to the best of my knowledge, a new subject of study. The characteristics of this new form of love may be identified as follows.

*Coral* indicates that this love is "of the heart," and is essentially internal. A line is drawn between inside and outside: in contemporary terms, Jean de Meun's *escorce* and *moële*.[4] True inner worth is distinguished from external appearances: in Jean's terms, *la robe ne faict pas le moine*.[5]

The distinction between internal and external permits the existence of a private space, in which the external world's values (political, social, economic, and hierarchical) have no place. Although he makes no mention of *amor coral* and presents limited literary evidence for what is essentially a historical argument, it is Georges Duby who best describes the larger social phenomenon, which may be seen as the broader context for our new notion of love, and that may be aligned with what has been described elsewhere as a pre-modern individuality or subjectivity.[6] "Courtly" codes of conduct and constraints on behavior no longer necessarily come into play.

Two further characteristics are associated with those above. First, private individuals are in a private space that they create themselves, with its own rules—or, rather, their own rules—and truth at its core. *Amor coral* is an idea of human relations based not in power-hierarchies, feudality, and fealty, but in free gift and exchange, in relations of equality and mutuality.[7] From the perspective of medieval women, this is an improvement on their status as objects, chattels, voiceless and devoid of will. There remains, as we shall see, plenty of room for

---

[3] For recent histories of the courtly love debate and argument syntheses, see particularly R. Boase, *The Origin and Meaning of Courtly Love* (Manchester: Manchester University Press, 1977); Sarah Kay, "Courts, Clerks, and Courtly Love," in *The Cambridge Companion to Medieval Romance*, ed. Roberta L. Krueger (Cambridge: Cambridge University Press, 2000), 81–96; and Juliet O'Brien, "*Trobar Cor(s)*: Erotics and Poetics in *Flamenca*" (Ph.D. diss., Princeton University, 2006), chap. 1.

[4] Guillaume de Lorris and Jean de Meun, *Le Roman de la Rose*, ed. Félix Lecoy (Paris: Champion, 1965–1970), ll. 11828 and 11830.

[5] *Le Roman de la Rose*, 11028.

[6] See Georges Duby, *De l'Europe féodale à la Renaissance*, *Histoire de la vie privée*, vol. 2 (Paris: Seuil, 1985).

[7] See Moshe Lazar, *Amour courtois et "fin'amors" dans la littérature du XIIe siècle* (Paris: Klincksieck, 1964).

cynicism, manipulation, and abuse. Second, when courtesy is no longer necessarily a sign of virtue let alone identical with it—and, indeed, if it becomes the opposite—its discussion may become incorporated into nostalgic tropes decrying falling standards and the growth of hypocrisy.

The idea evolves over the course of the twelfth and thirteenth centuries. About a century before *Flamenca*, and around the time of Chrétien de Troyes, *amor coral* appears in the poetry of the Occitan *trobador* Bernart de Ventadorn. Bernart is synonymous with the double identity of poet and lover and is one of the earliest poets to write about *amor cortesa*, especially in relation to the imprisonment of *amor cortesa* and its self-delusional quality (*En cossirer et en esmai*). He also portrays an emphatically anti-courtly love in several poems that create links between *cor* [body/heart], love, and truth or sincerity. [8] All trappings of the outside world, of the court and feudality, are irrelevant in the inside world of these lovers. *Amor coral* is used interchangeably with *amor cortesa* and with love that is *fin', bon, dreit,* or *vers.* [9]

Both *amor cortesa* and *amor coral* seem to be lost in northwards translation, via the Aquitainian courts of the late twelfth century, moving Occitan poets through France, England, and Germany, although *amor coral* seems to have entered the Catalan and Iberian languages and, via the post-Albigensian-crusade exile, into the poetry and languages of Italy. Its Occitan presence diminishes from the beginning of the thirteenth century onwards. Poetry shifts its attention from love to more temporal matters, as the lyric *canso* wanes and the political *sirventes* waxes, due in part to political instability in the region and to French invasion and the turmoils of the Albigensian crusade. The rare later thirteenth-century instances of *amor coral* tend to be in a satirical or *post facto* melancholy mode.

*Flamenca* provides one of the greatest concentrations of "courtly love" and its correlates in medieval Romance literature, such as the phrase that is often cited as evidence for the medieval existence of courtly love: *fenera d'amor cortes* (1197). [10] Yet *Flamenca* is also the richest source for instances of *amor coral*, and presents a very different idea of the relationship between *amor cortesa* and *amor coral* from that of the twelfth-century *trobadors*. Indeed, *fenera d'amor cortes* also provides a good example of *Flamenca*'s critical approach to the subject: and it is to this

----

[8]  Bernart de Ventadorn, *The Songs of Bernart de Ventadorn: Complete Texts, Translations, Notes, and Glossary*, ed. and trans. Stephen G. Nichols Jr., John A. Galm, A. Bartlett Giamatti, et al. (Chapel Hill: University of North Carolina, 1962). *Can la verz folha s'espan*: 151–52; *Estas ai com om esperdutz*: 91–93; *Gent estera que chantes*: 94–95; *Lancan vei la folha*: 112–13; *Lonc tems a qu'eu no chantei mai*: 119–20; *Can lo boschatges es floritz*: 157–59.

[9]  For a list of some other examples of *amor coral* in medieval literature, see O'Brien, "Erotics and Poetics."

[10]  As observed by Ferrante, *"Cortes' amor,"* and echoed by Kay, "Courts, Clerks, and Courtly Love." All further commentary is mine.

phrase that I shall return, after a brief introduction to the work as a whole, as it is not well-known outside medieval Occitanist circles.

## *Flamenca*: an introduction

*Flamenca*'s date of composition remains an uncertain factor. The manuscript is late thirteenth to early fourteenth century; *Flamenca* is the only text in it; and it is anonymous and lacunary, lacking amongst other things a beginning and end. [11] If *Flamenca* is at least contemporaneous with the *vidas* and *razos*, then it must date from the late thirteenth to early fourteenth centuries. Like its contemporaries the (mainly expatriate) *chansonniers*, Matfré Ermengaud's *Breviari d'Amors*, and Occitan and Catalan poetics treatises, *Flamenca* presents an attempt to catalogue a whole literary corpus, a body of knowledge, and even to preserve the ruins of a culture. It is, in addition, a work of debate and criticism, thanks in part to the choice of mode of writing. It combines Occitan and French elements and is written in Occitan, "the" language of lyric poetry, but as a romance, the French form *par excellence*. Cultural juxtaposition and fusion are treated with sophisticated ambiguity, leaving interpretation open — ranging potentially from a wistful wish for harmonious hybridity to an ironic form of *translatio*, subversive reappropriation and theft by an underdog. This openness parallels other dialogic elements in the work: three different character-based focalizations, several distinct narrative voices (ranging from a distant and clinical observer to an untrustworthy manipulator who toys overtly with the audience), and the romance's middle-portion construction around a dialogue between a pair of prospective lovers.

A synopsis of *Flamenca*'s main plot lines is appropriate at this juncture. Archimbaut of Bourbon marries Flamenca of Nemours, but is stage-managed into brooding jealousy by the queen, and this jealousy drives him mad. He cuts himself off from the outside world, and locks up his wife in a tower, along with her maids. Flamenca is allowed out only to go to church and to the local baths. Archimbaut will spy on the three ladies throughout the course of their imprisonment; and they are aware of his observation.

This section of the narrative starts out in a courtly setting, with events reported at a distance through third-person commentary, until the point when

---

[11] Bibliothèque municipale de Carcassonne, manuscript 34; the only other manuscript presence of *Flamenca* is the appearance of ll. 2713–2720 in the 14th-century Catalan Vega-Aguiló codex. For descriptions, see Rita Lejeune, "Le Manuscrit de *Flamenca* et ses lacunes," in *Littérature et société occitane au Moyen Âge* (Liège: Marche Romane, 1979), 331–39; Nadia Togni, "Les Lacunes du manuscrit de *Flamenca*," *Revue des langues romanes* 104 (2000): 379–97.

Archimbaut starts to progress into madness, when focalization shifts to him.[12] This shift also signals a movement into the mode and pace of the main body of our romance: concentration on matters of internal psychology; distance from external events, featuring little action but much thought and discussion; and protagonist-centred focalization.

News of Flamenca's imprisonment having reached him, Guillem de Nevers, a nice young man, sallies forth to rescue the damsel in distress. The rescue involves the incidental imprisonment of the prospective liberator, as he spends most of his time in his room, gazing out the window at the tower and tying himself up in knots in lengthy rumination. This section of the narrative is from Guillem's point of view.

Flamenca and Guillem will become lovers, in several subversions of the outside world and its norms. Guillem assumes clerical disguise, enabling the pair to meet at Mass—right under Archimbaut's nose. The briefest of opportunities is afforded at the moment when Guillem gives Flamenca the peace. As she kisses the psalter and their heads are close together, there is enough time for one of them to speak very quietly, during the time of that kiss. The time of a kiss is also the time of a single breath, and for one person to utter two syllables, sufficiently under the breath to pass as "amen." A succession of such meetings at Mass constitutes the first phase of relations, during which focalization will alternate between

---

[12] I use the term "focalization" in the twentieth-century narratological sense: narration of events from the point of view of a particular protagonist, "focused" on him and his perception of them and of the world, and with the option of seeing into his internal musings. The classic discussion of *focalisation* is Gérard Genette, *Nouveau discours du récit* (Paris: Le Seuil, 1983).

The term is particularly appropriate for *Flamenca*. The idea of *focus* on a character may be observed throughout the romance. *Flamenca* also deploys focalization in the strong or specialised sense: that is, not just point of view and view through one set of eyes, but angle of approach and its motion, the photographic or cinematographic "focus"—with a zooming-in to a narrower field of vision—to which Genette's idea is indebted. Each of the three principal protagonists demonstrates a restriction of vision (and movement in and out of this limitation): Guillem first sees Flamenca through a spy-hole, and glimpses only small portions of her (e.g., hands); Archimbaut spies on Flamenca through another peep-hole; Flamenca's first sightings of Guillem are impeded by her downcast head. Focus and focalization in *Flamenca* are described in full detail in O'Brien, "Erotics and Poetics," chaps. 2–4.

See also Sophie Marnette, *Narrateur et points de vue dans la littérature française médiévale: une approche linguistique* (Bern: P. Lang, 1998); eadem, *Speech and Thought Perception in French: Concepts and Strategies* (Amsterdam: John Benjamins, 2005), 212–13; A.C. Spearing, *The Medieval Poet as Voyeur: Looking and Listening in Medieval Love-Narratives* (Cambridge: Cambridge University Press, 1993), 48–50, 87–89; idem, *Textual Subjectivity: The Encoding of Subjectivity in Medieval Narratives and Lyrics* (Oxford: Oxford University Press, 2005).

the lovers. The first encounter is recounted from Guillem's point of view: deciding what he will say, saying it, observing Flamenca's reaction, and then wondering how she has taken it and how she will respond. We then move to Flamenca and her maids, and their reactions and formulation of a response; and so on, through the course of these encounters, as each "reads" the other's last response and "composes" a reply, in a double focalization.

This whole central section of *Flamenca* is constructed as a dialogue-poem with attached commentary by Guillem and Flamenca, the protagonist-poets: a cross between a *tenso* and a *razo*, as an expanded *vida*. There is a complete absence of commentary by any outside observer's narrative voice. At about 2500 lines long, the section constitutes about a third of the work and is its longest section. The lovers' idyll as a whole — including Guillem's section and the next (Flamenca's) one — occupies around 5500 lines, over half the romance's total length (in its present lacunary state).

The alternation of declaration and question allows Guillem and Flamenca to move rapidly beyond flirtatious uncertainties and comic misunderstandings and come to an "understanding" (*entendemen*), setting up the second, proper, hands-on stage of the affair. Full contact happens in the underground baths and then in Guillem's chambers, via a secret tunnel he has had dug from the baths: he creates the lovers' own, private, idyllic space in an ingenious subterfuge that is, quite literally, a subversion of the outside world.

Towards the end of this central section, focalization moves subtly to Flamenca: subtle as it is enabled by a move from the alternating double focalization to couple-centred focalization with the lovers presented as a single unit (with use of plural verbs and pronouns), and events represented from a joint point of view. Flamenca begins to see a little more clearly, with her reason less clouded by love. She puts an end to the affair, sends Guillem away on the tourneying circuit, and is at least superficially reconciled with Archimbaut, newly cured of his madness. This section is quite short, and much interrupted by lacunae at significant junctures, such as where the reader would expect to find some explanation for and elaboration on Archimbaut's cure.

After the most sizeable lacuna in the romance, Archimbaut holds a court, to which Guillem is invited. The lovers enter into a new phase of their affair that is public, *within* the court, and accepted — indeed, actively aided and abetted — by Archimbaut. Three days into the jousting, our narrative ends, left suspended by another lacuna. This final section moves out from protagonist-centred focalization and back to a distanced observation and reporting of events, which have now moved back to a courtly setting.

Representing these moves in focalization diagrammatically:

| Lines | Focalization | | | |
|---|---|---|---|---|
| *1–152* | *Court* | | | |
| 153–1562 | | Archimbaut | | |
| 1563–3949 | | | Guillem | |
| 3949–6659 | | | | Guillem+Flamenca (in alternation) |
| 6660–7181 | | | | Flamenca |
| *7182–8095* | *Court* | | | |

Putting together the first and last sections, the romance can be seen to have an outer courtly frame. The outer frame picks up the middle part's themes of poetic composition, reading, misreading, and interpretation. The main shift between middle and outer sections is one from internal to external. The same happens in a shift from a discussion of poetry associated with protagonist-poets to its being associated with more external poets: a first-person commentating voice, generalized reference to poets and poetry in this courtly world, and reference to poets and poetry in the real external world (Ovid, Horace, and Marcabru are named). Indeed, these movements in an outwards direction continue, as *Flamenca* weaves together complex layers of literary reference, of many kinds and degrees, from charged vocabulary (e.g., *trobar*) to entire narratives (e.g., *Tristan*).[13] It assimilates a substantial corpus of earlier (mainly twelfth-century) Occitan lyric and (twelfth–thirteenth centuries) French romance, bound together through the use of techniques that draw on the French romance with lyric inserts (early thirteenth century, e.g., Jean Renart's *Roman de la Rose*) and the later Occitan *vida* and *razo* traditions (in *chansonniers* from the late thirteenth to early fourteenth centuries). The fact that *Flamenca* is a genuinely polyphonic narrative is crucial to its success as an extreme form of *compilatio,* a highly allusive literary *summa.*

---

[13] O'Brien, "Erotics and Poetics," chap. 1. On *compilatio*, see Elizabeth Wilson Poe, Compilatio: *Lyric Texts and Prose Commentaries in Troubadour Manuscript H (Vat. Lat. 3207)* (Lexington: French Forum, 2000). *Flamenca* may be read as a literary *summa*, "meta-romance," and "supertext." On meta-romance, see Clare Kinney, "The Best Book of Romance: *Sir Gawain and the Green Knight*," *University of Toronto Quarterly* 59 (1990): 457–73; eadem, "Chivalry Unmasked: Courtly Spectacle and the Abuse of Romance in Sidney's *New Arcadia*," *Studies in English Literature* 35 (1995): 35–52. On the supertext, see John V. Fleming, "Carthaginian Love: Text and Supertext in the *Romance of the Rose*," in *Assays: Critical Approaches to Medieval and Renaissance Texts*, ed. Peggy A. Knapp and Michael A. Sturgin (Pittsburgh: University of Pittsburgh Press, 1981), 51–72.

# Methods

The above schema and the analysis that follows in the section after this were developed first through reading and research, then through computer-assisted analysis. Having obtained a digitized copy of the text and a printout of its concordance,[14] I applied to this new version of *Flamenca*—essentially the same data as contained in a print edition, but in a different format, and rearranged in the case of the concordance—some of the techniques of reading and analysis peculiar to the *Charrette Project*. These techniques may be summarized in simple and pragmatic terms:

> Pattern recognition: an expectation—informed by past experience—leads to a certain repetition being observed, and noted as significant—statistically and semantically—is then tested against evidence provided (or not) by computational "search and find" operations on a digitized text;

> Data collection and the systematic logging of repetitions: proceeding in the opposite manner, the observation of phenomena leads to the production of hypotheses.

The course of action was as follows. I made several copies of the text, marked them up, and tabulated the resulting data, each one focusing on a different feature. The features were selected based on lexical and thematic associations—for example, true love and truth and their synonyms: true, clear, good, right, fine, sensitive, understanding, comprehension, and also expressions of light, fire, blinding, illumination, and seeing. Some features were lexical; some grammatical (e.g., personal pronouns; and the use of impersonal, negative, and hypothetical constructions); some syntactic (e.g., direct and indirect speech, and first-person voice); and others narrative (protagonists' appearances).

Each copy of the text had its key feature marked up in a visually distinct way: highlighted in a different colour, for example. This facilitated the reading of *Flamenca*'s multiple layers, one at a time. The marked-up copies could also be "overlaid" in any combination, enabling the tracking of connected layers and of relationships between layers. Eventually this led to the production of a database. One feature often led to another, often through unexpected new patterns found in the marked-up text.

It should be stressed that the method is a mixture of the two basic techniques outlined above, in several stages. While intuition remains the main factor determining the *choice* of feature to track and reading path to follow, it is an intuition informed by the first, precomputational stages of research: the orthodox

---

[14] With thanks to F.R.P. Akehurst for kindly providing both.

background legwork.[15] This adds to a mental stockpile, the *imaginatio* of criticism as a compositional process like any other.

Pattern recognition is an important factor in such research, as it enables the reading of a text in layers, the reading of the interrelationship between layers, and detection of more subtle shifts between layers: folds and gaps, but also flow and seepages.[16] This proved, for example, to be important to a close reading of those passages in *Flamenca* where focalization did not move suddenly and in a clear-cut manner, but rather in more sophisticated transitions. It was very important indeed to attempting to make sense of transitions abbreviated by lacunae; and to finding distinct compositional layers in the text and transitions between them. The same stylistic features were examined as had been done in studying compositional layers in the *Charrette,* allowing distinctions to be made between the hands of Chrétien de Troyes, Godefroy de Legny, and Guiot. This is a reading of layers and movement between them, with emphasis on the movement of accrual but also on the contrary motion of crumbling, seepage, and decay. As such, this kind of reading recalls the "taphonomy" of forensics and archaeology, suggesting a methodological neologism: "fluid taphonomics."

Layers, their relationships to each other, and networks of relations, may just about be visualised and navigated by the mind's eye: but this can be greatly assisted by the use of technology offering the illusion of four dimensions: for instance, the interplay of layers in a text as reproduced in a simple PowerPoint slide show.[17] Computers are an integral part of a research that is essentially still *reading*, helping the researcher to spend time more effectively: less time on the spade-work of data collection; more on its analysis; and an end product that is verily a "reading," an interpretation and commentary.

### *Amor cortesa* and *amor coral* in *Flamenca*

One of the first patterns I found regarded "courtly love," investigated in response to Karl Uitti's mention of one instance of *amor cortes* (the famous l. 1197).

---

[15] The method thus lays no claim to being *scientifique* in the traditional philological sense, though it aims to be "scientific" in the modern Popperian sense, for example in testability and openness to refutation.

[16] On folds and gaps, see Gilles Deleuze, *Le Pli: Leibnitz et le baroque* (Paris: Minuit, 1988); specifically in *Flamenca*, see Roger Dragonetti, *Le Gai savoir dans la rhétorique courtoise: Flamenca et Joufroi de Poitiers* (Paris: Le Seuil, 1982); Francesca Nicholson, "Reading the Unreadable in *Flamenca*," paper at the British Branch of the International Courtly Love Society Conference, April 2003; J. O'Brien, "Making Sense of a Lacuna in the *Romance of Flamenca*," *TENSO: Bulletin of the Société Guilhem IX* 20 (2005): 1–25.

[17] See Alvarado, in this volume, for further discussion of electronic representation and visualization of textual poetics.

The phrase *fenera d'amor cortes* is spoken by Flamenca's jealous husband Archimbaud, tortured by his fear of possible cuckolding to the point of madness. He refers to *donnejador*— "ladies' men" with, also, some effeminate qualities (1149) —who, he swears, *non sai trobaran huis ubert* (1151) [will not find open house here]. Later, alone, he will ponder the possibility that this might indeed happen:

| | |
|---|---|
| E que faria s'us truanz, | [But what if some vile adversary, |
| que-s **fenera d'amor cortes** | A courteous faker of love— |
| e non sabra d'amor ques es, | A thing that he knows nothing of — |
| l'avia messa en follia? | Should make her virtue go astray?] |
| (1196–1199) [18] | |

The line looks, at first glance, as though it links *amor* to *cortes*: "a faker of courtly-love." But *cortes* is actually an attribute of the *fenera*, as both are masculine singular, whereas *amor* is—as always in Occitan—feminine. So rather than the *fenera* being the negative thing that sullies the positive *amor cortes(a)*, we have instead the doubly-repugnant *fenera cortes* playing with *amor*: so the whole line translates not as a "faker of courtly love," but rather as a "courtly faker of love." So courtliness or courtesy is not necessarily a positive attribute.

Shortly before, in a comment on Archimbaud's unfortunate condition, we have met the term *gelos fins*, a parodic contrary of *fin' amans* [fine, true lover]. [19] Read in the context of *gelos fins*, *fenera d'amor cortes* heralds *Flamenca*'s sardonic critique of love: crucially, it is a critique not only of *courtly* love, but of *all* love.

I searched a digital copy of the *Flamenca* text for further instances of the *am-* and *cort-* lexemes and of their conjunction, producing a marked-up copy and table of occurrences. In reading *Flamenca* for *amor cortesa*, I also found *am-* being

---

[18] Text: Peter T. Ricketts, Alan Reed, F.R.P. Akehurst, John Hathaway, and Cornelius Van Der Horst, eds., *Concordance of Medieval Occitan Literature, CD 1: Lyric Texts, CD 2: Verse Narrative Texts*, 2 vols. to date (Turnhout: Brepols, 2001); based on *Le Roman de Flamenca: nouvelle occitane du XIIIe siècle*, ed. Ulrich Gschwind (Berne: Francke, 1976); graciously provided (*Flamenca* text alone, excerpted from the whole CD-ROM) by F.R.P. Akehurst. The translation is Hubert and Porter, which I have sometimes modified when their translation significantly changes the sense of the original: *The Romance of Flamenca*, ed. Marion E. Porter, trans. Merton Jerome Hubert (Princeton: Princeton University Press, 1962). Here, for example, *que-s fenera d'amor cortes* (1197) was misleadingly translated as "aping the wiles of courtly love." This line is vital to the argument that Flamenca distinguishes between "love" and "courtesy/courtliness."

[19] 1172: *es ar sabon per lo pais / qu'en Archimbautz es gilos fins*—"and it was known throughout the land / that Sir Archimbaut was a true and perfect jealous anti-lover."

tied to *coral*, and *cortes* portrayed as negative: *Amor* is associated with the *cortes*, and seen as an enemy of true love.[20]

| | |
|---|---|
| Ben pensson conssi mais no-s dol[l]on | [Thinking that any bliss denied |
| per negun plazer que oblidon; | Might cause them later to regret, |
| soven envidon e revidon, | They lay their stakes, wager and bet, |
| lo jors, la mostra e la presa. | Maneuvering with art and skill. |
| Et **Amors fai coma cortesa** | Love, generous and gracious, will |
| quar non consent que i aia triga, | Not brook any impediment. |
| quar **tant era corals amiga** | Flamenca is so excellent |
| **Flamenca** que non sap jugar | A mistress that she'll play the game |
| ab son amic mais a **joc par,** | Only on terms that are the same |
| e per aisso tot o gasaina. | For each of them. Therefore she won. |
| Pero, abanz que-l juecs remaina, | And yet, before the game was done, |
| cascus o a tot gazainat, | They both have won, neither has lost: |
| et anc non n'escaperon dat, | Each one successfully has tossed |
| car negus non s'irais ni jura | The dice, and no complaint is heard. |
| Fin'Amors tan los assegura | For Love has given them his word |
| qu'ades **lur** dis que ben soven | That many times again will they |
| **poiran** jugar e longamen; | Be able to repeat their play.] |
| (6504–6520) | |

*Flamenca*'s three intertwined narratives present, from the protagonists' various points of view, each one's relationship with courtly love and the contrary proposition he or she explores in an attempt to escape from its dominion. In this debating mode, the protagonists grapple with their preconceptions of courtly love and how to be courtly lovers, and, eventually, with how to escape the constraints of this love, through which the audience sees that courtly love is a constraint, and is not identical with true love. *Flamenca* presents a critique of courtly love—and a critical exploration of notions of love more generally—through the multi-pronged attack emanating from the different perspectives of those involved: husband, lover, wife, and court.

Yet love in *Flamenca* is not a simple opposition between *amor coral* and *amor cortesa*, with a straightforward battle of good and evil that culminates in the former supplanting the latter. Rather, *Flamenca* seems to include two different steps in the amorous process, neither of which is "true, fine, sincere, perfect" love, or "love-as-a-whole." In a preliminary stage, we see a game of flirtation played by rules, in courtesy. In a next stage, lovers admit they are both interested and move from play to new relations: this is the *coral* stage of love. Once this stage has been entered into, we see that comparison can be made with the previous one, as the

---

[20] The other instances of *amor coral* are in 2368, 2822, 4272, 5397–5398, 6011, 6208, 6286–6287, 6500, 6510, 6569, and 7641. Not that *a/Amors* presents a very strong ambiguity between abstract noun and personification, as Occitan uses the same gender for both.

two are different. It is at this point that we perceive that *amor cortesa* is false and concerned with appearances, and the contrasting *amor coral* is true and sincere. When these two stages of love are put together, we see how a love that comprises both is closer to being "perfect"—in its literal sense—than is the first—"court-ly"—stage alone.

While *Flamenca* represents *amor cortesa* as a tainted love, this is not to say that the *coral* is all positive, nor that there is not a place for the *cortes* in the amorous and psychological quest of a romance such as *Flamenca*.[21] *Amor coral* may appear to have supplanted *amor cortesa* as the new *amor* under discussion in this romance; but it does not procure happiness ever after, and is rejected in favour of playing the courtly game. This is where the really stimulating problems arise. The constituent parts of pairs are necessary to one another's existence—inside/outside, truth/appearance, truth/falseness—so the courtly game and true love are symbiotically entwined: there can be no privacy and no intimate secrets without a public stage; and these secrets are, paradoxically, at once lies to the public and inner truth. Is *amor coral* the subversion of a courtly game, out-courtlying the courtly? How can that be compatible with the rejection of *cortes*?

### *Flamenca*: amor coral and beyond

Shortly after entering into the idyll of *amor coral*, *Flamenca*'s lovers separate. They come back together later at the husband's court, in a renewal of relations as an apparent combination of true *coral* under a superficial layer of *cortes*, under the noses of husband and court, and with their approval. What we see in this final part of the romance is not *amor coral* plain and simple, but rather its combination with *amor cortesa* into something new.

The previous (central) part's split focalization on the lovers—alternating between them, and showing their inner musings—moves now to a distanced third-person focalization, with a complete closing-down of all insight on the lovers' internal workings. The reader now sees from the external point of view, that of the court; the rare remarks interpreting behaviour are based on observation and supposition. In tune with the courtly setting, we have a dizzying increase of uncertainties, double-readings, and indeed a multiplication of untrustworthy narrative voices. The reader knows, from the previous parts of the romance, what has

---

[21] More recent work on medieval *amor* has moved towards its perception as a large and fluid idea: for example, in more sophisticated treatment of the "did they do it?" question, this new amorous idea must be treated with particular attention to being wary of reducing potential complexities into simple dichotomies and simplistic paradigm shifts. The hypothesis about a new kind of medieval *amor* presented here carries the further *caveat* that it is based on the study of a single work, from a disrupted and fragmented literature.

happened and is—surmising, based on past experience—going on between the lovers; she interprets some of their comments as she believes herself to be in on the joke, that is, references to past, private events, producing public speech with a double meaning through the secret code. The reader will also realize that she is now occupying the same voyeuristic position with regard to the narrative and its persons, as did Archimbaut with regard to the lovers; and that she is just as prone to misprision and misinterpretation, and to both of these being manipulated by characters who are conscious of the limitations of the viewer's direction and angle of vision. Archimbaut has a small cell built with a specially-constructed small peephole (*pertuis*, 1315), from which to look into the imprisoned ladies' chambers.

Once the affair is over, with Archimbaut the jealous husband returned to sanity and rehabilitated, the narrative enters its final section and closing frame, in which the three central protagonists are reintegrated at and into the court. At this point, the affair is renewed—but now at court, watched and enjoyed by its spectators. The lovers' idyll occupying the middle and main part of our text has been only a preliminary to the public staging of a courtly entertainment. The court itself becomes a protagonist, a single being with a single voice and gaze:

| | |
|---|---|
| L'endeman de [la] Pantecosta | [The day that followed Whitsunday, |
| dreg a Nemurs **li cortz s'ajosta** | The court at Namur made display |
| bela e rica e pleniera. | Of splendor gorgeous, rich and rare.] |
| (187–189) | |

One of the distinctions I drew earlier between the middle part of *Flamenca* and its outer frame is a shift towards a different kind of focalization. In the outer frame, we do not follow the point of view of any single character, but look on at a distance, apparently impartially and objectively, and accompanying only as far as an outside observer could do—as, say, would do a lurker in corridors and participant in feasts and jousts. In so doing, the reader is actually seeing from the point of view of the court. Initial readings suggest a contrast between outer frame and middle sections based on a shift from observation, reporting, and commentary to protagonistcentred focalization. But, further, the court actually acts as a protagonist in the narrative, and narration from its point of view can be read as a protagonist-based focalization, just like those in the middle part.

Our principal protagonists become part of the court in the closing frame. In a positive sense, this is the happy ending of reconciliation. An earlier gazing scene (from Flamenca's wedding feast) is recapitulated, but now includes the lovers Flamenca and Guillem, and shows light radiating from all faces concerned, including Flamenca's:

Ben son servit a lur talen,
Mais ben i ac plus de .V. cen
que cascuns esgarda e mira
Flamenca, e can plus cossira
sa faiso ni sa captenenza,
e sa beutat c'ades agenza,
sos oilz ne pais a l'esgardar
e fai la bocca jejunar;
(524–530)

[Thus lavishly they all are served,
Yet more than five hundred observed
Flamenca, and while they gazed
Upon her loveliness, bemazed
By the sheer beauty of her face,
Her charm of manner and grace,
They fed their eyes delightfully,
But left their mouths starving and dry.]

Ben fo-l palais enluminatz,
quar **de las donas venc clardatz**
**que monstreron tota lur cara;**
**mais la plus bella e la plus clara**
**fon de Flamenca que sezia**
**josta Guillem,** ...
(7555–7560)

[With shining light the palace gleamed,
As from the ladies' faces beamed
The glow of beauty radiant.
The fairest and most brilliant
Shone where Flamenca sat, right next
To William, ...]

Courtly interactions are highly formalized, staged, and performed in the romance's outer frame.[22] Courtly performances of the romance's first section are recalled chiasmically towards the end of the romance, as Guillem and Flamenca are integrated into the courtly spectacle and spectator sport, in terms that pick up the courtly games that open the romance:

car ben conois e ve e sap
que si dons laissus estaria
per los cadafals qu'el vezia.
(7274–7276)[23]

[Knowing that for the tournament
His lady would be close at hand
To watch him from this new-built stand.]

Flamenca and Guillem lose individuality when they become part of the general *mêlée* of tourneying and feasting. The ending (as it stands) is sinister: the three days' worth of resumed joyous courtliness are repetitive, and could potentially continue in unending repetition — a courtly nightmare. Worse still, although the lovers may now be together openly, they are trapped in someone else's play, forced to perform for this society of spectacle in a Neverland of eternal play:

---

[22] See, for example, 722–723, 732–733, and 782–792. The first two examples show this in the form of a dance, and the third, of similar mood, is a different sort of staged spectator sport.

[23] See also 7707–7710.

Flamenca s'es dese vanada
que sa marga sera donada
a cel que prumiers jostara
e cavallier derocara.
Ges non ac ben lo mot complit
que **tut ensems levon un crit**
e dison ques ades la parca
del braz, . . .
(7715–7722)

[Immediately Flamenca vowed
That her own sleeve would be bestowed
Upon that gentleman who first
His brave antagonist unhorsed.
Scarce had she spoken when a loud
Outcry arose from all the crowd
Bidding her give the sleeve . . .]

Shortly thereafter the barons gather together and declare that the knight to whom the lady gave her sleeve has rightly earned the tourney's laurels (8038–8044).

The sleeve may be viewed as a metaphor for what is happening "inside" it in the lovers' narrative, and as a hint of their perpetual return, trapped in a never-ending Moebius strip of a story. This sleeve-scene should be contrasted with an earlier one, in the opening courtly section of the romance. During Archimbaut's nuptial festivities, the king is seen jousting and sporting a sleeve suspected to belong to Flamenca, and that she may have given him. The queen transmits this information—and her suspicion—to Archimbaut. She does so in a curiously flirtatious manner, and her manipulative intervention gives rise to Archimbaud's crazed jealousy.[24] In this symmetrical repetition, in a sense "closing" this "fold" in the tale, Flamenca gives her sleeve to Guillem, publicly, through an intermediary. This stands in contrast to the earlier sleeve transmission, which was unseen, allegedly secret, and the subject of malevolent whisperings. It is also a parody of an earlier scene's transmission of *salutz*—an amorous epistle—from Flamenca to Guillem via the intermediary of the unfortunate husband, Archimbaut, as Guillem will carry the sleeve inside his shield, close to his heart. The couple attempts to deal resourcefully with all that is *cortes* by undermining it from within, inserting the private space of *amor coral* inside the public one.

The subterfuge is not successful, as the lovers are now back under courtly control, interacting mechanically, especially in their dulled speech, which has obvious in-jokes but is otherwise rather unexciting. Tilde Sankovitch reads the characters as acting like "puppets" manipulated by the external poet, Love, and the external forces she represents.[25] Sankovitch's idea may be extended to their manipulation by the court in the outer frame. Far from being a secret token of

---

[24] The scene features no protagonist-based focalization, but third-person comments designed to suggest protagonist intention and deliberation. Potential misreadings are left ambiguous: it is possible that the king and queen orchestrate the whole affair, as a narrative whose opening and closing acts are staged publicly at court. Narrative voice—avatar(s) of the *Flamenca* poet—and the court thus collude in deceiving and controlling the reader.

[25] Tilde Sankovitch, "The *Romance of Flamenca*: The Puppeteer and the Play," *Neophilologus* 60 (1976): 8–19.

love shared by the lovers, the sleeve is public property and its gift sanctioned (8038–8044) and controlled (7720–7722) by the court. In a final cutting comment on love at court, and the possibilities of the private subverting the public or coexisting harmoniously with it, the court appears to win. Returning to the scene at Flamenca's nuptials, it may be reread as a portent of the court's need to use and abuse its creatures; although while it may "feed" from them in a parasitic way, the court must draw the line at draining or destroying individuals.

| | |
|---|---|
| Ben son servit a lur talen, | [Thus lavishly they all are served, |
| Mais ben i ac plus de .V. cen | Yet more than five hundred observed |
| que cascuns esgarda e mira | Flamenca, and while they gazed |
| Flamenca, e can plus cossira | Upon her loveliness, bemazed |
| sa faiso ni sa captenenza | By the sheer beauty of her face, |
| e sa beutat c'ades agenza, | Her charm of manner and grace, |
| sos oilz ne pais a l'esgardar | They fed their eyes delightfully, |
| e fai la bocca jejunar; | But left their mouths starving and dry.] |
| (524–530) | |

Love-affairs involving comic episodes at court with public cuckolding are hardly rare in medieval Romance literature; nor is the conflict between private and public. The lacunary state of *Flamenca's* unique manuscript does leave the ending deliciously open. Yet the extant end part of *Flamenca* departs from type in its depiction of relations that are both *coral* and *cortes* (or something else derived from both—a new kind of love, the ingenious creation of our lovers). The narrative avoids the more formally expected endings—tragic deaths of the lovers, death of the lover, or death of the spouse and marriage of the lovers—expected, that is, because two of *Flamenca's* strongest intertextual relationships are with the *Tristan* textual family and with the Occitan *novas* and pseudo-biographical *vidas e razos*.[26] Instead, it offers a resolution, albeit an uncomfortable and inconclusive one. We are left with a *ménage à trois* that includes an impotent voyeur, perhaps in a practical comment on the real implications of adulterous love as life which, in *Flamenca* as in the real world, would probably just go on.

What *Flamenca* does with love that is remarkable (and worthy of twenty-first-century comment) is to discuss and debate an idea, and to do so by playing with it, and putting it into play. Sarah Kay proposes that *amour courtois* is a group of ideas in circulation at the time of Chrétien de Troyes, one played with in an imaginative and discursive mode and not to be thought of as a fixed idea and doctrine but as a fluid "agenda."[27] Her reading echoes Paris's portrayal of *amour*

---

[26] In the latter category, resonances should be particularly noted with the narrative poetry of the Catalan Raimon Vidal de Besalú, such as the love-triangle in his *Castía gilos* and the representation of the *cor noble* in *Abrils issi' e mays intrava*. See O'Brien, "Erotics and Poetics," chap. 3 and Conclusion.

[27] Kay, "Courts, Clerks, and Courtly Love."

*courtois* as an idea rather than a concrete entity spelled out in black and white, and dovetails with part of Uitti's 1972 critique of F.X. Newman:

> I have argued that representations of love in courtly texts do not constitute a doctrine, but an agenda which reflects the preoccupations of medieval courts; their concern with decorum, elegance, display, and affluence, but above all with limiting the potential for schism, and trying to negotiate the lay and clerical interests of the various courtiers and their masters. [28]

A key text illustrating the phenomena of amorous ideas and of their being in circulation is Andreas Capellanus's *De Amore* (1170s-80s). This is the second of the twin pillars supporting Paris's idea of *amour courtois*, and the one providing the crux and dramatic culmination of his argument. Paris's article, when read as a whole, produces a very different view of courtly love from the standard stereotype: it is emphatically *not* a stable or static set of fixed rules, but essentially fluid, mobile, debated; and in the hypothetical mode. The idea of love as a game is vital. Paris argues that courtly love had a limited place in the real world at courts centered around ladies such as Marie, sitting in judgement on amorous questions. I tend not to view this idea of "game" as government by rules and set moves, and action in a fixed pattern and progression. Instead, I side with Kay in focusing on the play of moving around parameters ingeniously, akin to the virtuoso play of scholastic debate. This is an activity with a play-acting side (e.g., the ladies' courts of love), and a kind of play that is conscious of being a game, and of not being real. It is an imaginative exercise, both in the contemporary sense of *imaginatio* and in the modern sense of the imagination. Finally, it should be emphasized that in this sort of game there is no necessary end result, nor any necessity for there to be one.

*De Amore*'s dialogues may be seen as deliberately and necessarily unsatisfied and open-ended, as is the work's double and apparently contradictory structure, in an attempt to engage the audience as active readers in making sense of the work. But *De Amore* can be read as containing a dialogic rather than prescriptive pedagogy; a text that leaves open the possibility for discussion continuing afterwards, in the manner of the protagonists' own conversations, rather than as a manual presenting a codification of "The Rules." Its structure bears such a strong resemblance to that of *Flamenca* and its several stages of love that it suggests a reading of the romance as a commentary on the treatise. [29]

---

[28] K. Uitti, "Remarks on Old French Narrative: Courtly Love and Poetic Form (I)," *Romance Philology* 26 (1972): 77–93, here 92. Responding to F.X. Newman, ed., *The Meaning of Courtly Love: Papers of the First Annual Conference of the Center for Medieval and Early Renaissance Studies, State University of New York at Binghamton, March 17–18, 1967* (Albany: SUNY Press, 1968).

[29] In its preface, *De Amore* sets itself up as amorous advice given to a young man. The first book comprises a theoretical treatise on love, and a middle section illustrating these

*Flamenca* features playful dialogue in the shape of the lovers' conversations; further, debate about love is what ties the romance together: what kinds of love are represented, whether or not they are true, whether or not this is perceived by protagonists, indeed how they perceive — and comically misperceive — their own love. It is a discursive narrative at all those levels: a narrative that both depicts discussion and is about it. As a critical work about love, *Flamenca* is also narratologically discursive, deploying techniques of a discursive nature: a plurality of narrative focalizations runs parallel to a multiplicity of narrative voices offering more or less clearly dubious guidance, misreading situations, and playing with the audience.

This structure offers the audience at least three kinds of involvement with *Flamenca*'s central debates (that is, the specific case, and amorous casuistry in general): most obviously, where they would position themselves, in sympathy with which of the three principal protagonists (Archimbaut, Guillem, Flamenca). Secondly and less obviously, in choosing to follow any of the narrative comments, and in discussion after the end of the romance, not least as the work is, in our only extant manuscript, left suspended. Thirdly and more subtle still, the romance features other protagonists of varying realities, who do not coincide in real time nor in a single space (Amor, the king of France, Archimbaut of Bourbon, Guillem of Nevers, Guillem of Montpellier, etc.), providing an *effet de l'irréel* paradoxically closer to the bone than realism would have been. There is a greater concentration of these crossover persons in the romance's outer frame, such as a number of narrative voices, references to real poets (and to poetry in general), and the court.

In the opening frame, we see the most important role of the court in *Flamenca* — and in its construction and control over its events: the affair is caused by the gossip-mill, of which poets and poetry are a major part. While the queen's reporting of her suspicions to Archimbaut provokes the liaison, it would have come to nothing if news of his subsequent descent into madness had not been spread by the poets and their mocking songs heard on every tongue (1171–1178).

---

principles, pitting men and women against each other in dialogues of (male-instigated) seduction. The second book considers the possible consequences of a successful seduction: the retention, continuation, and end of love. Once again, there is an embedded practical, dialogic section: here, cases of love brought before the court for arbitration, and judgements passed by the arbiters, courtly ladies. Another embedded narrative culminates in the King of Love's thirty-one rules. The final book is a cynical and misogynist rejection of love, in favour of abstention and religious devotion. It may be read — following authorial comments to this effect — as a practical and negative counterbalance to the first part's positive theory of love, as would be proper in any form of medieval intellectual disputation (e.g., Aquinas). Otherwise, the concluding book may be a later continuation, perhaps in an attempt to save the work from condemnation. See also K. Andersen-Wyman, *Andreas Capellanus On Love?* (New York: Palgrave, 2007).

Meanwhile Guillem first hears of Flamenca, and her habit and repute—greatly accentuated by inaccessibility—through the combination of general news and poetic information.[30]

| | |
|---|---|
| **Per moutas gens au et enten** | [Now many people had related |
| com tenia Flamenca presa | How he who thought to watch o'er her |
| cel que la cuj'aver devesa, | Had kept Flamenca prisoner. |
| **et au dir per vera novella** | Truly, men said, she was the best, |
| que-l miellers es e li plus bella | The fairest and the loveliest. |
| e-l plus **cortesa** qu'el mon sia. | In grace no woman was above her. |
| **En cor li venc que l'amaria** . . . | So he made up his heart to love her . . .] |
| (1761–1780) | |

It is poetry itself that is responsible for setting up and controlling the affair. The narrative's events take place through poets and the poetic/courtly rumour-mill; and the story ends with our three protagonists trapped forever at a perpetual court in an unended poem. Court and poets work together, in a voyeuristic hierarchy created by a chain of events: manipulative action, its observation, and then its reporting. Poetic activity is associated with that of the court, and not always in the most pleasant way. Like the court, poets may reap the benefits of a particularly piquant affair: besides providing pure entertainment, it provides valuable material for the entertainment industry of court-based poetry. Further performances then continue the spread of poetry to further audiences, who may, it is hoped, be capable of *entendemen* and thus continue the virtuous circle of applied poetry.

The audience is here, included in this gaze of apparently cold and distant observation, of a play on the stage that *is* courtly life: we are included in the work as protagonists. This is *Flamenca*'s most frightening critique of the courtly world, and indeed of courtliness itself. One by one, *Flamenca*'s protagonists attempt to escape their imprisonment, yet end up resigning themselves to courtly life, trapped in perpetual play-acting; and so might the audience.

*Flamenca*'s metanarrative aspect spills over into reading, and poetic activity may be extended to encompass readings. If *Flamenca*'s audience is left with an open text and some potentially deeply cynical or frightening lessons, these do still generate the poetic continuation and application that is discussion. Discussion itself is the closest we may come to understanding a "true love" that, as we

---

[30] The *vera novella* of 1777 is both "news" and the poetic form. One of the many formal labels applied to *Flamenca* is *novas*—akin to the Italian *novella* and French *nouvelle*—by an earlier first-person voice comment: *pero a mas novas vos torn*, "but let me return you to my tale" (250). The double sense of *novella / novas* is important: this is renewal and refashioning, as poetry is kept fresh and alive, and maintains relevance and applicability. This may also be interpreted as a tardy attempt at *translatio studii*, in a peculiarly Occitan and poetic form.

have seen, includes both *amor cortesa* and *amor coral,* in a relationship that may be characterised as symbiotic and discursive.

*Flamenca*'s discussion has had two historical continuations. The first comprises contemporary reading, performance, and critical appreciation of *Flamenca*; refashionings and *reprises* of some of its material, such as in the *Livre du voir dit*; and, most importantly, in the application of the *translatio studii* principle to ideas of love.[31] *Flamenca*'s second continuation is in its contributions to modern scholarly discussion about love in medieval literature. The *Charrette* and *De Amore* are key to making sense of the Northern move towards *amour courtois* or *courtoisie*, away from Occitan ideas of an *amor* that is interchangeably good, true, *fin'*, *cortesa*, and *coral*. *Flamenca* is, in turn, key to understanding a later refinement. Looking back on the corpus of courtly literature, it acts as a literary *summa* placing Occitan French literary traditions and their respective amorous ideas in literary discussion with one another, and engages in its own metaliterary discussion with them. This should be put in a larger context. Coming as it does from the period when works such as Jofre de Foixà's *Regles de trobar* and Dante's *De Vulgari eloquentia* provide an early instance of polemic about cardinal poetic issues, *Flamenca* constitutes a vital early step not just in the courtly love debate, but also in the history of literary criticism and theory.

---

[31] Little is known of *Flamenca*'s actual contemporary reception, as the *unicum* manuscript is not mentioned in contemporary sources and disappears from view until the early 19th century. It is mentioned in a 14th-century Catalan letter: see Stefano Asperti, "*Flamenca* e dintorni: Considerazioni sui rapporti fra Occitania e Catalogna nel XIV secolo," *Cultura neolatina* 45 (1985): 59–104. On *Flamenca* and performance, see Evelyn Birge Vitz, "Performance in, and of, *Flamenca*," in *"De sens rassis": Essays in Honor of Rupert T. Pickens*, ed. Keith Busby, Bernard Guidot, and Logan E. Whalen (Amsterdam: Rodopi, 2005), 683–98. Instances of performance *in* the work—as is the case for many other details in the narrative, such as the wedding—provide us with extremely useful information on performance *around the time of writing*. Unfortunately, this does not add any material evidence to hypothetical arguments around the reading and reception of *Flamenca* at the time of its writing. Tracing *Flamenca*'s echoes in later literature is useful for piecing together some part of its reception history; albeit later, as close as is possible to the immediately contemporary.

# Inversion and Parody: Generic Implications of the Digitization of Old French *Fabliaux*

Katherine A. Brown
Princeton University

The Old French *fabliaux* furnish a compelling example for electronic analysis, particularly in their capacity as parody of courtly genres. The study of parody promotes intertextual comparisons because it presupposes linguistic connections between the parodic text and its model. For this reason, parody lends itself to a number of algorithms and programs, including searching, counting, sorting, and indexing.[1] I intend to demonstrate how analysis of the language of the *fabliaux* facilitates comparisons with romance and highlights the linguistic inversions and parodic elements of the *fabliaux*. These comparisons bring to light the generic specificity of the *fabliaux* and, reciprocally, underscore the specificity of the language of courtly narrative. In order to demonstrate the role of textual encoding of the *fabliaux*, I shall give examples of inversion and parody, limiting the references to the courtly tradition, and shall suggest—showing whenever possible with current resources—the precise ways in which electronic analysis can further comparative studies and ultimately furnish material for new readings of texts.

Specific tools are necessary for the textual encoding and markup of *fabliaux* and other texts in order to better an understanding of the texts themselves and to contribute to larger generic, linguistic, and rhetorico-poetic studies of the Old French literary tradition. The level of encoding and markup of the *Charrette Project*[2] serves as an example. Specifically, the use of repetition and rhetorico-poetic devices, as defined and used in the *Charrette Project*, informs my reading of

---

[1] For a general introduction to textual encoding and markup, see Susan Hockey, *Electronic Texts in the Humanities: Principles and Practice* (Oxford: Oxford University Press, 2000) and Jean-Philippe Genet and Antonio Zampolli, eds., *Computers and the Humanities* (Aldershot: Dartmouth Publishing Company/European Science Foundation, 1992).

[2] For the *Charrette Project* and sister-sites, see http://www.princeton.edu/~lancelot/ ss/. For information on the general methodology of the Project, see the articles collected in *Œuvres & Critiques* 27.1 (2002).

Gina L. Greco and Ellen M. Thorington, eds., *Dame Philology's Charrette: Approaching Medieval Textuality through Crétien's 'Lancelot': Essays in Memory of Karl D. Uitti.* MRTS 408. Tempe: ACMRS, 2012. [ISBN 978-0-86698-456-0]

parody as a literary device in which conscious imitation of a model is observable on the level of words and rhetoric. While the definitions and applications of the rhetorico-poetic devices of the *Charrette Project* are specific to Chrétien's text, the methodology is arguably applicable to a variety of Old French texts. The type of textual encoding demonstrated by the *Charrette Project* has led me to question previous understandings of parody in the *fabliaux*, particularly how parody participates in the process of rewriting, and how inversion and parody in the *fabliaux* may be studied on situational, stylistic, and rhetorical levels with the aid of search and sorting tools.

To illustrate the projected utility of textual encoding, I shall examine an example provided by Per Nykrog in his study of the *fabliaux*. He posits that the introduction to Jean Bodel's *fabliau Des Deus Chevaus* (below left) is a courtly burlesque of the introduction to Chrétien de Troyes's *Cligés* (below right) since, in both cases, the narrator or clerkly figure enumerates the titles of his other compositions.[3]

| | |
|---|---|
| Cil qui trova del *Morteruel* | Cil qui fist d'Erec et d'Enide |
| Et del mort *Vilain de Bailluel* | Et les Commandemenz Ovide |
| Qui n'ert malades ne enfers, | Et l'Art d'Amours au romanz mist, |
| Et de *Gombert et des .ii. Clers*, | Et le Mors de l'Espaule fist, |
| Que il mal atrait a son estre, | Del roi Marc et d'Iseut la Blonde |
| Et de *Brunain* la vache au prestre | Et de la Hupe et de l'Aronde |
| Que Blere amena, ce m'est vis, | Et del Rossignol la Muance |
| Et trova le *Songe des Vis* | Un nouvel conte recomance. . .[5] |
| Que la dame paumoier dut | |
| Et du *Leu que l'Oue decut*, | |
| Et des *Ii. Envieus* cuiviers, | |
| Et de *Barat* et de Travers | |
| Et de lor compaignon Haimet, | |
| D'un autre fablel s'entremet . . .[4] | |

---

[3] Per Nykrog, *Les Fabliaux* (Geneva: Droz, 1973), 82–84.
[4] Cited by Nykrog, *Les Fabliaux*, 82–83.
[5] Cited by Nykrog, *Les Fabliaux*, 83.

[He who composed in verse about *Mort-eruel*, and about the death of the *Vilain de Bailleul* who was neither ill nor infirm, and about *Gombert et les deus Clers* whom he wrongly invited to his hearth, and about *Brunain*, the priest's cow that Blère brought, it seems to me, and who composed in verse the *Songe des Vis* that the lady was about to brandish, and about the *Leu que l'Oue decut*, and about the two *Envieus cuiviers*, and about *Barat* and Travers and about their companion Haimet, troubles himself with another fabliau . . .][6]

[He who told of *Erec* and of *Enide* and the *Commandemenz Ovide* and who put the *Art d'Amours* in verse, and who made the *Mors de l'Espaule*, of king Marc and of Yseut the Blonde, and of the Hupe et l'Aronde, and of the *Rossignol la Muance*, begins in turn a new story . . .]

A digital search tool can locate titles and lists of titles such as these (provided titles are marked or tagged separately). Searching and indexing tools such as those developed for the *Charrette Project* already have this capability, but within the context of the *Charrette Project* this is currently only true for a single text, Chrétien's *Le Chevalier de la Charrette* (*Lancelot*). A similar encoding of other works would allow for intertextual and generic comparisons. In this example, the two passages have no titles in common, so a search for a specific title would not connect these texts, but the device of listing titles in succession does link them. What distinguishes this example as a specific burlesque of *Cligés* as opposed to a more general parody of *clercs'* invocation of their own works is the particular phrase "cil qui fist/trova." Since some *fabliaux* and a number of romances are already digitized in the *Base de Français Médiéval*,[7] it is possible to conduct some lexical searches. A search of the expression "Cil qui fist/mist/trova/escrit" yielded three other occurrences of which only one was followed by a reference to writing or a text.[8] The use of the same phrase at the beginning of the text suggests that Jean Bodel was consciously repeating or imitating Chrétien's work; consequently,

---

[6] All English translations are my own unless otherwise noted.

[7] The *Base de Français Médiéval* is an internet database and linguistic tool dedicated to preserving and providing linguistic data for texts in Old and Middle French. Copyrighted texts and materials on the site are available only for lexical searches. There are currently twelve *fabliaux* in the database. For more information on the *BFM*, consult the website, *BFM: Base de Français Médiéval*, 26 October 2006, Lyon: UMR ICAR / ENS-LSH. 2005, http://bfm.ens-lsh.fr/.

[8] In the search, "Cil" is capitalized for a case-sensitive search intended to restrict occurrences to the first position of the verse-line. A few synonyms of "fist" were included in the search to maximize results. Below is the only other result from the *Roman de la Rose ou de Guillaume de Dole*: "**Cil qui mist** cest conte en romans, ou il a fet note . . ." (1). It should be noted that this search is limited to the texts already encoded in the *BFM* and therefore represents in no way an exhaustive search of medieval French literature.

this reinforces the notion of burlesque posited by Nykrog. As this example using the *BFM* shows, a search program is effective when the texts under consideration share similar language. This example also has generic implications, since parodic language involves imitation of a model. As my examination will emphasize — perhaps contrary to Nykrog's understanding — the instances of parody within the *fabliaux* tradition do not systematically subvert or undermine courtly literature and ideals, but rather reinforce them.

Before proceeding to the textual analysis of a specific example of parody, it would be expedient to discuss the use of the terms 'parody' and 'burlesque' in order to clarify their use by previous critics and in the present study. In his discussion of the *fabliaux*, Nykrog argues that parody (or rather courtly burlesque) constitutes one of the salient features of the genre.[9] Critics generally agree that the *fabliaux* draw on medieval texts from a variety of genres, but not all of the humor of the *fabliaux* is necessarily derived from parodic or satirical recastings of courtly texts, nor can all references and allusions to other texts within the *fabliaux* tradition be categorically defined as parody or burlesque. Moreover, although Nykrog's definitions of parody and burlesque remain implicit, if inherently connected to his generic definition of the *fabliaux*, the meaning of these terms is not self-evident. Since the words parody, burlesque, and travesty, among others, are ambiguous and often used interchangeably, even by Heinrich Lausberg who gives them as synonyms of each other, the present paper will discuss only parody as defined below.[10]

The word parody is derived from the Classical Greek παρῳδία (*parodia*), meaning a "song sung in imitation of another."[11] Mikhail Bahktin's definition of parody as "citation" or the "language of another"[12] lends itself to applications in search programs and other electronic analysis. For Bakhtin, parody is of language, not of subject, and is essentially dialogical, relating the language that

---

[9]  See Nykrog, *Les Fabliaux*, esp. 72–104.

[10]  For a discussion of parody in the Middle Ages, see Paul Lehmann, *Parodie im Mittelalter* (Munich: Drei Masken, 1922). For an attempt at the disambiguation of the terms 'parody,' 'burlesque,' and 'travesty,' see Margaret A. Rose, *Parody//Meta-Fiction: An Analysis of Parody as a Critical Mirror to the Writing and Reception of Fiction* (London: Croom Helm, 1979), esp. 39–55. See also Heinrich Lausberg, *Handbuch der Literarischen Rhetorik* (Munich: Max Hüber, 1960), who defines parody as "a work in prose or verse where one makes a joke of other works by using the same expressions and ideas in a ridiculous mischievous sense" and *burlesque* as "that which provokes laughter through contrast between the lowness of style and the dignity of the characters; that which provokes laughter through a kind of joke or caricature" (§1246, my translations). Lausberg apparently relies on sixteenth- and seventeenth-century conceptions of these terms, and neither term seems entirely appropriate to explain the relation between *fabliaux* and romance or other genres.

[11]  Rose, *Parody*, 18, 33.

[12]  Mikhaïl Bakhtin, "De la préhistoire du discours romanesque," in *Esthétique et théorie du roman*, trans. Daria Olivier (Paris: Gallimard, 1978), 401–37.

parodies to that which is parodied.[13] Since parody remains at the level of language, computer-assisted analysis can help to focus on the language(s) of parody by locating what is similar in texts and comparing what is different (although to my knowledge there are no searching and indexing tools designed specifically for the study of parody). Such analysis would further an understanding of the specificity of the diction for each text and each case. The differences, however, are often in the form of an inversion. Computers can easily be made to signal textual similarities that locate examples of linguistic inversions or announce parodic inversions for a large corpus of texts.

The device of parody in the *fabliaux* assumes two dominant forms: targeted imitations of a particular work and broader imitations of a genre or *topos*. Analyses of both specific and general parody can be assisted by detailed textual encoding because, ultimately, it is the language of the texts that will furnish distinctions between specific references and general or topical allusions among texts. Without the proper tools, it is difficult at best to attempt a lexical analysis of numerous texts and extensive passages. Searches in the *BFM* are designed for linguists, and are therefore limited to selections of words, usually those words with high occurrences in the texts under consideration. Accordingly, the context of each result must be compared systematically and there is as yet no tool to aid in these comparisons. While the *BFM* provides an excellent search and indexing tool and is invaluable for tracing specific words and phrases, and for listing concordances among a broad range of Old and Middle French texts, it does not include markup beyond the single word or morpheme, nor does it provide disambiguation and dictionary forms for various occurrences, as the *Charrette Project* does. The use of rhetorico-poetic figures like those currently marked up in the *Charrette Project* can conceivably call attention to the prevalence of inversion in the *fabliaux* and reinforce the notion of parody within the genre, or alternatively highlight characteristics of certain *topoi*.

## The *Fabliau* and *Perceval*

The *fabliau La Damoiselle qui ne pooit oïr parler de foutre* exists in three distinct versions; the present discussion will consider the second version[14] because it has the most extensive and profound relation to romance. In this version, the daughter of a wealthy rustic is renowned for her prudishness and feigns illness at the slightest mention of lewdness. Having heard about this "precious girl,"[15] a young

---

[13] Bakhtin, "De la préhistoire," 430–31.

[14] For a discussion and presentation of all three versions, see Jean Rychner, *Contributions à l'étude des fabliaux: variantes, remaniements, dégradations*, 2 vols. (Geneva: Droz, 1960).

[15] Nykrog refers to her as a "précieuse ridicule du XIIIe siècle" (*Les Fabliaux*, 78).

man named David, who knows a lot about trickery and guile ("qui mout savoit barat et guile," 33),[16] decides to try and profit from the situation. He goes to the rustic and asks for lodging. When the father warns him about the interdiction on using vulgar words, David imitates the girl's prudish reaction in her presence, stating that the mention of lewdness causes his heart great pain ("grant dolor au cuer me prant," 95). Delighted by David's apparently similar sensibilities, the girl offers to share her bed with him where the two proceed in turn to explore and rename the various parts of the body with more seemly nomenclature. The text culminates in the natural conclusion of the sexual metaphor: the young couple consummate their relationship.

This *fabliau*'s relation to courtly literature may be shown through references to Chrétien de Troyes's romance *Le Conte du Graal*, and through the language of the extended sexual metaphor found in the final lines. Roy Pearcy has observed the similarity in premises between the second version of *La Damoiselle qui ne pooit. . .* and the beginning of *Le Conte du Graal*, drawing a parallel between the father and daughter of the *fabliau* and Perceval and his mother in the romance:

> The whole situation in the fabliau constitutes a familiar kind of comic inversion, with the doting father anxious to protect his naïve daughter from exposure to knowledge about the facts of life substituting for the doting mother anxious to protect her son from exposure to knowledge about the facts of chivalry.[17]

The *fabliau* exploits both gender inversion and the substitution of chivalry for lewdness in this example. While the father is seemingly over-protective, "et ses peres l'avoit tant chiere / Por ce que plus enfanz n'avoit / Q'a son voloir trestot faisoit; / Plus ert a li que ele a lui," (10–13) [and her father showed her so much affection, because he had no other children, that he did what she wanted; he belonged to her more than she to him] he does not benefit from their isolation because he has no one to help him with his work:

> . . . Ses peres ne ose
> Avoir sergent un mois entier,
> S'an aust il mout grant mestier
> A ses blez batre et a vener
> Et a sa charrue mener
> Et a faire s'autre besoigne. (24–29)

---

[16] All citations of *La Damoiselle qui ne pooit oïr parler de foutre* (version II), unless otherwise noted, are from *Nouveau Recueil Complet des Fabliaux* (*NRCF*), ed. Willem Noomen and Nico van den Boogaard, 10 vols. (Assen/Maastricht: Van Gorcum, 1983–1998), 4: 84–89.

[17] Roy J. Pearcy, "Intertextuality and *La Damoiselle qui n'ot parler de foutre qu'i n'aust mal au cuer*," *Zeitschrift für Romanische Philologie* 109 (1993): 526–38, here 530.

[. . . Her father does not dare have a servant for an entire month, yet he had great need of one to beat and fan his wheat and to drive his plow and to do his other work.]

The rustic essentially capitulates to his daughter's desires. He raises no objections to David's sharing a bed with his daughter, and is almost complicit; thus, he fulfills his role as the opposite or inversion of Perceval's mother. Although the similarities between the texts are strictly situational, and inversions at that, this type of comparison, once identified, lends itself to a computer-assisted search. Sorting and indexing programs can then be used to compare the diction of each text to determine which words occur most often; which parts of speech constitute these common or shared words (nouns, verbs, adjectives, etc.); whether the anxious parents use the same language or whether the father in the *fabliau* inverts that language; whether their innocent children (Perceval and the daughter) use the same or inverted language; what words the narrator uses to describe them; whether the passages share any rhymes, verse-lines, or other rhetorico-poetic figures, and so forth. Textual encoding could further an understanding of the interrelation of these texts—and possibly their variants and other texts—as well as the role of language in parody. While these types of comparisons between two or even three texts may be carried out without computer assistance, comparisons among more than three texts and among extended passages would be tedious and time-consuming at best, and impossible at worst, without computer-assisted search and sorting tools. Thus, computer programs facilitate textual analysis, but the duty of interpretation ultimately lies with the scholar.

The parallel Pearcy cites between *Le Conte du Graal* and the first version of *La Damoiselle qui ne pooit. . .* is indicative of the type of search that can be facilitated by textual encoding and searching tools. He notes that Perceval's mother's reaction to the mention of chivalry and the girl's reaction to lewdness is the same, for both women faint. [18] The appearance of the same verb in both instances ("se pasmer") supports a clear connection between the texts, but encoding and tagging syntactico-grammatical functions could help to differentiate them by quickly supplying other instances of the verb in each text and by indicating relevant information such as person, tense, and mood for each occurrence. This type of lexical connection supports the idea that this *fabliau* draws from and plays off *Le Conte du Graal.* [19]

---

[18] "La mere se pasme a cest mot, / Que chevalier nomer li ot" (Chrétien de Troyes, *Conte du Graal* (*Perceval*), ed. Charles Méla, in *Chrétien de Troyes, Romans*, gen. ed. Michel Zink [Paris: Librairies Générale Française/Livre de Poche, 1994], 403–4) and ". . . ne pooit oïr parler / De foutre ne de culeter / Ne de rien qui a ce tornast / Que maintenant ne se pasmast" (*La Damoiselle qui ne pooit. . .* (I), 7–10).

[19] While true for the first version of the *fabliau*, this does not apply to the version currently under consideration or to the third version in which the girl merely feels ill.

Pearcy continues his study by demonstrating the resemblance between scenes of the girl's sexual initiation and Perceval's chivalric initiation in which Perceval encounters and questions a knight, and the girl meets and questions David in bed:

A sa lance sa main li tant,
Si prant et dit: "Biaus sire chiers,
Vos qui avez non chevaliers,
Que est ice que vos tenez?"
– [. . .] "Je cuidoie ores, dox amis,
Noveles apanre de toi,
Et tu les viaux savoir de moi.
Jo te dirai: ce est ma lance."
[. . .] Li vallez au pam de l'escu
Lo prant et dit tot en apert:
"Ce que est et de coi vos sert?
– [. . .] Je[l] te dirai, commant qu'il praigne,
Car a toi volantiers m'acort.
Escuz a non ce que je port.
–Escuz a non? –Voire, fait il,
Ne lo doi mie tenir vil,
Car il m'e[s]t tant de bone foi
Que se nus lance o trait a moi
Encontre toz les cos se trait,
C'est li servises qu'il me fait." (182–185,
188–191, 206–208, 216–224)[20]

Lors li reprist a demander
Et ses choses a detaster,
Tant qu'el l'a par lo vit saisi:
"Hé, demande, que est ici,
Daviet, si roide et si dur
Que bien devroit percier un mur?
– Dame, fait cil, c'est mes polains,
Qui mout est et roides et sains,
Mais il ne manja des ier main."
Cele remet aval sa main,
Si trove la coille velue;
Les deus coillons taste et remue,
Si redemande: "Daviet,
Que est or ce, en ce sachet,
Fait ele, sont ce deus luisiaus?"
Daviz fu de respondre isniaus:
"Dame, ce sont dui mareschal,
Qui ont a garder mon cheval,
Qant pest en autrui compagnie;
Tot jorz sont en sa compeignie:
De mon polain garder sont mestre."
(167–187)

[He reaches out his hand to his lance, takes it and says: "Fair sir, you who are called knight, what is this that you are holding?" (. . .) –"I thought, dear friend, that I would now learn news from you, but you want to know them from me. I will tell you: it is my lance." The young man touches the front of the shield and says in the open: "What is this and how is it used?" (. . .) –"I will tell you, come what may, since it agrees with me to do so. What I am carrying is called a shield." –"It's called a shield?" –"Truly," he said, "and I must never think it vile, for it is of such good service to me that if anyone uses a lance or shoots at me, it stands up against all the blows; that is the service it renders me."]

[Then she began again to ask and to touch his things until she seized him by the member: "So, she asks, what is this here, David, so straight and hard that it could easily pierce a wall?" –"Lady," he says, "that is my foal that is very straight and healthy, but he has not eaten since yesterday morning." She moves her hand down and finds the hairy scrotum. She touches and moves the two testicles, and asks again: "David, what is this now in this sack," she says, "are they two balls?" David answered right away: "Lady, they are two marshals who have to guard my horse when it grazes in other people's territory. They are always in his company: they are the masters of guarding my horse."]

---

[20] The citation of this passage in Pearcy's article differs somewhat from that above.

Both passages employ the same expository device: the *clerc*/narrator describes a physical object, the naïve character asks what it is, and the knowledgeable character turned instructor provides an answer. If the audience was not already familiar with these objects, the *clerc*/narrator supplies the appropriate word before either Perceval or the girl learns what it is, thereby creating a comic effect in both texts. This scene in *Le Conte du Graal* already constitutes a type of inversion, as the knight proves when he explains that he is answering questions rather than having his questions answered (188–190). The *fabliau* is parody, then, as a reworking or transformation of this part of the romance for comic effect.

Although the device of naming is similar, the language of the texts differs significantly. To say, however, that the language of the *fabliau* undermines that of *Le Conte du Graal* or of romance in general is to misunderstand its purpose. The *clerc*/narrator and the instructor essentially fulfill the same narrative function in both texts, informing the naïve character and the audience about the objects mentioned. Whereas the language of *Le Conte du Graal* is direct and explicit, the *fabliau* utilizes indirect and metaphorical language to couch the unfitting, indeed non-courtly terms of sexual language. In the *fabliau* there are two words to signify each object or rather two "signs" (*signa*) representing one "thing" (*res*)[21] and it is David, not the *clerc*/narrator who makes use of this "courtly" language. Part of the comic irony — aside from the obvious distance between object and name — is the contrast and even inversion of the narrator's use of non-courtly diction with the characters' insistence on diction that is courtly and decorous. It should be noted that this device is used twice in the *fabliau*, in the passage cited above and earlier on when David explores the girl's body:

> Et Daviez sa main avale
> Droit au pertuis desoz lo vantre,
> [. . .] Puis demande que ce puet estre.
> "Par foi, fait ele, c'est mes prez,
> Daviet, la ou vos tastez,
> Mais il n'est pas encore floriz."
> – "Par foi, dame, ce dit Daviz,
> N'i a pas d'erbe encor planté.
> Et que est ce en mi cest prés,
> Ceste fosse soeve et plaine ?"
> – "Ce est, fait ele, ma fontaine . . ." (134–135, 140–148)

[David moves his hand down right to the hole below the stomach (. . .) then he asks what it can be. "To be sure," she says, "it is my meadow, David, that which you are touching, but it has not yet blossomed." – "To be sure, Lady,"

---

[21] See *De Doctrina Christiana*, esp. 1.2 (PL 34. 19–20 ff.) for Augustine's discussion of signs and things.

David says, "there is not yet any grass planted. And what is this in the middle of this meadow?" –"It is, she says, my fountain . . ."]

Here, the girl initiates the use of metaphorical and "courtly" language, and David follows to the point of repeating her exclamation "par foi" at the beginning of his own speech. The girl teaches David the language of love, or rather her language of love, in much the same way that a *domna* such as Guenièvre instructs her knight. In continuing the girl's metaphor, David serves his lady.

The rapport between lewdness and chivalry becomes clear in this passage since the metaphor in the *fabliau* links the two. David's foal—which stands in contrast to the powerful battle horse (*destrier*) of romance—must silence the one who sounds the horn (*cornerre*, 152) in order to enter the meadow and drink from the fountain; the sexual metaphor borrows from the language of chivalric quest in a way that assimilates the acts of chivalry and lewdness. In this *fabliau*, the characters' diction and actions subvert the vulgar language and thus reinforce courtly diction. There is no need for metaphor when the knight explains chivalry to Perceval because knighthood forms part of the foundation of courtly society and, as such, often functions as a metaphor in itself for the language of love. The connection between love and knighthood in this example is clear through its metaphorical presentation in this *fabliau*, as well as through its topical treatment in romance narrative in general, because *Le Conte du Graal* associates love and knighthood especially through the character of Perceval. While his introduction to knights and knighthood occurs at the beginning of the romance, it is not until after Perceval leaves Arthur's court that he receives his true indoctrination into the worlds of chivalry and love with his defeat of Clamadieu and his first acquaintance with Blanchefleur (1253–2913). For Perceval as for David and the girl, love and chivalry are interconnected.

In this example, the use of digital tools can demonstrate that the two passages have few words in common, but that within each text, a small number of words are repeated. Although the following comparisons were executed by hand because the texts under consideration are not currently encoded for searches, indexing, and sorting, the present analysis shows the type of information that can be found and collected more quickly, accurately, and throughout longer passages and across manuscript variants with the aid of digital tools. For the passage of *Le Conte du Graal*, the words *escuz* and *lance* appear three times, emphasizing the importance of chivalry as Perceval learns and discovers new objects. In the *fabliau*, however, the "objects" being discovered are mentioned only once by their real names, and then a second time by their "courtly" names, suggesting that the scene is less about instruction than verbal play and substitution. The verbs of each text show the nature of the scenes, for "avoir non" [to be named] appears three times in *Le Conte du Graal* and supports the notion that this scene involves learning, an initiation, because everything, including the knight, is named, whereas the verb that appears the most often in the *fabliau* is "demander" [to ask] which highlights the dialogical nature of that scene. The girl is not learning words as does Perceval—certainly she must already know these names or else she would not be able to object to hearing about them—she does not need to ask what the "objects" are called because she creates a language as she learns about the "things" (*res*) and the act. Perceval merely learns the words, the "things" (*res*) and their function, but unlike the girl in the *fabliau*, he has no experience of them.

Thus far the relation between the *fabliau* and romance narrative has been general and situational, although at times focused on the language of each genre. In order to better an understanding of the systematic inversions of diction, it is useful to consider a more specific and restricted example. In his comparison of *La Damoiselle qui ne pooit. . .* to *Le Chevalier au Lion*, Keith Busby has suggested that the description of the girl is "reminiscent of the haughty *domna* of romance: *. . .une damoisele / Qui molt par estoit orgoilleuse / Et felonesse et dedaigneuse* (2–4)" and that even the physical description of the girl "is in true courtly style: *. . .molt ert avenanz et bele, / Blanche ot la char con flor d'espine: / S'ele fust fille de raïne, / Si fust ele bele a devise*" (124–127) [a young lady who was very haughty and terrible and disdainful . . . she was very gracious and beautiful, she had white skin like a whitethorn flower: If she were the daughter of a queen, she would be as beautiful as any].[22] Even though these passages present a vague rapport between *fabliau* and romance, merely a topical comparison of disdainful ladies, they nevertheless offer an opportunity for a more profound analysis of their diction. Complimenting Busby's comparison to romance, Pearcy has remarked that the second passage hides a reference to Blancheflor, the name of Perceval's lady, thereby strengthening an argument for a specific connection between these works.[23] A search in the *BFM* for a few of the words from these quotations—such as *felonesse*, *desdaigneuse*, *avenanz*—confirms the dependence of these passages on romance diction, for the vast majority of occurrences appear in romance narratives, most often those of Chrétien.[24] The ironic difference between the courtly use of the word *desdaigneuse* and its use in the *fabliau* is found precisely in the object of the lady's disdain. It should be noted, however, that the *domna* of romance is primarily disdainful of love, an example of which is best seen in *Cligés* where ". . . Soredamors, / Qui desdeigneuse estoit d'amors, / N'onques n'avoit oï parler / D'ome qu'ele deignast amer" (445–448)[25] [Soredamors, who was disdainful of love, had never heard speak of a man she'd deign to love] whereas the girl of the *fabliau* "n'oïst parler de foutre" (6) [would not hear talk of screwing]. This is precisely the

---

[22] Keith Busby, "Courtly Literature and the Fabliaux: Some Instances of Parody," *Zeitschrift für Romanische Philologie* 102 (1986): 67–87, here 80.

[23] Pearcy, "Intertextuality," 532.

[24] A search for "felonese" gave 8 occurrences; for "desdaigneuse," 5 occurrences; and for "avenanz," 33, most of which were from Chrétien's romances.

[25] Chrétien de Troyes, *Cligés*, ed. Charles Méla and Olivier Collet, in *Chrétien de Troyes, Romans*, 285–494.

type of inversion that characterizes the diction of many *fabliaux*, ostensibly placing the courtly ideals of *amour* in opposition to the vulgarity of *foutre*.

Certainly *foutre* is stylistically opposed to *amour*, for it is not commensurate
with courtly diction, but does stylistic opposition necessarily imply ideological
undermining? If this opposition is the crux of the inversion, then it suggests that
*amour*, the ideal of love, and *foutre*, the physical act, are opposed and perhaps
even mutually exclusive. Among the most contested issues in debates on courtly
love, the separation of physical from sentimental love presupposes the platonic
nature of *amour courtois*.[26] In order for the definition of parody as subversion to
apply to this *fabliau*, the word *foutre* would have to undermine any implication
of physical love associated with the word *amour*; consequently, love for and of a
worthy and courtly lady—such as Soredamors—would necessarily preclude any
physical dimension. Certainly Soredamors herself (mother of Cligés) and Enide
both violate any prohibition against physical love with their knights/husbands,
as do, of course, Iseut and Guenièvre. Predictably, Chrétien's texts are well represented in this brief list of (female) models of courtly lovers whose love also has
a physical dimension. The overwhelming literary evidence against such an im-
passable divide between physical and spiritual love challenges claims that the
physical acts of love in this and all *fabliaux* comprise the parody of these texts.
Whether the act of consummation undermines the ideals of courtly love is not
the issue at hand,[27] but evidence in favor of this argument is to be found primarily within the courtly tradition of romance texts, not outside in the *fabliaux*. Perhaps, as Karl Uitti has suggested, it is the role of the *fabliaux* to show that there
is indeed some *ameur*[28] in *amour*.

It may be concluded that, in this example, the opposition established between *foutre* and *amour* is essentially a stylistic inversion, and that the *fabliau*
does not subvert its courtly model. This initial opposition, however, ignores the
true object of the girl's disdain, which is not the act of love itself, but of hearing
talk of it (*parler de foutre*). The text supports the notion that the young lady is not
opposed to the act itself, for, in the final lines, the girl's suggestion initiates the
consummation of the couple's relationship: "David met lou en mon pré pestre /
Ton biau polain se deus te gart" (188–189) [David, put your pretty horse in my

---

[26] An excellent article on the debate is Jean Frappier, "Sur un procès fait à l'amour
courtois," *Romania* 93 (1972): 145–93.

[27] For more on this conception of courtly love, see Denis de Rougemont, *L'Amour et
l'Occident* (1st ed. 1939; repr. Paris: Plon, 1972) and Jean Markale, *L'Amour courtois ou le
couple infernal* (Paris: Imago, 1987).

[28] In modern French, *ameur* means "rutting" and refers to the physical act of love,
specifically for animals, but Gaston Paris notes its use in Old French as well. For an explanation of *ameur* and examples, see Gaston Paris, "Phonétique Française," *Romania* 10
(1881): 36–62, here 44 and Antoine Thomas, "Nouvèles variétés étimolojiqes" [sic], *Romania* 44 (1915–1917): 321–56, here 321.

meadow to graze, may God save you]. At this point the girl's ignorance is feigned at best and her disdain is clearly directed at vulgar language and the individuals who practice it. Language, particularly courtly language, is the primary object of consideration in this *fabliau*, not the sexual act. The character of the girl in her prudishness supports courtliness, at least in speech, through her insistence on sexual euphemisms and intolerance of vulgarity. Although comic, the girl's behavior and relation to language does not undermine courtly diction; inversion and parody are not synonymous with subversion.

On the other hand, the *clerc*/narrator of this text frequently makes use of vulgar and non-courtly speech in describing the language to which the girl objects and ultimately the act that she and David describe in their pseudo-courtly metaphor.[29] The disconnect between the *clerc*'s diction and the characters' use of language establishes another level of linguistic irony and comedy. This type of text lends itself well to computerized figural markup—particularly to the markup of direct and indirect discourse—since it facilitates comparison of the clerkly voice among texts and genres, as well as helps to demonstrate the ironic gaps between the diction of the narrator and the characters in this and other *fabliaux*.

*La Damoiselle qui ne pooit. . .* exemplifies the generic dependence of *fabliaux* on romance narrative and is representative of a number of *fabliaux* where the comic appeal arises from the divorce of *signum* from *res*. Not only does the separation of sign and thing provide the characteristic humor and sources for parody in the genre, it is an expression of the nature of literary language, both literal and allegorical, in the Old French vernacular that endorses the ideals of romance narrative and *courtoisie*. *La Damoiselle qui ne pooit. . .* also represents a particular and limited sub-section of *fabliaux* that exploit the device of sexual metaphors. While most of the *fabliaux* in this particular sub-section typically involve the sexual initiation of a maiden, there are at least two instances of a sexually ignorant young man whose education results in comic misunderstandings and word plays.[30] Gender issues aside, it is the overdeveloped euphemisms and extended metaphors of this sexual language, the language of *ameur*, that parody courtly language and deserve further consideration through electronic analysis.

Although not considered here, other applications of textual encoding and digital tools to the *fabliaux* would permit the tracing of references and allusions to various texts. As this examination of the *fabliaux* has shown, search tools can

---

[29] For definitions and a discussion of direct and indirect discourse and the role of the *clerc* in the *Chevalier de la Charrette*/(*Lancelot*), see K. Sarah-Jane Murray, "*Cil qui fist . . . cil qui dist*: *Oratio* and *Lettreüre* dans *Le Chevalier de la Charrette*," *Œuvres & Critiques* 27 (2002): 84–134.

[30] Other notable examples of this type are *Cele qui fu foutue et desfoutue*, *L'Esquiriel*, and *La Pucele qui voloit voler*, *fabliaux* 30, 58, and 65 respectively in the *Nouveau Recueil Complet des Fabliaux* (*NRCF*), ed. Noomen and Boogaard. The *fabliaux* about ignorant young men are *Jouglet* and *Le sot Chevalier*, *fabliaux* 10 and 53 respectively in the *NRCF*.

help to distinguish between general, topical references and specific allusions, and can conceivably be applied to a large corpus of digitized texts. Aside from helping to locate references to titles and characters from a range of works, encoding a larger corpus of Old French texts and the creation of a tool with functions similar to the grammatico-lexical database of the *Charrette Project*[31] has the capacity to facilitate the identification of specific words, phrases, and even themes and parodies of other texts. Since parody demands either direct or indirect models of recognizable works or types of works, a search tool that allows comparisons of language among texts and supposed models may prove invaluable: this type of search can target references to specific texts and their parodies, provided that parodies reuse words in the same semantic fields as their models. Similarly, grammatical and figural markup of texts can assist in analyzing the stylistic and formal characteristics of literary *topoi*. Within the *fabliaux* corpus, electronic searches of words, phrases, and entire verse-lines will yield more precise references to courtly literature, thereby facilitating comparisons that will enhance our readings of these texts and our knowledge of Old French.

The prevalence of *adnominatio*[32] and word-plays in the *fabliaux* corpus also furnishes another practical use for digital analysis. Simple lexical search tools do not disambiguate various parts of speech. The *fabliau* entitled *Le Chevalier qui fist les cons parler* illustrates the semantic possibilities encountered with word plays on *con* and *conte*: the *BFM* shows that there are approximately 80 occurrences in slightly more than 600 lines. These occurrences of word-plays are more easily traced and analyzed with the aid of a tool that divides words by lemma or dictionary form as opposed to orthography, thereby enabling the program to distinguish between *conte* (modern French *comte* meaning a "count") and *conte* (story) by semantic and grammatical function.

The majority of *fabliaux*, moreover, are characterized by Nykrog as *contes à triangle*, tales in which a married woman finds a way to deceive her husband in order to receive her lover. These types of *fabliaux* are clearly parodic transformations of courtly love triangles because they supply a husband who, by definition, cannot respond to the demands of *fin'amors* and thereby establish a need or motive for a lover. Textual encoding can facilitate comparisons between the language of love and lovers in romance and *fabliaux*, drawing out set phrases and formulae to show how they are reused or transformed in *fabliaux*.[33] The role of

---

[31] For information on the grammatico-lexical database of the *Charrette Project*, see Molly Robinson, "L'Analyse lexicale et grammaticale du *Chevalier de la Charrette* (*Lancelot*)," *Œuvres & Critiques* 27 (2002): 20–51.

[32] For a definition of *adnominatio*, see Deborah Long, "*Il joue un jeu joyeusement*: Chrétien et l'*adnominatio*," *Œuvres & Critiques* 27 (2002): 70–82.

[33] Anne Cobby's study of parody in the *fabliaux* establishes a connection between the use of formulae, or formulaic diction, and its parodic significance in *fabliaux*: *Ambivalent Conventions: Formula and Parody in Old French* (Amsterdam: Rodopi, 1995), esp. 23–54.

chiasmus[34] could also be of interest in relation to other genres, since it is sometimes used as a figure of physical and semantic exchange in the *fabliaux*.

In discussing generic transformation, Karl Uitti stated that "one of the salient characteristics of medieval French romance, a characteristic directly related to the principle of restoration, is that each romance text by definition responds to a previous romance text or even to the body of romance texts in general."[35] Indeed, this assessment seems to be equally valid for *fabliaux* because they are dependent on previous (romance) texts and literary forms, citing, reshaping, and "correcting" them to serve their purposes of entertainment, humor, and for their *raison d'être*.

---

[34] For a definition and examples of chiasmus, see Catherine Witt, "Le chiasme et la poésie courtoise de Chrétien de Troyes," *Œuvres & Critiques* 27 (2002): 155–220.

[35] Karl D. Uitti, "Renewal and Undermining of Old French Romance: *Jehan de Saintré*," in *Romance: Generic Transformation from Chrétien de Troyes to Cervantes*, ed. K. Brownlee and M. S. Brownlee (Hanover: University Press of New England, 1985), 135–54, here 141.

# AFTERWORD

# Jumping Off the Cart:
# The Future of *Charrette* Studies

Matthieu Boyd
Harvard University

and

K. Sarah-Jane Murray
Baylor University

For all that Chrétien's romance is entitled *The Knight of the Cart*, the knight does not spend very long, comparatively speaking, in the cart. At the end of the day he jumps off. The cart is never seen again. It was only a prologue, however indispensable, to other adventures.

Likewise, the philological approaches showcased in this volume take us only so far. As the organization of the volume suggests, there is a persistent separation between two forms (or fields) of scholarship: digital philology, and what we might call "traditional," "conventional," or "paper-based" philology—"non-digital," for lack of a better term. We can expect there to be an explosion of electronic projects devoted to the study of manuscripts and medieval textuality; at the same time, scholars will keep using non-digital methods. Both approaches are valid and necessary. The question is whether they, like Lancelot and Gauvain, need follow such distinct paths. Can we imagine an academy where the two realms converge and interact? This Afterword will explore certain possibilities in this direction.

The first section deals with a "non-digital" philological issue, that of translation—how to evaluate and possibly improve the access which English-speaking readers have to the *Knight of the Cart*, if they cannot read Old French. The second section looks at how current Old French scholarship—with its emphasis on "Codex and Context," to borrow Keith Busby's terminology—urges us to improve the *Charrette Project* itself, and to work towards a new kind of electronic library. Finally, the third section proposes new avenues of research into Chrétien de Troyes's romances, which have lost none of their reputation as foundational works of Old French courtly literature.

Gina L. Greco and Ellen M. Thorington, eds., *Dame Philology's Charrette: Approaching Medieval Textuality through Crétien's 'Lancelot': Essays in Memory of Karl D. Uitti*. MRTS 408. Tempe: ACMRS, 2012. [ISBN 978-0-86698-456-0]

## Basis for evaluating existing translations /
## Basis for a new translation

Compelling descriptions of Chrétien's "consummate artistry"[1] are not hard to find. Still, the *Charrette Project* has helped us reach an understanding of Chrétien's poetic art which is unprecedented in its fullness and its specificity. Users of the *Figura* database (see Rafael Alvarado, this volume) can systematically observe the poetic and rhetorical devices that he favors, and how often, in what combinations and contexts, he deploys them. As Ellen Thorington's study of rich rhyme (this volume) indicates, there are "striking" differences between Chrétien's style and that of Godefroi de Leigny, who claims to have finished the romance. Further, attention to the individual manuscripts has shown that scribes were sometimes quite discerning literary critics, and complemented Chrétien's artistry in various ways.

The question follows: is this kind of understanding good only for specialists? If not—if some of the *Charrette Project*'s findings would interest and benefit the general reader, or undergraduates who are asked to "be familiar with" Chrétien as one component of a survey course—then there is a challenge. The great majority of those who read Chrétien will only ever do so in translation. A significant percentage might, of course, use French translations, which often have an edited text on the facing page.[2] English translations usually do not. The English translations we currently have are those by Comfort (1914), Kibler (1981), Rogers (1984), Owen (1987), Cline (1990), Staines (1993), Raffel (1997), and Kibler (2004 [1991]).[3] Only Kibler's 1981 publication gives an edited text, and only it along with Cline and Raffel's versions are laid out in verse. The Penguin Classics volume (Kibler, 2004) is likely to be the text of choice in most institutional

---

[1] For example, William W. Kibler, trans., *Chrétien de Troyes: Arthurian Romances* (London and New York: Penguin, 2004 [1st ed. 1991]), 15–20.

[2] For example, *Le Chevalier de la Charrette (Lancelot)*, ed. and trans. Alfred Foulet and Karl D. Uitti, Classiques Garnier (Paris: Bordas, 1989).

[3] *The Knight of the Cart (Lancelot)*, trans. William W. Comfort, in *Arthurian Romances* (London: J. M. Dent & Sons, Inc., 1914); *Lancelot or, The Knight of the Cart*, ed. and trans. William W. Kibler (New York: Garland, 1981); *Lancelot, The Knight of the Cart*, trans. Deborah Webster Rogers, intro. W. T. H. Jackson, Records of Civilization: Sources and Studies 97 (New York: Columbia University Press, 1984); *Lancelot*, trans. D. D. R. Owen, in *Chrétien de Troyes: Arthurian Romances*, Everyman Classics (London and Melbourne: Dent, 1987); *Lancelot or the Knight of the Cart*, trans. Ruth Harwood Cline (Athens, GA, and London: University of Georgia Press, 1990); *The Knight of the Cart*, trans. David Staines, in *The Complete Romances of Chrétien de Troyes* (Bloomington and Indianapolis: Indiana University Press, 1993); *Lancelot: The Knight of the Cart*, trans. Burton Raffel (New Haven and London: Yale University Press, 1997); and *The Knight of the Cart (Lancelot)*, trans. William W. Kibler, in *Chrétien de Troyes: Arthurian Romances* (see n. 1).

settings. "Certainly," as Kibler notes, "no translation can hope to capture all the subtlety and magic of Chrétien's art."[4] Nevertheless, a given translation is often all that will be seen of it. When we uncover new dimensions of "subtlety and magic" — as the *Charrette Project* has allowed us to do — it is proper to revisit the question of what translators can genuinely hope to capture.

A basic question might be whether it misrepresents Chrétien to publish a prose translation of his work. Special attention might again be drawn to Kibler, who published facing-line translations of *Lancelot*, *Yvain*, and *Perceval*, which he recast as prose in the Penguin edition. A first-time reader of a prose translation might well overlook the fact that Chrétien actually wrote in verse, or might conclude that this cannot have been a fundamental aspect of his art. The second possibility may be more problematic. Cline asserted that "a prose translation can convey Chrétien's story but cannot give an impression of his style or artistry."[5] Her rhyming translation is a considerable achievement. Perhaps Cline's rhymes will not suit all tastes: they do not tell us very much about Chrétien's own distribution of rich rhymes,[6] and there has been a trade-off with respect to other features, such as Chrétien's enjambment,[7] and the overall tone, which turns out rather jaunty. But the weaknesses of any one attempt at verse translation do not invalidate the whole enterprise. A remarkable convergence of poetic sensibilities may be necessary for it to succeed, as Seamus Heaney's translation of *Beowulf* (2004) and Robert Fagles's translations of the *Iliad* and *Odyssey* (1990 and 1996) may be said to succeed, better than any prose translation could; but that is little reason for us not to try. One translator has suggested the following standard:

> [to allow] the modern reader some reasonably clear view of Chrétien's swift, clear style, his wonderfully inventive story-telling, his perceptive characterizations and sure-handed dialogue, his racy wit and sly irony, and the vividness with which he evokes, for us his twentieth-century audiences, the emotions and values of a flourishing, vibrant world.[8]

One achievement of the *Charrette Project* has been to discover or clarify which poetic devices are most fundamental to the character of Chrétien's work, and which are most desirable to translate. One example is this overarching chiasmus, which associates Chrétien and Godefroi with each other, as well as with the *Charrette* itself:

---

[4] *The Knight of the Cart (Lancelot)*, trans. Kibler (2004 [1991]), 20.

[5] *Lancelot or the Knight of the Cart*, trans. Cline, xxxiv.

[6] Cf. Thorington, this volume.

[7] Cf. Julia Zarankin, "Rupture et conjointure: l'enjambement dans *Le Chevalier de la Charrette (Lancelot)*," *Œuvres & Critiques* 27 (2002): 221–39.

[8] Raffel, "Translator's Preface," in *Lancelot: The Knight of the Cart*, trans. idem, quoting idem, "Translator's Preface," in *Yvain: The Knight of the Lion*, trans. idem (New Haven and London: Yale University Press, 1987).

In the Prologue, Chrétien writes: 'Del <u>Chevalier de la Charrette</u> / Comance *Crestïens* son livre . . .' (vv. 25–26).[9] Godefroi begins the epilogue in
a similar fashion: '*Godefroiz de Leigni*, li clers / A parfinee <u>la Charrette</u> . . .'
(vv. 7124–7125).[10] At the heart of these two passages of *oratio recta*, the romance is presented as a collaborative initiative undertaken by Chrétien, and
continued by Godefroi: »<u>Chevalier de la Charrette</u> / *Crestïens* / *Godefroiz de
Leigni* / <u>Charrette</u>«. [. . . T]he chiasmus poetically binds the two authors,
together, with the textual artifact *Le Chevalier de la Charrette*.[11]

This chiasmus is of paramount importance. Any good translation should contain
it. That way, a teacher can present it using the text that students have actually
read, without having to rely on Old French. As it turns out, some translations
have the overarching chiasmus, and others do not. Here is a sample:

> Kibler 1981: "Chrétien begins his book / About the Knight of the Cart" (3);
> "The clerk Godefroy de Leigni / Has put the final touches on the Knight
> of the Cart" (295).

> Kibler 2004: "Chrétien begins his book about the Knight of the Cart" (207);
> "The clerk Godefroy de Lagny has put the final touches on *The Knight of the
> Cart*" (294).

> Rogers: "Of *The Knight in the Cart* Chrétien here begins his book" (1); "The
> clerk Godfrey de Leigny has finished *The Cart*" (119).

> Cline: "The story of *The Knight of the Cart:* / now Chrétien begins his book"
> (1); "Though Godefroy de Leigny, clerk, / has put the last hand to The Cart"
> (196).

> Raffel: "As Chrétien begins this tale / Of Lancelot, the Knight / Of the
> Cart" (2); "Godfrey of Lagny, a learned / Cleric, has ended this romance"
> (224).

It would be useful to take this chiasmus, and other significant findings published
by members of the *Charrette Project*, and assemble a list of fundamentally important poetic devices that stand a reasonable chance of surviving translation (the

---

[9]  'Of *The Knight of the Cart* Chrétien begins his book . . .'
[10]  'Godefroi de Leigni, the *clerc*, has carried to term the *Cart* . . .'
[11]  K. Sarah-Jane Murray, "Medieval Scribes, Modern Scholars: Reading *Le Chevalier de la Charrette* in the Twenty-First Century," in *Literatur und Literaturwissenschaften
auf dem Weg zu den digital Medien—Eine Standortbestimmung* [*Literature and Literary
Studies on Their Way Towards the Digital Media—Where Are We?*] (Bern: Germanistik,
2005), 145–63, here 151. We preserve here the use of both underline and italics to emphasize the four parts (ABB'A') of the chiasmus.

distribution of rich rhymes might not satisfy this last criterion). Such a list would help teachers evaluate the extant translations, to see how well they can be used to show the latest scholarly insights into the subtleties of the romance. If none of them do it well enough, the list could offer guidelines for a new translation.

Here are thoughts about this final possibility. There are two kinds of barriers to understanding what Chrétien has done in writing *Lancelot*. Some are linguistic and others conceptual. Judicious translation consists of removing as many of the linguistic barriers as possible while deciding how many of the conceptual barriers to leave in place. Leaving them requires that the reader learn to deal with them—this is often the "significant learning"[12] that one tries to achieve while teaching a course. We would like to see some barriers remain, at least partially, to facilitate learning objectives essential to familiarity with Chrétien's work.

For example, Peter Dembowski (this volume) calls attention to "the importance of variants, and hence to one of the central tenets of endeavors such as the *Charrette Project*." Translations tend to illustrate this poorly. Usually there will be remarks about "the manuscript tradition" which enumerate the manuscripts and acknowledge the existence of variants.[13] The problems with this approach are that (i) the non-specialist reader, uninformed about "the fundamentally dynamic nature of medieval textuality"[14] and associated concepts such as *mouvance* and *variance*,[15] does not realize the significance of this information; (ii) the variants are consistently presented as obstacles to the production of "a readable coherent text"[16] which should be as close as possible to "that of the great Champenois poet."[17]

(ii) is explained by the fact that translators almost always base their work on critical editions; they are constrained by the thinking that produced those editions.[18] Murray noted that "[w]hatever advantages the monumental printed book may have that results from th[e] process [of producing critical editions of

---

[12] L. Dee Fink, *Creating Significant Learning Experiences: An Integrated Approach to Designing College Courses* (San Francisco: Jossey-Bass, 2003).

[13] Here we are concerned with variants that change the meaning, or that prejudice interpretation—for the latter, see Murray, "Medieval Scribes, Modern Scholars," on 'poetic punctuation' (153)—as against those which are purely orthographical or dialectal, and thus impossible to render in another language.

[14] Murray, "Medieval Scribes, Modern Scholars," 146.

[15] See Paul Zumthor, *Essai de poétique médiévale* (Paris: Seuil, 1972); Rupert T. Pickens, "Transmission et *translatio:* mouvement textuel et variance," *French Forum* 23 (1998): 133–45; and Bernard Cerquiglini, *Éloge de la variante: histoire critique de la philologie* (Paris: Seuil, 1989).

[16] *Lancelot or the Knight of the Cart*, trans. Cline, xxxii.

[17] *The Knight of the Cart (Lancelot)*, trans. Kibler (2004 [1991]), 23.

[18] See David F. Hult, "Reading It Right: The Ideology of Text Editing," in *The New Medievalism*, ed. M. S. Brownlee, K. Brownlee, and S. G. Nichols (Baltimore and London: Johns Hopkins University Press, 1991), 113–30, for an overview of "the ideology of text editing."

the usual type] [. . .] the subtleties of *variance*, celebrated by Cerquiglini, are lost and in the end a good deal of precious information is discarded."[19] One of the triumphs of the *Charrette Project* (see Greco, this volume) has been to relieve us of an absolute need to resolve variants. The project contains the whole manuscript tradition, in all of its frustrating richness. Of course, the *Figura* database searches only the Foulet-Uitti critical edition. Even so, the critical edition is resituated as a guide to the richness of the manuscript tradition, as against an attempt to render that richness academic, in the pejorative sense of the word.

Most translators of Chrétien are scholarly and conscientious. They write careful explanatory notes, and so forth, which mention controversial variants. But the translation itself goes by either the Sword Bridge or the Bridge Under Water, as it were, with respect to these: it doesn't offer both on an equal footing. It is always a "readable coherent text." This is a great achievement by the translator. But you cannot use it to teach students about the fundamentally dynamic nature of medieval textuality because the "readable coherent text" that the students have before them, which at this point will be indistinguishable from the author's text, will undermine whatever you try to do. Students who compare translations (even Kibler 1981 and Kibler 2004) will see another kind of variation, and may realize some of the nuances of Chrétien's language, but this does not precisely make the point about the manuscript tradition.

Actually, students today will be able to understand the manuscript tradition by drawing an analogy that was unavailable even two decades ago. This analogy is to the way texts circulate online. Folklorists have observed that "netlore," or urban legends disseminated via the Internet,[20] exhibit many of the features of oral transmission; really what they have observed is that a sample of these texts exhibits variation, which is a defining feature of both oral and manuscript traditions. Here is an admittedly rather crass example that should be familiar to anyone who is used to receiving email:

1.  After all the genuine stuff—with no more trim!
    P.E.P. are tasting hot right this time! This is the
    real thing not a forgery! One of the very exceptionals, absolutely unique product is on sale around the world!

2.  Ultimately the original thing—with no more trickery! P.E.P. are hot right now! Well this is the true stuff not an imitation! One of the very exceptionals, absolutely unique produce is easy accessible at any place!

---

[19] Murray, "Medieval Scribes, Modern Scholars," 146.
[20] For an interesting collection, see The Urban Legend Reference Pages, http://www.snopes.com.

3. Ultimately the original thing—no more swindle!
   P.E.P. are piping hot at the time! This is the real stuff not an imitation!
   One of the very prominents, totally unique produce is on the market
   everywhere![21]

Clearly these are all the "same" piece of obnoxious spam. The nuances of "same,"
and the significance of the variant readings, are only marginally interesting in
the case of the spam, which probably results from the use of an automated thesaurus script to fill various slots. Otherwise the texts are comparable to various
manuscripts of a medieval work. One could ask students to "edit" this email,
which would alert them to some of the issues involved in textual editing. To the
extent that we credit medieval scribes with intelligence and deliberation, and respect their judgment as literary critics, the differences that we observe in manuscripts are more worthy of respect. They are informative in the same way that differences between full-scale revisions of the same material can be informative (see
the essays by Kelly and Armstrong, this volume), but more subtle. Further, there
is a compelling scholarly interest in reminding the reader that the critical edition
upon which a given translation is based is not what Chrétien wrote.

A translation could at various points divide in half,

like the two knights parting ways, but
without the suggestion that one path
leads successfully to Gorre and the other to frustrated bobbing up and down,
like Gauvain. Of course, this technique
might need to be applied judiciously,
i.e., only to meaningful variants. Every
time the knights passed to either side of
a single tree, as it were, one might not
see cause to represent the fact.

like this. Another possibility would be
to translate the text of a single manuscript, such as MS Bibliothèque Nationale f. fr. 794, "Guiot's copy," which
would simulate, albeit in a limited way,
the experience of reading a medieval
book—even if "this ultra-conserva-
tive approach resulted in a text that in
many instances was demonstrably not
that of the great Champenois poet."[22]

But why stop there? The Internet has an unlimited capacity to run texts in parallel. The *Charrette Project*'s archive of diplomatic transcriptions is designed to take
advantage of this. Translating each of these transcriptions (which, to avoid du-
plication of labor and ensure that similarity is conveyed wherever it exists, could
be done by adapting a translation of the Foulet-Uitti critical edition to the individual cases) is a very satisfactory answer to the problems raised here. The reader
would have a choice of texts based on authentic language (the closest thing to
reading from the manuscripts themselves), and could display them simultaneously in different windows, or alternate freely between them, to make comparisons.

---

[21] Excerpts of pseudonymous email received at the address of the Harvard Celtic
Colloquium in June 2007.
[22] *The Knight of the Cart (Lancelot)*, trans. Kibler (2004 [1991]), 23.

No information contained in the manuscript tradition would be lost unless it simply could not be expressed in English (polysemic vocabulary might require some extra accommodation, such as hyperlink glosses). The need to judge individual variations either trivial or significant—by deciding whether or not a single translation ought to represent them by, for example, breaking into columns as suggested above—could be avoided almost entirely ("almost" because a translation may by necessity represent one feature at the cost of another); this judgment would be left to the reader, as it should be.

We do not, of course, recommend a total neglect of the Old French text, nor suggest that students should stop learning medieval languages. But the fact remains that millions of people will encounter Chrétien de Troyes's genius only in translation—although some might turn to Old French when they become fascinated with the complexity of translating him. The challenge, briefly stated, is to ensure that the theoretical innovations associated with the *Charrette Project* (described by Greco, this volume), and certain specific observations about rhetorico-poetic features, are allowed to form part of the most basic understanding of Chrétien's romance—the understanding that the general reader or beginning student is expected to form. One way to do this is through translation guided by the same principles that have guided the *Charrette Project* until now. The result will be a model for the treatment of other works preserved in multiple manuscripts, especially those whose text varies more considerably. As many scholars have implied (e.g., Busby; Foulet and Uitti; Foulet and Speer; Taylor; Pignatelli, this volume),[23] to study Old French romance outside of its manuscript context is not really to study it at all.

## Of Codex and Context: Reconsidering the Digital Facsimile

The problems posed by translation are one way in which philology issues an important challenge to digital projects. More generally, we need to consider what it really means to study Old French romance within a codicological context, and how the *Charrette Project*, or other projects of a similar nature, could become more helpful.

---

[23] See, for example, Keith Busby, *Codex and Context: Reading Old French Verse Narrative in Manuscript*, Faux Titre 221–222, 2 vols. (Amsterdam: Rodopi, 2002); Alfred Foulet and Karl D. Uitti, "On Editing Chrétien de Troyes, *Lancelot*: Two Steps and their Concern," *Speculum* 63 (1988): 271–92; Alfred Foulet and Mary Speer, *On Editing Old French Texts*, Edward C. Armstrong Monographs on Medieval Literature 1 (Lawrence, KS: Regents Press of Kansas, 1979); and Andrew Taylor, *Textual Situations: Three Medieval Manuscripts and Their Readers* (Philadelphia: University of Pennsylvania Press, 2002).

The late twentieth and early twenty-first centuries have given rise to numerous studies on manuscripts, including Sylvia Huot's *From Song to Book*, Andrew Taylor's *Textual Situations*, Keith Busby's *Codex and Context,* and the two-volume *Manuscrits de Chrétien de Troyes* edited by Busby, Terry Nixon, Alison Stones, and Lori Walters.[24] These studies teach the importance of the codex and point to its integrity as artifact. It matters how the codex was assembled. Why, for example, was Benedeit's *Voyage de saint Brendan* copied by the same scribe after the *Fables* of Marie de France in MS York Minster XVI K/12 [I]? In some cases, texts were brought together for thematic reasons. At other times, it may have been a purely practical decision—thus one often finds a selection of shorter tales (e.g., *fabliaux*) serving as "fillers" at the end of a manuscript. Sometimes the relationship is ambiguous. It has become increasingly clear that the study of a manuscript copy is not complete until its relationship to its neighbors in the codex (if there are any) has been carefully examined. For the moment at least, this is one area in which the *Charrette Project* falls short. It does not represent whole codices. Some scholars might even like to see the binding and the flyleaves, in addition to the whole codex from which the images of any manuscript are taken. Thus current philological research suggests that it is time for the *Charrette Project* to develop somewhat, so that it lives up to one of Uitti's initial motivations: "to prepare," as Greco puts it (this volume), "a new type of edition—or, rather, presentation of the text—that [will continue to] reflect [new] theories and allow textual scholarship to respond to the theoretical discussion underway."

As the essays by Juliet O'Brien and Katherine Brown (this volume) demonstrate, the *Charrette Project* model is adaptable to other texts and manuscript traditions. Perhaps the most extensive adaptation is the Digby 23 Project at Baylor University (http://timaeus.baylor.edu), which will include images of an entire codex with two constituent manuscripts, searchable diplomatic transcriptions, English translation, searchable database, critical apparatus, and tools for teaching. Its subject is the Oxford University codex containing the earliest surviving copy of the *Chanson de Roland*, preceded by Plato's *Timaeus* in a Latin translation by Calcidius. Both texts were copied during the twelfth century, and bound together at a later date.[25] They present a number of challenges, not least because one of them is a Latin work. These include, most notably, how to deal with scribal abbreviations not found in the *Charrette* manuscripts, and, on a much more

---

[24] Sylvia Huot, *From Song to Book: The Poetics of Writing in Old French Lyric and Lyrical Narrative Poetry* (Ithaca: Cornell University Press, 1987); Taylor, *Textual Situations;* Busby, *Codex and Context*; and Keith Busby, Terry Nixon, Alison Stones, and Lori Walters, eds., *Les Manuscrits de Chrétien de Troyes–The Manuscripts of Chrétien de Troyes*, Faux Titre 71–72, 2 vols. (Amsterdam: Rodopi, 1993).

[25] See K. Sarah-Jane Murray, "Plato's *Timaeus* and the *Song of Roland*: Poetry and Humanism in Oxford Bodleian MS Digby 23," *Philological Quarterly* 83 (2004): 115–26, on the possible thematic affinities of these two works.

complex level, how to address the presence of abundant Latin glosses. Even the Old French *Roland*, a *chanson de geste*, is of a different genre than the *Charrette*, and the version preserved in Digby 23 is of Anglo-Norman provenance.

The increasing availability of such digital facsimiles, and the development of tools that enable scholars to manipulate the data preserved within the manuscripts themselves, raise some interesting cultural as well as philological issues. Given their place within the Old French canon, the *Timaeus* and the *Roland* both provide important literary and cultural contexts for reading Chrétien's *Charrette*; why not involve other works? Many studies of Chrétien's romances have done so, examining how Chrétien draws upon Ovid, how he builds upon the antique romances, how he responds to the troubadours, to the *Tristan et Iseut* stories, and so on. Involving further manuscripts will enable students and scholars to read Chrétien de Troyes within the medieval intellectual context. Saints' *Lives* will also make an interesting complement, as will key texts by medieval theologians (e.g., St. Bernard, St. Anselm) and philosophers (e.g., Abelard) as well as commentaries on the Bible. The relationship between Chrétien's romances—indeed much vernacular literature—and the philosophical or theological realms is still not fully understood.

One might envision, then, yet another phase of the *Charrette Project* itself in which we would use the electronic technologies now available to us to study not just one manuscript tradition but, rather, the evolution of the Old French literary canon. The resulting database would be truly interdisciplinary, drawing on a multiplicity of genres, so as to situate Chrétien's *oeuvre* and the works of other Old French authors within their respective literary, philosophical, and theological contexts. For Chrétien's *Charrette* alone, this could mean including—in addition to images (and eventually transcriptions) of each manuscript in its entirety—manuscripts of Ovid, the *Enéas*, Bernard of Clairvaux, troubadour poetry, Benoît de Sainte-Maure, Virgil, Martianus Capella, and Guillaume de Lorris. If such a project were ever to come to fruition, users would have at their disposal an immensely rich virtual library of key medieval works, existing side by side in cyberspace much as one might have found them in a medieval court library.

### Envisioning the Future of *Charrette* Studies

How, finally, might we respond to the *Knight of the Cart* and Chrétien's other romances in the future? Or is it time to jump off the *Charrette* and start other endeavors?

The proposed Timaeus Project has already shown some avenues of future study. A further topic that merits discussion is the relationship of Chrétien de Troyes to his source material, or influences. Chrétien's work emerges from the confluence of two main intellectual or cultural currents: the first might be described as "Classical" or "Mediterranean," the second as "Celtic" or "Atlantic." This observation has to do with the hoary distinction between the matters "of Rome" and "of Britain," but Chrétien's matter is so thoroughly composite that it may be time to question whether these categories are in any way an accurate description of his work.[26] As Uitti discovered,[27] *Erec et Enide* is in fact a *mout bele conjointure* 'a most beautiful conjoining' (14) of two stories: *De nuptiis Mercurii et Philologiae* 'The Marriage of Mercury and Philology' by the late-antique author Martianus Capella, and a Celtic tale which to some extent survives in the Welsh *Mabinogion*.[28] *Cligés*, which might be thought to constitute a kind of super-romance in combination with *Erec et Enide*, is also synthetic. But Chrétien did much more than synthesize. He created Arthurian romance, an entirely new genre.[29]

As Busby has noted, a more fully integrated approach to Chrétien's use of sources is necessary.[30] His classically-oriented clerkly training must be squared with his creative use of Celtic matter; the fact that he conjoins both has to be a basic premise of everything that is done in *Charrette* studies from now on. Scholars who have made a careful study of one or the other of these aspects must not fail to consider their interplay.

A number of questions on the Celtic side, such as how Chrétien became acquainted with Celtic sources, at what remove, and who the vectors of transmission were, remain intractable. It may be said that the Celtic influence on Old French literature deserves sober reevaluation after the well-intentioned excesses of Roger Sherman Loomis and the sometimes equally excessive dismissal of his ideas. To do this responsibly will require scholars of Old French to become familiar with medieval Celtic literature and Celtic folklore, or, failing that, to consult trained Celticists.[31]

---

[26] K. Sarah-Jane Murray, *From Plato to Lancelot: A Preface to Chrétien de Troyes* (Syracuse, NY: Syracuse University Press, 2008).

[27] Karl D. Uitti, "A propos de Philologie," *Littérature* 41 (1981): 20–46.

[28] This is the story of Geraint son of Erbin.

[29] The so-called "Three Romances" in the *Mabinogion*, including *Geraint*, show signs of his influence. For "the Arthur of the Welsh" prior to Chrétien, see, e.g., Rachel Bromwich, A. O. H. Jarman, and Brynley F. Roberts, eds., *The Arthur of the Welsh: The Arthurian Legend in Medieval Welsh Literature* (Cardiff: University of Wales Press, 1991, repr. 1995); O. J. Padel, *Arthur in Medieval Welsh Literature*, Writers of Wales Series (Cardiff: University of Wales Press, 2000); and Ceridwen Lloyd-Morgan, ed., *Arthurian Literature XXI: Celtic Arthurian Material* (Cambridge: D.S. Brewer, 2004).

[30] Keith Busby, "France: Medieval Arthurian Romance," in *Medieval Arthurian Literature: A Guide to Recent Research*, ed. N. J. Lacy (New York: Garland, 1996), 121–209.

[31] The *Charrette Project 2* has tried to encourage research in this area, sponsoring a session on "Medieval Literature and Celtic Studies" (organized by Matthieu Boyd) at the 42nd International Congress on Medieval Studies at Western Michigan University, 11 May 2007. John Carey, in *Ireland and the Grail* (Aberystwyth: Celtic Studies Publications, 2007), makes a hugely significant contribution in the matter of the Celtic sources

Michael Faletra is one scholar who has specifically addressed the question of "The Celtic Sources of Chrétien's *Chevalier de la Charrette*." His argument was that while the *Charrette* "[w]ith its echoes both of the Christian Harrowing of Hell narrative and of stories of various Celtic missions to the Otherworld [. . .] challenges us with its hermeneutic excessiveness," it is possible that it contains "a very loaded reference to William I's alleged 'liberation' of the land of Gorre (= the Gower peninsula) from its native Welsh overlords in 1081": "The *Charrette* [. . .] exploits the alienness of its possible Celtic sources as a means of mystifying the workings of Norman-Angevin territorial acquisition in Wales, Brittany, and beyond."[32] We do not necessarily endorse Faletra's suggestions (they are debatable, which is a good thing; we have no space to debate them here), but his approach provides us with a basis for observing that there are two extremes which need to be avoided. These are: source study that neglects what the text in question is actually saying (i.e., the text is more than the sum of its sources), and theoretically-motivated close reading of the text that more or less entirely excludes source study.

Many years ago, Loomis offered analogues from early Irish and Welsh sources to argue that elements of the basic plot of the *Charrette* (Lancelot's journey to Gorre, and some related issues) were of Celtic origin.[33] Tom Peete Cross also used analogues to test the claim that some of the *lais* of Marie de France, and other so-called Breton *lais*, plausibly derived from Celtic sources.[34] What remained to be seen was how these Celtic sources, assuming they were something like the extant analogues, had been adapted by the Old French authors, and for what purpose. If an Old French text had motifs in common with a Celtic text, was their function in the story still the same? And so forth. Failure to proceed to this discussion has, in recent years, put the useful practice of considering analogues somewhat out of fashion. In fact, when the Welsh *Gereint* is used to supplement Uitti's comparison of *Erec et Enide* with Martianus Capella's *De nuptiis*, it becomes apparent that the *De nuptiis* underlies more seemingly minor details of *Erec et Enide* than Uitti himself may have suspected, such as the numbers of

of Chrétien's *Conte du Graal* and some related works; Carey is a specialist in medieval Irish literature.

[32] Michael Faletra, abstract for "The Celtic Sources of Chrétien's *Chevalier de la Charrette*," 42nd International Congress on Medieval Studies at Western Michigan University, 11 May 2007.

[33] Roger Sherman Loomis, *Celtic Myth and Arthurian Romance* (New York: Columbia University Press, 1927) and idem, *Arthurian Tradition and Chrétien de Troyes* (New York: Columbia University Press, 1949).

[34] See, for example, Tom P. Cross, "The Celtic Origin of the Lay of *Yonec*," *Revue Celtique* 31 (1910): 413–71, and idem, "The Celtic Elements in the Lays of *Lanval* and *Graelent*," *Modern Philology* 12 (1915): 585–644.

knights and giants in each group that attacks Erec.[35] Insofar as Faletra sought to "look at the ways in which [the *Charrette*'s] very ambiguity is founded upon the perceived Otherness of its ostensibly 'Celtic' *matiere*,"[36] he engaged the question of Chrétien's creative use of sources. This question remains at the cutting edge of *Charrette* studies whether we like it or not. See Kelly, in this volume, for further exploration of this issue.

As suggested above, it is also time for a closer look at the theological and ethical dimension of Chrétien's romances. While Chrétien's identity as a Christian author is scarcely debated (and that of his audience even less), the shortage of studies on, for example, the relationship of his romances to the writings of St. Bernard of Clairvaux (especially *On Loving God*) or Peter Abelard (e.g., the doctrine of intentionality, particularly important in *Cligés*) is striking. Work in this area is likely to reveal that Chrétien did not suddenly become preoccupied with Christian themes and ideals in the *Conte du Graal*, but that the human preoccupation with what Thomas Aquinas would later qualify as "the ultimate end of the intellectual creature" (*Compendium of Theology*, ch. 104) is already at the heart of his earlier works, if only implicitly. We are advocating an interdisciplinary approach to Chrétien, without sacrificing the scholarly rigor expected of a specialist. The article by Lori Walters in this volume is a good example.

Like Michel de Montaigne, Chrétien de Troyes was in the business of making "well-made heads" rather than "well-filled" ones, and his romances raise profound ethical questions. What is the nature of marriage? What is love? How does one reconcile Love and Duty, or the Private and the Public? What are the responsibilities of citizens who are in this world, but not necessarily of it? And so forth. These avenues of inquiry will interest not only specialists, but also students in French or even general survey courses, where Chrétien is being read in translation. For it is perhaps Chrétien's preoccupation with what it means to be human (in all our finitude, glory, and even — as Anselm reminds us — in our wretchedness) that "distinguishes him from all other poets of the Latin races between the close of the [Roman] empire and the arrival of Dante."[37] If, following John's example in *Cligés*,[38] we can only learn to open the hidden doors in the text, Chrétien's works have not ceased yielding their treasures.

---

[35] Full discussion in Murray, *From Plato to Lancelot*, 188–97.

[36] Faletra, "Celtic Sources."

[37] *The Knight of the Cart (Lancelot)*, trans. Comfort, xviii.

[38] Michelle Freeman, *The Poetics of* Translatio Studii *and* Conjointure: *Chrétien de Troyes's* Cligés, French Forum Monographs 12 (Lexington, KY: French Forum, 1979).

# Bibliography

## Original Sources

Adam de Perseigne. "*Soliloquium* d'Adam de Perseigne, 2: texte et traduction," ed. and trans. Jean Bouvet. *Collectanea cisterciensia* 50 (1988): 133–71.

Adenet le Roi. *Cleomadés*. Vol. 5 of *Les Œuvres d'Adenet le Roi*, ed. Albert Henry. Université Libre de Bruxelles: Travaux de la Faculté de philosophie et lettres 46. Brussels: Éditions de l'Université de Bruxelles, 1971.

André le Chapelain. *Le Traité de l'amour courtois*, trans. Claude Buridant. Paris: Bibliothèque française et romane, 1974.

Augustine. *The City of God Against the Pagans*, ed. and trans. R. W. Dyson. Cambridge: Cambridge University Press, 1998.

———. *Confessiones, Books I–IV*, ed. Gillian Clark. Cambridge Greek and Latin Classics. Cambridge: Cambridge University Press, 1996.

———. *Confessions*, text and comm. J.J. O'Donnell. Oxford: Oxford University Press, 1992. Also available online at www.georgetown.edu/faculty/jod/augustine/.

———. *De Doctrina Christiana*, ed. and trans. R. P. H. Green. Oxford: Oxford University Press, 1995.

———. *Saint Augustine: Confessions*, trans. Henry Chadwick. Oxford: Oxford University Press, 1998 (1ˢᵗ ed. 1991).

———. *Soliloquies: Augustine's Inner Dialogue*, ed. John E. Rotelle, trans. Kim Paffenroth. New York: New City Press, 2000.

*Beowulf*, trans. Seamus Heaney. New York: Farrar, Straus, and Giroux, 2000.

Bernard of Clairvaux. *Bernard of Clairvaux: Selected Works*, ed. Ewart H. Cousins, trans. G. R. Evans, intro. Jean Leclercq. New York: Paulist Press, 1987.

Bernart de Ventadorn. *The Songs of Bernart de Ventadorn: Complete Texts, Translations, Notes, and Glossary*, ed. and trans. Stephen G. Nichols Jr., John A. Galm, A. Bartlett Giamatti, et al. Chapel Hill: University of North Carolina Press, 1962.

Béroul. *The Romance of Tristran*, ed. A. Ewert. Oxford: Blackwell, 1967 (1ˢᵗ ed. 1939).

*Biblia Sacra iuxta Vulgatam versionem*, ed. Bonifatius Fischer and Robert Weber. Stuttgart: Württembergische Bibelanstalt, 1969.

Boccaccio, Giovanni. *Il Filostrato e il Ninfale fiesolano*, ed. Vincenzo Pernicone. Bari: Laterza, 1937.

Challoner, Richard, et al. *The Holy Bible: containing the entire canonical scriptures according to the decree of the Council of Trent: translated from the Latin Vulgate . . .: the Old Testament first published . . . at Douay, A.D. 1609, the New Testament . . . at Rheims, A.D. 1582*. N.p.: n.p., 1884.

Chaucer, Geoffrey. *Troilus and Criseyde*, ed. Robert K. Root. Princeton: Princeton University Press, 1926.

———. *The Works of Geoffrey Chaucer*, ed. F. N. Robinson. The New Cambridge Edition. 2nd ed. Boston: Houghton Mifflin, 1957.

Chrétien de Troyes. *Cligés*, ed. Stewart Gregory and Claude Luttrell. Arthurian Studies 28. Cambridge: Brewer, 1993.

———. *Cligès*, ed. Charles Méla and Olivier Collet. In *Chrétien de Troyes: Romans*, gen. ed. Michel Zink. Paris: Librairie Générale Française/Livre de Poche, 1994.

———. *Conte du Graal (Perceval)*, ed. Félix Lecoy. 2 vols. Paris: Champion, 1972, 1975.

———. *Conte du Graal (Perceval)*, ed. Charles Méla. In *Chrétien de Troyes: Romans*.

———. *Der Karrenritter (Lancelot)*. In *Sämtliche erhaltene Werke nach allen bekannten Handschriften* IV, ed. Wendelin Foerster. Halle: Niemeyer, 1899.

———. *Erec et Enide*, ed. Peter F. Dembowski. In *Œuvres complètes*, gen. ed. Daniel Poirion, 1–169. Bibliothèque de la Pléiade. Paris: Gallimard, 1994.

———. *Guillaume d'Angleterre*, ed. Anne Berthelot. In *Œuvres complètes*, 953–1036.

———. *The Knight of the Cart*, trans. David Staines. In *The Complete Romances of Chrétien de Troyes*. Bloomington and Indianapolis: Indiana University Press, 1993.

———. *The Knight of the Cart (Lancelot)*, trans. William W. Comfort. In *Arthurian Romances*. London: J. M. Dent & Sons, Inc., 1914.

———. *The Knight of the Cart (Lancelot)*, trans. William W. Kibler. In *Chrétien de Troyes: Arthurian Romances*. London and New York: Penguin. 2004 [1st ed. 1991].

———. *Lancelot*, trans. D. D. R. Owen. In *Chrétien de Troyes: Arthurian Romances*. Everyman Classics. London and Melbourne: Dent, 1987.

———. *Lancelot or the Knight of the Cart*, trans. Ruth Harwood Cline. Athens, GA, and London: University of Georgia Press, 1990.

———. *Lancelot or, The Knight of the Cart*, ed. and trans. William W. Kibler. New York: Garland, 1981.

———. *Lancelot: The Knight of the Cart*, trans. Burton Raffel. New Haven and London: Yale University Press, 1997.

————. *Lancelot, The Knight of the Cart*, trans. Deborah Webster Rogers, intro. W. T. H. Jackson. Records of Civilization, Sources and Studies 97. New York: Columbia University Press, 1984.

————. *Lancelot, ou Le Chevalier de la Charrette*, ed. Daniel Poirion. In *Œuvres complètes*, 505–682.

————. *Le Chevalier au Lion ou le Roman d'Yvain*, ed. David F. Hult. Lettres Gothiques. Paris: Librairie Générale Française, 1994.

————. *Le Chevalier de la Charrete*, ed. Mario Roques. Paris: Champion, 1958.

————. *Le Chevalier de la Charrette (Lancelot)*, ed. Alfred Foulet and Karl D. Uitti. Classiques Garnier. Paris: Bordas, 1989.

————. *Le Roman de Perceval*, ed. William Roach. Geneva: Droz, 1959.

————. *Le Roman de Perceval ou Le Conte du Graal*, ed. Keith Busby. Tübingen: Niemeyer, 1993.

————. *Yvain: The Knight of the Lion*, trans. Burton Raffel. New Haven and London: Yale University Press, 1987.

Christine de Pizan. *La Cité des Dames* (*La Città delle Dame*), ed. Earl Jeffrey Richards. Milan: Luni Editrice, 1997.

————. *L'Epistre au Dieu d'amours*. In *Œuvres poétiques*, ed. Maurice Roy, 2:1–27. Paris: Firmin Didot, 1886.

Cornelius à Lapide. *Commentaria in quatuor prophetas maiores*. Antwerp, 1703.

d'Arbois de Jubainville, Henri. *Histoire des Ducs et des Comtes de Champagne*. 7 vols. Paris: Durand, 1861.

Evrart de Conty. *Le Livre des Eschez amoureux moralisés*, ed. Françoise Guichard-Tesson and Bruno Roy. Bibliothèque du moyen français 2. Montréal: CERES, 1993.

[*Flamenca*]. *Le* Roman de Flamenca, ed. and trans. Paul Meyer. Paris: A. Franck, 1865.

————. *Le* Roman de Flamenca: *nouvelle occitane du XIII*ᵉ, ed. Ulrich Gschwind. Berne: Francke, 1976.

————. *Le* Roman de Flamenca, *publié d'après le manuscrit unique de Carcassonne [. . .] 2è édition entièrement refondue*, ed. Paul Meyer. Vol. 1 of intended 2; 2ⁿᵈ vol. (trans. and comm.) never appeared. Paris: Bouillon, 1901.

————. In *Les Troubadours*, ed. René Lavaud and René Nelli, trans. Paul Meyer [1901], 1: 619–1064. Bruges: Desclée de Brouwer, 1960–1966.

————. *The* Romance of Flamenca, trans. E.D. Blodgett. New York: Garland, 1995.

————. *The* Romance of Flamenca, ed. Marion E. Porter, trans. Merton Jerome Hubert. Princeton: Princeton University Press, 1962.

————. "The *Romance of Flamenca*," ed. and trans. John Leonard Ryan. Ph.D. diss., University of New Mexico, 1974.

Gerson, Jean. *Jean Gerson: Early Works*, trans. and intro. Brian Patrick McGuire, pref. Bernard McGinn. Classics of Western Spirituality 92. New York: Paulist Press, 1998.

*Les Grandes Chroniques de France*, ed. Jules Viard. 10 vols. Paris: Champion, 1920–1953.

Guillaume de Lorris, and Jean de Meun. *Le Roman de la Rose*, ed. Félix Lecoy. 3 vols. Paris: Champion, 1965–1970.

———. *The Romance of the Rose*, trans. Charles Dahlberg. Princeton: Princeton University Press, 1971; repr. Amherst: University Press of New England, 1983.

Hilton, Walter. *The Goad of Love*, ed. and intro. Clare Kirchberger. London: Faber and Faber, 1952.

Homer. *Iliad*, trans. Robert Fagles. New York: Viking Press, 1990.

———. *Odyssey*, trans. Robert Fagles. New York: Viking Press, 1996.

Horace. *Satires, Epistles and Ars poetica, with an English Translation*, ed. and trans. H. Rushton Fairclough. Loeb Classical Library 194. Cambridge, MA: Harvard University Press, 1929.

Jehan. *Les Mervelles de Rigomer*, ed. Wendelin Foerster and Hermann Breuer. Gesellschaft für romanische Literatur 19, 39. 2 vols. Dresden: Gesellschaft für romanische Literatur, 1908–1915.

*The Jerusalem Bible*, ed. Alexander Jones. New York and London: Darton, Longman, and Todd, 1966.

Noomen, Willem, and Nico van den Boogaard, eds. *Nouveau Recueil Complet des Fabliaux*. Assen/Maastricht: Van Gorcum, 1983–1998.

Orm. *The Ormulum, with the Notes and Glossary of Dr. R. M. White*, ed. Robert Holt. Oxford: Clarendon Press, 1879.

*La Queste del Saint Graal*, ed. A. Pauphilet. Paris: Champion (CFMA), 1978.

*The Quest of the Holy Grail*, trans. Pauline Matarasso. London: Penguin, 1969.

Rudel, Jaufré. *The Songs of Jaufré Rudel*, ed. Rupert T. Pickens. Studies and Texts 41. Toronto: Pontifical Institute of Medieval Studies, 1978.

*Sir Gawain and the Green Knight*, ed. J. R. R. Tolkien and E. V. Gordon, 2nd ed., rev. Norman Davis. Oxford: Clarendon Press, 1967.

Ulrich von Zatzikhoven. *Lancelet: A Romance of Lancelot*, trans. Kenneth G. T. Webster, rev. and intro. Roger Sherman Loomis. New York: Columbia University Press, 1951.

*The Vulgate Version of the Arthurian Romances*, ed. H. O. Sommer, vol. 1: *Lestoire del Saint Graal*. Washington, DC: Carnegie Institute, 1909.

Wace. *Le Roman de Brut*, ed. Ivor Arnold. 2 vols. Paris: SATF, 1938–1940.

———. *The Roman de Rou*, trans. Glyn S. Burgess, ed. Anthony J. Holden, annot. Glyn S. Burgess and Elisabeth van Houts. Jersey: Société Jersiaise, 2002.

## Secondary Works

Ahl, Frederick. *Metaformations: Soundplay and Wordplay in Ovid and Other Classical Poets.* Ithaca: Cornell University Press, 1985.

Andersen-Wyman, K. *Andreas Capellanus On Love?* New York: Palgrave, 2007.

Andrieux-Reix, Nelly. "Transcription, lisibilité, transgression: quelques problèmes posés par les éditions de textes médiévaux." In *Le Moyen Français: le traitement du texte (édition, apparat critique, glossaire, traitement électronique). Actes du IX<sup>e</sup> colloque international sur le moyen français, Strasbourg, 29–31 mai 1997*, ed. Claude Buridant, 55–63. Strasbourg: Presses Universitaires de Strasbourg, 2000.

Alvarado, Rafael C. "Of Media, Data and Documents: An Argument for the Importance of Relational Technology to the Project of Humanities Computing." In *Proceedings of the ACH-ALLC 1999 International Humanities Computing Conference, Charlottesville, VA, 10 June 1999.* http://www.iath2. virginia.edu/ach-allc.99/proceedings/alvarado.html.

Armstrong, Grace. "Father and Son in the *Queste del Saint Graal.*" *Romance Philology* 21 (1977): 1–16.

Arseneau, Isabelle. "Lancelot échevelé: la parodie dans *Les Merveilles de Rigomer.*" In *La Chevelure dans la littérature et l'art du Moyen Âge: actes du 28<sup>e</sup> Colloque du CUER MA, 20, 21 et 22 février 2003*, ed. Chantal Connochie-Bourgne, 9–21. Senefiance 50. Aix-en-Provence: Publications de l'Université de Provence, 2004.

Asperti, Stefano. "*Flamenca* e dintorni: Considerazioni sui rapporti fra Occitania e Catalogna nel XIV secolo." *Cultura neolatina* 45 (1985): 59–104.

Astell, Ann W. *The Song of Songs in the Middle Ages.* Ithaca: Cornell University Press, 1990.

Bakhtine, Mikhaïl. "De la préhistoire du discours romanesque." In idem, *Esthétique et théorie du roman*, trans. Daria Olivier, 401–37. Paris: Gallimard, 1978.

Barthes, Roland. "De l'œuvre au texte." *Revue d'esthétique* 3 (1971): 225–32.

———. "From Work to Text," trans. Stephen Heath. In idem, *Image-Music-Text*, 155–64. New York: Hill and Wang, 1977.

———. *S/Z.* Paris: Seuil, 1970.

Baumgartner, Emmanuèle. *Chrétien de Troyes: Yvain, Lancelot, la charrette et le lion.* Paris: PUF, 1992.

———. "Robert de Boron et l'imaginaire du livre du Graal." In *Arturus Rex, Vol. II: Acta Conventus Lovaniensis 1987*, ed. Willy Van Hoecke, Gilbert Tournay, and Werner Verbeke, 259–68. Mediaevalia Lovaniensia, ser. I: Studia 17. Leuven: Leuven University Press, 1991.

———. *L'Arbre et le pain: essai sur la* Queste del Saint Graal. Paris: SEDES, 1981.

Belting, Hans. *L'Image et son public au Moyen Âge.* Trans. Fortunato Israel. Paris: Gérard Monfort, 1998 (1ˢᵗ ed. 1981).

Benton, John F. "The Court of Champagne as a Literary Center." *Speculum* 36 (1961): 551–91.

Besamusca, Bart, Willem P. Gerritsen, Cory Hogetoorn, and Orlanda S. H. Lie, eds. *Cyclification: The Development of Narrative Cycles in the* Chansons de Geste *and the Arthurian Romances.* Koninklijke Nederlandse Akademie van Wetenschappen: Verhandelingen, Afdeeling Letterkunde N. R. 159. Amsterdam: North-Holland, 1994.

Bird, Stephen, and Mark Liberman. "Annotation Graphs as a Framework for Multidimensional Linguistic Data Analysis." In *Proceedings of the Workshop Towards Standards and Tools for Discourse Tagging,* 1–10. Somerset, NJ: Association for Computational Linguistics, 1999. http://papers.ldc.upenn.edu/DTAG1999/dtag.pdf.

BFM: Base de Français Médiéval. 26 October 2006. Lyon: UMR ICAR / ENS-LSH. 2005. http://bfm.ens-lsh.fr/.

Boase, Roger. *The Origin and Meaning of Courtly Love.* Manchester: Manchester University Press, 1977.

Boers, Willy. "La Genèse d'Evrat." *Scriptorium* 61 (2007): 74–149.

Bouvet, Jean, and Jean Longère. "Adam de Perseigne." In *Dictionnaire des Lettres Françaises: le Moyen Âge,* ed. Geneviève Hasenohr and Michel Zink, 13–15. Paris: Fayard, 1992 (1st ed. 1964).

Bromwich, Rachel, A. O. H. Jarman, and Brynley F. Roberts, eds. *The Arthur of the Welsh: The Arthurian Legend in Medieval Welsh Literature.* Cardiff: University of Wales Press, 1991, repr. 1995.

Bruckner, Matilda T. "*Le Chevalier de la Charrette*: That Obscure Object of Desire, Lancelot." In *A Companion to Chrétien de Troyes,* ed. Joan Grimbert and Norris J. Lacy, 137–55. Cambridge: Boydell and Brewer, 2005.

———. *Chrétien Continued: A Study of the* Conte du Graal *and its Verse Continuations.* Oxford: Oxford University Press, 2009.

———. "Intertextuality." In *The Legacy of Chrétien de Troyes,* ed. Norris J. Lacy, Douglas Kelly, and Keith Busby, 1:223–65. Faux Titre 37. Amsterdam: Rodopi, 1987.

———. "Rewriting Chrétien's *Conte du Graal*—Mothers and Sons: Questions, Contradictions, and Connections." In *The Medieval "Opus": Imitations, Rewriting, and Transmission in the French Tradition. Proceedings of the Symposium Held at the Institute for Research in Humanities, October 5–7, 1995, The University of Wisconsin-Madison,* ed. Douglas Kelly, 213–44. Faux Titre 116. Amsterdam: Rodopi, 1996.

———. "Why Are There So Many Interpretations of Le Chevalier de la Charrette?" In *Lancelot and Guinevere: A Casebook,* ed. Lori J. Walters, 55–78. New York: Garland, 1996. Repr. London: Routledge, 2002. Originally published in *Romance Philology* 40 (1986): 159–80.

Buridant, Claude. *Grammaire nouvelle de l'ancien français*. Paris: SEDES, 2000.

Burke, Kenneth. "On Musicality in Verse." In idem, *The Philosophy of Literary Form: Studies in Symbolic Action*, 369–78. 2nd ed. Baton Rouge: Louisiana State University Press, 1967.

Busby, Keith. *Codex and Context: Reading Old French Verse Narrative in Manuscript*. Faux Titre 221–222. 2 vols. Amsterdam: Rodopi, 2002.

———. "Courtly Literature and the Fabliaux: Some Instances of Parody." *Zeitschrift für Romanische Philologie* 102 (1986): 67–87.

———. "Diverging Traditions of Gauvain in Some of the Later Old French Verse Romances." In *The Legacy of Chrétien de Troyes*, ed. Lacy, Kelly, and idem, 93–109.

———. *Gauvain in Old French Literature*. Degré Second 2. Amsterdam: Rodopi, 1980.

———. "France: Medieval Arthurian Romance." In *Medieval Arthurian Literature: A Guide to Recent Research*, ed. N. J. Lacy, 121–209. New York: Garland, 1996.

———, Terry Nixon, Alison Stones, and Lori Walters, eds. *Les Manuscrits de Chrétien de Troyes—The Manuscripts of Chrétien de Troyes*. Faux Titre 71–72. 2 vols. Amsterdam: Rodopi, 1993.

Bynum, Caroline Walker. "Patterns of Female Piety in the Later Middle Ages." In *Crown and Veil: Female Monasticism from the Fifth to the Fifteenth Centuries*, ed. Jeffrey F. Hamburger and Susan Marti, 172–90. New York: Columbia University Press, 2008.

Cambronne, Patrice. "Augustin et l'Église Manichéenne: jalons d'un itinéraire." *Vita Latina* 115 (1989): 22–36.

Cantor, Norman F. *The Civilization of the Middle Ages*. New York: HarperCollins, 1993.

Carapezza, Francesco. "Le Fragment de Turin du Rigomer: nouvelles perspectives." *Romania* 119 (2001): 76–112.

Cerquiglini, Bernard. *Éloge de la variante: histoire critique de la philologie*. Paris: Seuil, 1989.

*The Charrette Project 2*, ed. Rafael C. Alvarado, Gina Greco, K. Sarah-Jane Murray, et al. 2005. Baylor University. 4 April 2007. http://lancelot.baylor.edu/.

Chênerie, Marie-Luce. *Le Chevalier errant dans les romans arthuriens en vers des XII<sup>e</sup> et XIII<sup>e</sup> siècles*. Publications romanes et françaises 172. Geneva: Droz, 1986.

———. "Un recueil arthurien de contes populaires au XIII<sup>e</sup> siècle? Les *Merveilles de Rigomer*." In *Réception et identification du conte depuis le Moyen Âge: actes du colloque de Toulouse, janvier 1986*, ed. Michel Zink and Xavier Ravier, 39–49. Travaux de l'Université de Toulouse-Le Mirail A41. Toulouse: Service de Publications UTM, 1987.

Cizek, Alexandru N. Imitatio et tractatio: *die literarisch-rhetorischen Grundlagen in Antike und Mittelalter.* Rhetorik-Forschungen 7. Tübingen: Niemeyer, 1994.

Cobby, Anne. *Ambivalent Conventions: Formula and Parody in Old French.* Amsterdam: Rodopi, 1995.

Codd, E.F. "A Relational Model of Data for Large Shared Data Banks." In *Communications of the ACM* 13 (1970): 377–87. http://doi.acm.org/10.1145/362384.362685.

Colish, Marcia. *Medieval Foundations of the Western Intellectual Tradition, 400–1400.* New Haven: Yale University Press, 1997.

Combes, Annie. *Les Voies de l'aventure: réécriture et composition romanesque dans le "Lancelot" en prose.* Nouvelle Bibliothèque du Moyen Âge 59. Paris: Champion, 2001.

Copeland, Rita. *Rhetoric, Hermeneutics, and Translation in the Middle Ages: Academic Traditions and Vernacular Texts.* Cambridge Studies in Medieval Literature 11. Cambridge: Cambridge University Press, 1991.

Cremonesi, Carla. "Guilhem IX." In *Dictionnaire des Lettres Françaises: le Moyen Âge,* ed. Hasenohr and Zink, 592–95.

Cross, Tom P. "The Celtic Elements in the Lays of *Lanval* and *Graelent.*" *Modern Philology* 12 (1915): 585–644.

———. "The Celtic Origin of the Lay of *Yonec.*" *Revue Celtique* 31 (1910): 413–71.

———, and William A. Nitze. *Lancelot and Guenevere. A Study on the Origins of Courtly Love.* Chicago: University of Chicago Press, 1930.

De Cornulier, Benoît. "La cause de la rime: Réponse à Jean Molino et Joëlle Tamine." *Poétique* 52 (1982): 498–508.

———. "La rime n'est pas une marque de fin de vers." *Poétique* 46 (1981): 246–56.

———. "Rime 'riche' et fonction de la rime: Le Développement de la rime 'riche' chez les romantiques." *Voix et figure du poème* 59 (1985): 115–23.

Dees, Anthonij. *Atlas des formes et des constructions des chartes françaises du XIIIᵉ siècle.* Tübingen: Niemeyer, 1980.

———. *Atlas des formes linguistiques des textes littéraires de l'ancien français.* Tübingen: Niemeyer, 1987.

———. *Étude sur l'évolution des démonstratifs en ancien et moyen français.* Groningen: Wolters-Nordhoff, 1971.

Deleuze, Gilles. *Le Pli: Leibnitz et le baroque.* Paris: Minuit, 1988.

DeRose, Steven. "Markup Overlap: A Review and a Horse." In *Proceedings of Extreme Markup Languages 2004,* Montreal, Québec, 2–6 August 2004. http://www.mulberrytech.com/Extreme/Proceedings/html/2004/DeRose01/EML2004DeRose01.html.

*Dictionnaire des Lettres francaises (Le Moyen Âge),* ed. Geneviève Hasenohr and Michel Zink. 1964; repr. Paris: Fayard, 1992.

Diessel, Holger. *Demonstratives: Form, Function, and Grammaticalization.* Amsterdam and Philadelphia: John Benjamins Publishing Company, 1999.

Diverres, Armel. "The Grail and the Third Crusade: Thoughts on *Le Conte del Graal* by Chrétien de Troyes." *Arthurian Literature* 10 (1990): 13–104.

Dragonetti, Roger. *Le Gai savoir dans la rhétorique courtoise: Flamenca et Joufroi de Poitiers.* Paris: Le Seuil, 1982.

Duby, Georges. *De l'Europe féodale à la Renaissance: Histoire de la vie privée*, 2. Paris: Seuil, 1985.

Duggan, Joseph J. *The Romances of Chrétien de Troyes.* New Haven: Yale University Press, 2001.

———. *The 'Song of Roland': Formulaic Style and Poetic Craft.* Berkeley, Los Angeles, and London: University of California Press, 1973.

Eggert, Bruno. "Entwicklung der normandischen Mundart im Département de la Manche und auf den Inseln Guernsey und Jersey." *Zeitschrift für Romanische Philologie* 13 (1889): 353–403.

Erlande-Brandenburg, Alain. "La Priorale Saint-Louis de Poissy." *Bulletin monumental* 129 (1971): 85–112.

Esnos (Hasenohr), Geneviève. "Les Traductions médiévales françaises et italiennes des *Soliloques* attribuées à Saint Augustin." *Mélanges d'archéologie et d'histoire* 79 (1967): 299–366.

The FAUX Charrette. *The Princeton Charrette Project.* 24 August 2006. 1 October 2006. http://www.princeton.edu/~lancelot/ss/materials.shtml#faux.

Ferrante, Joan M. "*Cortes' Amor* in Medieval Texts." *Speculum* 55 (1980): 686–95.

The Figura Database. *The Princeton Charrette Project.* 24 August 2006. 1 October 2006. http://www.princeton.edu/~lancelot/ss/materials.shtml#figura.

Faletra, Michael. Abstract for "The Celtic Sources of Chrétien's Chevalier de la Charrette." 42nd International Congress on Medieval Studies at Western Michigan University, 11 May 2007.

Fink, L. Dee. *Creating Significant Learning Experiences: An Integrated Approach to Designing College Courses.* San Francisco: Jossey-Bass, 2003.

Fleming, John V. "Carthaginian Love: Text and Supertext in the *Romance of the Rose.*" In *Assays: Critical Approaches to Medieval and Renaissance Texts*, ed. Peggy A. Knapp and Michael A. Sturgin, 51–72. Pittsburgh: University of Pittsburgh Press, 1981.

———. *Reason and the Lover.* Princeton: Princeton University Press, 1984.

Flutre, Louis-Fernand. *Table des noms propres avec toutes leurs variantes figurant dans les romans du Moyen Âge écrits en français ou en provençal et actuellement publiés ou analysés.* Poitiers: Centre d'Études Supérieures de civilisation médiévale, 1962.

Foerster, Wendelin. "Zur altfranzösischen Uebersetzung der Isidorschen *Synonyma.*" *Zeitschrift für romanische Philologie* 1 (1877): 397–402.

Forsyth, Ilene H. *The Throne of Wisdom*. Princeton: Princeton University Press, 1972.

Foulet, Alfred. "Guenevere's Enigmatic Words: *Lancelot*, vv. 211–13." In *Jean Misrahi Memorial Volume: Studies in Medieval Literature*, 175–79. Columbia, SC: French Literature Publications, 1977.

———, and Mary Speer. *On Editing Old French Texts*. Edward C. Armstrong Monographs on Medieval Literature 1. Lawrence, KS: Regents Press of Kansas, 1979.

———, and Karl D. Uitti. "On Editing Chrétien de Troyes, *Lancelot*: Two Steps and their Concern." *Speculum* 63 (1988): 271–92.

François, G. "L'émergence de la majuscule dans la Chanson de Roland." *Revue de Linguistique Romane* 70 (2006): 41–52.

Franks, M. R. *The Universe and Multiple Reality*. New York: iUniverse, 2003.

Frappier, Jean. "Sur un procès fait à l'amour courtois." *Romania* 93 (1972): 145–93.

Freeman, Michelle. *The Poetics of* Translatio Studii *and* Conjointure: *Chrétien de Troyes'* Cligés. French Forum Monographs 12. Lexington: French Forum, 1979.

Friis-Jensen, Karsten. "The *Ars Poetica* in Twelfth-Century France: The Horace of Matthew of Vendôme, Geoffrey of Vinsauf, and John of Garland." *Cahiers de l'Institut du Moyen Âge grec et latin, Université de Copenhague* 60 (1990): 319–88, 61 (1991): 184.

Fulton, Rachel. *From Judgment to Passion: Devotion to Christ and the Virgin Mary, 800–1200*. New York: Columbia University Press, 2002.

———. "Horace and the Early Writers of Arts of Poetry." In *Sprachtheorien in Spätantike und Mittelalter*, ed. Sten Ebbesen, 360–401. Tübingen: Narr, 1995.

Gaylord, Alan. "Uncle Pandarus as Lady Philosophy." *Papers of the Michigan Academy of Science, Arts, and Letters* 46 (1961): 571–95.

Genet, Jean-Philippe, and Antonio Zampolli, eds. *Computers and the Humanities*. Aldershot: Dartmouth Publishing Company/European Science Foundation, 1992.

Genette, Gérard. *Nouveau discours du récit*. Paris: Le Seuil, 1983.

Gerdts, William H., Jr. "The Sword of Sorrow." *Art Quarterly* 17 (1954): 213–29.

Gier, Albert. "Das Verwandschaftsverhältnis von afr. sens und sen." *Romanistisches Jahrbuch* 28 (1977): 54–72.

Godefroy, Frédéric. *Dictionnaire de l'ancienne langue française et de tous ses dialectes du XIᵉ au XVᵉ siècle*. Paris: Bouillon, 1880–1902.

Gossen, Carl Theodor. *Grammaire de l'ancien picard*. Paris: Klincksieck, 1970.

Gouttebroze, Jean-Guy. "'Sainz Pos le dit, et je le lui': Chrétien de Troyes lecteur." *Romania* 114 (1996): 524–35.

Greco, Gina L. "L'édition électronique de textes médiévaux: théorie et pratique." In *L'Épopée romane: Actes du XVe Congrès International Rencesvals (Poitiers, 21–27 août 2000)*, ed. G. Bianciotto et C. Galderisi, 2:1045–50. Poitiers: Université de Poitiers, 2002.

——, and Peter Shoemaker. "Intertextuality and Large Corpora: A Medievalist Approach." *Computers and the Humanities* 27 (1993): 349–55.

——, Peter Shoemaker, and Toby Paff. "The *Charrette Project*: Manipulating Text and Image in an Electronic Archive of a Medieval Manuscript Tradition." *Computers and the Humanities* 30 (1996/1997): 407–15.

Guillot, Céline. "Démonstratifs et déixis discursive: Analyse comparée d'un corpus écrit de français médiéval et d'un corpus oral de français contemporain." *Langue Française* 152 (2006): 56–69.

Haskins, Charles H. *The Renaissance of the Twelfth Century*. Cambridge, MA: Harvard University Press, 1921.

Hany-Longuespé, Nicole. "Les vestiges de Saint-Etienne au trésor de la cathédrale de Troyes." In *Splendeurs de la cour de Champagne au temps de Chrétien de Troyes: Catalogue de l'exposition de la Bibliothèque municipale de Troyes (18 juin–11 septembre 1999)*, ed. Patricia Stirnemann, Thierry Delcourt, Xavier de la Salle, and Danielle Quéruel, 30–35. Troyes: Association Champagne historique, 1999.

Harf-Lancner, Laurence. *Les Fées au Moyen Âge: Morgane et Mélusine. La Naissance des fées*. Nouvelle Bibliothèque du Moyen Âge 8. Paris: Champion, 1984.

Hedeman, Anne D. *Of Counselors and Kings: The Three Versions of Pierre Salmon's Dialogues*. Urbana and Chicago: University Press of Illinois, 2001.

——. *The Royal Image: Illustrations of the* Grandes Chroniques de France, *1274–1422*. Berkeley: University of California Press, 1991.

Henderson, Jane Frances Anne. "A Critical Edition of Evrat's *Genesis*: Creation to the Flood." Ph.D. diss., University of Toronto, 1977.

Himmelmann, Nikolaus P. "Demonstratives in Narrative Discourse: A Taxonomy of Universal Uses." In *Studies in Anaphora*, ed. Barbara Fox, 205–54. Amsterdam-Philadelphia: John Benjamins Publishing Company, 1996.

Hindman, Sandra. *Sealed in Parchment: Rereadings of Knighthood in the Illuminated Manuscripts of Chrétien de Troyes*. Chicago: University of Chicago Press, 1994.

Hockey, Susan. *Electronic Texts in the Humanities: Principles and Practice*. Oxford: Oxford University Press, 2000.

Hollahan, Patricia. "Daughter of Sion, Daughter of Babylon: Images of Woman in the Old English Psalms." *Essays in Medieval Studies* 2 (1985): 27–39.

Hollander, Robert. "Il Dartmouth Dante Project." In *Letteratura italiana e arti figurative*, ed. A. Franceschetti, 1:277–85. Florence: Olschki, 1988.

——. "Il Dartmouth Dante Project: i commenti danteschi consultabili via Internet." In *Macchine per leggere: tradizioni e nuove tecnologie per comprendere i testi (Atti del Convegno di studio della Fondazione Ezio Franceschini e della Fondazione IBM Italia)*, ed. C. Leonardi, M. Morelli, and F. Santi, 83–90. Spoleto: Centro italiano di studi sull'alto medioevo, 1994.

———. "The Dartmouth Dante Project." *Quaderni d'italianistica* 10 (1989): 287–98.

———, and Stephen Campbell. "The Dartmouth Dante Project." *Computational Lexicology and Lexicography: Linguistica Computazionale* 6 (1992): I, 163–79.

Hult, David F. "Reading It Right: The Ideology of Text Editing." In *The New Medievalism*, ed. M. S. Brownlee, K. Brownlee, and S. G. Nichols, 113–30. Baltimore and London: Johns Hopkins University Press, 1991.

Huot, Sylvia. *From Song to Book: The Poetics of Writing in Old French Lyric and Lyrical Narrative Poetry*. Ithaca: Cornell University Press, 1987.

———. "The Manuscript Context of Medieval Romance." In *The Cambridge Companion to Medieval Romance*, ed. Roberta L. Krueger, 60–77. Cambridge: Cambridge University Press, 2000.

Javelet, Robert. *Image et ressemblance au douzième siècle: de Saint Anselme à Alain de Lille*. Paris: Letouzey et Ané, 1967.

Kay, Sarah. "The Contradictions of Courtly Love and the Origins of Courtly Poetry: The Evidence of the *Lauzengiers*." *Journal of Medieval and Renaissance Studies* 6 (1996): 209–53.

———. *Courtly Contradictions: The Emergence of the Literary Object in the Twelfth Century*. Stanford: Stanford University Press, 2001.

———. "Courts, Clerks, and Courtly Love." In *The Cambridge Companion to Medieval Romance*, ed. Krueger, 81–96.

———. "Who was Chrétien de Troyes?" *Arthurian Literature* 15 (1997): 1–35.

Kelly, Douglas. *The Art of Medieval French Romance*. Madison: University of Wisconsin Press, 1992.

———. "The *Fidus Interpres*: Aid or Impediment to Modern Translation and *Translatio*?" In *Translation Theory and Practice in the Middle Ages*, ed. Jeanette Beer, 47–58. Studies in Medieval Culture 38. Kalamazoo: Medieval Institute Publications, Western Michigan University, 1997.

———. "How Did Guiolete Come to Court? Or, the Sometimes Inscrutable Paths of Tradition." In *"De sens rassis": Essays in Honor of Rupert T. Pickens*, ed. Keith Busby, Bernard Guidot, and Logan E. Whalen, 309–23. Faux Titre 259. Amsterdam: Rodopi, 2005.

———. "Interlace and the Cyclic Imagination." In *A Companion to the "Lancelot-Grail Cycle*," ed. Carol Dover, 55–64. Arthurian Studies 54. Cambridge: Brewer, 2003.

———. *Medieval French Romance*. Twayne's World Authors Series 838. New York: Twayne, 1993.

———. "Multiple Quests in French Verse Romance: *Mervelles de Rigomer* and *Claris et Laris*." *L'Esprit créateur* 9 (1969): 257–66.

————. Sens *and* Conjointure *in the Chevalier de la Charrette.* The Hague: Mouton, 1966.

Kennedy, Elspeth. *Lancelot and the Grail: A Study of the Prose "Lancelot."* Oxford: Clarendon Press, 1986.

————. "The Making of the Lancelot-Grail Cycle." In *A Companion to the "Lancelot-Grail Cycle,"* ed. Dover, 13–22.

Kieckhefer, Richard. "Mystical Experience and the Definition of Christian Mysticism." In *The Comity and Grace of Method: Essays in Honor of Edmund F. Perry,* ed. Thomas Ryba, George D. Bond, and Herman Tull, 198–234. Evanston, IL: Northwestern University Press, 2004.

Kinney, Claire. "The Best Book of Romance: *Sir Gawain and the Green Knight.*" *University of Toronto Quarterly* 59 (1990): 457–73.

————. "Chivalry Unmasked: Courtly Spectacle and the Abuse of Romance in Sidney's *New Arcadia.*" *Studies in English Literature* 35 (1995): 35–52.

Kinoshita, Sharon. *Medieval Boundaries: Rethinking Difference in Old French Literature.* Philadelphia: University of Pennsylvania Press, 2006.

Kleiber, Georges. "L'opposition CIST/CIL en ancien français, ou comment analyser les démonstratifs?" *Revue de Linguistique Romane* 51 (1987): 5–35.

————. "Sur la sémantique des descriptions démonstratives." *Lingvisticae Investigationes: Revue Internationale de Linguistique Française et de Linguistique Générale* 8 (1984): 63–85.

Krahmer, Shawn M. "Bernard's Virile Bride of Christ." *Church History* 69 (2000): 304–27.

Kunstmann, Pierre. "Ancien et moyen français sur le Web: textes et bases de données." *Revue de Linguistique Romane* 64 (2000): 17–42.

Kupfer, Marcia. "... *lectures...* plus vrayes*: Hebrew Script and Jewish Witness in the Mandeville Manuscript of Charles V." *Speculum* 83 (2008): 58–111.

Lacy, Norris J. "Les Merveilles de Rigomer and the Esthetics of 'Post-Chrétien' Arthurian Romance." *Arthurian Yearbook* 3 (1993): 77–90.

Laidlaw, J.C. "Rhyme, Reason and Repetition in *Erec et Enide.*" In *The Legend of Arthur in the Middle Ages: Studies Presented to A. H. Diverres by Colleagues, Pupils, and Friends,* ed. P.B. Grout, 129–37. Arthurian Studies 7. Cambridge: Brewer, 1983.

Lausberg, Heinrich. *Handbuch der Literarischen Rhetorik.* Munich: Max Hüber, 1960.

Lazar, Moshe. *Amour courtois et "fin'amors" dans la littérature du XIIe siècle.* Paris: Klincksieck, 1964.

Le Goff, Jacques. *Saint Louis.* Paris: Gallimard, 1996.

Lehmann, Paul. *Parodie im Mittelalter.* Munich: Drei Masken, 1922.

Lejeune, Rita. "Le Manuscrit de *Flamenca* et ses lacunes." In *Littérature et société occitane au Moyen Âge,* 331–39. Liège: Marche Romane, 1979.

Lloyd-Morgan, Ceridwen, ed. *Arthurian Literature* XXI: *Celtic Arthurian Material.* Cambridge: D.S. Brewer, 2004.

Long, Deborah. "*Il joue un jeu joyeusement*: Chrétien et l'*adnominatio*." *Œuvres & Critiques* 27 (2002): 70–82.

Loomis, Roger Sherman. *Arthurian Tradition and Chrétien de Troyes*. New York: Columbia University Press, 1949.

———. *Celtic Myth and Arthurian Romance*. New York: Columbia University Press, 1927.

Lowden, John. *The Making of the 'Bibles moralisées.'* Vol. 1: *The Manuscripts*. University Park: Penn State University Press, 2000.

Mackay, Charles. *Extraordinary Popular Delusions and the Madness of Crowds*. New York: Farrar, Straus and Giroux, 1972.

Maddox, Donald. "Cyclicity, Transtextual Coherence, and the Romances of Chrétien de Troyes." In *Transtextualities: Of Cycles and Cyclicity in Medieval French Literature*, ed. Sara Sturm-Maddox and idem, 39–52. MRTS 149. Binghamton, NY: Medieval and Renaissance Texts and Studies, 1996.

———. "Lancelot et le sens de la coutume. " *Cahiers de Civilisation Médiévale* 29 (1986): 330–53.

Marchello-Nizia, Christiane. "Deixis and Subjectivity: The Semantics of Demonstratives in Old French (9ᵗʰ-12ᵗʰ century)." *Journal of Pragmatics* 37 (2004): 43–68. http://authors.elsevier.com/sd/article/S0378216604000864.

———. "Du subjectif au spatial: l'évolution sémantique des démonstratifs en français." In *Le Démonstratif en français*, ed. Céline Guillot, spec. no. of *Langue française* 152 (2006): 114–26.

———. "From Personal Deixis to Spatial Deixis: The Semantic Evolution of Demonstratives from Latin to French." In *Space in Languages*, ed. M. Hickman and Stéphane Robert, 103–20. Amsterdam and New York: John Benjamins, 2006.

———. "La sémantique des démonstratifs en français: une neutralisation en progrès?" In *Le Français parmi les langues romanes*, ed. Mario Barra Jover, spec. no. of *Langue française* 141 (2004): 69–84.

———. *L'Évolution du français: Ordre des mots, démonstratifs, accent tonique*. Paris: Armand Colin, 1995.

———. "'Se voz de ceste ne voz poéz oster, Je voz ferai celle teste coper.' (*Ami et Amile* 753): La sphère du locuteur et la déixis en ancien français." In *Mémoire en temps advenir: hommage à Theo Venckeleer*, ed. A. Vanneste, P. De Wilde, S. Kindt, and J. Vlemings, 413–27. Louvain-la-Neuve: Peeters, 2003.

Markale, Jean. *L'Amour courtois ou le couple infernal*. Paris: Imago, 1987.

Marnette, Sophie. *Narrateur et points de vue dans la littérature française médiévale: une approche linguistique*. Bern: P. Lang, 1998.

———. *Speech and Thought Perception in French: Concepts and Strategies*. Amsterdam: John Benjamins, 2005.

Matarasso, Pauline. *The Redemption of Chivalry*. Geneva: Droz, 1979.

McCarty, Willard. "Depth, Markup and Modelling." In *Proceedings of the ACH-ALLC 2004 International Humanities Computing Conference*. Athens, GA. 30

May 2003. http://www.digitalstudies.org/ojs/index.php/digital_studies/article/viewArticle/67.

McCash, June Hall. "Chrétien's Patrons." In *A Companion to Chrétien de Troyes*, ed. Grimbert and Lacy, 15–29.

———. "*Eructavit cor meum*: Sacred Love in a Secular Context at the Court of Marie de Champagne." In *Earthly Love, Spiritual Love, Love of the Saints*, ed. Susan J. Ridyard, 159–78. Sewanee, TN: University Press of the South, 1999.

———. "Marie de Champagne's *Cuer d'ome et cors de fame*: Aspects of Feminism and Misogyny in the Twelfth Century." In *The Spirit of the Court: Selected Proceedings of the Fourth Congress of the International Courtly Literature Society, Toronto, 1983*, ed. Glyn S. Burgess and Robert A. Taylor, 234–45. Liverpool: D.S. Brewer, 1985.

McKenzie, Allan Dean. "The Virgin Mary as the Throne of Solomon in Medieval Art." 2 vols. Ph.D. diss., New York University, 1965.

McMahon, Robert. "Book 13: The Creation of the Church as the Paradigm for the *Confessions*." In *A Reader's Companion to Augustine's Confessions*, ed. Kim Paffenroth and Robert P. Kennedy, 207–23. Louisville, KY: Westminster, John Knox Press, 2003.

———. *Understanding the Medieval Meditative Ascent: Augustine, Anselm, Boethius, and Dante*. Washington, DC: Catholic University of America Press, 2006.

McWebb, Christine. "Female City Builders: Hildegard of Bingen's *Scivias* and Christine de Pizan's *Livre de la cité des dames*." *Magistra: A Journal of Women's Spirituality in History* 9 (2003): 52–71.

Meade, Marion. *Eleanor of Aquitaine: A Biography*. London: Ted Smart, 1977.

Ménard, Philippe. *Le Rire et le sourire dans le roman courtois en France au Moyen Âge (1150–1250)*. Publications romanes et françaises 105. Geneva: Droz, 1969.

Meyer, Paul. "Maître Pierre Cudrifin, horloger, et la ville de Romans (1422–1431)." *Romania* 21 (1892): 39–52.

———. "Recettes médicales en français, publ. d'après le Ms. B. N. Lat. 8654 B." *Romania* 37 (1908): 358–61.

Micha, Alexandre. *La Tradition manuscrite des romans de Chrétien de Troyes*. Paris: Droz, 1966 (1ˢᵗ ed. 1939).

Minnis, A. J. *Medieval Theory of Authorship: Scholastic Literary Attitudes in the Later Middle Ages*. London: Scolar Press, 1984.

Mohrmann, Christine. Review of Maurice Testard, *Saint Augustin et Cicéron*. *Vigiliæ Christianæ* 13 (1959): 239.

Moignet, Gérard. *Grammaire de l'ancien français*. Paris: Klincksieck, 1988 (1st ed. 1973).

Molino, Jean, and Joëlle Tamine. "Des rimes, et quelques raisons. . ." *Poétique* 52 (1982): 487–98.

Monsonégo, Simone, and Madeline Henin. "Le traitement des groupements variables de morphèmes: Aspects lexicaux." In *Le Moyen Français: le traitement du texte (édition, apparat critique, glossaire, traitement électronique). Actes du IX^e colloque international sur le moyen français, Strasbourg, 29–31 mai 1997*, ed. Buridant, 149–64.

Morier, Henri. *Dictionnaire de poétique et de rhétorique*. Paris: PUF, 1961.

Murray, K. Sarah-Jane. "*Cil qui fist . . . cil qui dist*: Oratio and *Lettreüre* dans *Le Chevalier de la Charrette*." *Œuvres & Critiques* 27 (2002): 84–134.

———. *From Plato to Lancelot: A Preface to Chrétien de Troyes*. Syracuse, NY: Syracuse University Press, 2008.

———. "Informatique et textualité médiévale: l'exemple du Projet Charrette." *Cahiers de Civilisation Médiévale* 48 (2005): 219–26.

———. "Medieval Scribes, Modern Scholars: Reading *Le Chevalier de la Charrette* in the Twenty-First Century." In *Literatur und Literaturwissenschaften auf dem Weg zu den digital Medien—Eine Standortbestimmung (Literature and Literary Studies on Their Way Towards the Digital Media—Where Are We?)*, 145–63. Bern: Germanistik, 2005.

———. "Plato's *Timaeus* and the *Song of Roland*: Poetry and Humanism in Oxford Bodleian MS Digby 23." *Philological Quarterly* 83 (2004): 115–26.

Newman, F. X., ed. *The Meaning of Courtly Love: Papers of the First Annual Conference of the Center for Medieval and Early Renaissance Studies, State University of New York at Binghamton, March 17–18, 1967*. Albany: SUNY Press, 1968.

Nicholson, Francesca. "Reading the Unreadable in *Flamenca*." Paper at the British Branch of the International Courtly Love Society Conference, April 2003.

Nitze, William A. "The Bleeding Lance and Philip of Flanders." *Speculum* 21 (1946): 303–11.

———. "Conjointure in *Erec*, vs. 14." *Modern Language Notes* 69 (1954): 180–81.

———. "Sans et matière dans les œuvres de Chrétien de Troyes." *Romania* 44 (1915): 14–36.

Nixon, Terry. "Catalogue of Manuscripts." In *Les Manuscrits de Chrétien de Troyes*, ed. Busby et al., 2:1–85.

Noble, Peter S. "Le comique dans *Les Merveilles de Rigomer* et *Hunbaut*." *Arthurian Literature* 19 (2003): 77–86.

———. "The Role of Lorie in *Les Merveilles de Rigomer*." *Bibliographical Bulletin of the International Arthurian Society* 48 (1996): 283–90.

Nykrog, Per. *Les Fabliaux*. Geneva: Droz, 1973.

O'Brien, Juliet. "Making Sense of a Lacuna in the *Romance of Flamenca*." *TENSO – Bulletin of the Société Guilhem IX* 20 (2005): 1–25.

———. "*Trobar Cor(s)*: Erotics and Poetics in *Flamenca*." Ph.D. diss., Princeton University, 2006.

Ó Corráin, Donnchadh. "Historical Need and Literary Narrative." In *Proceedings of the Seventh International Congress of Celtic Studies, Oxford, 1983*, ed. D. Ellis Evans, 141–58. Oxford: Oxbow, 1986.

Ouy, Gilbert. "Introduction." In idem, *La librairie des frères captifs: Les manuscrits de Charles d'Orléans et Jean d'Angoulême*, 7–25. Turnhout: Brepols, 2007.

Padel, O.J. *Arthur in Medieval Welsh Literature*. Writers of Wales. Cardiff: University of Wales Press, 2000.

Paffenroth, Kim. "Book Nine: The Emotional Heart of the *Confessions*." In *A Reader's Companion to Augustine's Confessions*, ed. idem, 137–54.

Paris, Gaston. "Études sur les romans de la table ronde." *Romania* 10 (1881): 465–96.

———. "Études sur les romans de la Table Ronde: Lancelot." *Romania* 12 (1883): 459–534.

———. "Phonétique Française." *Romania* 10 (1881): 36–62.

Payen, Jean-Charles. *Le Motif du repentir dans la littérature française médiévale (des origines à 1230)*. Publications romanes et françaises 98. Geneva: Droz, 1968.

Pearcy, Roy J. "Intertextuality and *La Damoiselle qui n'ot parler de foutre qu'i n'aust mal au cuer*." *Zeitschrift für Romanische Philologie* 109 (1993): 526–38.

Pellen, René. "Conclusion: Internet, une situation contrastée et ambiguë." *Le Médiéviste et l'Ordinateur* 37 (1998): 42–45. http://lemo.irht.cnrs.fr.

———. "L'édition critique à l'âge d'Internet." In *L'Épopée romane: Actes du XV<sup>e</sup> Congrès International Rencesvals* (Poitiers, 21–27 août 2000), ed. G. Bianciotto and C. Galderisi, 2:1059–68. Poitiers: Université de Poitiers, 2002.

———. "Les textes sur Internet d'après Ménéstrel: lacunes et problèmes." *Le Médiéviste et l'Ordinateur* 37 (1998): 7–10. http://lemo.irht.cnrs.fr.

Pickens, Rupert T. "Jaufré Rudel et la poétique de la mouvance." *Cahiers de Civilisation Médiévale* 20 (1977): 323–37.

———. "Transmission et *translatio*: mouvement textuel et variance." *French Forum* 23 (1998): 133–45.

Pierpont Morgan Library. *In August Company: The Collections of the Pierpont Morgan Library*. New York: The Library, 1993.

Pignatelli, Cinzia. "Présence et fréquence de la ponctuation dans les manuscrits en vers du XIIIe siècle: les huit manuscrits du *Chevalier de la Charrette* au banc d'essai." In *Systèmes graphiques de manuscrits médiévaux et incunables français: ponctuation, segmentation, graphies*. Actes de la Journée d'étude de Lyon, ENS LSH, 6 juin 2005, ed. Alexei Lavrentiev, 85–105. Chambéry: Université de Savoie, 2007.

———. "Une approche de la tradition textuelle du *Chevalier de la Charrette*: la quantification des phénomènes régionaux." In *Cinquante années d'études médiévales: À la confluence de nos disciplines, Actes du Colloque organisé à l'occasion du cinquantenaire du CESCM (Poitiers 1er-4 septembre 2003)*, ed. C.

Arrignon, M.-H. Debiès, C. Galderisi, and E. Palazzo, 741–52. Turnhout: Brepols, 2006.

Plumer, Eric. "Book Six: Major Characters and Memorable Events." In *A Reader's Companion to Augustine's Confessions*, ed. Paffenroth, 89–105.

Poe, Elizabeth Wilson. Compilatio: *Lyric Texts and Prose Commentaries in Troubadour Manuscript H (Vat. Lat. 3207)*. Lexington: French Forum, 2000.

Poirion, Daniel. "Avant-Propos." In *Le Chevalier de la Charrette (Lancelot)*, ed. Alfred Foulet and Karl D. Uitti, iii–xxi.

Powell, Morgan. "Translating Scripture for Ma Dame de Champagne: The Old French 'Paraphrase' of Psalm 44 (*Eructavit*)." In *The Vernacular Spirit: Essays on Medieval Religious Literature*, ed. R. Blumenfeld-Kosinski, D. Robertson, and N. Warren, 83–103. New York: Palgrave, 2002.

*The Princeton Charrette Project*, ed. Karl D. Uitti. 1994. Trustees of Princeton University. 2006. Dept. of French and Italian, Princeton University. 3 April 2007. http://www.princeton.edu/~lancelot.

Provost, William. "Marie de France." In *Women in the Middle Ages: An Encyclopedia*, ed. Nadia Margolis and Katharina M. Wilson, 2: 596–99. Westport, CT: Greenwood Press, 2004.

Putter, Ad. "Knights and Clerics at the Court of Champagne: Chrétien de Troyes's Romances in Context." In *Medieval Knighthood: Papers from the Fifth Strawberry Hill Conference*, ed. S. Church and R. Harvey, 243–66. Woodbridge: Boydell and Brewer, 1994.

Quéruel, Danielle. "Une cour intellectuelle au XIIᵉ siècle." In *Splendeurs de la cour de Champagne au temps de Chrétien de Troyes*, 1–18.

Raciti, G. "Un opuscule inédit d'Adam de Perseigne: le livre de l'amour mutuel." *Cîteaux* 31 (1980): 297–341.

Rahner, Hugo. *Symbole der Kirche: Die Ekklesiologie der Väter*. Salzburg: Otto Müller Verlag, 1964.

Ribard, Jacques. *Chrétien de Troyes*, Le Chevalier de la Charrette*: essai d'interprétation symbolique*. Paris: Nizet, 1972.

Ricketts, Peter T., Alan Reed, F.R.P. Akehurst, John Hathaway, and Cornelius Van Der Horst, eds. *Concordance of Medieval Occitan Literature*. CD 1: lyric texts. CD 2: verse narrative texts. 2 vols. to date. Turnhout: Brepols, 2001-.

Robertson, D. W. "A Further Note on *Conjointure*." *Modern Language Notes* 70 (1955): 415–16.

———. *A Preface to Chaucer*. Princeton, Princeton University Press, 1962.

———. "Some Medieval Literary Terminology, with Special Reference to Chrétien de Troyes." *Studies in Philology* 48 (1951): 669–92.

Robinson, Molly. "L'Analyse lexicale et grammaticale du *Chevalier de la Charrette (Lancelot)*." Œuvres & Critiques 27 (2002): 20–51.

Rockwell, Paul Vincent. "'Je ne suiz mie soffisanz': Insufficiency and Cyclicity in the Lancelot-Grail Cycle." In *Transtextualities: Of Cycles and Cyclicity in Medieval French Literature*, ed. Sturm-Maddox and Maddox, 71–91.

Roques, Mario. "Le Manuscrit fr. 794 de la Bibl. Nat. et le scribe Guiot." *Romania* 73 (1952): 177–99.

Rose, Margaret A. *Parody//Meta-Fiction: An Analysis of Parody as a Critical Mirror to the Writing and Reception of Fiction.* London: Croom Helm, 1979.

Rossi, Luciano. "Carestia, Tristan, les troubadours et le modèle de saint Paul: encore sur D'Amors qui m'a tolu a moi (RS 1664)." In *Convergences médiévales: épopée, lyrique, roman: mélanges Madeleine Tyssens,* 403–19. Brussels: De Boeck Université, 2000.

Rougemont, Denis de. *L'Amour et l'Occident.* Paris: Plon, 1972 (orig. 1939).

Rouse, Richard and Mary. "The Crusade as Context: The Manuscripts of *Athis et Prophilias.*" In *Courtly Arts and the Art of Courtliness: Selected Papers from the Eleventh Triennial Congress of the International Courtly Literature Society, University of Wisconsin-Madison, 29 July-4 August 2004,* ed. Keith Busby and Christopher Kleinhenz, 49–104. Cambridge: Boydell and Brewer, 2006.

Rychner, Jean. *Contributions à l'étude des fabliaux: variantes, remaniements, dégradations.* 2 vols. Université de Neuchâtel, Recueil de travaux publiés par la Faculté des lettres 28. Neuchâtel: Faculté des lettres; Geneva: Droz, 1960.

Rydberg, Gustav. *Geschichte des französischen ɔ.* Uppsala: Almqvist & Wiksells Buchdruckerei, 1907.

Sankovitch, Tilde. "The *Romance of Flamenca*: The Puppeteer and the Play." *Neophilologus* 60 (1976): 8–19.

Sargent-Baur, Barbara Nelson. "The Missing Prologue of Chrétien's *Chevalier au Lion.*" *French Studies* 41 (1987): 385–94.

Schmolke-Hasselmann, Beate. *Der arthurische Versroman von Chrestien bis Froissart: zur Geschichte einer Gattung.* Beihefte zur Zeitschrift für romanische philologie 177. Tübingen: Niemeyer, 1980.

Schuler, Carol M. "The Sword of Compassion: Images of the Sorrowing Virgin in Late Medieval and Renaissance Art." Ph.D. diss., Columbia University, 1987.

Séguy, Mireille. *Les Romans du Graal ou le signe imaginé.* Nouvelle Bibliothèque du Moyen Âge 58. Paris: Champion, 2001.

Spearing, A. C. *The Medieval Poet as Voyeur: Looking and Listening in Medieval Love-Narratives.* Cambridge: Cambridge University Press, 1993.

———. *Textual Subjectivity: The Encoding of Subjectivity in Medieval Narratives and Lyrics.* Oxford: Oxford University Press, 2005.

Speer, Mary B. "Editing Old French Texts in the Eighties: Theory and Practice." *Romance Philology* 35 (1991): 7–43.

———. "Wrestling with Change: Old French Textual Criticism and *Mouvance.*" *Olifant* 7 (1980): 311–26.

Sperberg-McQueen, Michael, and Lou Burnard. "The Design of the TEI Encoding Scheme." In *Text Encoding Initiative: Background and Context,* ed. Nancy Ide and Jean Veronis, 17–40. Berlin: Springer, 1995.

Staines, David. "The Medieval Cycle: Mapping a Trope." In *Transtextualities: Of Cycles and Cyclicity in Medieval French Literature*, ed. Sturm-Maddox and Maddox, 15–37.

Stirnemann, Patricia. "Une bibliothèque princière au XII<sup>e</sup> siècle." In *Splendeurs de la cour de Champagne au temps de Chrétien de Troyes*, 36–42.

———, and Thierry Delcourt. "Biographies." In *Splendeurs de la cour de Champagne au temps de Chrétien de Troyes*, 43–47.

———, and Geneviève Hasenohr. "Description of BNF fr. 794." In *Splendeurs de la cour de Champagne au temps de Chrétien de Troyes*, 66.

Taylor, Andrew. "The Myth of the Minstrel Manuscript." *Speculum* 66 (1991): 43–73.

———. *Textual Situations: Three Medieval Manuscripts and Their Readers*. Philadelphia: University of Pennsylvania Press, 2002.

———. "Was There a Song of Roland?" *Speculum* 76 (2001): 28–65.

Testard, Maurice. *Saint Augustin et Cicéron*. 2 vols. Paris: Études Augustiniennes, 1958.

Thomas, Antoine. "Nouvèles variétés étimolojiqes" [sic]. *Romania* 44 (1915–1917): 321–56.

Thorington, Ellen M. "'De conter un conte par rime': Rimes riches dans *Le Chevalier de la Charrette (Lancelot)*." *Œuvres & Critiques* 27 (2002): 132–54.

Tobler, A., and E. Lommatzsch. *Altfranzösisches Wörterbuch*. Berlin-Wiesbaden: Franz Steiner Verlag, 1915–2002.

Togni, Nadia. "Les Lacunes du manuscrit de *Flamenca*." *Revue des langues romanes* 104 (2000): 379–97.

Trachsler, Richard. *Clôtures du cycle arthurien: étude et textes*. Publications romanes et françaises 215. Geneva: Droz, 1996.

———. *Disjointures–conjointures: étude sur l'interférence des matières narratives dans la littérature française du Moyen Âge*. Romanica Helvetica 120. Tübingen: Francke, 2000.

———. "Lancelot aux fourneaux: des éléments de parodie dans les *Merveilles de Rigomer*?" *Vox Romanica* 52 (1993): 180–93.

———. *Les Romans arthuriens en vers après Chrétien de Troyes*. Bibliographie des écrivains français 11. Paris: Memini, 1997.

Uitti, Karl D. "A propos de Philologie." *Littérature* 41 (1981): 20–46.

———. "Autant en emporte li funs: Remarques sur le Prologue du *Chevalier de la Charrette* de Chrétien de Troyes." Romania 105 (1984): 270–91.

———. "Background Information on Chrétien de Troyes's *Le Chevalier de la Charrette*." 1997. *The Princeton Charrette Project*. Trustees of Princeton University. 1 October 2006. http://www.princeton.edu/~lancelot.

———. *Chrétien de Troyes Revisited*. New York: Twayne Publishers, 1995.

———. "From *Clerc* to *Poète*: The Relevance of the *Romance of the Rose* to Machaut's World." In *Machaut's World: Science and Art in the Fourteenth*

*Century*, ed. Madeleine Pelner Cosman and Bruce Chandler, 209–16. New York: New York Academy of Sciences, 1978.

———. "Historiography and Romance: Explorations of *Courtoisie* in the *Chronique de Morée*." In *Autobiography, Historiography, Rhetoric*, ed. Mary Donaldson-Evans et al., 265–86. Amsterdam: Rodopi, 1994.

———. "Informatique et textualité médiévale: l'exemple du 'Projet Charrette.' *Le Médiéviste et l'Ordinateur* 37 (1998): 25–36. http://lemo.irht.cnrs.fr.

———. "Remarks on Medieval *Courtoisie*: Poetry and Grace." *Modern Philology* 92 (1994): 199–210.

———. "Remarks on Old French Narrative: Courtly Love and Poetic Form (I)." *Romance Philology* 26 (1972): 77–93.

———. "Renewal and Undermining of Old French Romance: *Jehan de Saintré*." In *Romance: Generic Transformation from Chrétien de Troyes to Cervantes*, ed. K. Brownlee and M. S. Brownlee, 135–54. Hanover: University Press of New England, 1985.

———, and Gina L. Greco. "Computerization, Canonicity and the Old French Scribe: The Twelfth and Thirteenth Centuries." *TEXT* 6 (1994): 133–52.

The Urban Legend Reference Pages. Barbara and David P. Mikkelson. 1995–2009. http://www.snopes.com.

Vitz, Evelyn Birge. "Performance in, and of, *Flamenca*." In *"De sens rassis": Essays in Honor of Rupert T. Pickens*, ed. Busby, et al., 683–98.

von Wartburg, W. *Französisches Etymologisches Wörterbuch*. Bonn: F. Klopp, 1928–2003.

Walters, Lori. "Christine de Pizan comme biographe royal," trans. Laurence Costa. In *Le passé à l'épreuve du présent: Appropriations et usages du passé au Moyen Âge et à la Renaissance*, ed. Pierre Chastang and Michel Zimmermann, 223–36 + four accompanying plates. Paris: Presses de l'Université Paris-Sorbonne, 2007.

———. "The Creation of a 'Super Romance': Paris, Bibliothèque Nationale, fonds français, MS 1433." *Arthurian Yearbook* 1 (1991): 3–25 + accompanying plates.

———. "Female Figures in the Illustrated Manuscripts of *Le conte du Graal* and its Continuations: Ladies, Saints, Spectators, Mediators." In *Text and Image: Studies in the French Illustrated Book from the Middle Ages to the Present Day*, ed. David J. Adams and Adrian Armstrong, spec. no. of *Bulletin of the John Rylands University Library of Manchester* 81.3 (1999): 7–54.

———. "The Formation of a Gauvain Cycle in Chantilly Manuscript 472." *Neophilologus* 78 (1994): 29–43.

———. "Jeanne and Marguerite de Flandre as Female Patrons." *Dalhousie French Studies* 28 (1994): 15–27.

———. "The King's Example: Arthur, Gauvain, and Lancelot in Rigomer and Chantilly, Musée Condé 472 (anc. 626)." In *"De sens rassis": Essays in Honor of Rupert T. Pickens*, ed. Busby et al., 675–93.

————, ed. *Lancelot and Guinevere: A Casebook*. New York: Garland, 1996; repr. New York: Routledge, 2002.

————. "Le rôle du scribe dans l'organisation des manuscrits des romans de Chrétien de Troyes." *Romania* 106 (1985): 303–25.

————. "*Magnifying the Lord*: Prophetic Voice in *La Cité des Dames*." *Cahiers de Recherches médiévales* 13 (2006): 237–53.

————. "Reconfiguring Wace's Round Table: Walewein and the Rise of the National Vernaculars." *Arthuriana* 15 (2005): 39–58.

————. "Re-Examining Wace's Round Table." In *Courtly Arts and the Art of Courtliness*, ed. Busby and Kleinhenz, 721–44.

————. Review of K. Busby, *Codex and Context: Reading Old French Verse Narrative in Manuscript*. *Speculum* 78 (2003): 1260–63.

Watt, Mary Alexandra. *The Cross That Dante Bears: Pilgrimage, Crusade, and the Cruciform Church in the Divine Comedy*. Gainesville, FL: University Press of Florida, 2005.

Wells, M.A. *The Secret Wound: Love-Melancholy and Early Modern Romance*. Stanford: Stanford University Press, 2007.

Wenzel, Siegfried. "Chaucer's Troilus of Book IV." *PMLA* 79 (1964): 542–47.

West, G. D. *An Index of Proper Names in French Arthurian Prose Romances*. University of Toronto Romance Series 35. Toronto: University of Toronto Press, 1978.

————. *An Index of Proper Names in French Arthurian Verse Romances 1150–1350*. University of Toronto Romance Series 15. Toronto: University of Toronto Press, 1969.

Witt, Catherine. "Le chiasme et la poésie courtoise de Chrétien de Troyes." *Œuvres & Critiques* 27 (2002): 155–220.

Zarankin, Julia. "Rupture et conjointure: L'Enjambement dans *Le Chevalier de la Charrette (Lancelot)*." *Œuvres & Critiques* 27 (2002): 221–39.

Zink, Gaston. *Morphologie du français médiéval*. Paris: PUF, 1997 (1$^{st}$ ed. 1989).

Zumthor, Paul. *Essai de poétique médiévale*. Paris: Seuil, 1972.

————. "Intertextualité et mouvance." *Littérature* 41 (1981): 8–16.